POLITICS AND DEVELOPMENT
India's Changing Landscape

About the Editors

Prof. (Dr.) M.R. Biju, is currently Dean, School of Social Sciences, Dean, School of Legal Studies and Head, Department of Public Administration and Policy Studies, Central University of Kerala, Kasaragod. The Chairperson of Board of Studies, Public Administration and Policy Studies, he is also working as Member of the Court of the University. He is the Editor of *South Asian Journal of Socio-Politic~l Studies* (SAJOSPS) and Editor-in-Chief of *International Journal of Political Science* (IJOPS). He is a prolific writer on socio-political and developmental issues and published Twenty-Nine (30) books, One Hundred and Seventy (175) research papers, Seventeen (23) book chapters, and has reviewed over Nine Hundred books for South Asian Journal of Socio-political Studies.

His teaching and research experience, spanning more than 26 years, includes several achievements such as completion of three major research projects funded by Ministry of Panchayati Raj, Government of India and University Grants Commission, New Delhi and the Post-doctoral fellowship awarded by the UGC in 2004. He has successfully guided doctoral students of the University of Kerala.

He is consistently making professional academic contributions in the capacity of an Associate Board member of Economics and Management, a prestigious journal published by the Technical University of Liberec, Czech Republic, as the Director and Member Secretary of the Asian Institute of Development Research (AIDR), and a life Member of several Academic and Professional Bodies. He is also serving on the Editorial Board of International Journal of Business, Innovation and Administration. He is a member of the PG Board of Studies of Political Science and Public Administration of the Central University of Rajasthan and Gandhigram Rural Institute, Dindugal.

M.R.B. Anantha Padmanabha, is working as Deputy Editor of South Asian Journal of Socio-Political Studies (SAJOSPS), has to his credit a few books (co-author) and research papers published in international and national journals. He has also presented papers in National Seminars. Currently, he is studying Political Science and International Relations at Pondicherry University.

POLITICS AND DEVELOPMENT
India's Changing Landscape

Edited by

M.R. Biju
M.R.B. Anantha Padmanabha

CONCEPT PUBLISHING COMPANY PVT. LTD.
NEW DELHI-110059

ISBN-13: 978-93-88937-95-5

First Published 2021

Published and Printed by

Concept
Since 1974

Concept Publishing Company Pvt. Ltd.
A/15-16, Commercial Block, Mohan Garden,
New Delhi-110059 (India)
T: 91 11 25351460, 91 11 25351794
E : publishing@conceptpub.com, *W*: www.conceptpub.com

Cataloging in Publication Data--Courtesy: D.K. Agencies (P) Ltd. <docinfo@dkagencies.com>

Politics and development : India's changing landscape / edited by M.R. Biju, M.R.B. Anantha Padmanabha.
pages cm
Includes bibliographical references and index.
ISBN 9789388937955

1. Elections—India. 2. Democratization—India. 3. Decentralization in government—India. 4. Women in development—India. 5. India—Politics and government—2014- I. Biju, M. R., 1965- editor. II. Anantha Padmanabha, M. R. B., editor.

LCC JQ292.P65 2021 | DDC 324.954 23

Preface

When the Constituent Assembly of India was concluding its historical work on 25th November, 1949, Dr. B.R. Ambedkar had prophesied: "Times are changing. People including our own are being moved by new ideologies. They are getting tired of government by the people and of the people. They are prepared to have government for the people and are indifferent whether it is the government of the people and by the people." After the attainment of Independence, we adopted the British model of parliamentary democracy. Naturally we continued the colonial model of legislative, administrative and judicial institutions and practices developed on the Indian soil by the British colonial masters. In fact, masters changed from white to brown but the style of governance remained as such. The public component in our democratic republic was the least remembered except during the election time. In political debates, when one side accuses the other of corruption the response is not denial or defence but of counter-charges saying 'you too'. Justice, education and healthcare are all too expensive to be within the reach of the poor who constitute the lion's share of Indian democracy. India today has more of the poor and illiterates than at the time of Independence. When a large number of women and children die in hospitals due to medical negligence when almost every-day innumerable women and children face inhuman brutality how can we take pride in the state of our democracy.

It is said that all public offices in India are open to all citizens equally without any discrimination on the grounds of caste, gender, religion etc. without making any generalization or commenting on the choice of high functionaries, the hard fact is that equality before law, equality of opportunity or status and equal protection of laws remain only as paper guarantees of the Constitution. For example, just we can take the case of political leadership. In our democratic polity, politics is led by or dominated by a few families and often leadership gets transferred from one person to another within the same family. Barring few exceptions, prime ministerial, chief ministerial and even ministerial positions have largely revolved around a few privileged families. Further, democracy has to work to unite and not to divide the people or electorate. Indian democracy as conceived by Mahatma Gandhi was that of power vesting in the people at the grassroots and from their rising upwards through concentric circles in a bottom-up approach but, we are still following the colonial model of a top to down approach with power staying at the top or the centre and then a bit of it trickling down to the people at the grassroots.

Democracy is a dynamic process. There never been a fully developed democratic polity. Each nation evolves its own system according to its ethos, needs, challenges and of course circumstances of the times. For India, we have ample historical evidences which categorically proves that we had a full-fledged self-governing institution existed from the Vedic period. naturally it can be treated as the cradle of our democracy. In the past 72 years after Independence, temporary aberrations like emergency, democracy has survived and thrived in India. Freedom, national unity, independence of judiciary, freedom of the press were to a large extent insured in our system without much agonies and pitfalls. Whatever problems we faced hitherto were to a large extent, resolved within the framework of democracy and constitutionalism. Our democracy can take legitimate pride in having from panchayats to parliament some 3.6 million elected representatives, 1.5 of them women. The journey of 72 years traversed by our democratic republic was most eventful and not fully free from challenges too. We had successfully conducted seventeen Lok Sabha elections and hundreds of elections to the state legislative assemblies, which were largely acknowledged as free and fair.

Indian politics has no doubt undergone fundamental transformation in the recent past. It has been influenced by demographic changes such as a multi-fold increase in the size of middle class, penetration of social media, withering away of old hierarchies and systematic changes in the nature of electoral battle. The social, political and geographical expansion of the BJP since 2014 has altered the political landscape which has resulted through the marginalization of the Congress party. The period after 2014 also witnessed an erosion in the electoral strength of the left parties in general and state level and regional parties in particular. Based on the aforesaid narration of India's Political Saga, the authors would like to project the following observations:

- The party politics in India is highly ideological and divisions on the appropriate role of the state have influenced the changes in the Indian party system since the country's Independence. The different ideas on whether the state should intervene in social norms and whether it should single out disadvantaged groups for special treatment have long historical lineages.
- The national political scenario also witnessed the transition from the Congress dominant system to a multi-party competition to a party system centred around the BJP.
- The long-term structural decline especially the organisational pitfalls of the Congress party and the absence in bringing up a new and vibrant leadership both at the national and state levels created an atmosphere favourable to the right-wing parties, which was capitalised by the BJP.

The political and administrative discourses of India in 2019 and 2020 were to a large extent determined by two individuals —Prime Minister Narendra Modi and Mr. Amit Shah. From Jammu & Kashmir to Kanyakumari and from Kutch to Kohima, the impact of their political decisions was felt across the length and breadth of the nation. A mammoth tally of seats in the House of People and a near majority in the Council of States along with its allies ensured that both could translate their ideological will into a legislative action without much resistance from the opposition. But Modi government have to face serious threats from two fronts – economic and political. It is now an accepted fact that India's economy is in the doldrums with immediate and effective interventions required from the Centre to put the system back on track. So far, the corrective measures of the sender have failed to produce any tangible results and therefore, all eyes will be on the future course of actions— political administrative and economic.

Keeping this background in view, an attempt has bee made in his volume to address the issues pertaining to a wide-ranging areas and aspects of the recent Indian Politics, viz. Constitution and Democracy: 70 Years, of Experience Lok Sabha Polls 2019 in India, in Kerala and in Maharashtra, Citizenship (Amendment) Act 2019, RTI (Amendment) Act, 2019, Gandhian, Sarvodaya Concepts of Democracy, Role of the State in Governance, Economic Status and Living Standards of Agricultural Sector, Reproduction of Marginality through Developmentalism, Gender Inequality, Gender and Development, Maternal and Child Health Care, Subaltern Resistance, CSR Practices in relation to Corona Virus Pandemic, Threats to Indian Democracy, Interrogating Citizenship and Political Economy. The chapters are contributed by senior academics and development experts with rich experience on the core areas of the study. In their submission the authors have highlightened the existing problems faced by Indian polity, economy and society and put forward solid suggestions to revamp the system.

M.R. Biju
M.R.B. Anantha Padmanabha

Acknowledgements

We would like to express our deep sense of gratitude to those who have been kind enough to help us in the preparation of this volume. We wish to express our heartfelt thanks to the esteemed contributors to this anthology of articles. The views and opinions expressed by the contributors are of great value for the researchers, academics and administrators for framing policies and strategies on Indian Polity, Development and Governance. Also thankful to Shri Ashok Kumar Mittal of Concept Publishing Company Pvt. Ltd., New Delhi, who brought out this book in an elegant form.

M.R. Biju

M.R.B. Anantha Padmanabha

Contents

PART 2

Governance, Gender and Subaltern Resistance

Contributors

Dr. D. Indrakumar, Deputy Director, National Institute of Labour Economics, Research and Development, Plot-25, Sector A-7, Institutional Area, Narela, Delhi.

Dr. D. Pulla Rao, Senior Professor, Department of Economics, Andhra University, Visakhapatnam-530003.

Dr. Deepak Kumar Pandey, Assistant Professor, GDC, Bazpur, US Nagar, (Uttarakhand).

Dr. P Lazarus Samraj, Professor, Department of Politics and International Studies, Pondicherry University.

Dr. Vineeth Thomas, Assistant Professor, Christ University, Bangalore.

Gothanda Moorthy C., Department of Politics and International Studies, Pondicherry University.

M.R.B. Anantha Padmanabha, Deputy Editor, South Asian Journal of Socio-Political Studies (SAJOSPS).

Prof. (Dr.) Mrudul Nile, Professor, Department of Civics and Politics, University of Mumbai.

Prof. (Dr.) Nagendra Ambedkar Sole, Department of Public Policy, Law and Governance, Central University of Rajasthan.

Dr. Padmalaya Mahapatra, Associate Professor, P.G. Department of Public Administration, Utkal University, Bhubaneswar, Odisha.

Dr. Phulmoni Das, Assistant Professor, Department of Political Science, Dibrugarh University, Dibrugarh, Assam.

Prof. (Dr.) M.R. Biju, Dean, School of Social Sciences, Dean, School of Legal Studies and Head, Department of Public Administration and Policy Studies, Central University of Kerala, Kasargode-671316, Kerala.

Prof. (Dr.) R.L.M. Patil, Formerly Chairman, Department of Political Science, University of Bangalore, Karnataka.

Dr. Santhosh Mathew, Associate Professor, Centre for South Asian Studies, Pondicherry University, Puducherry.

Soumya Sagarika Sahoo, Ph.D. Research Scholar, P.G. Department of Public Administration, Utkal University, Bhubaneswar, Odisha.

Dr. Sujit Lahiry, Associate Professor of Political Science, Panjab University, Regional Centre, Sri Muktsar Sahib-152026, Punjab.

Tanvi Yadav, Ph.D. Scholar, Department of Public Policy, Law and Governance, Central University of Rajasthan.

Dr. Valentina Fusari, University of Pavia, Corso Street Nuova, 65, 27100, Pavia, Italy.

Dr. Venkatanarayanan, S., Andaman Law College, Port Blair-744101, Andaman & Nicobar Islands, India.

Introduction

M.R. Biju and *M.R.B. Anantha Padmanabha*

When the Constituent Assembly of India was concluding its historical work on 25th November, 1949, Dr. B.R. Ambedkar had prophesied: "Times are changing. People including our own are being moved by new ideologies. They are getting tired of government by the people and of the people. They are prepared to have government for the people and are indifferent whether it is the government of the people and by the people." After the attainment of independence, we adopted the British model of parliamentary democracy. Naturally we continued the colonial model of legislative, administrative and judicial institutions and practices developed on the Indian soil by the British colonial masters. In fact, masters changed from white to brown but the style of governance remained as such. The public component in our democratic republic was the least remembered except during the election time. In political debates, when one side accuses the other of corruption the response is not denial or defence but of counter-charges saying 'you too'. Justice, education and healthcare are all too expensive to be within the reach of the poor who constitute the lion's share of Indian democracy. India today has more of the poor and illiterates than at the time of Independence. When a large number of women and children die in hospitals due to medical negligence when almost everyday innumerable women and children face inhuman brutality how can we take pride in the state of our democracy.

It is said that all public offices in India are open to all citizens equally without any discrimination on ground of caste, gender, religion etc. without making any generalization or commenting on the choice of high functionaries, the hard fact is that equality before law, equality of opportunity or status and equal protection of laws remain only as paper guarantees of the Constitution. For example, just we can take the case of political leadership. In our democratic polity, politics is led by or dominated by a few families and often leadership gets transferred from one person to another within the same family. Barring few exceptions, prime ministerial, chief ministerial and even ministerial positions have largely revolved around a few privileged families. Further, democracy has to be worked to unite and not to divide the people or electorate. Indian democracy as conceived by Mahatma Gandhi was that of power vesting in the people at the grassroots and from their rising upwards through concentric circles in a bottom-up approach but, we are still following the colonial model of a top down approach with power staying at the top or the centre and then a bit of it trickling down to the people at the grassroots.

Democracy is a dynamic process. There have never been a fully developed democratic polity. Each nation evolves its own system according to its ethos, needs, challenges and of course, circumstances of the times. For India, we have ample historical evidences which categorically proves that we had a full-fledged self-governing institution existed from the Vedic period. Naturally it can be treated as the cradle of our democracy. In the past 72 years after Independence, temporary aberrations like emergency, democracy has survived and thrived in India. Freedom, national unity, independence of judiciary, freedom of the press where to a large extent insured in our system without much agonies and pitfalls. Whatever problems we faced hitherto were to a large extent resolved within the framework of democracy and constitutionalism. Our democracy can take legitimate pride in having from panchayats to parliament some 3.6 million elected representatives, 1.5 of them women. The journey of 72 years traversed by our democratic republic was most eventful and not fully free from challenges too. We had successfully conducted seventeen Lok Sabha elections and hundreds of elections to the state legislative assemblies, which were largely acknowledged as free and fair.

Significance of 17th Lok Sabha Elections 2019

The Bharatiya Janata Party-led NDA won the elections with the BJP itself winning a clear majority. The BJP became the single largest party in the House and surpassed expectations to win 303 seats, with its alliance partners bringing the NDA to a total of 353 seats. Reasons attributed to the victory included the personal popularity of Narendra Modi, effective voter turnout drives by the NDA, a surge in public nationalism following the Pulwama attack, the consolidation of Hindu voters in a multi-caste coalition and the successful implementation of social welfare programmes during the First Modi ministry's term.

With the results, the BJP was able to gain 21 more seats in the House, having won 282 in the 2014 Indian general election. It was the second time in India's independent history that voters re-elected the same party to power with a bigger majority to the Lok Sabha—India's lower house of parliament. The BJP's total vote share stood at 37.4 per cent, an increase of over 6 percentage points from 31.34 per cent in 2014. The National Democratic Alliance secured a vote share of 45 per cent, compared to 38 per cent in 2014. In contrast, the vote share of Indian National Congress remained the same at 19.5 per cent. About 1.04 per cent of the voters in India chose to vote for None Of The Above (NOTA) in the 2019 elections, with Bihar leading with 2.08 per cent NOTA voters.

Modi became the only Indian prime minister in history whose government was re-elected with both an increase in the total percentage of votes along with a full majority. His opponent, Rahul Gandhi, ran in two constituencies, winning from Wayanad, but losing from the Amethi constituency—the seat he, his mother (Sonia Gandhi), his father (Rajiv Gandhi), and his uncle (Sanjay Gandhi) had collectively held for decades. In addition, many candidates who were members of popular political dynasties were defeated across India in favour of the BJP or other parties' candidates.

The election had been called a referendum on Modi and the BJP's Hindu nationalistic policies and advocacy. According to *The Wall Street Journal*, Modi's victory "sets (sic) the stage for further economic change in one of Asia's fastest-growing economies." Alasdair Pal and Mayank Bhardwaj, in an article published by *Reuters*, claimed that the result was a mandate for business-friendly policies and tougher national security positions, reinforcing "a global trend of right-wing populists sweeping to victory, from the United States to Brazil and Italy, often after adopting harsh positions on protectionism, immigration and defence."

Reasons for the Success of the BJP

The 2019 Lok Sabha election results have been marked by the poor performance of parties that are perceived to be family-run enterprises. Narendra Modi pilloried the Gandhis for not having worked their way up in politics. By doing so, he tapped into the growing disenchantment with the politics of entitlement—in particular, with political families of 'social justice' parties, such as Samajwadi Party and Rashtriya Janata Dal in the north and Janata Dal (Secular) in the south. Today, the Samajwadi Party, Bahujan Samaj Party and Rashtriya Janata Dal are staring at a bleak future, having won five, 10 and zero seats this time. Their performance was no less dismal five years ago. On both occasions, they were swept aside by the Modi wave. Their style of politics has also been rejected. Having set out to challenge feudal tendencies in society, they are paying the price for internalising them." With Amit Shah and Modi at the helm, the BJP has managed to project itself as the mascot for determined, self-made individuals who break out of their socio-economic constraints. They have termed this the New India—impatient with categories of not just caste, but more disconcertingly, 'secularism'. It is a sizeable force, which identifies with the rugged confidence of the present BJP top leadership; it is, of course, true that local BJP leaders have fielded their kith and kin who have won, riding the Modi wave.

While this is a new subalternism, it does not mean that 'caste' as a political category is on the wane. The BJP has, in fact, consolidated its hold on the lower castes whose aspirations were not addressed by traditional social justice parties—this is even as Modi said in his victory address that there were only two castes, 'the poor and those who serve the poor'. Issues of caste need to be seen through the prism of a young, upwardly mobile society which disregards the politics of entitlement. If the 2014 Lok Sabha elections were marked by anti-incumbency, pro-incumbency was the keynote of the 2019 elections as BJP decimated the opposition. The BJP juggernaut rolled across its bastions in the north and west of the country—in bellwether state UP its vote share shot up from 42.6% in 2014 to 49.5%, negating the impact of SP, BSP and RLD joining hands—while making significant incursions into the south (Karnataka, Telangana) and east (Bengal, Odisha). At last count BJP had wins/leads in 303 seats and its allies in 50 seats, giving NDA a thumping majority in the Lok Sabha.

What accounts for the shift from anti-incumbency in 2014 to pro-incumbency in 2019? It is not as if the economy has changed much. On the positive side inflation was managed well during NDA's first term (but faces upward pressure now). On the negative side joblessness appears to have grown more acute. One could attribute BJP's success to better administration of welfare schemes, the Balakot strikes which retaliated against Pakistan's sponsorship of terror groups, and Prime Minister Narendra Modi's personal popularity. But while all these factors may have played a role they do not, even in combination, satisfactorily account for the magnitude of BJP's sweeping victory.

It is possible some deep structural shifts are taking place in the Indian polity. The so-called "secular" model many other parties have followed is to work with conservative Muslim clerics to secure the Muslim vote, and then add on specific castes as each party's USP relying on post-Mandal social engineering. Thus, SP is the party of Yadavs, BSP of Jatavs and so on. This model, however, offers plenty of opportunity for counter-mobilisation. BJP has moved into this vacuum swiftly and effectively. It may have capitalised, for example, on the unseen backlash to aggressive expansion of caste reservations, cementing its support among upper castes with the EWS quota. Hindu upper castes would comprise a solid bloc that can neutralise the Muslim vote (which, in any case, is split among several parties). Alongside, Modi also projects a different kind of backward caste identity that is fluid, aspirational, upwardly mobile and less dependent on specific caste networks. As smartphones spread and cities expand, this style may appeal more to Hindu lower castes. BJP alone has around 300 Lok Sabha seats which gives it the power to override even its allies in the next government. With great power, however, must come great responsibility. The Indian polity is dynamic and the voter can never be taken for granted. Now that BJP has acquired enough confidence in government it must utilise the first hundred days of its second tenure to launch the transformative leap that the economy badly needs—more so since global headwinds are growing—even as it fully respects constitutional values in letter and spirit. BJP started on the right, reformist note in 2014 but veered off track following Congress accusations of it being anti-poor, lurching later into radical socialist experiments such as demonetisation.

"Factor" markets of land, labour and capital need market-oriented reform for efficient allocation of resources; so do agriculture and education. At the same time, the state must step in and provide quality inputs where the market cannot provide these (such as healthcare, basic education). Unproductive subsidies must be cut, and the autonomy of public institutions respected and expanded. Such reforms, whose objective is to ramp up India's global competitiveness, may be painful at the beginning. But BJP has the mandate and trust of the people, and must be bold enough to push them through. A powerhouse economy and its spinoff benefits will, in turn, yield a political bonanza for BJP by the time the next general election come round in 2024.

Systematic Election Strategies

The time bound, systematic and behind the scenes outreach programmes of the BJP and its leadership played a crucial role in its electoral victory. The party chief Amit Shah was cautioning party workers that anything short of complete enthusiasm and hard work for the Lok Sabha polls could lead to defeat and a decline of the BJP and Sangh Parivar. A large part of the BJP's strategy was around Prime Minister Modi as its most charismatic leader who commanded votes Amit Shah at the BJP National Convention in New Delhi on January 11 across categories. It also worked to create a category of voters who would vote above parochial concerns. The opposition's disarray with regards to leadership helped drive home this point of a decisive leader. Beneficiary as voter six months before the polls, a list of beneficiaries of the Modi government's welfare programmes was shared with every Lok Sabha constituency, and party workers were asked to reach out to them. Party president Amit Shah had also revealed that around 161 call-centres had been set up by the party with over 15,000 callers to help with the outreach.

"The benefits, unlike under previous governments, were not specific to one community and helped the party break caste barriers and identity issues," said a senior leader. After the seventh phase of polling revealed that women, for the first time in independent India's history, had come out to vote in as many numbers as men and as the results, started pouring in on Thursday, the party was assured of victory. "Women and young people 'who saw welfare programmes being delivered created a set of voters who helped break caste arithmetic," said a senior party leader. The party's greatest challenge was the formidable caste arithmetic of Uttar Pradesh's Mahagathbandhan of Bahujan Samaj Party (BSP) and Samajwadi Party (SP). Senior leaders said the aggression among the support bases of both these parties helped along a process of "reverse-polarisation." "Our voters saw this aggression by SP and BSP voters and consolidated firmly behind us—non-Yadav OBCs, non-Jatav *dalits* and upper castes. Added to women and the young, this was a formidable combination," said the source. Real time feedback and the addressing of it by Prime Minister Modi was reflected in his tour plans that mostly concentrated on seats where the party needed a boost rather than go to strongholds. The BJP's planning for the Lok Sabha polls began nearly three years ago with Shah coming out with focus areas for the party's expansion. A list of 120 seats mostly in what he termed as the "Coromandel Coast", where the BJP hadn't won ever but had registered some votes in

2014, were concentrated on. In Odisha as in West Bengal, the BJP slowly ate up the Congress and Left's space as the opposition, giving it nearly 30 extra seats.

Leadership of Narendra Modi

One factor stands out in the verdict of the 2019 general election the ringing endorsement of a single leader, Narendra Modi. It was Mr. Modi all the way except in some states of the South where his party, the BJP, has no presence and where his Hindi oratory is ineffectual. Across the rest of India, the voters wanted someone who made them feel secure. No one else inspired similar trust—not Rahul Gandhi, Mayawati, Akhilesh Yadav, Mamata Banerjee, N. Chandrababu Naidu, K. Chandrasekhar Rao and not even Sharad Pawar. What were the fears driving the voter and where did they originated. The structural origins of these fears can be traced to the less than robust liberal revolution that India experienced over the past seven decades. The liberal push in India led to a forced restructuring of society through an ever expanding agitation for granting special rights not only to *dalits*, tribals, minorities and the other backward classes, but also to women, the disabled, gays and transgenders. Such restructuring was not very successful, nor consistent, yet it threatened traditional social, cultural, religious hierarchies.

The liberal reshaping of India was resisted at every step. Counter-revolutionary social-forces were always waiting in the wings. They took various forms from the periodic cow protection agitations led by *sadhus* to the movement for the destruction of the Babri Masjid and construction of a Ram Temple at the site, to the lynching of cow traders and beef-eaters. To say that Rahul Gandhi was no match for Modi begs the real question. Rahul Gandhi and the OBC parties offered the protection and continuation of an evolving liberal vision. They may have different perspectives and horizons of operationalising this vision, but they were broadly for the ongoing expansion of the rights of marginalised sections of society. This election was against that vision in all its forms.

The counter-revolution taps into fear. Prime Minister Narendra Modi tapped into the fears that the liberals aroused. First and foremost, he tapped into the fear of the Hindu majority that they were being marginalised in their "own country" and their privileges were shrinking because of the expanded rights of others. The latter was addressed directly by Prime Minister Modi by announcing a 10 per cent job quota for the upper castes. He probably knew that his pronouncement that a Hindu could never be terrorist may sound like pure rhetoric, but it assuaged many of his listeners that their religion was better than others and it was time that other religious communities recognised it. By constantly rubbishing the Metropolitan elite, his wordsmiths consistently coined new phrases to denigrate and criminalise them (Lutyens' gang, Half-Maoists, Urban Naxals, Khan Market gang etc.), and Prime Minister Modi tapped into the fear that the system was being manipulated to partisan ends by a small urban elite. By constantly hammering that Indian liberals were friends of Pakistan (and therefore anti-national), he created the fear that they not only under-estimated. Islamic terror, but by speaking out for the minorities, starting a dialogue with Kashmiri leaders for better relations with Pakistan, they encouraged terrorism. On the eastern borders of India, he heightened the existing anxiety about Muslim illegal immigrants (potential recruits for Islamic terror) outnumbering Hindus and promised citizenship to Hindu immigrants. Many of these fears exist historically across India, especially because of the lingering trauma of Partition. (Bharat Bhushan, 2019).

BJP secured 50 per cent Vote Share in 200 Seats

The BJP secured over 50 per cent vote share in more than 200 constituencies across the country, according to the tentative figures of the Election Commission. The party's share crossed the halfway mark in all the 26 constituencies of Gujarat and about 40 seats in Uttar Pradesh. The same trend was noticed in 25 constituencies of Madhya Pradesh, 23 of Rajasthan, 20 of Karnataka, 14 in Bihar and nine of the 10 constituencies of Haryana. In all the seven seats of Delhi, it bagged over 50 per cent vote share. In the eight constituencies of Mumbai North, Bhilwara, Navsari, Surat, Vadodara, Faridabad, Karnal and Kangra, the BJP got over 70 per cent share of the votes polled. The highest of 74.73 per cent was in Navsari, as per the data available through the Election Commission's website at 6 p.m. on Thursday. It did not secure 50 per cent share in any of the constituencies in Odisha. State-wise analysis revealed that the highest gain of 23.29 per cent—from 34.70 per cent to 57.99 per cent—for the BJP was registered in Haryana, where it is in power. In 2014 also, it had bettered its performance as compared to 17.21 per cent in 2009.

The second highest gain of about 21.5 per cent, from the previous figure of 18 per cent, was recorded in West Bengal, where the party came close to the 43.54 per cent vote share of the Trinamool Congress. While in Himachal Pradesh, the party's vote share went up by more than 15 per cent to 68.93 per cent, about 10 per cent gain was reported from Arunachal

Pradesh, Jharkhand and Delhi. In Karnataka and Tripura also, the figure increased by about 8 per cent compared to 2014.

The Debacle of the Congress

When the Bharatiya Janata Party (BJP) led by Narendra Modi stormed to power in 2014, the Congress was reduced to 44 seats in the Lok Sabha. In 2019, the Congress has suffered another colossal defeat. It won 52 seats, still not enough to claim the post of the Leader of the Opposition in the Lok Sabha. This dismal result shows that the revival of the once-dominant power-house is not happening any time soon. Modi's re-election with an even larger majority sanctifies the structural shift to the right and the BJP's overarching dominance of the political system—that is why the Congress's spectacular defeat in this election is far more consequential than it was in 2014. The Modi landslide in 2019 is not based on any pretence of development, but on the basis of Hindutva consolidation and majoritarian triumphalism. The divide-and-rule strategy has succeeded in securing an unprecedented electoral endorsement for Hindu nationalism as large numbers voted for the BJP as the party that best represents, protects and propagates Hindu interests and rejected the pluralistic vision of India.

The 2019 outcome was powered by a hyper-nationalist agenda and Modi's strong advocacy of it. This election was all about the political persona of Modi and what he symbolised: a strongman standing against a divided Opposition. Gandhi is a genial and affable figure, but that seems to put him at a disadvantage when pitted against Modi's muscular leadership in 'new India'. The Congress made a strategic mistake when it decided to focus its attack entirely on Modi. Many voters had said that although they felt that the BJP had not delivered on its promises, they would vote for him because they believe a strong decisive leadership can solve India's numerous problems. Gandhi appeared to see the danger of personalising the campaign, but even then he persisted in repeating the slogan '*chowkidar chor hai*' to dent Modi's image as a scrupulously honest leader, rather than remake his message. In almost every speech he would begin and conclude with the Rafale issue. But it didn't excite anyone except possibly the committed Congress voters attending his rallies. The real gains for the Congress would have come from disappointment in the Modi government's economic performance and policies, but the BJP shrewdly sidestepped its governance record by diverting to a three-point campaign of nationalism (national security, Pakistan and terrorism),

Hindutva (Hindus everywhere, minorities nowhere) and anti-corruption (blasting the Congress's record, ignoring its own). Modi did not run on his track record but on teaching Pakistan a lesson. He has been re-elected on this plank. The economic down run and shrinking employment opportunities didn't matter in this election.

After the Pulwama terrorist attack and India's response with the Balakot airstrikes, the BJP mixed national security with a muscular nationalism, which completely derailed the Opposition as Modi used this narrative to project himself as the strong leader of a '*mazboot sarkar* (solid government)'. The Congress could not counter this narrative. It tried to change the subject by returning the focus to people's issues. The Nyuntam Aay Yojana (NYAY) income guarantee proposal was part of this attempt, but it came too late and the party did not carry it to the people. Consequently, NYAY did not become a talking point in the campaign; it did not even figure prominently in Gandhi's speeches. The Congress now lacks a distinct social base, and its ability to retain its supporters is dwindling. To regain its influence, it needs to decentralise and build broad based social coalitions at the State level. The party's decline is not irreversible. But in the long road ahead, it has to figure out what it actually stands for, and what it will take to stand up to Modi's BJP. The real key to rejuvenation lies in mass contact, a distinctive and far savvier campaign on an egalitarian platform and the leadership's ability to communicate this to the people—rather than depending on the eternal verities (and varieties) of dynastic leadership.

Performance of the Left Parties

While the election results have brought cheer to the saffron camp, the Left is seeing red with almost negligible presence across the country. The Left, which once held West Bengal and Tripura as fortresses and held 53 Lok Sabha seats only 10 years ago has been reduced to a mere four seats in the 2019 polls and drew a blank in their traditional bastions. Even in Kerala, where they rule the state in an alliance, it managed to cobble up only one victory. Their tally in the 2014 elections came down drastically from 53 to 10. Surprisingly, the Left has done well in Tamil Nadu, where it is in an alliance with the Congress and the DMK, which has swept almost all the seats in the state. Political experts say the Left's unwillingness to change to adapt to current political scenario is leading to their successive defeat and erosion from the political spectrum. "The Left still is living in the past. It needs to adopt and mould its campaign and ideology to suit the present times. In a day and age where the other parties are using innovative campaign techniques, the Left is stuck with the traditional methods," Left historian Pradip Datta said. To their credit, the Left has tried to return to political relevance by supporting farmers on their issues and pressurized them to make their voice heard. They must push for issues more aggressively and learn to compromise a little to yield better dividends or the day won't be far where they will not be present in the political scenario of the country.

Regional Parties

The gigantic saffron wave that swept through the country which smashed the hopes of many regional parties, which tried to punch above their weight. Most of the aspiring parties—NCP, BSP, SP, JD(S), AAP, AIADMK and TDP—have been reduced to single digits in the Lok Sabha. West Bengal's Trinamool Congress led by Mamata Banerjee, who was eyeing the PM's post, suffered a big blow as the BJP made deep in-roads into her territory. TMC, which had scored 34 in the 2014 Modi wave, was reduced to 22 after Thursday's results.

Similarly, after winning four seats in 2014, the RJD had registered a remarkable performance in the 2015 Bihar Assembly polls under the leadership of Tejashwi Yadav. However, it could not carry forward as the party, along with allies Congress and RLSP lost most of the seats in the 2019 Lok Sabha (LS) polls. The RJD failed to win even a single seat, making it the worst-ever drubbing since its formation about three decades ago. Similarly, the JD(S) had into limelight in 2018 when it stitched an alliance with the Congress in the wake of the fractured mandate in the Karnataka Assembly polls. However, it was reduced to one seat in the LS polls. Sharad Pawar-led NCP, which was also considering itself as one of the king-makers, is facing similar crisis. The party, which had presence on six seats in 2014, could win only four seats this time.

Shibu Soren-led Jharkhand Mukti Morcha was winning just one seat till late evening as against its presence on two seats in 2014. The party suffered a major blow with even Soren losing his seat in the tribal State. "The TRS, which was expecting a hung Parliament and aspiring to play a key role in putting together a third front, was reduced to 8 seats. The party had scored impressive win in the last Assembly polls, but it could not repeat the performance in the LS elections. AIADMK is another big loser as its tally came down to meagre 1 (2019) from a remarkable 37 seats in 2014 in the Lok Sabha: The only saving grace for the party is that it is part of the

NDA. Arvind Kejriwal-led AAP repeated its 2014 performance this time as well, scoring zero. Ditto with the Left parties, which registered its worst poll performance in six decades. Kerala's ruling party CPI (M) had won nine seats in 2014. But, it lost 19 out of 20 seats in the state this time.

SP-BSP's Poor Performance

The big battle of 2019 ended in Uttar Pradesh, the state with the largest number of Lok Sabha seats, on Thursday, springing a huge surprise. It was in UP where the non-BJP parties were expected to make a stand, if the Modi wave 2.0 swept away rivals in most states. It did not happen. The Samajwadi Party, Bahujan Samaj Party and Rashtriya Lok Dal combine would have, by the sheer weight of their social arithmetic, been capable of stopping a repeat of the 2014 saffron tide in 57 out of the 80 seats. Even going by the vote share last time, they were ahead with 60 seats. Then, what happened? The NDA tally of 64 is only part of the story; not reflective of what transpired entirely. Yet, the BJP-led juggernaut's show is spectacular, for it generated a repeat wave—unprecedented in UP's electoral history—and shook the rival formations to the roots to the extent that the best known politician outside UP—Rahul Gandhi, too, capitulated. Had he seen it coming?

The Modi magic singularly overwhelmed the statistics, trumping caste barriers. The result: Saffron, which even at its 2014 strike rate stood to lose about 50 seats, managed to brilliantly reverse the damage, even taking its vote share to over 50 per cent from 43 per cent of 2014 while winning less seats. It will be difficult for Congress chief Rahul Gandhi to reconcile to the Amethi shocker as would it be for SP chief Akhilesh Yadav, who is another big loser in the alliance. Contesting 37 out of 80 seats, SP vote share fell to 4 per cent—a clear indication that BSP cadres did not vote SP. It also failed to improve upon its 2014 performance, winning five seats again losing family bastions—Kannauj (Dimple), Firozabad (Akshay Yadav) and Badaun (Dharmendra Yadav). Similarly, RLD lost all three seats it contested. Even Chaudhury Ajit Singh failed to save his Jat pride in Muzaffarnagar. BSP chief Mayawati, however, emerged a gainer, cashing SP votes to win 11 seats against none in 2014. BSP had contested 38 of 80 seats.

Social Justice Politics under Threat

The 2019 verdict bas also dismantled social justice parties in Uttar Pradesh and Bihar, two States that together send 120 members to the Lok Sabha. The rise of Hindutva since the 1980s had a parallel—new wave of backward caste mobilisation in parts of northern and western India, which questioned the Nehruvian elite's grip on power. While parties based on social justice politics or regional pride weakened the Congress, they also viewed the BJP with skepticism despite their occasional association with it. Through deft coalition building, the BJP used many non-Congress outfits to further its own growth and gobbled them up in several States, much as Gujarat. In U.P. and Bihar, social justice parties with deep-rooted support among the Hindu backward castes, in alliance with the considerable Muslim population in these States, became the biggest roadblock to the Hindutva project. In 2014, the BJP upended that dynamic and swept both States in 2019 which proved that the phenomenon is enduring.

The Rashtriya Janata Dal in Bihar and the Samajwadi Party, the Bahujan Samaj Party and Rashtriya Lok Dal in U.P. usurped by their leaders as personal and family enterprises and sunk in corruption charges, collapsed. But outfits such as Ram Vilas Paswan's Lok Janashakti Party in Bihar and the Shiv Sena in Maharashtra, guilty of the same since, have flourished in their alliance with the BJP. The 2019 outcome must thus be seen as one powered by the hyper-nationalist agenda that was the mainstay of Modi's five-year term in government, though corruption and nepotism of the BJP's opponents could have been supplementary factors. The welfare schemes of the Modi government did play a role. Along with the Welfare Programmes the Pulwama terrorist strike and India's response to it dovetailed into the BJP's campaign.

Reduced Number of Muslim Members

Nearly 150 million Muslims will only have 24 representatives in the 17th Lok Sabha, according to trends shown on the Election Commission website till late Thursday evening. While Muslims constitute 10.5 per cent of the total population, its percentage representation in the new Lok Sabha will be 4.42 per cent. Notably, neighbouring Bangladesh has a better representation of minorities with 21 of its members belonging to the minority community. This constitutes 8.8 per cent representation of their total strength. Pakistan, on the other hand, fares poorly than India as only 2.9 per cent of its members belong to the minority community.

However, the representation of Muslim is in India has gone up by two seats this time if compared to 2014, when it hit an all-time low in the last 50 years. BJP which won with a thumping majority will not have a single Muslim MP as was the case in 2014. The highest number of Muslims have come from Uttar Pradesh with three each from Samajwadi Party and Bahujan Samajwadi party. Among the winners is firebrand Samajwadi leader Azam Khan. Notably U.P., which has the highest population of Muslims, had sent no Muslim MP to the Lok Sabha in 2014. The second highest number of five Muslim MPs is from West Bengal with four MPs from the Trinamool and one from the Congress. Jammu & Kashmir, which is a Muslim majority state, has three MPs, all from National Conference. The three MPs are party president Farooq Abdullah, Mohammad Akbar Lone and Hasnain Masoodi. Bihar, which had sent four MPs to the Lok Sabha last time, has only two Muslims this time—one each from Congress and Janata Dal (United). About half of the country's Muslims live in the states of Uttar Pradesh, Bihar, and Bengal. Kerala and Assam also have two MPs each who belong to the minority community. Maharashtra, with a Muslim population of around 11 per cent, has elected one Muslim MP—Imtiaz Jaleel Syed of All India Majlis-E-Ittehadul Muslimeen. Punjab, Telangana and Lakshadweep also have one Muslim MP each. The only encouraging statistics on Muslim representation is the fact that this time the contribution of Muslim MPs comes from 10 states while in the last elections, the Muslim MPs hailed from just seven states.

The definitive nature of the Bharatiya Janata Party's victory in the 17th general election marks an unmistakable inflection point in the journey of the Republic. If the 16th general election in 2014 catapulted the BJP as the primary pole of the Indian politics, relegating the Congress to a distant second, 2019 establishes it as the overarching hegemony. For good reasons, this result is being viewed as an endorsement of Prime Minister Narendra Modi's persona, and his imprint on this victory is distinctive. But it will be a folly to ignore the underlying structural reasons that made this victory possible, and its sweep so deep and wide. It takes strong personalities to popularise an idea, but it is those ideas that outlive personalities that define the course of a people or a nation. The outcome, hence, must be understood as an electoral endorsement of Hindutva, or Hindu nationalism, the creed that guided the BJP and it forebears for nearly a century since Vinayak Damodar Savarkar wrote the treatise by the same title. Narendra Modi, who counts Savarkar as a critical influence, has been the catalyst and the alchemist of the transformation in the way India imagines itself. In recess, if not in irreversible decline, is the idea of India that had grown from the freedom movement, and had prevailed for most part of the history of the Republic.

Championed by the first Prime Minister of India, Jawaharlal Nehru, it sought inspiration from the millennia old civilisation, the Vedas and the Upanishads, but also strived to build India into a modern society with a scientific temper and liberal values. The idea outlived Nehru, but it had begun to fade soon after his passing. Nehru and his mentor, Mahatma Gandhi, were the prime targets of derision for the proponents of Hindutva in the early years. With the 2019 result, Hindutva has pushed Nehruvian secularism to the margins of Indian politics. The Congress, now led by Nehru's great-grandson Rahul Gandhi, did better than in 2014, but not enough to even be recognised as the official Opposition in the Lok Sabha. Now, BJP is bound to uphold secular ideals or to protect the integrity of existing institutions may amount to demanding an abandonment of its very core beliefs. Gaining the trust of all citizens will be a necessary prerequisite for Modi to drive India's continuing journey to become a global leader. It is only reasonable that the government and the Prime Minister be asked to live up to the promise they continuously make *sabka saath, sabka vikas* (with all development for all)'. These tenets must be felt in the daily lives of the marginalised sections of the population, and Narendra Modi must add a third tenet to make his *mantra* meaningful: *sabka vishwas* (the trust of all).

Indian voters have shown remarkable maturity and thoughtfulness in delivering a stable government at the Centre. They realise the necessity of a stable government, and so often vote differently in National and State elections. Forecasts of political and economic instability made in 2014, when the macro-economy was vulnerable, proved incorrect. Similar forecasts were made this year, based on the Bharatiya Janata Party (BJP-led National Democratic Alliance's losses in the Karnataka, Madhya Pradesh and Rajasthan Assembly elections. The *pundits* should bow to the greater wisdom of the people—in this election, the BJP has swept the same States. The Congress underestimated the voters' continuing need for good governance. The Congress did not choose dynamic Chief Ministers when it had the option. It also underestimated the voters need for a positive narrative. Talking of slow job growth and farmer distress did not work. The Nyuntam Aay Yojana scheme (the Congress's proposed social welfare programme) was not acceptable as a substitute for jobs. On the other hand, the BJP promised to improve ease of living, beyond just the ease of doing business, and strengthen the self-respect and ability of the average citizen to do more, which is exactly the right approach for an aspirational India.

There was fear of competitive populism in the event of a weak government being elected at the Centre. Now the BJP will hopefully focus, as promised in its manifesto, on infrastructure, housing, technology, health, education, water, the environment, and facilitate the move away from agricultural jobs to raise farmer incomes. Only 23 per cent of rural income now comes from farming, and there is a major ongoing shift to add value in agriculture. Apart from this, administrative reforms should be the focus. There are police and judicial reforms on the anvil. Well-targeted direct benefit transfers will efficiently deliver relief to the really distressed at low cost. Humility should come with strength. After an exceptionally bitter election season, the NDA will hopefully follow a constructive and inclusive agenda and encourage moderate progressive stances. Institutions are the backbone of any economy and must be strengthened. The people know the government took difficult decisions to clean up the system, and chose to give it a second chance. It is time to meet their expectations.

Thus, Indian politics has no doubt undergone fundamental transformation in the recent past. It has been influenced by demographic changes, such as a multi-fold increase in the size of middle class, penetration of social media, withering away of old hicrarchies and systematic changes in the nature of electoral battle. The social, political and geographical expansion of the BJP since 2014 has altered the political landscape which has resulted through the marginalization of the Congress party. The period after 2014 also witnessed an erosion in the electoral strength of the left parties in general and state level and regional parties in particular. Based on the aforesaid narration of India's political Saga, the authors would like to project the following observations:

- The party politics in India is highly ideological and divisions on the appropriate role of the state have influenced the changes in the Indian party system since the country's Independence. The different ideas on whether the state should intervene in social norms and whether it should single out disadvantaged groups for special treatment have long historical lineages.
- The national political scenario also witnessed the transition from the Congress dominant system to a multi-party competition to a party system centred around the BJP.
- The long-term structural decline especially the organisational pitfalls of the Congress party and the absence in bringing up a new and vibrant leadership both at the national and state levels created an atmosphere favourable to the right-wing parties, which was capitalised by the BJP.

The political and administrative discourses of India in 2019 and 2020 were to a large extent determined by two individuals and Prime Minister Narendra Modi and Amit Shah. From Jammu and Kashmir to Kanyakumari and from Kutch to Kohima, the impact of their political decisions was felt across the length and breadth of the nation. A mammoth tally of seats in the House of People and a near majority in the Council of States along with its allies ensured that both could translate their ideological will into a legislative action without much resistance from the opposition. But Modi government have to face serious threats from two fronts—economic and political. It is now an accepted fact that India's economy is in the doldrums with immediate and effective interventions required from the Centre to put the system back on track. So far, the corrective measures of the sender have failed to produce any tangible results and therefore, all eyes will be on the future course of actions— political, administrative and economic.

Contents of the Volume

In the inaugural paper **Prof. R.L.M Patil** examines the working of the Constitution and Democracy of India. He has made a detailed survey on the constitutional development and democratic practices of the last seven decades. To him, the experiment of Constitutional democracy has faced odds all over the world except in a few countries. Constitutions have been scrapped or replaced almost all over Asia, Africa, Latin America and even Europe for reasons of unworkability and changing circumstances. Pakistan, Bangladesh, Sri Lanka are some of the leading examples in our own neighbourhood. It is heartening to see that in India the Constitution, launched in 1950, is working well. Democracy and Constitution have helped each other well here. The performance of any institution or idea can never be perfect. The Indian laboratory for experimenting the joint working of democracy and Constitution has indeed been satisfactory although there is room for improvement.

In chapter two the **Volume Editors** have presented a paper on the 17th General Elections in India. According to the authors, about 900 million people were eligible to vote and turnout was over 67 per cent—the highest ever as well as the highest participation by women voters. The Bharatiya Janata Party won 303 seats, further increasing its substantial majority and the BJP-led National Democratic Alliance won 353 seats. The Indian National Congress won 52 seats, and the Congress-led United Progressive Alliance won 91. Other parties and their alliances won 98 seats. The

Congress again failed to secure the requisite 10 per cent of the seats (54 seats) in the Lok Sabha. Hence, India remains without an official Opposition party. Legislative assembly elections in the states of Andhra Pradesh, Arunachal Pradesh, Odisha and Sikkim were held simultaneously with the general election, as well as by-elections to twenty two seats of the Tamil Nadu Legislative Assembly. The whole study has been categorized under six major heads. Part-I unfolds the pre-poll scenario, Part-II examines the content of the poll manifestoes of various political fronts, parties and alliances, Part-III evaluates the Political Alliances and Combinations made by various parties, Part-IV deals with the reasons laid to the overwhelming success of BJP and its allies, Part-V critically studies the debacle of the Congress party, and Part-VI brings together the major findings of the study.

After making a detailed enquiry the authors came to the conclusion that, Indian voters have shown remarkable maturity and thoughtfulness in delivering a stable government at the Centre. They realise the necessity of a stable government, and so often vote differently in National and State elections. Forecasts of political and economic instability made in 2014, when the macro-economy was vulnerable, proved incorrect. Similar forecasts were made this year, based on the Bharatiya Janata Party (BJP-led National Democratic Alliance's) losses in the Karnataka, Madhya Pradesh and Rajasthan Assembly elections. The pundits should bow to the greater wisdom of the people—in this election, the BJP has swept the same States. The Congress underestimated the voters' continuing need for good governance. The Congress did not choose dynamic Chief Ministers when it had the option. It also underestimated the voters need for a positive narrative. Talking of slow job growth and farmer distress did not work. The Nyuntam Aay Yojana scheme (the Congress's proposed social welfare programme) was not acceptable as a substitute for jobs. On the other hand, the BJP promised to improve ease of living, beyond just the ease of doing business, and strengthen the self-respect and ability of the average citizen to do more, which is exactly the right approach for an aspirational India.

There was fear of competitive populism in the event of a weak government being elected at the Centre. Now the BJP will hopefully focus, as promised in its manifesto, on infrastructure, housing, technology, health, education, water, the environment, and facilitate the move away from agricultural jobs to raise farmer incomes. Only 23 per cent of rural income now comes from farming, and there is a major ongoing shift to add value in agriculture. Apart from this, administrative reforms should be the focus. There are police and judicial reforms on the anvil. Well-targeted direct benefit transfers will efficiently deliver relief to the really distressed at low cost. Humility should come with strength. After an exceptionally bitter election season, the NDA will hopefully follow a constructive and inclusive agenda and encourage moderate progressive stances. Institutions are the backbone of any economy and must be strengthened. The people know the government took difficult decisions to clean up the system, and chose to give it a second chance. It is time to meet their expectations.

After presenting the national scenario of the 17th Lok Sabha Polls in Chapter 3 the same authors have presented another paper on the Lok Sabha Polls [2019] in Kerala. According to the authors, when the Congress suffered drubbing in most parts of the country, Kerala bucked the trend and stood firmly with it, handing the party-led United Democratic Front a landslide. While the UDF won 19 of the 20 seats on offer, the Communists suffered a humiliating defeat, winning only one seat in their only remaining bastion. The verdict was almost a repeat of 1977 when the UDF won all 20 seats. The Sabarimala factor made its impact, but not as predicted. While the CPM-led Left Democratic Front suffered a debacle, the BJP-led NDA failed to win even a single seat. The BJP, riding on Sabarimala sentiments, had entertained hopes of winning at least two seats, but the best the party could achieve was a runner-up position in Thiruvananthapuram. In all other seats, the NDA finished third. However, the BJP was able to bag close to 3 lakh votes in Pathanamthitta and Thrissur. In their study the authors further state that for the left parties in Kerala it is the time for a clear introspection. Unless they adopt stringent corrective measures, they may soon be on the road to elimination. Arrogance of some top most leaders of the Left parties and violence promoted by a section are primarily responsible for the party's decline in the State. While the Kannur model of violence practiced by party workers across the State has had a drastic impact, even other factors cannot be neglected. While instances of apparent double speak led to a loss of credibility, a sour lack of connect with the masses too may have contributed to the rout. The authoritarian style of functioning of the state Chief Minister also contributed a lot. For example on issues like Sabarimala, the stand of the CM was not in tune with the ground realities prevailed in the State. The Hindus comprising the Ezhavas and Nairs have been main supporters of the CPM. The way the order of the Apex Court on Sabarimala was handled by the state government forced a large section of the Hindu women to desert the party. Further, the Left parties unlike the past are unable to convince the people outside the party and take them into confidence. The leadership even refused to listen the pulse of the common man, naturally the sympathizers began dwindling.

The authors summed up their study with the following observations:

- The Congress and UDF which gained tremendously in the elections have to face the uphill task of rising up to the aspirations of the people who had given a landslide mandate to the party and the front. KPCC president Mullappally Ramachandran had recently said it is a 'fearsome result,' clearly hinting at the responsibility the people of the state have vested in the Congress and its affiliates in the UDF. The Congress knows the votes polled by its candidates were mostly anti-incumbency ones against Pinarayi and Modi. The party leadership feels majority and minority consolidation has taken place in its favour. While the majority voted in protest against the political stand of the Chief Minister on the Sabarimala issue, the minority votes went in favour of Rahul Gandhi, against the Narendra Modi Government and its policies. Party think-tanks were surprised that around 10 lakh votes were removed from the voters list and that the Left front had meticulously planned electioneering by posting mostly Left-leaning officers for election duty. The non-functioning of the party machinery is the major reason the party leadership found behind such a large number of votes being removed from the list. The immediate challenge before the front is the local body polls in 2020. The front knows it has to rise up to the level of the present mandate and for that the organisational machinery has to be intact and proper. The Congress leadership knows the performance of the elected party MPs will be a major barometer for the public to vote in its favour in the local body polls as well as the 2021 assembly polls. Mullappally, who said priority will be given to a total revamp of the organisation from top to booth level, is seeking the support of the AICC president and his team for the same. With the party machinery in place, the Congress knows it can take on the challenge posed by the Left and the NDA in the next local body and assembly polls. The major contention the party and the front have to face will be the performance of the MPs. The leadership knows with a proper organisational machinery in place and the MPs performing according to the wishes of the people, then a repeat of the present success is not a difficult proposition. One can only keep one's fingers crossed.

- The vote share of the UDF, which won 19 out of 20 seats, has jumped from 42.08 per cent in the 2014 elections to 47.25 per cent in the 2019 elections. The LDF's share dipped from 40.23 per cent in 2014 to 35.2 per cent this time. While the BJP-led NDA failed to win even a single seat, its vote share has gone up. In 2014, the NDA had bagged 10.85 per cent of the votes. In 2019, the front's share has risen to 15.20 per cent, with the BJP accounting for 12.93 per cent of the votes, as per EC data. Party-wise, the Congress took home 37.27 per cent of the votes in 2019. Five years ago, the grand old party's Kerala unit had managed 31 per cent. The CPI(M) which contested 16 seats in 2019 as against the 15 in 2014, also increased its individual vote share from 22 per cent to 25.83 per cent, as per EC data. The Communist Party of India, which failed to score a single victory, saw its vote share dipping from 8 per cent in 2014 to 6.05 per cent.
- For the left parties in Kerala it is the time for a clear introspection. Unless they adopt stringent corrective measures, they may soon be on the road to elimination. Arrogance of some top most leaders of the left parties and violence promoted by a section are primarily responsible for the party's decline in the State. While the Kannur model of violence practiced by party workers across the state has had a drastic impact, even other factors cannot be neglected. While instances of apparent double speak led to a loss of credibility, a sour lack of connect with the masses too may have contributed to the rout. The authoritarian style of functioning of the state Chief Minister also contributed a lot. For example on issues like Sabarimala, the stand of the CM was not in tune with the ground realities prevailed in the state. The Hindus comprising the Ezhavas and Nairs have been main supporters of the CPM. The way the order of the Apex Court on Sabarimala was handled by the State government forced a large section of the Hindu women to desert the party. Further, the Left parties unlike the past are unable to convince the people outside the party and take them into confidence. The leadership even refused to listen the pulse of the common man, naturally the sympathizers began dwindling.
- The IUML's share remained constant with the party taking home 5.45 per cent of the votes. Kerala Congress (Mani) and the RSP

accounted for 2.07 per cent and 2.45 per cent respectively this time, a slight increase from 2014. In Vadakara, one of the keenly watched constituencies, K. Muraleedharan cornered over 5.26 lakh votes, increasing the UDF share from 43.48 per cent (Mullapally Ramachandran in 2014) to 49.6 per cent.

- In high-profile Wayanad, the candidature of 'Rahul Gandhi ensured that the UDF share climbed to a whopping 64% from 41.2 per cent. Ramya Haridas of the UDF wrested Alathur from the LDF by claiming over 50 per cent of the votes. The BJP, despite ending up third in Pathanamthitta, managed to bag almost 30 per cent of the votes. Same went for Thrissur where actor Suresh Gopi increased the saffron party's share to around 28 per cent. In Thiruvananthapuram, Shashi Tharoor, performing a hat-trick, increased his share from 34.2 per cent to around 41 per cent in the process.
- The popular narrative was that it was a 'minority consolidation' which facilitated the dream like run of the Congress-led United Democratic Front and the rout of the Left Democratic Front in the Lok Sabha election in Kerala. This reductionist view seems to be a gross under-reading of a very decisive political vote and a devaluation of a significant democratic resistance by a sizeable chunk of the electorate. The "minority consolidation theory" gained traction during the unending TV debates that followed exit poll results. It says that one of the two major reasons for the spectacular victory of the UDF with a success rate of 95 per cent was the consolidation of the Muslim vote in Malabar and the Christian vote in the central Kerala and coastal regions of the State.
- The other reason, according to this line of thinking, is the Sabarimala effect, which forced a substantial section of the Hindu faithful to vote for Congress. This, the claim goes, was to teach the LDF a lesson for tinkering with a Hindu religious practice. In effect, the UDF wave was triggered by the "majority consolidation" originating from a religious cause and the "minority consolidation originating from fear. However, in the popular narrative the minority consolidation is communal and other is not. True, Muslims and Christians, who made up 45 per cent of the electorate, did vote for the UDF in higher numbers this time than any other recent elections. Dubbing this as communal would be unfair. Rather, it was a decisive political vote which carried a clear political message that a majority

of the minority communities in Kerala did not want Modi as their Prime Minister, moreover elections in a democracy is exactly for this to choose your government and your ruler. More than a pro-UDF or anti-LDF vote, this was anti-Modi vote. It was a decisive political act aimed to unseat the BJP governance at the National Level.

In chapter four, **Prof. Mrudul Nile** presented a study on the performance of Maharashtra in the general elections 2019. Maharashtra, according to the author has a legacy of progressive social movements which are deep rooted in its social and political history. The state of Maharashtra has been one of the leading states contributing immensely to the social policies of the nation. A state that boasts of Gokhale, Agarkar, Lokmanya Tilak who contributed to the freedom struggle in India, to Mahatma Jyotirao Phule, Savatri Bai Phule and Dr. B.R. Ambedkar, who are the founders of the social thought of not only in Maharashtra but also in the entire country, left great impact on politics of today. Prof. Nile concluded his study by stating that,

- the voting pattern of Maharashtra which affects the Central government was seen in 2019 elections too. Earlier, the Congress used to replicate the pattern but now since 2014, BJP too has been successful to replicate the pattern.
- BJP exploited every opportunity to win the election. Pulwama was a life saving incident for the BJP.
- Congress's strategy to lure the people failed. Rahul Gandhi, the then Congress President, came with a slogan *'Chowkidar Chor Hai'* and tried to expose the issue of Rafael deal. But with the Pulwama attack, BJP stressed the need for it. Congress could not actually muster the support of the public sector undertakings which were being considered for privatisation, the bank employees strike, the farmers march, the *dalits* and Muslims.
- The Vanchit Bahujan Aghadi (VBA) was one of the most important factor which influenced the results in almost ten out of forty eight constituencies. In many places, VBA occupied third position.
- The Shiv Sena completely depends on BJP's campaign and more importantly derived the benefits of the Pulwama attack. Shiv Sena could not take up local issues effectively during the entire campaign of General Elections 2019.

The Citizenship (Amendment) Act, 2019 is the subject of discussion in chapter five. The **volume editors** have examined the constitutional and legal dimensions of the subject in this chapter. According to the authors, this new legislation gives an opportunity to illegal migrants who entered India on or before 31 December, 2014 for Indian Citizenship. The Act also specified that illegal migrant category includes Hindus, Sikhs, Buddhists, Jains, Parsis and Christians who came from Afghanistan, Pakistan and Bangladesh. It also seeks to relax the requirement of residence in India for citizenship by naturalisation from 11 years to 5 years for these migrants. The Act excludes Muslims from such eligibility. The Union Cabinet cleared the Bill on 4th December, 2019. It was passed by Lok Sabha on 10 December, 2019 and subsequently in the Rajya Sabha on 11 December, 2019. Keeping this in background this chapter attempts to examine the constitutional, legal and political implications of this legislation. The study has been classified under six broad heads—introduction, background of CAA provisions of granting citizenship, argument for and against CAA, its impact on north-east and finally views of various political parties on it.

No doubt, the CAA is a very serious move with far-reaching consequences and deeper impact on the basic character of the Constitution and therefore, it needs a closer look. It seeks to give shelter and protection to persecuted minorities in Bangladesh, Pakistan and Afghanistan. This ushers in a fundamental change in country's process of citizenship by naturalisation which allows foreigners to become Indians. Under the current legal dispensation, illegal immigrants cannot apply for Indian citizenship. Current law bars Hindu migrants from Bangladesh, who have entered India without papers to become citizens. It also excludes anyone who has entered using a legal document but has overstayed visa. At the same time, the CAA also shortens the waiting period for naturalisation for these chosen communities who would now require a six-year residence instead of the previous condition of having been a resident of India for at least 11 out of the last 14 years. Thus, once again creating two kinds of citizens that is a serious violation of fundamental rights granted to Indian citizens by the Constitution.

In the concluding observation the authors further states that the CAA aims to provide Citizenship to those who had been forced to seek shelter in India because of religious persecution or fear of persecution in their home countries—Afghanistan, Pakistan and Bangladesh. It is primarily meant Hindus, Sikhs, Jains, Buddhists, Parsis and Christians. This is a drastic shift from the professions of the Citizenship Act of 1955 that labels a person as an 'illegal immigrant', if he or she has entered India without travel documents or has overstayed the date specified in the documents. It therefore amends the 1955 Act to grand exemptions to illegal migrants from the above mentioned countries, who reached India on or before December 2014. Further, according, this new Act, the Amendment will not be applicable to the tribal areas of Meghalaya, Mizoram or Tripura as included in the 6th Schedule to the Constitution and in the areas covered under the 'inner line' notified under the Bengal Eastern Frontier Regulation of 1873. Finally, it also proposes to incorporate a sub-section (D) in Section 7, providing for cancellation of Overseas Citizenship of India (OCI) registration where the OCI card holder has violated any provision of the Citizenship Act or any other law in force.

After the submission of a chapter on Citizenship (Amendment) Act, 2019 the **same authors** came out with another chapter on the Right to Information (Amendment) Bill, 2019. According to the authors, Right to Information (RTI) is Act of the Parliament of India to provide for setting out the practical regime of the right to information for citizens and replaces the erstwhile Freedom of Information Act, 2002. Under the provisions of the Act, any citizen of India may request information from a "public authority" (a body of Government or "instrumentality of State") which is required to reply expeditiously or within thirty days. The Act also requires every public authority to computerise their records for wide dissemination and to proactively certain categories of information so that the citizens need minimum recourse to request for information formally. This law was passed by Parliament on 15 June, 2005 and came fully into force on 12 October, 2005. Everyday, over 4800 RTI applications are filed. In the first ten years of the commencement of the Act over 17,500,000 applications had been filed.

Transparency seems to be the only means for sustaining democratic governance. That is why the right to information has been legislated in about 70 countries of the world, and another 30 countries are in the process of legislation. It was in this context that the RTI was enacted in India in 2005. The experience of 5 years shows that the response to this Act has been very positive and optimistic. It has also been widely welcomed by the people at all levels. They have been seeking various types of Information from different authorities. The RTI Act confers on all citizens the right to seek information and makes it the duty of the public authorities to disseminate the same for better governance and accountability. It covers the Central, State and Local governments and recipients of Government Grants but does not apply to the intelligence and security organisations except if the information released to the allegations of corruption. Against this backdrop, an attempt has been made here to examine the fundamental linkages and differences between RTI Act, 2005 with the Right to Information Amendment Bill, 2019.This chapter has been categorized under five major heads—Part-I examines the legislating right to information in Indian context, Part-II makes an indepth critical enquiry on the features as well as working of the RTI Act, 2005. Part-III unearths the salient features of the Right to Information (Amendment) Bill, 2019. This part also makes a comparative appraisal of these two historic legislations and Part-IV presents the concluding observations.

The authors summed up their study with the following comments:

- Every citizen has the right to know how the government is functioning. Right to information empowers every citizen to obtain information from the government. It is duty of public authorities to maintain records for the easy access and to publish within 120 days the name of the particular officer who should give information and in regard to the framing of the rules and regulations. All informations shall be disseminated widely and in such form and manner which is easily accessible to the public. It has been provided that it is required that the request to be disposed of within 30 days: provided that where information sought for concerns life or liberty of a person, the same shall be provided within 48 hours. If a request is rejected it shall be communicated giving reasons and specifying the procedure for appeal and the designation of the appellate authority. The Act also exempts granting information where it would disproportionately divert the resources of the public authority or would be detrimental to the safety and preservation of the record in question.
- Knowledge and information is the prerequisite for the enjoyment of this right because the lack of authentic information on matters of public interest leads to the wild rumors. Freedom of speech and expression includes the right to receive and collect information. Since the democracy is the government of the people who are the sovereign masters. There can be no government by the people if they are ignorant of the issues to be resolved, the argument for and against different solutions and the facts underlying those arguments. The taxes collected by the government belong to the people. They have the right to know in what manner they are being governed and how their money is

being spent. The business of the government should be a participatory process. The fact should be made public. Only a fully informed citizenry can be better equipped for the performance of these duties.

- The Right to Information Act enables the citizens to get the required information for the redressal of the grievances within a specified time from the date of filing application. Any citizen can ask for information under this law by applying in writing or through electronic means to the Public Information Officer (PIO), specifying the particulars of the information sought for. The right to information has been judicially recognized as a part of the fundamental right to speech and expression. Information is *sine qua non* for the efficient functioning of democracy. It keeps the people informed about the socio-political and economic affairs and issues. In a developing country like India, the availability of the information is required to be assured to the people in a simple and speedy manner because the development process depends on it.
- Over the past few years, RTI has gained increasing importance in the human rights discourse as well as the larger democratic discourse. Since a democratic government must be sensitive to the public opinion for which information must be made available by it to the people. Effective accountability rests on the peoples' acquaintance with the information. A system that operates in secrecy tends to loose the faith of the people as much as its own legitimacy and credibility. Openness and full access to the information are the two pillars of the democratic state. It will equip the citizens to participate meaningfully in the democratic and political process. Governance is undoubtedly strengthened by the RTI. That is why the RTI has been recognized as an essential requirements of the good governance. The enactment of the RTI Act, 2005 is a bold step. The Act covers not only the public sector but also the NGOs and the private sector to some extent. In addition to this, it has various other positive features like provision of First and Second Appellate Authorities. It is also one of the toughest legislations in the world, as it is the only RTI Act imposing penalty for any contravention of the provisions of the Act.
- However, mere conferment of the right is not enough. Its successful implementation in the true spirit is needed. The

revision and review of legislations contrary to this right is required. Suitable amendments in the conduct rules for public servants, attitudinal change in the behaviour of the bureaucracy, creation of efficient information management system, more frequent use of this right by press and will of the citizens are also required. Many loopholes need to be plucked. However, despite the weaknesses, it is a *Magna Carta* for introducing reforms in the governance of the country and will go a long way in strengthening the roots of democracy by introducing transparency and accountability in governance.

It is further observed that serious problems highlighted above with regard to the amendment proposals and the justification underlying them, it is advisable that the Amendment Bill has to be redrafted and recasted thoroughly. Instead the requisite orders may be issued to upgrade the salaries of the Information Commissioners at all levels in accordance with the provisions of the RTI Act as they exist today and initiate measures to improve their functioning by providing them with an adequate number of staff of high calibre for quickly disposing appeals and complaints.

In chapter seven **Tanvi Yadav** and **Prof. Nagendra Ambedkar Sole** also presented a paper titled "RTI (Amendment) Act, 2019: A Threat to Participatory Democracy". According to the authors in a Democracy, awareness of people is the only source of surviving. Right to information is considered as the fundamental human right under the preview of UDHR at International level. In India, Right to Information was enacted to bring out transparency and accountability in governance. The evolution of Right to Information includes enormous debates, discussions and several battles in social as well as the legal field in the form of movements and petitions, respectively. After such a long struggle, when the time has come to make the Information Commission as a constitutional body, Government is cutting the powers and independence of Information Commissioners through the amendment in RTI Act. The 2019 amendment in the RTI Act is a threat to participatory democracy and autonomy of the Information Commission. People can be free when they have the right to participate in democracy through their knowledge about their freedom. The chapter explores the journey of RTI in India from evolution to judiciary commitment and examines how the current amendment is a threat to Right to Information.

The authors concluded their study with the following comments and observations:

- Spirit of any democracy can be justified by the Right of the people to inspect those in power. Without discussion and dispute, the establishment of democracy will be empty at its centre. After Independence, among the progressive laws of India, RTI Act is accepted and considered as dynamic law in the nation. It is the most sincere hope to survive the dying democracy of India.
- Now when the time has come to make Information Commission as a constitutional body, the government is trying to destroy its soul by threatening the independent position of Chief Information Commissioner and Information Commissioner by taking advantage of Information Commission not being a constitutional body. However, the Government cannot "punish" an independent-minded IC by removing them. The provision of the RTI Act governing the removal of ICs is not affected by this amendment, and the rules cannot be changed to cut short the tenure of anyone IC without falling a foul of the principal RTI Act. Though, the steps of government make it clear that there is a threat to the government in revealing Information to the people.
- Right to Information promotes the public interest by promoting openness in administration, discouraging arbitrariness in decision-making and making administration responsible towards ordinary people. It can be used as a tool of corruption check and prevent arbitrary state actions. Aruna Roy and Nikhil Dey rightly pointed out that the RTI has been and will be used for transparency and accountability in India and government will realise that they can amend a law but cannot stop a movement.
- Right to information with the upliftment of judiciary can be a great check and balance of governance in India. As Abraham Lincoln said in 1861, "Let the people know the facts, and the country will be safe", it is necessary to the development and security of the country to make the people aware. However, the present RTI amendment is not only a threat to RTI but also to the notion of participatory democracy.

In chapter eight, **Prof P. Lazarus Samraj, Gothanda Moorthy** and **Vineeth Thomas** intends to throw light on the major factors which are affecting the peculiar conditions of Indian democracy, namely Money, Media and Corporate. This chapter keenly analyses each factor and finally puts forward practical solutions to contain these three factors. According to the authors, Democracy is the only highly acceptable effective *modus* *operandi* for the peaceful transfer of power between competing political groups. Rich legacy of democracy in UK and USA and the decolonisation process after Second World War played a catalytic role in the adoption of democracy throughout the world. Orange revolution, Bulldozer revolution, Jasmine revolution, revolts against authoritarian regimes in Tunisia, Libya, Egypt, Nepal and Myanmar are some of the visible examples of aspirations of humanity to adopt democracy.

India, the largest democracy in the world is experimenting constitutional democracy since her Independence during mid-twentieth century. There are plenty of factors that are corroding Indian democracy. Only the time tested constitution and well established political institutions can pull the transitional Indian democracy to the level of mature democracy. It is historically proven fact that attaining democratic maturity is a time consuming process. For instance, British who had started practising democracy in thirteenth century attained maturity only in twentieth century by undergoing lots of turmoil, bloodshed, instability etc.

In chapter nine, **Soumya Sagarika Sahoo** and **Prof. Padmalaya Mahapatra** have presented a paper on the role of state administration in accelerating farmers' income. It is a study based on Odisha. According to the authors, agriculture and allied activities is an important sector of the economy of Odisha, providing livelihoods, reducing poverty, ensuring food security and giving a boost to industry and service sectors. As the economy progresses, countries have experienced the movement of labour and capital from extractive and commodity production sectors to value added activities—both in manufacturing and service sector. This has occurred in Odisha as well. However, this does not diminish the importance of the agricultural sector; rather, it allows scope to improve productivity as technology changes and facilitates growth in the economy. Agriculture sector in 2018-19 posted high growth after a sharp downturn in the preceding year. The agriculture sector is also the largest employer in the state. As per the Periodic Labour Force Survey of 2017-18, 48.8 per cent of workers [aged 15 and above as per Usual Principal and Subsidiary Status (UPSS)] are engaged in agriculture and allied activities. This sector is a major source of employment, especially in rural areas; 56 per cent of the total rural workers are employed in the agriculture sector. The target of doubling farmers' income in a short period requires identification of sources of income growth and enabling conditions for harnessing their growth potential. The chapter concludes with an observation effective coordination between Centre and States is important in mainstreaming and channelising policies and investment to achieve the target of doubling farmers' income.

Prof. D. Pulla Rao in chapter ten came out with a paper on the economic status and living standards of agricultural women workers. It is a case study of Vishakapatanam district of Andhra Pradesh. According to Prof. Rao, in the lower socio-economic level of the society, women do more hazardous manual labour than men. Women do more than half of the agricultural works in India. Still men are considered to be the bread winners. This sense of women being inferior is passed on from one generation through psychological conditionings. The most widespread and de-humanising discriminations and assault against women are on the psychological level. The female psyche is being crushed at the very childhood. The female psyche is brutalised long before bodily violence is inflicted on her. They are conditioned to accept inferior positions in society. Women from childhood undergo a slow unconscious process of destructive or denial of their self-worth. Society, through a process of conditioning, creates in girls at home and in school certain thinking patterns, which ascribed to the female sex an inferior status.

Besides, society gradually trains them to make this value system their own. Usually baby girls are given bangles, anklets etc. thus communicating a sense of fragility. Another result of the social conditioning is that man either as father, brother or husband considers women as socio-economic gift of his household. A woman's value judged, not so much in terms of her worth as a person with rights and dignity as in terms of her utility to man. Expression of this mentality is found in different language and society. For example, in national language Hindi, girl is called '*paraya dhan*' and boy '*apana dhan*'. Any assessment of the status of women has to start from the social framework, social structures, cultural norms and value systems that influence social expectations regarding the behaviour of both men and women and determine women's roles and their position in the society.

In chapter eleven, **Dr. Santhosh Mathew** made an explorative study on gender inequality and women empowerment. According to Dr. Mathew women make 49.6 per cent of world population and 48.17 per cent of Indian population. India is at 191st position out of 201 countries in terms of female to male ratio. Among Asian countries, India is at 43rd position out of 51 countries on the basis of UN (world population prospects) and Ministry of Statistics and Programme Implementation (MOSPI), India. There is no contradict of the truth, that women in India after a long struggle achieved a considerable development in approximately seventy years of freedom, however they have still to fight against many cultural barriers and social restrictions in the country. Everyday we see that in the society from ancient to till date to the privileges, responsibilities and opportunities of women, it depends on the cultural traditions and customs of the family and society. Women empowerment is the practice by which women gain power and control more than their own lives and attain the capabilities to form their choices. This is very important because throughout the world women are still facing biased in access to education, work and economic assets and participation in government. India has slightly improved in World Economic Forum (WEF)'s wage equality for similar work indicator, where it stood at 72nd place. The country has also closed its tertiary education enrolment gap for the first time in 2018 has managed to keep its primary and secondary gap closed for the third year running. Interestingly, India has the second largest Artificial Intelligence (AI) workforce but one of the largest AI gender gaps, with only 22 per cent of roles filled by women. So, women empowerment is a one of the major achievement to Sustainable Development. In this chapter we are trying to find out gender equality and women empowerment indices based on 8 population indicators of the 29 States and 7 Union Territories of India, from 4th National Family Health Survey (NFHS). In this study we are trying to cluster the groups based on urban and rural populations of the 36 States/UTs of India using Cluster Analysis. It is useful for policy-makers to take decisions for women development activities and empowerment.

In chapter twelve, **Prof. Padmalaya Mahapatra** presented her second paper on gender and development. It is a study of maternal and child health care policies in the state of Odisha. This present study is based on both primary and secondary sources of data. The chapter attempts to analyse the impact of maternal health care policies on women's health status in Odisha. It mainly focuses on maternal mortality relating to socio-economic characteristics of deceased, status of antenatal care, major causes that led to maternal death, major steps taken through various policies and programmes initiated by Government of India/Government of Odisha and their achievement. According to the author, gender discourse within the field of development has come a long way from building a case of 'inclusive' growth which prevents the marginalisation of women to questioning of the predominant notions of development itself. The body of feminist critique continues to traverse new terrains and posit new challenges. The neo-liberal vision of society with a strong undercurrent of economic determinism often celebrates the atomistic, unconnected, self-maximising individual— a conception which largely inhibits the space of both culture and development. Women's limited access to and control of material resources and limited decision-making power within the household can produce high fertility rates, under-investment in aspects of family welfare, such as child nutrition and education, and sub-optimal allocations of human capital in the economy. Maternal morbidity and mortality along with infant mortality rate is universally considered as human development indicators in a country and determines the health status of the people. In spite of very good plans and programmes, the reduction in MMR & IMR is much below the target set in Odisha.

Dr. Indra Kumar in chapter thirteen presents an evaluative and assessment study of the organized *versus* unorganised manufacturing industries in India. According to Dr Kumar, there was drastic growth in the manufacturing industries in the country in recent years. As compared with the unorganised manufacturing the organised manufacturing industries has expanded at large scale. The adoption of new economic reforms in 1991 has helped the manufacturing sector to grow much faster. There is sharp rise in the large scale manufacturing industries in the country after this reform with the help of foreign direct investments. Country has become one of the most favoured industrial destinies of the world for certain manufacturing items like automobile industries. The present chapter aims to assess the contribution from the organised and unorganised segment of manufacturing industries in the country since 1980. The author further adds that there was drastic growth in the manufacturing industries in the country in recent years. As compared with the unorganised manufacturing the organised manufacturing industries has expanded at large scale. The implementation of new economic reforms in 1991 has helped the manufacturing sector to grow much faster. There is sharp rise in the large scale manufacturing industries in the country after this reform. Country has become one of the most favoured industrial destiny of the world for certain manufacturing items like automobile industry.

In chapter fourteen, **Tanvi Yadav** and **Prof. Nagendra Ambedkar Sole** presented their second submission titled, 'Legal Interventions and Women Empowerment against Witch Hunting in Rajasthan'. According to the author, empowerment of women is possible only when such superstition and unscrupulous beliefs are rooted out from the society. Prevailing laws in India have failed to address this issue. Different social activists, groups, and even judiciary have on numerous times voiced for the need of special laws to stop such inhuman activities, yet there is no national law on the subject, though some states have enacted special laws such as the Rajasthan Witch Hunting Prevention Act, 2015, enacted recently to curb growing menace of witch-hunting. The present chapter analyses the prevalence of the cultural violence in Rajasthan through case studies. This chapter will also investigate the need of legal reforms to stop such social evil and to empower victims of this evil practice, at the grassroots level.

In chapter fifteen, **Phulmoni Das** made a critical appraisal of the subaltern resistance in India. It is study of the identity movement of the tea garden community of Assam. Further this chapter is an attempt to trace out the theoretical understanding of the subaltern resistances in India since colonial period. India also has been witnessing the proliferation of subaltern movements in post-Independent period. This chapter also tries to highlight the quest for identity movement of the tea garden community of Assam, as this community has been recognised as the one of the most marginal and depressed group of section. Based on their marginality and subalternity this community is referred as subaltern. Deprivation of this identity has lead to another phase of movement among the tea garden community of Assam. Ever since India became Independent these people lost their Scheduled Tribe status in Assam and thus they were deprived of their educational, economic and political privileges guaranteed by the Constitution of India.

According to the author, Subaltern resistance led by the subaltern groups is not new phenomenon to Indian history as it has been deeply marked in a long historical time. But the struggles of the subaltern groups have not been added to the mainstream discourses of history writing for quite some time. It was the initiative of the Subaltern Studies Group who first tried to make a serious attempt to trace the missing linkages of Subaltern struggle and to bring it to the mainstream discourses. Indian politics is marked by the influence of different subaltern movements lead by different subaltern groups such as *dalits, adivasis*, rural landless, tribals, minorities etc. India became independent, these people lost their Scheduled Tribe status in Assam and thus they were deprived of their educational, economic and political privileges guaranteed by the Constitution of India.

In chapter sixteen, **Dr. Deepak Kumar Pandey** came out with a study, titled 'Interrogating Citizenship: A glimpse of Vantangia Community'. According to Dr. Pandey, since the outset of the societal institutions with power structure, the question of individual status *vis-à-vis* these structures have been enquired into. The quest to find some theorisation and to maintain the equilibrium between these two; leads too many theories, some tilted towards one end and some towards another. Some theories make efforts to have a proper balance between these two. From ancient Greek theorists to modern theorists, effort has been made to draw and point the line on which this balance could be made. What is the role of society, state or structures embedded with power? What are its need and limitations? For what purpose these are made? How their legitimacy be claimed? What is the role and status of individual *vis-à-vis* these structures? And if the individuals (on whom these powers have to be used) are the source of legitimacy; can they take their legitimacy out of these structures? What, if these structures will not work according to wish and needs of these individuals? And many more questions arise and have been enquired into deeply. Reciprocal needs, the basic chord of societal structure leads to the Aristotelian conclusion that man is social and political animal. What makes this social 'animal' along with reciprocal needs, which makes it 'political'? How to manage these reciprocal needs? Who will control and coordinate these needs? Need to control and coordinate these needs amongst the social 'animals' lead to power structure. But again, by which mechanism this power structure is to be used? How this mechanism will locate the individual in this power structure? Whether it is a kind of contract or kind of subjection? Again question arises, up to what level these power dynamics can be exercised? What would be the controlling areas and what would be the periphery of individual domain? Should any space be left out for those individuals, upon which these controlling power is to be exercised?

After his detailed enquiry Dr. Pandey concludes his study by stating that, state and political structures should ever-ready and open to accommodate the citizenry in the new developments and needs of the societal structure. State and its legal citizenship should not work as barrier for accommodating diversities and new developments, rather political and social structures should move and evolve in tandem to have better citizenry rights and political entitlements. Conceptualisation of *Public Sphere* by Habermas as a space for deliberation and democratic citizenship masks many of the inequalities and hierarchies. Citizenship should be viewed and should come out of its legal trap to accommodate its 'own' people, for their better life and subsistence. Coming out of legal trap does not mean that being illegal; rather it means that, legal structures should not be in the confines and their own shackles. There should be enough elasticity to cover the emerging and ongoing socio-political needs, moves and developments. We have to perceive the polity and its structures 'out of the box' of procedures and lock of the authority (or political power).

Because of Vantangia, thousands of Acre of land between Dehradun to Gorakhpur gets blessed with vast area of natural forest. But despite all their contributions to society and nation, they are still struggling for their citizenry rights and entitlements. Even after 66 years of independence they are forced to be second rate citizens. They are still waiting for their new dawn, in which they are seen and considered as equals as citizens. There is a need to break this 'disconnect', which is prevailing between the 'demos' and the polity. There is a need to adopt the sustainable local development approach, in which the 'people' at the periphery get the entitlements and opportunities in decision-making and a chance to have dignified life as a human being enriching citizenship in ever evolving mode, with new array of rights in their socio-political domain. "Democracy, in the modern sense, is going to be the institution of a space whose social function has had to emancipate itself from any concrete content... What is at stake is more than procedures; it is the institution of signifiers of a social lack resulting from the absence of God as fullness of Being."

From the human security perspective, they need urgent attention of government, society and other institutions. Bringing governance out of the shackles of legality and turning it into humane governance can only bring their citizenry entitlements. They should have been given the land rights and the duty to protect the forests to which they are emotionally and almost culturally associated, then only dawn of true independence will reach to these 'wretched of the earth' and then only being citizen become meaningful term for them.

In chapter seventeen, **Dr Sujit Lahiry** presents a study on Democracy, Secularism and Religio-Political Corruption in India. This chpater treats the mixing of religion and politics, i.e. religious politics as a manifestation of political corruption, especially as illustrated in contemporary India. It critically analyses the endemic communal and divisive politics of the Sangh Parivaar, ever since 2014, when the Narendra Modi government came to power. The Modi-Amit Shah duo had unleashed a reign of terror, which can be referred to as 'Hindu Terrorism'. The author further states that the framers of the Constitution of India had vowed to constitute India into a 'Sovereign, Socialist, Secular, Democratic, Republic'. And, the Indian state under Nehru avowedly followed this principle, both in letter and spirit. However, the rise of erstwhile Jan Sangh and later on BJP in the last two decades had fuelled the rise of Hindu-Muslim communal polarization. It is also envisioned in BJPs overzealous drive to create a 'Hindu Rashtra'. In other words, the state far from being a neutral arbiter in religious matters is trying to forge a dominant and majoritarian Hindu nationalism and democracy.

Studies and researches on Gender and Political Economy is the core area of discussion in chapter eighteen. This chapter is contributed by **Dr. S. Venkatanarayanan** and **Dr. Valentina Fusari.** According to them, the correlation between gender and political economy is intricate and contentious, as the precise nature of its nexus is complex to be comprehended. Gender roles are very rigidly practiced widely, similar to caste and class hierarchies entrenched in the social fabric. Gender organises social life and thus much of individual experiences. It also contributes to the gendered roles in neoliberal political economy—lack of security, opportunity, and empowerment, which ultimately lowers the quality of life. This article is an attempt to examine the relation between gender and neoliberalism to understand how women are socialised as a weaker gender within it. The nature of wage employment and its forms within neoliberalism reveals the gendered exploitation in this political economy. The article will elaborate the larger theoretical understanding of gender to understand the impact of neoliberal political economy in contemporary times. In the concluding chapter (nineteen) the **volume editors** presented a study on Gandhian concepts of Decentralisation and Democracy and its relevance in the present day context.

Keeping this background in view, an attempt has been made in his volume to address the issues pertaining to a wide-ranging areas and aspects of the recent Indian Politics.

REFERENCES

M.R. Biju, "Debacle of the Congress and Left in General Election," *South Asia Politics*, Vol. 18, No. 8, December 2019.

M.R. Biju, "General Elections 2019 in India: Political Interludes behind the Success of BJP and NDA," *Social Science in Perspective*, Vol. 11, No. 3 & 4, July-December 2019.

M.R. Biju, "Performance of the Non-BJP Parties in India's 17th General Elections, 2019," *Mainstream*, Vol. LVII, No. 47, November 9, 2019.

M.R. Biju, "Political Significance of 2019 General Elections in India," *Ideal Journal of Legal Studies*, Vol. 10, No. 10, August 2019.

M.R. Biju, "Regional and Social Parties in General Elections," *South Asia Politics*, Vol. 18, No. 10, February 2020.

M.R. Biju, "The 17th Lok Sabha Polls in Kerala: Decisive Political Vote," *South Asian Journal of Socio-Political Studies*, Vol. XX, No.1, July-December 2019.

M.R. Biju, "The Citizenship (Amendment) Act, 2019," *South Asia Politics*, Vol. 18, No. 9, January 2020.

M.R. Biju, "The RTI (Amendment) Bill," 2019, *South Asia Politics*, Vol. 18, No. 7, November 2019.

Rahul Verma, "How the BJP's Dominance changed India's Political Landscape?," *Times of India*, 29 December 2019.

Subhash C. Kashyap, State of Indian Democracy, *South Asia Politics*, Vol. 16, No. 5, September 2017.

PART 1

Political Dynamics in India

1

Constitution and Democracy

70 Years of India's Experience

R.L.M. Patil

The famous French general and statesman Napoleon Bonaparte had an argument with his adviser Talleyrand on what a constitution should be like. Napoleon's view was that it should be short and precise. Talleyrand said "No Sir, it should be long and flexible".

The makers of our Constitution seem to have taken the advice of Talleyrand seriously. Our experience in the last seventy years reflects the political correctness of the view. The constitution of modern democracies like the U.S. and France confirm that a constitution is not simply a legal document but also a political manifesto which contains compromises and contradictions. The textual theory and the practical necessities together determine the functioning of the constitution. To cite just one example: both U.S. and French Constitutions contemplate a parliamentary/congressional system of government and yet gave way to a presidential model of government because of the historic fact that a great figure happened to be elected the President of the Country, Gen. George Washington in the U.S. and Gen. Charles De Gaulle in France. In India if Pandit Nehru was to be the President and an ordinary politician the Prime Minister, our Constitution, too, would have worked out the Presidential way without a change of any provision in the Constitution!

Coming to the elements of contradictions and compromises one can cite competitive claims in the Constitution of India:

- Fundamental rights and restriction on them
- Fundamental rights and state directive principles

- Parliamentary supremacy and judicial supremacy
- President and Prime Minister
- Central and State governments
- America's federal and judicial characters, and British Parliamentary and unitary characteristics.

It is a tribute to the statesmanship of the past Prime Ministers, Presidents, Chief Ministers and Judges of the higher judiciary that our Constitution had mostly a smooth run so far. Now and then we have experienced a few hiccups. We have grown wiser with experience, no doubt. Yet, there is room for improvement. Democratic spirit and constitutional morality have to be nurtured continuously if the system has to bear fruit as Sri Pranab Mukherjee, a former President, observed a few months ago.

If the twin fundamentals of democratic spirit and constitutional morality have to be put in a nutshell, it may be that all the people of India should have freedom and equality with a sense of justice; political stability and economic development should be achieved along with national unity and security. Democracy and constitution should be able to feed one another. The process is long and complicated. In the light of experience gained so far, one may suggest a host of measures to avoid malevolent developments. A few novel features may also be mooted.

Supreme Court: The present day Supreme Court has come to gather power and significance which it did not have until 1980s. There are multiple reasons for this new development. A doubt arises that in the coming days it may be burdened with even more heavy load of work, and the institution may assume the role of an arbiter in all the spheres of the state activity, be it political, constitutional, economic, environmental, educational, administrative and even religious. The judicial system should not collapse under its own weight. Some urgent reforms apart, a new suggestion may be made to lessen its burden on deciding the constitutionality of an increasing number of legislative and executive decisions. In France the Supreme judicial body there does not have the jurisdiction of examining any parliamentary act and declaring it unconstitutional. This important job is entrusted to 'State Council'. Its views are sought by the French Parliament before an Act is passed or dropped. Thereafter, it cannot be questioned anywhere. If this is followed in India the Supreme Court would be relieved of a huge task. The Apex Court could concentrate on other issues arising from the original and the appellate jurisdictions.

Dr. B.R. Ambedkar when asked what, according to him, was the most important provision of the Constitution, said "Article 14" without hesitation. Though true to a great extent, this provision seems to be at odds with ruling of the judiciary that "bail is a rule where jail is a exception". This statement almost negates the most valuable promise made by the Constitution because tens of lakhs of poor and helpless people are awaiting in jails for a fair and prompt trial for their supposed 'crimes' for several years—sometimes for 20 or 25 years—while some of the powerful, rich and influential people like former or existing Chief Ministers (Lalu Prasad, Jayalalitha), ministers (Chidambaram), politicians, bureaucrats, businessmen, film actors and others could arrange for quick or delayed trial as per their wish. Important judicial reforms suggested by several committees are yet to be taken up for consideration by the Parliament and the Executive. In the meanwhile 'equality before law' is applauded by the Constitutional *pundits*.

Parliament: There is no common ground between Britain and India in matter of polity, economy, society and national character. In spite of this, the British 'parliamentary democracy' seems to have been lifted and planted in India. The calibre of the voters and the capability of the candidates in the electoral fray in the two countries differ vastly. Yet the transplanted system is supposed to work equally well here. Not only this, the 'Parliamentary procedure' which guides the working of the legislative system, also appears to be near identical in both the countries. Perhaps in UK the procedure undergoes changes as per the changed circumstances but in India this colonial hangover continues unabated. A few glaring out-of-date practices:

- Stages of consideration of a Bill.
- Speaker's election, privileges and powers.
- Budget-making and presentation (secrecy, date of commencement etc.).
- Privileges of the House/Members.
- Discipline in and productivity of the House's deliberations.
- The Committee System.

It would be worthwhile to look at how the legislature in the U.S. functions, for a change. The Committee-system followed in the U.K. and U.S. differs vastly in the purpose, method and efficiency. In the U.S. the Senate Committees for example on foreign affairs and defence issues are working phenomenally well. But we are following a non-descript system here.

Executive although not specifically stated anywhere in the Constitution, it is generally believed that the Constitution of India envisages a parliamentary system of governance as in the U.K. It has worked on this basis for the past seventy years. Norms, decorum and level of deliberations in the parliaments of the two countries differ so widely that it would be futile to say we work on the Westminster model of parliamentary democracy. No minister here resigns when allegations of corruption, misconduct or impropriety are levelled against him. He would mostly react by saying these allegations are part of conspiracy hatched by the opponents to make him resign. MPs and MLAs express no remorse for their misconduct inside the House during the proceedings. Many of them are found busy elsewhere and take little or no interest in the Parliamentary work.

Council of Ministers is the most significant component of the Parliamentary system. Headed by the Prime Minister it is the supreme executive arm of the state. In India it possesses no particular shape or size. Its composition does not necessarily reflect either merit or suitability, but only indicates that geographic, gender, caste, religion and special interests are taken into account. These considerations *per se* not bad, but indeed part of democratic forces. However, what worries is the fact that, in some cases a too flexible or too unwieldy Council is formed. In the Union Cabinet, Ministers/Ministries are found to be in-charge of the State subjects, like agriculture, forestry, drinking water, road transport etc. Once, there were three cabinet Ministers in the Central Government who dealt with Panchayati Raj, Rural Development and Dry-land Development! In the state of Uttar Pradesh, there were three Ministers for electricity: one for its production, another for its distribution and the third for its consumption affairs! Education is handled by several Ministries—Higher, Middle and Primary, Technical, Sports and Culture, Engineering, Medical, Agriculture, Law, Vocational and others.

In the U.S. the number of Ministries/Departments are limited to a specific number and subjects as per an Act of the Congress. In Switzerland, the Constitution itself enumerates what would be the Ministries. In India the size and specification of the Ministries are flexible beyond description. Once in Karnataka, the Chief Minister Sri Ramakrishna Hegde appointed Sri Poddar as Minister for Coffee while there were other Ministers for Sugar and Milk. Fortunately, there is limitation on the number of Ministers a state can have: 15 per cent of the MLAs and MLCs. Even this does not stand to reason fully. There are states as big as Uttar Pradesh, Madhya Pradesh, West Bengal etc. while small states like Goa, Manipur etc. also exist. Budgetary allocations matter, too. Ministries may be organised on a near-equal footing. Special consideration like tribal affairs etc. also needs to be taken in account. There is hierarchy among the ministers, too. Some are of the Cabinet rank while others are of the status of Ministers of State whatever it might mean! Sometimes, Ministers are appointed without their being a member of the legislature. Their term expires after six months. But no problem; they are reappointed the day after the expiry of the term. (It happened in Punjab). All in all, there is a need to take a fresh look at the composition, structure and functioning of the Council of Ministers.

We claim that the Westminster model is followed here. A significant matter we have ignored altogether in the model is the concept of Shadow Cabinet. As an alternative to the prevalent Councils of Ministers an opposition party in the U.K. draws up a list of possible Ministers in charge of different subjects who would train themselves to take over the responsibilities of a government if a chance permits them. Background preparation would have been provided by advance-training to the would-be ministers. Even in the ruling party a set of MPs could be enlisted to prepare themselves in the specific subjects so as to enable them to contribute to the debates in the House meaningfully. This measure, if followed by all the parties in the Parliament, would go a long way in heralding a healthy and meaningful deliberations in the House.

Time-sharing for Government: One of the principles of parliamentary democracy is that those who manage to secure 51 per cent of seats on the floor of Lower House of Parliament should form government while all others would sit in opposition (wilderness). If the loser party, or group of parties, were to command strength of 49 per cent, or near to it, should they necessarily be denied the opportunity of forming the government? For all the remaining time? Should it be then a proposition of zero-sum game? Why not make it a non-zero-sum game?

If there are only two major political parties, or even three, and each have won a sizeable number of seats, would it not be fair to allot a share in time to run the government according to their strength in the House? The total period of an Assembly is 60 months. Party A might have got 51 per cent of strength; Party B got 40 per cent and other(s) 9 per cent. In proportion to the seats why not they be entrusted with power to run the government for 30 months and 24 months respectively? This type of distributive justice may appear to be radical and unusual but it stands to reason. In Karnataka some time ago the Congress, BJP and JD (S) had held strength of 20 per cent each. Instead of making them share power cordially and constitutionally for 20 months each, they were forced to play power-game/political manipulation/immoral political opportunism and hold power for an equal period of time as per their strength of seats. They were driven around in the name of Constitutional morality. What was politically possible was constitutionally termed immoral. Ultimately the political possible was imposed on the Constitution. Instead, it would be prudent to write a provision in the text of the Constitution which would permit ('morality') formation of governments by different parties in proportion to their strength in the House. Of course, a minimum of time share, say, of 12 months, may be prescribed. The people who extended support to a political party at the time of election to the Assembly should not feel dejected or out-casted for the reason that they did not pass the 51 per cent mark. The Constitution should appear to them to be inclusive in its essence.

Electoral Considerations: The Election Commission of India has, no doubt, performed a stupendous task. But the electoral system needs to be tightened and the undesirable elements need to be prevented from entering the electoral fray. Firstly, any Tom, Dick and Harry need not contest the elections. To keep the process clean and purposeful the voters should be informed properly about the desirability and feasibility of the candidates from among whom they decide to elect one as their representative. The candidate should be: an educated person who can read, write and participate in the discussions in the Assembly/Parliament; should be a person who has a record of social service or be a professional (sometimes, the widow or son is put up as winnable candidate—that seems to be the only eligibility!); should declare his and family's income and assets/liabilities annually; paid all taxes, and refunded government or bank loans; should have a clean police record; and finally, should be prepared to provide a performance report to his constituency periodically. Political parties who choose and field candidates should also be asked to file application for registration before the Election Commission of India (ECI) every year compulsorily failing which they may be barred from election activities. Along with the application itself the parties should submit certified records of income/fund-raising/assets as well as expenditure, the charter of the party along with the muster of active members, proof of their functioning democratically in their internal matters and as per their own charter, and a general declaration that they will abide by the Constitution of India and laws of India. Individual or independent candidates would have to float their own parties and stand for elections on their behalf: this eliminates the scope for their escape from ECI's scrutiny in future. The ECI should be enabled to verify the various records and if they are proved to be dubious or unsatisfactory the party's registration should be suspended forthwith.

Apart from the above constructive suggestions, quite a few popular or even populist demands for electoral reforms need to be examined before they are supported uncritically. These are mainly:

Recall: In some countries, an elected representative on his failure to perform duties properly is called back by a popular petition and fresh elections are held. Should this practice be followed in India?

Yes	*No*
It will act as a deterrent and help improve the performance of people's representatives—MP's, MLA's etc.	What happens in Switzerland cannot be replicated in India. Here we have no signature-bank as in Switzerland whose officers can tally signatures of a petition for recall with authentic signatures of voters, recorded officially. Secondly, a petition for recall can be moved easily and successfully where in a constituency the winning candidate has a small margin of victory while the opponents of his put together command votes which would far exceed the requisite number for moving a recall-petition.

NOTA: This suggestion is supposed to instil fear in the hearts of unworthy candidates. But the details of the recording of NOTA reveal that no candidate/s could be disqualified on account of the NOTA votes even if these are more than the total votes gathered by the winning candidate. This anomaly has been witnessed in the last Gujarat Assembly elections.

State-Funding of Electoral Expenses

Yes	*No*
It is believed that many worthy aspirants are deterred from contesting elections for the reason of their poor financial conditions. Hence, the State should come forward to foot their bill for election expenses.	When crore-patis are in the field they do not need this flea-bite financial subsidy. On the other hand, the poor candidates cannot summon enough courage to challenge the multi-crore-patis with the help of a small subsidy from the State. Besides, accounting problems arise.

***Compulsory Voting*:** If electoral successes are to be read as popular support, it is found that in several instances the percentage of votes cast in an election to the Assembly or Parliament is pathetically poor. Often, the winning candidate carries no more than 10-15 percentage of registered voters in his constituency. This is not only unfair to the principle of representative democracy but also confirmation of apathy on the part of the people. To set right this impairment it is suggested that voting should be made compulsory in Parliamentary/Assembly elections.

Yes	*No*
It helps the democratic/ representative process.	If people don't come forward to cast their votes, how can they be made to do so compulsorily? Under the threat of penalty or imprisonment? How to trace and pin-point the offenders? How many more jails to house them? How to examine the *bona fide* of their excuses not to come to vote? This is a classic case of remedy being worse than disease.

Simultaneous Elections: This new suggestion is fraught with many problems.

Yes	*No*
Avoidance of wasteful and enormous amount of money; non-stopping of schemes and appointments to jobs during the recurrent cycles of elections, and the minimisation of work load of conducting the elections.	Several State Assemblies undergo political instability from time to time for a variety of reasons. If they have to wait for long to reconstitute their Assemblies in the wake of simultaneous elections, a lot of harm would have been done to governmental functioning as well as to democratic ethos.

For the information of the scrutinizer only: Under the first-past-the-post electoral system voters cast their votes for a candidate of their choice and the candidate who secures the highest number of votes is declared as winner. It is known as FPTP.

***Proportional Representation*:** This idea was dismissed, rightly so, by Pt. Jawaharlal Nehru as an excellent suggestion to usher in anarchy in the country. With all its faults, the first-past-the-post system is better than other systems for our vast and semi-literate country.

Governors: Governors of states in our Federal Constitution occupy a unique if not unenviable position. They have three masters to abide by—the Central Government, the State Chief Minister and their own conscience. Nobody knows exactly how and why Governors are chosen and even dismissed. Dr. Ambedkar during the Constituent Assembly debates took different stands on the exact Constitutional position they hold. The Rajamannar Committee and Sarkaria Commission in their respective Reports make detailed examination of the Governor's role etc. Their recommendations are worthy of acceptance by one and all. But Governments at the Centre have not been able to implement any of them. One novel idea may be to put forward. Instead of having Governors, have 29 Vice-Presidents of India, one for each State (28) and the senior-most of them all being made the presiding officer of Rajya Sabha. They can be given enough powers and made accountable. Their names can be picked by an all-India committee headed by the Prime Minister and the Leader of Opposition at the Centre. The nominees need not be affiliated to political parties in the recent past. Judges of the High Courts/Supreme Court, Padma Awardees, Generals, Vice-Chancellors or any distinguished personality could be put on the panel of eligible candidates. Governors, if need be, given a competent advisory legal assistance. The present practice of appointing Governors without a deep thought is going to hurt the image of Constitutional functionaries.

Rajya Sabha: In 1919, exactly a century ago, the Rajya Sabha (Council of States) was born. Its original purpose was to ensure the support as well as expert advice of Princely States to the ruling dispensation of the country. Gradually it moved into the place of a second chamber/upper chamber in the Central/federal legislative setup. After India gained Independence, Princely States ceased to exist, after the decision to frame a new Constitution for the country, the Council of States continued to exist as though no change has occurred at all. A mere cosmetic change took place in the number and manner of election of its members. It was, and still is, devoid of any federal characteristics seen in the Upper Chamber in any other federal system in the world. It may not be far wrong to state that it constitutes a harmless Parliamentary appendix. At its best, this House of elders is expected to hold dispassionate and learned debates on issues of national importance. But at worse times, the Rajya Sabha has witnessed undignified, partisan and unproductive debates. In the 1980s the ruling party Congress's members of the House behaved in such an ugly and unruly fashion that the Presiding Officer, Vice-President of India, Dr. Shankar Dayal Sharma, a very much Congressman himself, wept, sobbed and wiped off tears from his eyes and begged the elderly Members to behave. This was no isolated instance.

Addressing a conference of Political Science Association in December 1978 Prof. Aloo J. Dastur of Bombay University had said: "Perhaps, the time has come when we as political scientists, teachers and students of Parliamentary government, have to give serious thought to the conduct of the elders. It is necessary, or is it even useful to have a second chamber? The old English cry "either mend the House of Lords or end it" raised in the election of 1910 could very well be the rallying cry (here now). In the opinion of Prof. Bhavani Singh "the Rajya Sabha has become an exotic transplanted on our soil. It represents neither the people nor the Government nor the State Legislatures."

However well argued, the Rajya Sabha is not going to be abolished for the reason that politicians have a vested interest in keeping it. But, we can exert pressure for its reconstitution and make it more useful and meaningful.

For example, the members of Rajya Sabha may be all the nominees of State legislatures as in U.S., Germany and Switzerland. They may act as the guardians of the interests of the States. Further, this second chamber need not be entrusted with the burden of repeating the functions of the Lok Sabha. Instead, it may be endowed with powers special to the federal character of the polity. The President may be asked under Constitutional provisions, to obtain the approval of Rajya Sabha (only) for the following, before the Central Council of Ministers acts:

- Imposition of President's Rule in States.
- Appointment of Governors.
- Appointment of officers to the federal agencies like the U.P.S.C., U.G.C., Election Commission, Finance Commission etc.
- Perusal of Annual Reports of Performance of various bodies submitted to the Parliament annually.

The present practice of the Upper House acting as a brake on the Lok Sabha in legislation may be done away with except for specific cases involving federal issues.

Thus, it is advisable that the Rajya Sabha should be reoriented to serve better the interests of federalism, democracy, and the Constitution.

Generally speaking, the experiment of Constitutional democracy has faced odds all over the world except in a few countries. Constitutions have been scrapped or replaced almost all over Asia, Africa, Latin America and even Europe for reasons of unworkability and changing circumstances. Pakistan, Bangladesh, Sri Lanka are some of the leading examples in our own neighbourhood. It is heartening to see that in India the Constitution, launched in 1950, is working well. Democracy and Constitution have helped each other well here. The performance of any institution or idea can never be perfect. The Indian laboratory for experimenting the joint working of democracy and Constitution has indeed been satisfactory although there is room for improvement.

2

Political Significance of the 2019 General Elections in India

M.R. Biju and *M.R.B. Anantha Padmanabha*

The 2019 Indian general election was held in seven phases from 11 April to 19 May, 2019 to constitute the 17th Lok Sabha. The votes were counted and result was declared on 23 May. About 900 million people were eligible to vote and turnout was over 67 per cent—the highest ever as well as the highest participation by women voters. The Bharatiya Janata Party won 303 seats, further increasing its substantial majority and the BJP-led National Democratic Alliance won 353 seats. The Indian National Congress won 52 seats, and the Congress-led United Progressive Alliance won 91. Other parties and their alliances won 98 seats. The Congress again failed to secure the requisite 10 per cent of the seats (54 seats) in the Lok Sabha. Hence, India remains without an official Opposition party. Legislative assembly elections in the states of Andhra Pradesh, Arunachal Pradesh, Odisha and Sikkim were held simultaneously with the general election, as well as by-elections to twenty two seats of the Tamil Nadu Legislative Assembly.

Keeping this in background an attempt has been made in this chapter to examine the facets of the 17th Lok Sabha Polls in India. It has been categorised under seven major heads. Part-I unfolds the pre-poll scenario, Part-II examines the content of the poll manifestoes of various political fronts, parties and alliances, Part-III evaluates the Political Alliances and Combinations made by various parties, Part-IV deals with the reasons laid to the overwhelming success of BJP and its allies and Part-V critically studies the debacle of the Congress party and the Left, Part-VI studies the performance of Regional Parties, Social Justice Parties and Muslim League, and Part-VII brings together the major findings of the study.

Election Schedule

The election schedule was announced by Election Commission of India (ECI) on 10 March 2019, and with it the Model Code of Conduct came into effect. The election was scheduled to be held in seven phases. In Bihar, Uttar Pradesh and West Bengal, the election was held in all seven phases. The polling for the Anantnag constituency in the state of Jammu & Kashmir was held in three phases due to violence in the region.

PART-I
ELECTORAL ISSUES AND CONTROVERSIES

(a) Allegations of Undermining Institutions

The opposition parties have accused the NDA government is destroying democratic institutions and processes. Modi denied and blamed Congress and the Communists for undermining institutions including the police, CBI and the CAG, and cited the murder of BJP activists in Kerala and Madhya Pradesh. The Congress party, other opposition parties and a group of retired civil servants have accused the ECI as being compromised and as endorsing the model code of conduct violations by Narendra Modi and other BJP political leaders during their campaign. Another group of 81 retired civil servants, judges and academics disputed these allegations, made counter-allegations, and stated that the ECI acted fairly and similarly in alleged violations by either side. The group states that such political attacks on the ECI are a "deliberate attempt to denigrate and delegitimise the democratic institutions."

(b) Economic Performance

According to *The Times of India*, the major economic achievements of the incumbent NDA government include an inflation rate less than 4 per cent, the GST reform, the Insolvency and Bankruptcy Code. Its programmes, in recent years, that have positively touched many among the Indian masses, include the Jan Dhan Yojana, rural cooking gas and electricity for homes. According to the IMF, the Indian economy has been growing in recent years, its GDP growth rate is among the highest in the world for major economies, and India is expected to be the fastest growing major economy in 2019-20 and 2020-21, with real GDP projected to grow at 7.3 per cent. The GDP growth data has been disputed by a group of Indian social scientists, economists and the political opposition's election campaign, while a group of Indian chartered accountants has defended the data, the GDP calculation methodology, and questioned the motivations of those disputing the recent Indian GDP statistics.

The opposition's election campaign has claimed that both the demonetisation and GST law have "seriously hit small business, farmers and casual labour", states *The Times of India*. The incumbent has claimed that they inherited a country from the previous Congress-led government that was "a legacy of policy paralysis, corruption and economic fragility", and that the BJP-led government policies have placed India on better economic fundamentals and a fast gear. Modi claims that his government pursued demonetisation in the national interest, his government has identified and de-registered 338,000 shell companies, identified and recovered Rs. 130,000 crore (US$ 19 billion) in black money since 2014, and almost doubled India's tax base. The Congress party disputes the incumbents' claims, and has alleged that BJP offices have "become hubs of creating black money", and seeks a judicial inquiry into the Rafael deal with France and BJP's role in corruption.

(c) National Security and Terrorism

In response to the 2019 Pulwama attack, the Indian Air Force conducted airstrikes inside Pakistan—for the first time since the 1971 Indo-Pak war. The ongoing conflict with Pakistan became a significant factor in the election. The opposition parties accused of politicising the army, whilst the BJP countered their accusations by stating that such allegations raised by them were adversely affecting the morale of armed forces. According to the Pew Research Center, both before and after the outbreak of recent India-Pakistan tensions, their 2018 and 2019 surveys suggest that the significant majority of the voters consider Pakistan as a "very serious threat" to their country, and terrorism to be a "very big problem".

(d) Unemployment

According to the Pew Research Center, a majority of Indian voters consider the lack of employment opportunities as a "very big problem" in their country. "About 18.6 million Indians were jobless and another 393.7 million work in poor-quality jobs vulnerable to displacement", states the Pew report. A report on unemployment prepared by the National Sample Survey Office's (NSSO's) periodic labour force survey, has not been officially released by the government. According to *Business Today*, this report is the "first comprehensive survey on employment conducted by a government agency after Prime Minister Narendra Modi announced demonetisation move in November 2016." According to this report, the 2017-18 "usual status" unemployment rate in India is 6.1 per cent, which is a four-decade high. The government has claimed that the report was not final. According to the International Labour Organization (ILO)—a United Nations agency, unemployment is rising in India and the "unemployment rate in the country will stand at 3.5 per cent in 2018 and 2019—the same level of unemployment seen in 2017 and 2016", instead of dropping to 3.4 per cent as it had previously projected. According to the ILO's World Employment Social Outlook Report, the unemployment rate in India has been in the 3.4 to 3.6 per cent range over the UPA-government led 2009-2014 and the NDA-government led 2014-2019 periods.

Opposition parties have claimed in their election campaign that the unemployment in India has reached crisis levels. The NDA government has denied the existence of any job crisis. Prime minister Narendra Modi claimed that jobs are not lacking but the accurate data on jobs has been lacking. The opposition has attacked the NDA government's performance with the NSSO reported 6.1 per cent unemployment data. Modi and his government have questioned this job statistics report, stating that "most surveys that try to capture unemployment rate are skewed since these did not cover the unorganised sector, which accounts for 85-90 per cent of jobs."

(e) Agrarian and Rural Distress

The Congress party campaign has highlighted "agrarian distress" as an election issue. The BJP campaign has highlighted that the Congress party had been in power for five generations of the Nehru dynasty and its past promises and campaign issues have been empty. It claims that the recent farmer loan waivers by Congress have not reached "even 10 per cent of the farmers" nor has it helped the financial situation of the farmers. BJP highlights that its "Kisan Samman Nidhi" helps the small farmers at the time of seed planting through a direct deposit of Rs. 6,000 to their accounts. The opposition has accused this as being an attempt to lure voters. According to *The Times of India*, a group of farmer associations have demanded that the 2019 election manifesto of competing political parties should promise to "keep agriculture out of the World Trade Organization (WTO)" and that the interests of Indian farmers must not be compromised in global trade treaties. They have also demanded loan waivers and income support for the agriculture sector. According to the *Business Standard* and the United Nation's Food and Agriculture Organization, India has witnessed record crop harvests in recent years including 2017 when its farmers grew more foodgrains than ever before. However, the farmers consider the "low remunerative prices" they receive in the free market to be too low and a need for the Indian government to establish higher minimum support prices for agricultural products. These farmers consider this an issue for the 2019 general elections.

(f) Dynasty Politics

The BJP has highlighted that the Congress party has relied on Nehru's dynasty for leadership since India's Independence, its lack of internal party institutions and claimed that whenever Congress has been in power, the freedom of press and Indian government institutions have "taken a severe beating". During the election campaign, its leaders have mentioned the Emergency of 1975, the nepotism, corruption and widespread abuses of human rights under the Congress rule in the past. Congress-led alliance leader H.D. Kumaraswamy—the son of a former Prime Minister of India and the current Chief Minister of Karnataka, has countered that "India developed because of dynasty politics", stating that "dynasty politics are not the main issue, rather country's problems are." The Congress has alleged hypocrisy by the BJP, claiming that the BJP itself forms alliances with dynasty-based parties such as the Akali Dal in Punjab, and that family relatives of senior BJP leaders such as Rajnath Singh and Arun Jaitley have been in politics too.

According to an IndiaSpend report published by the Bloomberg Quint, the smaller and regional parties such as the Jammu and Kashmir National Conference, Lok Janshakti Party, Shiromani Akali Dal, Biju Janata Dal and Samajwadi Party have higher densities of dynasty-derived candidates and elected representatives in recent years. While both the Congress and the BJP have also nominated candidates from political dynasties, states the report, the difference between them is that in Congress "top party leadership has been handed down from generation to generation within the same family", while there has been a historic non-dynastic diversity in the top leadership within the BJP. According to the report, while BJP has also nominated candidates from political dynasties, its better public relations operation "can leap to its defence when attacked on the same grounds." In contrast to the IndiaSpend report, analysis of

Kanchan Chandra, a prominent Professor of Politics, of the 2004, 2009 and 2014 general elections included a finding that the Congress party has had about twice or more dynastic parliamentarians than the BJP at those elections, and higher than all major political parties in India except the Samajwadi Party. Many of these dynastic politicians in India who inherit the leadership positions have never held any jobs and lack state or local experience, states Anjali Bohlken—a professor and political science scholar, and this raises concerns of rampant nepotism and appointments of their own friends, relatives and cronies if elected. The BJP has targeted the Congress party in the 2019 elections for alleged nepotism and a family dynasty for leadership.

(g) Campaign Controversies

(i) Income Tax Raids

In April 2019, raids conducted by the Income Tax Department found bundles of unaccounted cash amounting to Rs. 281 crore (US$ 41 million), along with liquor and documentary evidence in premises of people with close connections to Madhya Pradesh Chief Minister Kamal Nath of the Congress. Modi has highlighted this evidence to attack the Congress in its election campaign, alleging corruption is part of Congress party's culture.

(ii) Social Media Abuses and Fake News

According to *The New York Times* and *The Wall Street Journal*, the election had attracted a systematic attempt to spread misinformation through social media. Facebook said that over a hundred of these advocacy accounts spreading disinformation were traced to "employees of the Pakistani military public relations wing". Some others have been linked to the INC and BJP. Political parties spent over Rs. 53 crore (US$ 7.7 million) with the largest spending by BJP on digital platforms for online advertisements. The BJP placed 2,500 advertisements on Facebook while the Congress placed 3,686 advertisements. According to a study by Vidya Narayanan and colleagues at the Oxford Internet Institute, social media was used by all the major parties and alliances, and all of them linked or posted divisive and conspiratorial content and images. According to Narayanan, "a third of the BJP's images, a quarter of the INC's images, and a tenth the SP-BSP's images were catalogued as divisive and conspiratorial." The

Narayanan *et al.* study added that "we observed very limited amounts of hate speech, gore or pornography in either platform samples" by BJP, Congress or SP-BSP, but the election did include proportionally more polarising information on social media than other countries except for the US Presidential election in 2016.

(iii) NaMo TV and Modi Biopic

According to *The Financial Times* and other news sources, on 31 March, 2019, the cable and satellite operators—such as Tata Sky, DishTV, and Videocon—added a new "NaMo TV" channel to the dozens of news and entertainment channels they already offer. Further, independently, a Bollywood biopic named "PM Narendra Modi" starring Vivek Oberoi was due for release in early April. The NaMo TV channel exclusively focuses on replaying Narendra Modi's speeches, the live coverage of rallies by Modi and key leaders of the Bharatiya Janata Party, and presenting the incumbent government's initiatives and achievements in the last five years to the audience that chooses to tune to the channel. The election time Bollywood biopic, states *The Financial Times*, is "adulatory, which depicts his rise from humble origins as the son of a railway station tea-seller to a strongman who vows to avenge Pakistani terror attacks."

The Indian opposition led by the Congress party and activists opposed to the incumbent Bharatiya Janata Party have expressed outrage and alleged that it violates India's election laws and the regulations on "broadcast channels" under the Programme Codes of the Cable TV Act of 1994. The Bharatiya Janata Party and its supporters claim that this is an exercise of the "Right to Free Speech" protected by the Article 19 of the Constitution of India, a means to address the bias against them and to communicate directly to the voters. They also claim that the NaMo TV does not violate any regulation or law, as similar "Direct-to-Home (DTH) operator channels" have already been distributed by cable and satellite operators in the past since 2006. Others state that the audience has a choice to ignore or tune into the channel, and "only Modi's most devoted loyalists were likely to tune in". However, they state that if the BJP pressures public facilities and commercial establishments to show it exclusively during the elections then that would lead to abuse. The Congress party and activists have filed a complaint to the Indian Election Commission, demanding that the NaMo TV channel be stopped. The Election Commission announced on 12 April that any content broadcast on the NaMo TV must be pre-approved by its committee, and only precertified content can be broadcast. On 13 April, 2019, the BJP submitted the contents of NaMo TV to the Election Commission designated "certification and monitoring committee" for its review and pre-certification. The Election Commission ruled on 19 April, 2019, that live speeches of Narendra Modi and other BJP leaders can be broadcast on NaMo TV as well as Twitter platform tweets can be broadcast by Rahul Gandhi and Congress leaders during the silence period. However, neither should mention the constituency or candidates covered by the silence period immediately prior to the polling date.

The ECI blocked the release of the Modi biopic while the election is in progress. The producers appealed this "stay" to the Supreme Court. The film was released on 24 May, 2019 finally.

(iv) EC Actions under Article 324

Election Commission curtailed West Bengal campaigning by one day, after a bust of 19th century Bengali icon Ishwar Chandra Vidyasagar was vandalised during 7th phase poll violence.

(v) Campaign Finance

Several organisations have offered varying estimates for the cost of election campaign. The Centre for Media Studies in New Delhi estimates the election campaign could exceed $7 billion. According to the Association for Democratic Reforms (ADR), an election watchdog, in the Financial Year 2017-18 BJP received Rupees 4,370,000,000 (US $63 million), about 12 times more donations than Congress and five other national parties combined.

The electoral bonds in denominations ranging from 1,000 rupees to 10 million rupees ($14 to $140,000) can be purchased and donated to a political party. The bonds do not carry the name of the donor and are exempt from tax. Factly—an India data journalism portal, traced the electoral bond donations for 2018 under India's Right to Information Act. According to Factly, electoral bonds worth about Rupees 10,600,000,000 (US$150 million) were purchased and donated in 2018. According to Bloomberg, this accounted for 31.2 per cent of political donations in 2018, while 51.4 per cent of the total donated amount were each below Rupees 20,000 (US$290) and these too were from unknown donors. About 47 per cent of the donations to political parties were from known sources. Between 1 January and 31 March, 2019, donors bought Rupees 17,100,000,000 (US$250 million) worth of electoral bonds and donated. The spending in elections boosts national GDP, and the 2009 election spending contributed about 0.5 per cent to GDP.

According to Centre for Media Studies, the BJP spent over Rs. 28,000 crore (or 45%) of the Rs. 60,000 crore spent by all political parties during the polls. Congress questions BJP over its poll expenditure.

PART-II
PARTY MANIFESTOS

(a) Highlights of the BJP Manifesto

- The BJP released its manifesto sub-titled Sankalpit Bharat, Sashakt Bharat (lit. "Resolute India, Empowered India") on 8, April. Some of its highlights:
- Double farmer incomes by 2022 by completing all major and micro-irrigation infrastructure projects, opening adequate markets and modern farm produce storage centres, implement minimum price supports for farmer produce, farmer loans and all-weather rural roads. Introduce a pension bill for small and marginal farmers to provide social security after 60 years of age.
- Bring all secondary schools under the national board quality purview. Invest Rs. 100,000 crore (US$14 billion) in higher education, open new and increase seats at existing engineering, management and law schools. Establish skills and innovations centre at block-level in every town. Enhance higher education opportunities for women by introducing financial support and subsidies programmes. Source 10 per cent of government procurement from companies with more than 50 per cent female employees.
- Ensure a *pucca* (lit. brick-solid, modern) house, safe potable water, toilet, LPG gas cylinder, electricity, and banking account for every family. Reduce the percentage of families living under the poverty line to a single digit by 2024.
- Double the length of national highways. Improve fuel quality by mandating 10 per cent ethanol in Petrol. Scale renewable energy capacity to 175 GW.

- Electrify and convert to broad gauge all railway tracks.
- Establish 150,000 health and wellness centres. Start 75 new medical colleges. Raise doctor-to-population ratio to 1:1400. Triple childcare facilities. Achieve 100 per cent immunisation of all babies.
- Raise India's ranking further in "ease of doing business". Double exports, introduce single-window compliance procedures for all businesses.
- Reduce air pollution by eliminating all crop residue burning.
- Digitise paperwork and proceedings, modernise the courts.
- Launch and promote a National Digital Library with e-books and leading journals to provide free knowledge accessible to all students. Launch a "Study in India" programme to bring foreign students to institutes of higher education.
- Zero tolerance for terrorism, fund resources to strengthen national security, guarantee veterans, and soldier welfare, modernise police forces.
- End special status and special rights to natives of Jammu & Kashmir under Articles 370 and 35A.

(b) Highlights of the Congress Manifesto

The Congress released its manifesto, titled Congress Will Deliver on 3 April. Some of its highlights are:

- Introduce a Nyuntam Aay Yojana welfare programme wherein Rs.72,000 (US$1,000) per year will be transferred directly to the bank account of a woman-member in each family in the poorest 20 per cent households.
- Create 1 million "Seva Mitra" jobs in rural and urban local Government bodies. Fill all 400,000 Central Government vacancies before March 2020, and encourage State governments to fill their 2,000,000 vacancies. Enact a law that requires all non-government controlled employers with over 100 employees to implement an apprentice program.
- Enact a permanent National Commission on Agricultural Development and Planning and introduce a "Kisan Budget" (Farmer Budget) in the Parliament every year. Waive all farmer loans in all states with any amount outstanding.
- Enact a Right to Homestead Act that will provide free land to every household who does not own a home.

- Enact a Right to Healthcare Act and guarantee every citizen free diagnostics, free medicines, free hospitalisation, and free out-patient care. Double spending on healthcare to 3 per cent of its GDP by 2024.
- Double spending on education to 6 per cent of its GDP by 2024.
- Revise the national GST law from three tax tiers to a single moderate rate of tax. Reduce taxes on exported products to zero. Exempt GST from the essential goods and services that are currently not exempt. Enact a new Direct Taxes Code.
- Augment and rapid construction of national highways. Modernise Indian railway infrastructure. Promote green energy. Manufacturing promotion.
- Increase defence spending.
- Enact a National Election Fund, wherein public funds will be distributed to recognised political parties to run their campaign.
- Preserve special status and special rights to natives of Jammu & Kashmir under Article, 370 and 35A.
- Amend the Armed Forces (Special Powers) Act, 1958. End the Sedition law (Section 124A of the Indian Penal Code).

(c) Other Major Parties

Other national and regional parties have released their manifestos too:

- **The Tamil Nadu-based regional parties AIADMK and DMK** released their manifesto on 18 March, 2019, with each promising to release the seven Tamils jailed after being found guilty for their role in the assassination of Rajiv Gandhi, a former Congress party leader and Prime Minister of India. The AIADMK promised to press for the political rights of the Tamil people in the Eelam region of Sri Lanka, while the DMK has promised Indian citizenship to all Sri Lankan expats. According to the *Deccan Herald*, the AIADMK has promised a cash transfer of Rupees 18,000 (US$260) per year to "all families below the poverty level, destitute women, widows without income, differently-abled, landless agricultural labourers, rural and urban manual labourers and destitute senior citizens." The AIADMK also promised to raise the tax exemption limit and revisions to the GST law. The DMK promised a probe into Rafale fighter jet deal, and a plan to distribute free sanitary napkins to working women along with starting martial arts schools for girls.

- **Biju Janata Dal (BJD)** released its manifesto on 9 April, 2019. It promised a Rs. 100,000 (US$1,400) zero-interest crop loan to farmers every year, a Rs. 500,000 (US$ 7,200) zero-interest loan to women-run self-help groups, 75 per cent jobs reservation in Odisha-based companies to Odisha youth, free education to all girls and a marriage assistance grant of Rupees 25,000 (US$ 360) to daughters of poor families. It also promised to complete two expressways.
- **Communist Party of India (Marxist) (CPIM)** manifesto promised to raise the minimum wage to Rs. 216,000 (US$ 3,100) per year, an old age pension of Rs.72,000 (US$ 1,000) per year and universal public distribution of 35 kilograms of foodgrains per family. It also stated the restoration of inheritance tax and an increase in the taxes on individuals and corporations. It also promised spending 6 per cent of GDP on education, enacting a Right to Free Health Care with 3.5 per cent of GDP on health in the short term and 5 per cent in the long term, introduction of price controls on essential drugs, breaking monopoly of drug multinationals, as well as enact a Right to Guaranteed Employment in urban areas.
- **Nationalist Congress Party (NCP)** promised to open talks with Pakistan on terrorism. It also promised to expand trade and political relationship with Russia, and seek to weaken Russia's ties with China and Pakistan.
- **Samajwadi Party** promised an annual pension of Rupees 36,000 (US$ 520) to poor families in a form of a cash transfer to women. It has also proposed a new property tax of 2 per cent on homes valued above Rupees 25,000,000 (US$ 360,000) as well as raising income taxes on the affluent. It also promised to create 100,000 new jobs every year.
- **Telugu Desam Party** released its manifesto on 5 April, 2019. It promised zero-interest loans to farmer without any caps, a grant of Rupees 15,000 (US$ 220) per year to each farmer as investment support, a grant of Rupees 100,000 (US$ 1,400) to each family with a daughter in the year of her marriage, an unemployment allowance of Rupees 3,000 (US$ 43) for any

youth who has completed intermediate education, and free laptops to all students at the intermediate level.

- **AITMC's manifesto** was released on 27 March, 2019. It promised a judicial probe into demonetization, a review of GST law, and sought to bring back the Planning Commission. It also promised free medical care, expanding the "100-day work scheme" currently operating in India to "200-day work scheme" along with a pay increase.
- **Aam Aadmi Party** released its manifesto on 25 April, 2019 promising full statehood for Delhi to give the Delhi government control over police and other institutions. The manifesto promised 85 per cent reservations in the Delhi-based colleges and jobs for the voters of Delhi and their families.

PART-III
PARTIES AND ALLIANCES

(a) Political Alliances

With the exception of 2014, no single party has won the majority of seats in the Lok Sabha since 1984, and therefore, forming alliances is the norm in Indian elections.

There were five main national pre-poll alliances. They are the National Democratic Alliance (NDA) headed by the BJP, the United Progressive Alliance (UPA) headed by the INC, Mahagathbandhan (or Grand Alliance), or MGB, Federal Front headed by All India Trinamool Congress, and the left front of Communist-leaning parties. Given the volatile nature of coalition politics in India, alliances may change during and after the election. The INC has not formed an alliance in states where it is in direct contest with the BJP. These states include Himachal Pradesh, Uttarakhand, Rajasthan, Gujarat, Madhya Pradesh, and Chhattisgarh. It has formed alliances with regional parties in Jammu and Kashmir, Bihar, Tamil Nadu, Maharashtra, Karnataka, Jharkhand, and Kerala. In January 2019, Bahujan Samaj Party and Samajwadi Party announced a grand alliance (Mahagathbandhan) to contest 76 out of the 80 seats in Uttar Pradesh leaving two seats, namely Amethi and Rae Bareli, for INC and another two for other political parties.

(b) Political Parties

More than 650 parties contested in these elections. Most of them were small with regional appeal. The main parties are the Bharatiya Janata Party (BJP) and the Indian National Congress (INC). It was the first time when BJP (437) contested more seats than Congress (421) in the Lok Sabha elections.

(c) Candidates

Altogether 8,039 candidates are in the fray for 542 parliamentary constituencies, i.e. 14.8 candidates per constituency on an average, according to PRS India, an NGO. About 40 per cent of the candidates fielded by Prime Minister Narendra Modi's Bharatiya Janata Party have a criminal case against them. Key opposition party Congress is not far behind with 39 per cent of the candidates with criminal charges, according to Association of Democratic Reforms analysis.

(d) Voter Statistics

According to the ECI, 900 million people were eligible to vote, with an increase of 84.3 million voters since the last election in 2014, making it the largest-ever election in the world. 15 million voters aged 18-19 years became eligible to vote for the first time. 468 million eligible voters were males, 432 million voters were females and 38,325 identified themselves belonging to third gender. Total 71,735 overseas voters also enrolled. The residents of the former enclaves exchanged under the 2015 India-Bangladesh boundary agreement voted for the first time.

(e) Electronic Voting Machines and Security

The ECI deployed a total of 1.74 million voter-verified paper audit trail (VVPAT) units and 3.96 million electronic voting machines (EVM) in 1,035,918 polling stations. Approximately 270,000 paramilitary and 2 million state police personnel provided organisational support and security at various polling booths. On 9 April, 2019, the Supreme Court ordered the ECI to increase VVPAT slips vote count to five randomly selected EVMs per assembly constituency, which means ECI has to count VVPAT slips of 20,625 EVMs before it certifies the final election results.

(f) Turnout

In the first phase, 69.58 per cent of the 142 million eligible voters cast their vote to elect their representatives for 91 Lok Sabha seats. The voter turnout was 68.77 per cent in the same constituencies in the 2014 general elections. In the second phase, 156 million voters were eligible to vote for 95 Lok Sabha seats and the turnout was 69.45 per cent, compared to 69.62 per cent in 2014. For the third phase, 189 million voters were eligible to elect 116 Lok Sabha representatives. According to ECI, the turnout for this phase was 68.40 per cent, compared to 67.15 per cent in 2014. In the fourth of seven phases, 65.50 per cent of the 128 million eligible voters cast their vote to elect 72 representatives to the Indian parliament while the turnout for the same seats in the 2014 election was 63.05 per cent. The fifth phase was open to 87.5 million eligible voters, who could cast their vote in over 96,000 polling booths. In the sixth phase, 64.40 per cent of the 101 million eligible voters cast their vote in about 113,000 polling stations. The final turnout stood at 67.11 per cent, the highest ever turnout recorded in any of the general elections till date. The percentage is 1.16 per cent higher than the 2014 elections whose turnout stood at 65.95 per cent. Over 600 million voters polled their votes in 2019 Indian general elections.

(g) Results–An Overview

The Bharatiya Janata Party-led NDA won the elections with the BJP itself winning a clear majority. The BJP became the single largest party in the House and surpassed expectations to win 303 seats, with its alliance partners bringing the NDA to a total of 353 seats. Reasons attributed to the victory included the personal popularity of Narendra Modi, effective voter turnout drives by the NDA, a surge in public nationalism following the Pulwama attack, the consolidation of Hindu voters in a multi-caste coalition and the successful implementation of social welfare programmes during the First Modi ministry's term.

With the results, the BJP was able to gain 21 more seats in the House, having won 282 in the 2014 Indian general election. It was the second time in India's independent history that voters re-elected the same party to power with a bigger majority to the Lok Sabha—India's lower house of parliament. The BJP's total vote share stood at 37.4 per cent, an increase of over 6 percentage points from 31.34 per cent in

2014. The National Democratic Alliance secured a vote share of 45 per cent, compared to 38 per cent in 2014. In contrast, the vote share of Indian National Congress remained the same at 19.5 per cent. About 1.04 per cent of the voters in India chose to vote for None Of The Above (NOTA) in the 2019 elections, with Bihar leading with 2.08 per cent NOTA voters.

Modi became the only Indian Prime Minister in history whose government was re-elected with both an increase in the total percentage of votes along with a full majority. His opponent, Rahul Gandhi, ran in two constituencies, winning from Wayanad, but losing from the Amethi constituency—the seat he, his mother (Sonia Gandhi), his father (Rajiv Gandhi), and his uncle (Sanjay Gandhi) had collectively held for decades. In addition, many candidates who were members of popular political dynasties were defeated across India in favour of the BJP or other parties' candidates.

The election had been called a referendum on Modi and the BJP's Hindu nationalistic policies and advocacy. According to *The Wall Street Journal*, Modi's victory "sets (*sic*) the stage for further economic change in one of Asia's fastest-growing economies." Alasdair Pal and Mayank Bhardwaj, in an article published by *Reuters*, claimed that the result was a mandate for business-friendly policies and tougher national security positions, reinforcing "a global trend of right-wing populists sweeping to victory, from the United States to Brazil and Italy, often after adopting harsh positions on protectionism, immigration and defence."

PART-IV
REASONS FOR THE OVERWHELMING SUCCESS OF THE BJP – A CLOSE WATCH

The 2019 Lok Sabha election results have been marked by the poor performance of parties that are perceived to be family-run enterprises. Narendra Modi pilloried the Gandhis for not having worked their way up in politics. By doing so, he tapped into the growing disenchantment with the politics of entitlement—in particular, with political families of 'social justice' parties, such as Samajwadi Party and Rashtriya Janata Dal in the north and Janata Dal (Secular) in the south. Today, the Samajwadi Party, Bahujan Samaj Party and Rashtriya Janata Dal are staring at a bleak future, having won five, 10 and zero seats this time. Their performance was no less dismal five years ago. On both occasions, they were swept aside by the Modi wave. Their style of politics has also been rejected. Having set out to challenge feudal tendencies in society, they are paying the price for internalising them." With Amit Shah and Modi at the helm, the BJP has managed to project itself as the mascot for determined, self-made individuals who break out of their socio-economic constraints. They have termed this the New India—impatient with categories of not just caste, but more disconcertingly, 'secularism'. It is a sizeable force, which identifies with the rugged confidence of the present BJP top leadership; it is, of course, true that local BJP leaders have fielded their kith and kin who have won, riding the Modi wave.

While this is a new subalternism, it does not mean that 'caste' as a political category is on the wane. The BJP has, in fact, consolidated its hold on the lower castes whose aspirations were not addressed by traditional social justice parties—this is even as Modi said in his victory address that there were only two castes, 'the poor and those who serve the poor'. Issues of caste need to be seen through the prism of a young, upwardly mobile society which disregards the politics of entitlement. If the 2014 Lok Sabha elections were marked by anti-incumbency, pro-incumbency was the keynote of the 2019 elections as BJP decimated the opposition. The BJP juggernaut rolled across its bastions in the north and west of the country —in bellwether state UP its vote share shot up from 42.6 per cent in 2014 to 49.5 per cent, negating the impact of SP, BSP and RLD joining hands—while making significant incursions into the south (Karnataka, Telangana) and east (Bengal, Odisha). At last count BJP had wins/leads in 303 seats and its allies in 50 seats, giving NDA a thumping majority in the Lok Sabha.

What accounts for the shift from anti-incumbency in 2014 to pro-incumbency in 2019? It is not as if the economy has changed much. On the positive side inflation was managed well during NDA's first term (but faces upward pressure now). On the negative side joblessness appears to have grown more acute. One could attribute BJP's success to better administration of welfare schemes, the Balakot strikes which retaliated against Pakistan's sponsorship of terror groups, and Prime Minister Narendra Modi's personal popularity. But while all these factors may have played a role they do not, even in combination, satisfactorily account for the magnitude of BJP's sweeping victory.

It is possible some deep structural shifts are taking place in the Indian polity. The so-called "secular" model many other parties have followed is to work with conservative Muslim clerics to secure the Muslim vote, and then add on specific castes as each party's USP relying on post-Mandal social engineering. Thus, SP is the party of Yadavs, BSP of Jatavs and so on. This model, however, offers plenty of opportunity for counter-mobilisation. BJP has moved into this vacuum swiftly and effectively. It may have capitalised, for example, on the unseen backlash to aggressive expansion of caste reservations, cementing its support among upper castes with the EWS quota. Hindu upper castes would comprise a solid bloc that can neutralise the Muslim vote (which, in any case, is split among several parties). Alongside, Modi also projects a different kind of backward caste identity that is fluid, aspirational, upwardly mobile and less dependent on specific caste networks. As smartphones spread and cities expand, this style may appeal more to Hindu lower castes. BJP alone has around 300 Lok Sabha seats which gives it the power to override even its allies in the next government. With great power, however, must come great responsibility. The Indian polity is dynamic and the voter can never be taken for granted. Now that BJP has acquired enough confidence in government it must utilise the first hundred days of its second tenure to launch the transformative leap that the economy badly needs—more so since global headwinds are growing—even as it fully respects constitutional values in letter and in spirit. BJP started on the right, reformist note in 2014 but veered off track following Congress accusations of it being anti-poor, lurching later into radical socialist experiments such as demonetisation.

"Factor" markets of land, labour and capital need market-oriented reform for efficient allocation of resources; so do agriculture and education. At the same time, the state must step in and provide quality inputs where the market cannot provide these (such as healthcare, basic education). Unproductive subsidies must be cut, and the autonomy of public institutions respected and expanded. Such reforms, whose objective is to ramp up India's global competitiveness, may be painful at the beginning. But BJP has the mandate and trust of the people, and must be bold enough to push them through. A powerhouse economy and its spinoff benefits will, in turn, yield a political bonanza for BJP by the time the next general election comes round in 2024.

Final Tally

NDA-352		*UPA – 91*		*Others-99*	
BJP	303	Congress	52	All India Trinamool Congress	22
Shiva Sena	18	DMK	23	YSR Congress Party	22
JD(U)	16	NCP	5	Biju Janata Dal	12
Lok Jana Shakti Party	6	J & K National Conference	3	Bahujan Samaj Party	10
Shiromani Akali Dal	2	IUML	3	Telangana Rashtra Samithi	9
Apna Dal (Soneylal)	2	JDS	3	Samajwadi Party	5
AIADMK	1	Jharkhand Mukti Morcha	1	Teiugu Desam Party	3
AJSU Party	1	Kerala Congress (M)	1	CPI (M)	3
Independent-BJP	1	Viduthalai Chiruthalgal Katchi	1	CPI	2
NDPP	1	Independent— Congress	1	AIMIM	2
Rashtriya Loktantrik Party	1			Independent	2
				Aam Aadmi Party	1
				AIUDF	1
				Sikkim Krantikari Morcha	1
				Mizo National Front	1
				Naga People's Front	1
				National People's Party	1
				Revolutionary Socialist Party	1

Source: *Business Line*, 25 May, 2019 – Election Cancelled for Vellore Constituency – Total Seats – 543.

	NDA		*UPA*		*OTHERS*	
	2019	*2014*	*2019*	*2014*	*2019*	*2014*
	NORTH					
Chandigarh	1	1				
Delhi	7	7				
Haryana	10	7		1		2
Himachal Pradesh	4	4				
Jammu & Kashmir	3	3			3	3
Punjab	4	6	8	3	1	4
Rajasthan	24	25	1			
Uttar Pradesh	64	71	1	2	15	7
Uttarakhand	5	5				
	WEST AND CENTRAL					
Chhattisgarh	9	10	2	1		
Dadar and Nagar Haveli		1			1	
Daman and Diu	1	1				
Goa	1	2	1			
Gujarat	26	26	-			
Madhya Pradesh	28	27	1	2		
Maharashtra	41	42	5	6	2	
	SOUTH					
Andhra Pradesh		2			25	23
Karnataka	25	17	2	11	1	
Kerala			19	12	1	8
Lakshadweep			1	1		
Puducherry		1	1			
Tamil Nadu	1	2	37			37
Telangana	4	1	3	2	10	14
	EAST					
Andaman & Nicobar Islands	1	1				
Bihar	39	33	1	7		
Jharkhand	12	12	2	2		
Odisha	9	1			12	20
Sikkim					1	1
West Bengal	16	2	2	4	22	36
	NORTH-EAST					
Arunachal Pradesh	2	1		1		
Assam	9	7	3	3	2	4
Manipur	1			2	1	
Meghalaya					1	1
Mizoram				1	1	
Nagaland	1	1				
Tripura	2					2

Source : *Business Line*, 24 May, 2019.

Systematic Election Strategies

The time bound, systematic and behind the scenes outreach programmes of the BJP and its leadership played a crucial role in its electoral victory. The party chief Amit Shah was cautioning party workers that anything short of complete enthusiasm and hard work for the Lok Sabha polls could lead to defeat and a decline of the BJP and Sangh Parivar. A large part of the BJP's strategy was around Prime Minister Modi as its most charismatic leader who commanded votes says Amit Shah at the BJP National Convention in New Delhi on January 11 across categories. It also worked to create a category of voters who would vote above parochial concerns. The opposition's disarray with regards to leadership helped drive home this point of a decisive leader. Beneficiary as voter six months before the polls, a list of beneficiaries of the Modi government's welfare programmes was shared with every Lok Sabha constituency, and party workers were asked to reach out to them. Party president Amit Shah had also revealed that around 161 call centres had been set up by the party with over 15,000 callers to help with the outreach.

"The benefits, unlike under previous governments, were not specific to one community and helped the party break caste barriers and identity issues," said a senior leader. After the seventh phase of polling revealed that women, for the first time in independent India's history, had come out to vote in as many numbers as men and as the results started pouring in on Thursday, the party was assured of victory. "Women and young people, who saw welfare programmes being delivered created a set of voters who helped break caste arithmetic," said a senior party leader. The party's greatest challenge was the formidable caste arithmetic of Uttar Pradesh's Mahagathbandhan of Bahujan Samaj Party (BSP) and Samajwadi Party (SP). Senior leaders said the aggression among the support bases of both these parties helped along a process of "polarisation." "Our voters saw this aggression by SP and BSP voters and consolidated firmly behind us—non-Yadav OBCs, non-Jatav *dalits* and upper castes, added to women and the young, this was a formidable combination," said the source. Real time feedback and the addressing of it by Prime Minister Modi was reflected in his tour plans that mostly concentrated on seats where the party needed a boost rather than go to strongholds. The BJP's planning for the Lok Sabha polls began nearly three years ago with Shah coming out with focus areas for the party's expansion. A list of 120 seats mostly in what he termed as the "Coromandel Coast", where the BJP hadn't won ever but had registered some votes in

2014, were concentrated on. In Odisha as in West Bengal, the BJP slowly ate up the Congress and Left's space as the opposition, giving it nearly 30 extra seats.

Leadership of Narendra Modi

One factor stands out in the verdict of the 2019 general election the ringing endorsement of a single leader, Narendra Modi. It was Mr. Modi all the way except in some states of the South where his party, the BJP, has no presence and where his Hindi oratory is ineffectual. Across the rest of India, the voters wanted someone who made them feel secure. No one else inspired similar trust—not Rahul Gandhi, Mayawati, Akhilesh Yadav, Mamata Banerjee, N. Chandrababu Naidu, K. Chandrasekhar Rao and not even Sharad Pawar. What were the fears driving the voter and where did they originated. The structural origins of these fears can be traced to the less than robust liberal revolution that India experienced over the past seven decades. The liberal push in India led to a forced restructuring of society through an ever expanding agitation for granting special rights not only to *dalits*, tribals, minorities and the other backward classes, but also to women, the disabled, gays and transgenders. Such restructuring was not very successful, nor consistent, yet it threatened traditional social, cultural, religious hierarchies.

The liberal reshaping of India was resisted at every step. Counter-revolutionary social forces were always waiting in the wings. They took various forms from the periodic cow protection agitations led by *sadhus* to the movement for the destruction of the Babri Masjid and construction of a Ram Temple at the site, to the lynching of cow traders and beef-eaters. To say that Rahul Gandhi was no match for Modi begs the real question. Rahul Gandhi and the OBC parties offered the protection and continuation of an evolving liberal vision. They may have different perspectives and horizons of operationalising this vision, but they were broadly for the ongoing expansion of the rights of marginalised sections of society. This election was against that vision in all its forms.

The counter-revolution taps into fear. Prime Minister Narendra Modi tapped into the fears that the liberals aroused. First and foremost, he tapped into the fear of the Hindu majority that they were being marginalised in their "own country" and their privileges were shrinking because of the expanded rights of others. The latter was addressed directly by Prime Minister Modi by announcing a 10 per cent job quota for the upper castes. He probably knew that his pronouncement that a Hindu could never be terrorist may sound like pure rhetoric, but it assuaged many of his listeners that their religion was better than others and it was time that other religious communities recognised it. By constantly rubbishing the Metropolitan elite, his Wordsmiths consistently coined new phrases to denigrate and criminalise them (Lutyens' gang, Half-Maoists, Urban Naxals, Khan Market gang, etc.), and Prime Minister Modi tapped into the fear that the system was being manipulated to partisan ends by a small urban elite. By constantly hammering that Indian liberals were friends of Pakistan (and therefore anti-national), he created the fear that they not only under-estimated. Islamic terror, but by speaking out for the minorities, starting a dialogue with Kashmiri leaders or better relations with Pakistan, they encouraged terrorism. On the eastern borders of India, he heightened the existing anxiety about Muslim illegal immigrants (potential recruits for Islamic terror) outnumbering Hindus and promised citizenship to Hindu immigrants. Many of these fears exist historically across India, especially because of the lingering trauma of Partition. (Bharat Bhushan: 2019).

Gains in Semi-rural Areas too

With the 2019 general election, the BJP has managed to shed its tag of being an out-and-out urban party by winning 123 rural seats, bettering its tally of 115 in 2014. The saffron party has also done well in the semi-rural belt and has enhanced its tally from 127 in 2014 to 141 in 2019. In its traditional stronghold of urban seats, the BJP has slipped marginally to 39 from 40 in 2014. Analysts say that the BJP moved into rural territories due to their welfare schemes. "For a rural voter, things like toilets, gas connections and houses are of utmost importance.

"The BJP, through schemes like Swachh Bharat, Awas Yojana and Ujjwala scheme, has helped it garner support from rural voters. They have successfully blurred the lines between rural and urban India," a political researcher at the Association of Democratic Reforms (ADR) said. In the traditional stronghold of urban areas, the BJP and its allies have done exceedingly well. In Delhi, the BJP won all the seven seats and swept through the six parliamentary constituencies of Mumbai. In the other two metros of Kolkata and Chennai, where the party had a negligible presence, the BJP won one seat while it drew a blank in Tamil Nadu. In other cities too, the BJP fared well by winning one of the four seats on offer in Hyderabad, both seats in Ahmedabad and one each in Pune, Chandigarh and Lucknow.

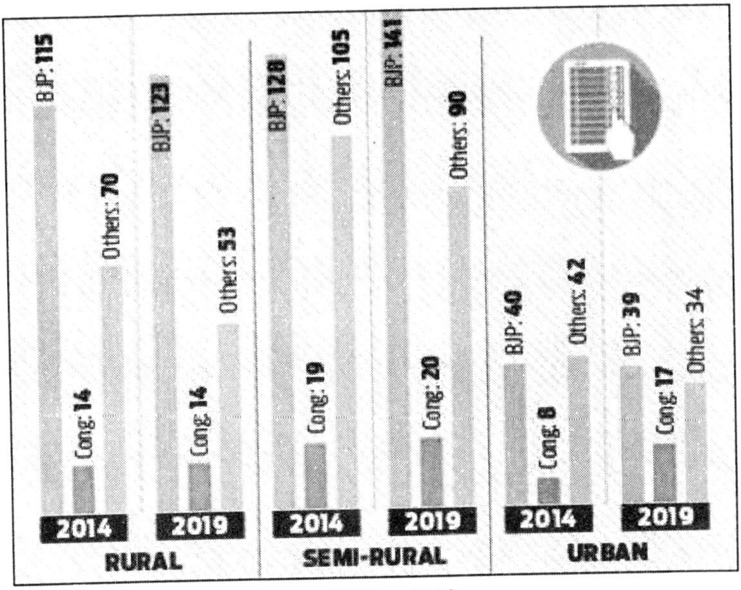

Source: *The New Indian Express,* 25 May, 2019.

BJP got 50 per cent Vote Share in 200 Seats

The BJP secured over 50 per cent vote share in more than 200 constituencies across the country, according to the tentative figures of the Election Commission. The party's share crossed the halfway mark in all the 26 constituencies of Gujarat and about 40 seats in Uttar Pradesh. The same trend was noticed in the 25 constituencies of Madhya Pradesh, 23 of Rajasthan, 20 of Karnataka, 14 in Bihar and 9 of the 10 constituencies of Haryana. In all the seven seats of Delhi, it bagged over 50 per cent vote share. In the eight constituencies of Mumbai North, Bhilwara, Navsari, Surat, Vadodara, Faridabad, Karnal and Kangra, the BJP got over 70 per cent share of the votes polled. The highest of 74.73 per cent was in Navsari, as per the data available through the Commission's website at 6 p.m. on Thursday. It did not secure 50 per cent share in any of the constituencies in Odisha. State-wise analysis revealed that the highest gain of 23.29 per cent—from 34.70 per cent to 57.99 per cent—for the BJP was registered in Haryana, where it is in power. In 2014 also, it had bettered its performance compared to 17.21 per cent in 2009.

The second highest gain of about 21.5 per cent, from the previous figure 18 per cent, was recorded in West Bengal, where the party came close to the 43.54 per cent vote share of the Trinamool Congress. While in Himachal Pradesh, the party's vote share went up by more than 15 per cent to 68.93 per cent, about 10 per cent gain was reported from Arunachal Pradesh, Jharkhand and Delhi. In Karnataka and Tripura also, the figure increased by about 8 per cent as compared to 2014.

Better Performance in the Reserved Constituencies

The SC/ST violence, which erupted in various parts of the country last year, was touted to be a major poll issue with *pandits* saying it could be a factor against the BJP which had won 63 out of 128 reserved in 2014. However, the BJP and Narendra Modi successfully warded off these fears and in 2019, emerged victorious in 78 reserved seats. With their allies, the count went up to 86, amounting to around 68 per cent.

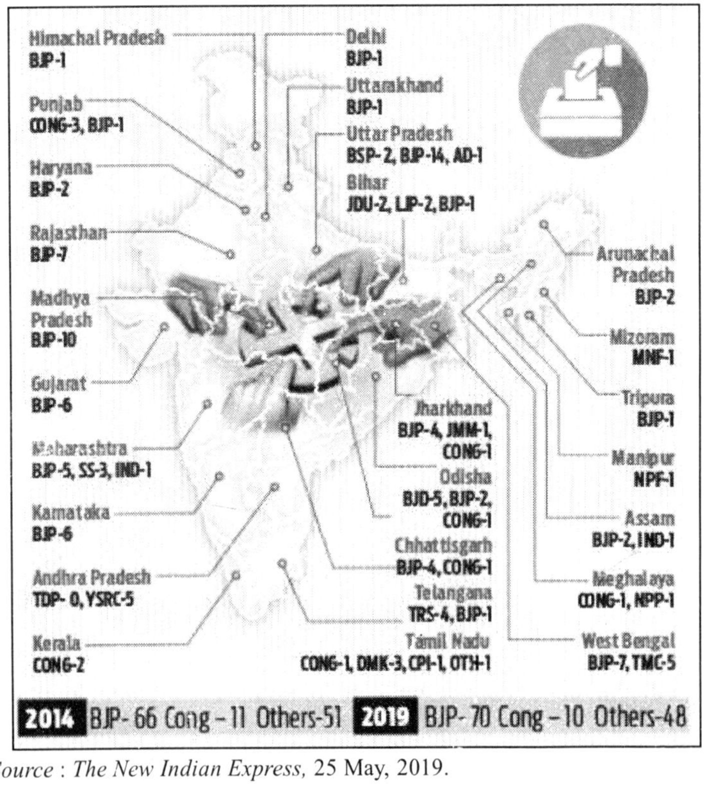

Source : *The New Indian Express,* 25 May, 2019.

According to political experts, the BJP, by making microscopic calculations, was able to do this. "They did not have a blanket strategy for wooing the SCs and Dalits. For example, they increased the representation of non-Jatavs in local governments and local bodies. Similarly, in other places, they had different welfare-based strategies," said Aditya Nigam, professor at the Centre for Studies on Developing Societies. Nigam felt that Dalit issues which hit the headlines like the Rohith Vemula case did not resonate with the people on an individual level. "It did not affect them hence they did not feel the need to be anti-BJP."

PART-V
THE DEBACLE OF THE CONGRESS AND THE LEFT PARTIES

(a) Indian National Congress

When the Bharatiya Janata Party (BJP) led by Narendra Modi stormed to power in 2014, the Congress was reduced to 44 seats in the Lok Sabha. In 2019, the Congress has suffered another colossal defeat. It won 52 seats, still not enough to claim the post of the Leader of the Opposition in the Lok Sabha. This dismal result shows that the revival of the once-dominant power-house isn't happening any time soon. Modi's re-election with an even larger majority sanctifies the structural shift to the right and the BJP's overarching dominance of the political system, that is why the Congress's spectacular defeat in this election is far more consequential than it was in 2014. The Modi landslide victory in 2019 is not based on any pretence of development, but on the basis of Hindutva consolidation and majoritarian triumphalism. The divide-and-rule strategy has succeeded in securing an unprecedented electoral endorsement for Hindu nationalism as large numbers voted for the BJP as the party that best represents, protects and propagates Hindu interests and rejected the pluralistic vision of India.

The 2019 outcome was powered by a hyper-nationalist agenda and Modi's strong advocacy of it. This election was all about the political persona of Modi and what he symbolised: a strongman standing against a divided Opposition. Gandhi is a genial and affable figure, but that seems to put him at a disadvantage when pitted against Modi's muscular leadership in 'new India'. The Congress made a strategic mistake when it decided to focus its attack entirely on Modi. Many voters had said that although they felt that the BJP had not delivered on its promises, they would vote for him because they believe a strong decisive leadership can solve India's numerous problems. Gandhi appeared to see the danger of personalising the campaign, but even then he persisted in repeating the slogan '*chowkidar chor hai*' to dent Modi's image as a scrupulously honest leader, rather than remake his message. In almost every speech he would begin and conclude with the Rafale issue. But it did not excite anyone except possibly the committed Congress voters attending his rallies. The real gains for the Congress would have come from disappointment in the Modi government's economic performance and policies, but the BJP shrewdly sidestepped its governance record by diverting to a three-point campaign of nationalism (national security, Pakistan and terrorism), Hindutva (Hindus everywhere, minorities nowhere) and anti-corruption (blasting the Congress's record, ignoring its own). Modi did not run on his track record but on teaching Pakistan a lesson. He has been re-elected on this plank. The economic downrun and shrinking employment opportunities did not matter in this election.

After the Pulwama terrorist attack and India's response with the Balakot air-strikes, the BJP mixed national security with a muscular nationalism, which completely derailed the Opposition as Modi used this narrative to project himself as the strong leader of a '*mazboot sarkar* (solid government)'. The Congress could not counter this narrative. It tried to change the subject by returning the focus to people's issues. The Nyuntam Aay Yojana (NYAY) income guarantee proposal was part of this attempt, but it came too late and the party did not carry it to the people. Consequently, NYAY did not become a talking point in the campaign; it did not even figure prominently in Gandhi's speeches. The Congress now lacks a distinct social base, and its ability to retain its supporters is dwindling. To regain its influence, it needs to decentralise and build broad-based social coalitions at the State level. The party's decline is not irreversible. But in the long road ahead, it has to figure out what it actually stands for, and what it will take to stand up to Modi's BJP. The real key to rejuvenation lies in mass contact, a distinctive and far savvier campaign on an egalitarian platform and the leadership's ability to communicate this to the people— rather than depending on the eternal verities (and varieties) of dynastic leadership.

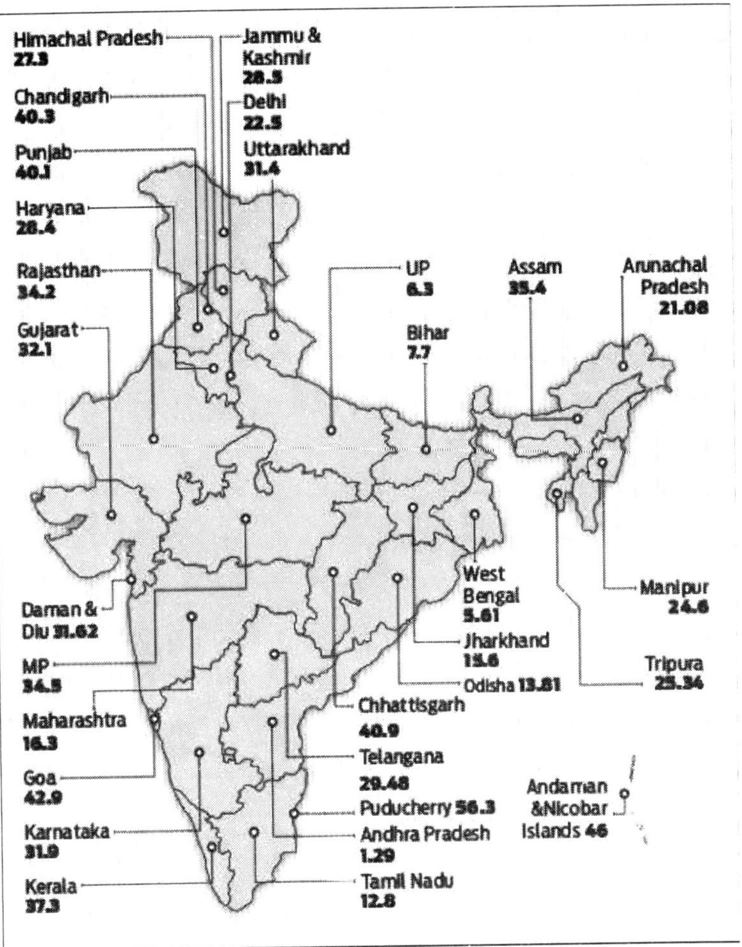

Vote Share in Percentage of the Congress in 2019

Source : *The New Sunday Express*, 26 May, 2019.

(b) Performance of the Left Parties

While the election results have brought cheer to the saffron camp, the Left is seeing red with almost negligible presence across the country. The Left, which once held West Bengal and Tripura as fortresses and held 53 Lok Sabha seats only 10 years ago has been reduced to a mere four seats in the 2019 polls and drew a blank in their traditional bastions.

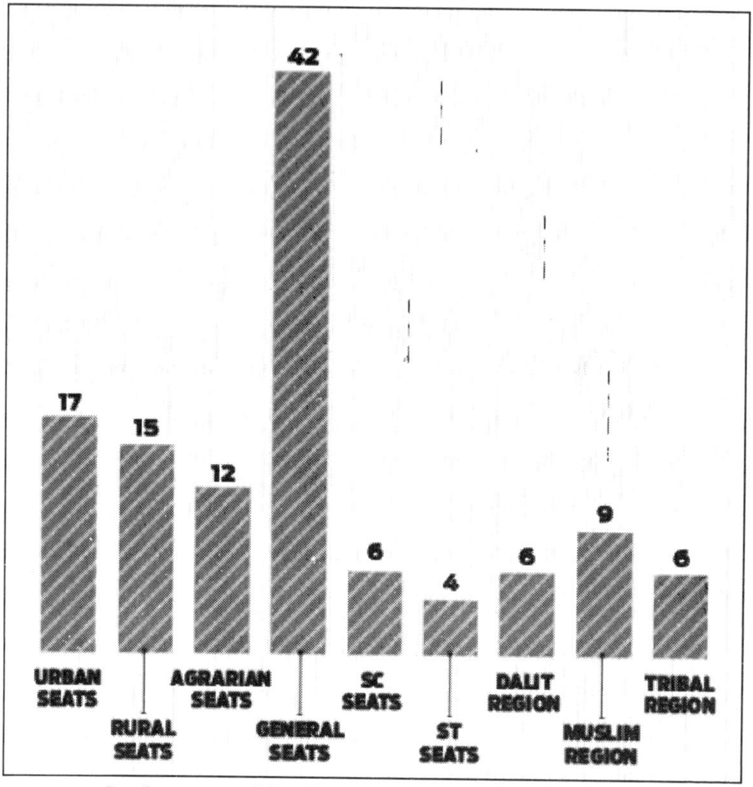

Performance of the Congress in Various Sectors, 2019

Source: *The New Sunday Express,* 26 May, 2019.

Even in Kerala, where they rule the state in an alliance, it managed to cobble up only one victory. Their tally in the 2014 elections came down drastically from 53 to 10. Surprisingly, the Left has done well in Tamil Nadu, where it is in an alliance with the Congress and the DMK, which has swept almost all the seats in the State. Political experts say the Left's unwillingness to change to adapt to current political scenario is leading to their successive defeat and erosion from the political spectrum. "The Left still is living in the past. It needs to adapt and mould its campaign and ideology to suit the present times. In a day and age where the other parties are using innovative campaign techniques, the Left is stuck with the traditional methods," Left historian Pradip Datta said. To their credit, the Left has tried to return to political relevance by supporting farmers on their issues and pressurized them to make their voice' heard. "They

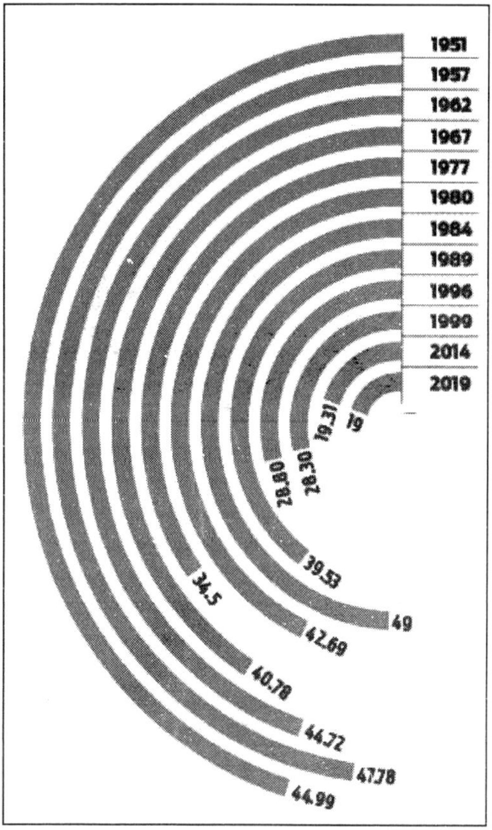

Vote Share in Percentage of the Congress from 1951 to 2019

Source: *The New Sunday Express*, 26 May, 2019.

must push for issues more aggressively and learn to compromise a little to yield better dividends or the day won't be far where they will not be present in the political scenario of the country.

PART-VI
PERFORMANCE OF REGIONAL, SOCIAL JUSTICE PARTIES AND MUSLIM LEAGUE

Regional Parties

The gigantic saffron wave that swept through the country which smashed the hopes of many regional parties, which tried to punch above their weight. Most of the aspiring parties—NCP, BSP, SP, JD(S), AAP, AIADMK and TDP—have been reduced to single digits in the Lok Sabha. West Bengal's Trinamool Congress led by Mamata Banerjee, who was eyeing the PM's post, suffered a big blow as the BJP made deep in-roads into her territory. TMC, which had scored 34 in the 2014 Modi wave, was reduced to 22 after Thursday's results.

Similarly, after winning four seats in 2014, the RJD had registered a remarkable performance in the 2015 Bihar Assembly polls under the leadership of Tejashwi Yadav. However, it could not carry forward as the party, along with allies Congress and RLSP lost most of the seats in the 2019 LS polls. The RJD failed to win even a single seat, making it the worst-ever drubbing since its formation about three decades ago. Similarly, the JD(S) had into limelight in 2018 when it stitched an alliance with the Congress in the wake of the fractured mandate in the Karnataka Assembly polls. However, it was reduced to one seat in the LS polls. Sharad Pawar-led NCP, which was also considering itself, as one of the king-makers, is facing similar crisis. The party, which had presence on six seats in 2014, could win only four seats this time.

Shibu Soren-led Jharkhand Mukto Morcha was winning one just seat till late evening as against its presence on two seats in 2014. The party suffered a major blow with even Soren losing his seat in the tribal State. "The TRS, which was expecting a hung Parliament and aspiring to play a key role in putting together a third front, was reduced to 8 seats. The party had scored impressive win in the last Assembly polls, but it could not repeat the performance in the LS elections. AIADMK is another big loser as its tally came down to meagre 1 (2019) from a remarkable 37 seats in 2014 in the Lok Sabha: The only saving grace for the party is that it is part of the NDA. Arvind Kejriwal-led AAP repeated its 2014 performance this time as well, scoring zero. Ditto with the Left parties, which registered its worst poll performance in six decades. Kerala's ruling party CPI (M) had won nine seats in 2014. But it lost 19 out of 20 seats in the state this time.

(d) SP-BSP Poor Performance

The big battle of 2019 ended in Uttar Pradesh, the state with the largest number of Lok Sabha seats, on Thursday, springing a huge surprise. It was in UP where the non-BJP parties were expected to make a stand, if the Modi wave 2.0 swept away rivals in most states. It did not happen. The Samajwadi Party, Bahujan Samaj Party and Rashtriya Lok Dal combine would have, by the sheer weight of their social arithmetic, been capable of stopping a repeat of the 2014 saffron tide in 57 out of the 80 seats. Even going by the vote share last time, they were ahead with 60 seats. Then, what happened? The NDA tally of 64 is only part of the story; not reflective of what transpired entirely. Yet, the BJP-led juggernaut's show is spectacular, for it generated a repeat wave—unprecedented in UP's electoral history—and shook the rival formations to the roots to the extent that the best known politician outside UP—Rahul Gandhi, too, capitulated, Had he seen it coming?

The Modi magic singularly overwhelmed the statistics, trumping caste barriers. The result: Saffron, which even at its 2014 strike rate stood to lose about 50 seats, managed to brilliantly reverse the damage, even taking its vote share to over 50 per cent from 43 per cent of 2014 while winning less seats. It will be difficult for Congress chief Rahul Gandhi to reconcile to the Amethi shocker as would it be for SP chief Akhilesh Yadav, who is another big loser in the alliance. Contesting 37 of 80 seats, SP vote share fell to 4 per cent—a clear indication that BSP cadres did not vote SP. It also failed to improve upon its 2014 performance, winning five seats again losing family bastions—Kannauj (Dimple), Firozabad (Akshay Yadav) and Badaun (Dharmendra Yadav). Similarly, RLD lost all three seats it contested. Even Chaudhury Ajit Singh failed to save his Jat pride in Muzaffarnagar. BSP chief Mayawati, however, emerged a gainer, cashing SP votes to win 11 seats against none in 2014. BSP had contested 38 of 80 seats.

(e) Social Justice Politics under Threat

'The 2019 verdict bas also dismantled social justice parties in Uttar Pradesh and Bihar, two States that together send 120 members to the Lok Sabha. The rise of Hindutva since the 1980s had a parallel—new wave of backward caste mobilisation in parts of northern and western India, which questioned the Nehruvian elite's grip on power. While parties based on social justice politics or regional pride weakened the Congress, they also viewed the BJP with skepticism despite their occasional association with it. Through deft coalition building, the BJP used many non-Congress outfits to further its own growth and gobbled them up in several States, such as Gujarat. In U.P., and Bihar, social justice parties with deep-rooted support among the Hindu backward castes, in alliance with the considerable Muslim population in these States, became the biggest roadblock to the Hindutva project. In 2014, the BJP upended that dynamic and swept both States in 2019 which proved that the phenomenon is enduring.

The Rashtriya Janata Dal in Bihar and the Samajwadi Party, the Bahujan Samaj Party and Rashtriya Lok Dal in U.P. usurped by their leaders as personal and family enterprises and sunk in corruption charges, collapsed. But outfits such as Ram Vilas Paswan's Lok Janashakti Party in Bihar and the Shiv Sena in Maharashtra, guilty of the same since, have flourished in their alliance with the BJP. The 2019 outcome must thus be seen as one powered by the hyper nationalist agenda that was the mainstay of Modi's five-year term in government, though corruption and nepotism of the BJP's opponents could have been supplementary factors. The welfare schemes of the Modi government did play a role, but these or the promise of economic development were not the real differentiators. The Pulwama terrorist strike and India's response to it dovetailed into the BJP's campaign.

(f) Reduced Number of Muslim Members

Nearly 150 million Muslims will only have 24 representatives in the 17th Lok Sabha, according to trends shown on the Election Commission website till late Thursday evening. While Muslims constitute 10.5 per cent of the total population, its percentage representation in the new Lok Sabha will be 4.42 per cent. Notably, neighbouring Bangladesh has a better representation of minorities with 21 of its members belonging to the minority community. This constitutes 8.8 per cent representation of their total strength. Pakistan, on the other hand, fares poorly than India as only 2.9 per cent of its members belong to the minority community.

However, the representation of Muslim in India has gone up by two seats this time if compared to 2014, when it hit an all time low in the last 50 years. BJP which won with a thumping majority will not have a single Muslim MP as was the case in 2014. The highest number of Muslims have come from Uttar Pradesh with three each from Samajwadi party and Bahujan Samajwadi party. Among the winners is firebrand Samajwadi leader Azam Khan. Notably UP, which has the highest population of Muslims, had sent no Muslim MP to the Lok Sabha in 2014. The second highest number of five Muslim MPs is from West Bengal with four MPs from the Trinamool and one from the Congress. Jammu & Kashmir, which is a Muslim majority state, has three MPs, all from National Conference. The three MPs are party president Farooq Abdullah, Mohammad Akbar Lone and Hasnain Masoodi, Bihar, which had sent four MPs to the Lok

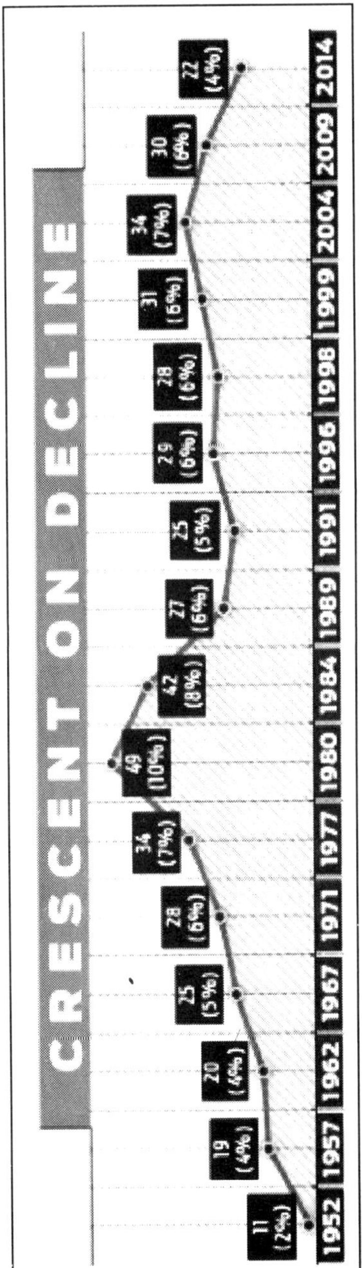

Source: The New Indian Express, 24 May, 2019.

Sabha last time, has only two Muslims this time—one each from Congress and Janata Dal (United). About half of the country's Muslims live in the states of Uttar Pradesh, Bihar, and and West Bengal. Kerala and Assam also have two MPs each who belong to the minority community. Maharashtra, with a Muslim population of around 11 per cent, has elected one Muslim MP—Imtiaz Jaleel Syed of All India Majlis-E-Ittehadul Muslimeen. Punjab, Telangana and Lakshadweep also have one Muslim MP each. The only encouraging statistics on Muslim representation is the fact that this time the contribution of Muslim MPs comes from 10 states while in the last elections, the Muslim MPs hailed from just seven states.

(g) 76 Women MPs in Lok Sabha

Thirty three per cent representation in the, Lower House of the Parliament is still a far cry but Indian women seem to have done their best this time as the election results were declared on Thursday. A total of 76 women candidates are set to, make it to the 17th Lok Sabha—the highest, since the first general elections—marking, a little over 14 per cent of the total 542 seat that had gone to the polls. In the last Lok Sabha, there were 66 women representatives. Uttar Pradesh and West Bengal are sending the highest number of women 11 each—to the Lok Sabha. There will also be a comparatively high number of women, MPs from Odisha and around six of them are from Biju Janta Dal. Among the most high profile, women MPs who will be seen in the Lower House are Sonia Gandhi, Maneka Gandhi, Hema Malini and Smriti Irani.

Another star candidate Jaya Prada, who, was a BJP candidate from UP's Rampur, however, lost to Samajwadi Party's Azam Khan. Bollywood actress Urmila Matondkar, too, lost from Mumbai north. A total of 34 women MPs in Parliament are from the ruling BJP, which had fielded just 47 women candidates. In comparison, TMC had fielded 41 per cent of women candidates while BJD had fielded 33 per cent. Marginally better performance by women candidates pleased many but some women rights activists sounded rather cautious except Bengal and Odisha there were fewer women candidates fielded than men. "So, the odds for winning then were naturally, higher for men than women," said a Delhi-based activist. "Secondly, the women fielded by winning parties tend to have a strong elite profile. So, it does not necessarily mean that representation of common women is getting any better in Parliament." Meanwhile, DMK of Tamil Nadu, which had fielded two women candidates, including, Sumathy Thangapandian from Chennai South and Kanimozhi Karunanidhi from Thoothukudi, saw them both winning their respective seats. In Andhra, four women candidates of YSR Congress, Goddeti Madhavi from Aruku, K.V. Satyavathi from Anakapalli, Chinta Anuradha from Amalapuram and Vanga Geetha from Kakinada also registered convincing victories. As many as 28 out of 41 sitting women MPs, including Sonia Gandhi, Hema Malini and Kirron Kher, are set to retain their seat in Lok Sabha.

(h) NOTA—Only a Marginal Change

The percentage of votes for NOTA, or the none-of-the-above option, this year has remained virtually unchanged from last time, according to data from the Election Commission (EC) website. In 2019, about 1.04 per cent of the voters felt that none of the candidates deserved their vote. In the 2014 Lok Sabha election, this was around 1.08 per cent of the voters. The 2019 Lok Sabha elections stretched over six weeks and registered the highest voter turnout in the history of the Lok Sabha election. The final voter turnout stood at 67.11 per cent, according to the EC. However, NOTA numbers varied widely across States, with a high of 2.08 per cent in Assam and Bihar to 0.65 per cent in Sikkim. According to records from the Association For Democratic Reforms (ADR), a research agency, the number of NOTA options in 2014 was about 60,00,197 with the highest percentage from Bastar, Chhattisgarh with 38,772 (5.04% votes) followed by Nilgiris in Tamil Nadu with 46,559 (4.99%) and Nabarangpur of Odisha with 44,408 (4.34%) votes. The NOTA option was introduced in India following a 2013 Supreme Court directive in the *People's Union for Civil Liberties* vs. *Union of India* judgment. It was first used in the 2013 Assembly elections in Chhattisgarh, Mizoram, Rajasthan and Madhya Pradesh and the former Union Territory of Delhi. In these States and Delhi, NOTA constituted 1.85 per cent of the total votes polled.

PART-VII
CONCLUSION

The definitive nature of the Bharatiya Janata Party's victory in the 17th general election marks an unmistakable inflection point in the journey of the Republic. If the 16th general election in 2014 catapulted the BJP as the primary pole of Indian politics, relegating the Congress to a distant second, 2019 establishes it as the overarching hegemon. For good reasons, this result is being viewed as an endorsement of Prime Minister Narendra

Modi's persona, and his imprint on this victory is distinctive. But it will be a folly to ignore the underlying structural reasons that made this victory possible, and its sweep so deep and wide. It takes strong personalities to popularise an idea, but it is those ideas that outlive personalities that define the course of a people or a nation. The outcome, hence, must be understood as an electoral endorsement of Hindutva, or Hindu nationalism, the creed that guided the BJP and its forebears for nearly a century since Vinayak Damodar Savarkar wrote the treatise by the same title. Narendra Modi, who counts Savarkar as a critical influence, has been the catalyst and the alchemist of the transformation in the way India imagines itself. In recess, if not in irreversible decline, is the idea of India that had grown from the freedom movement, and had prevailed for most part of the history of the Republic.

Championed by the first Prime Minister of India, Jawaharlal Nehru, it sought inspiration from the millennia old civilisation, the *Vedas* and the *Upanishads*, but also strived to build India into a modern society with a scientific temper and liberal values. The idea outlived Nehru, but it had begun to fade soon after his passing. Nehru and his mentor, Mahatma Gandhi, were the prime targets of derision for the proponents of Hindutva in the early years. With the 2019 result, Hindutva has pushed Nehruvian secularism to the margins of Indian politics. The Congress, now led by Nehru's great-grand son Rahul Gandhi, did better than in 2014, but not enough to even be recognised as the official Opposition in the Lok Sabha. Now, BJP is bound to uphold secular ideals or to protect the integrity of existing institutions may amount to demanding an abandonment of its very core beliefs. Gaining the trust of all citizens will be a necessary prerequisite for Modi to drive India's continuing journey to become a global leader. It is only reasonable that the government and the Prime Minister be asked to live up to the promise they continuously make *sabka saath, sabka vikas* (with all development for all). These tenets must be felt in the daily lives of the marginalised sections of the population, and Narendra Modi must add a third tenet to make his *mantra* meaningful: *sabka vishwas* (the trust of all) (*The Hindu,* 24 May, 2019).

Indian voters have shown remarkable maturity and thoughtfulness in delivering a stable government at the Centre. They realise the necessity of a stable government, and so often vote differently in National and State elections.. Forecasts of political and economic instability made in 2014, when the macro economy was vulnerable, proved incorrect. Similar forecasts were made this year, based on the Bharatiya Janata Party (BJP-led National Democratic Alliance's losses in the Karnataka, Madhya

Pradesh and Rajasthan Assembly elections. The *pandits* should bow to the greater wisdom of the people—in this election, the BJP has swept the same States. The Congress underestimated the voters' continuing need for good governance. The Congress did not choose dynamic Chief Ministers when it had the option. It also underestimated the voters need for a positive narrative. Talking of slow job growth and farmer distress did not work. The Nyuntam Aay Yojana scheme (the Congress's proposed social welfare programme) was not acceptable as a substitute for jobs. On the other hand, the BJP promised to improve ease of living, beyond just the ease of doing business, and strengthen the self-respect and ability of the average citizen to do more, which is exactly the right approach for an aspirational India.

There was fear of competitive populism in the event of a weak government being elected at the Centre. Now the BJP will hopefully focus, as promised in its manifesto, on infrastructure, housing, technology, health, education, water, the environment, and facilitate the move away from agricultural jobs to raise farmer incomes. Only 23 per cent of rural income now comes from farming, and there is a major ongoing shift to add value in agriculture. Apart from this, administrative reforms should be the focus. There are police and judicial reforms on the anvil. Well-targeted direct benefit transfers will efficiently deliver relief to the really distressed at low cost. Humility should come with strength. After an exceptionally bitter election season, the NDA will hopefully follow a constructive and inclusive agenda and encourage moderate progressive stances. Institutions are the backbone of any economy and must be strengthened. The people know the government took difficult decisions to clean up the system, and chose to give it a second chance. It is time to meet their expectations.

REFERENCES

Ajay Gudavathy, History Repeats Itself for TDP, *Ibid.*

Anubhav Mishra, How Chowkidar became a Brand, *Business Line*, 25.02.2019.

Ashima Goyal, The NDA has its Task Cut Out, *Ibid.*

Bharath Bhushan, Tectonic Shift towards a very Different India, *Deccan Chronicle*, 25.05.2019.

Facing the Debacle, Editorial, *The Hindu*, 25.05.2019.

George, T.J.S., All Set for the Next 20 Years, *Ibid.*

Harish Khare, The 2019 Vote: An Intoxicating Verdict, *The Hindu*, 24.05.2019.

How India Voted: Verdict 2019, *Business Line*, 24.05.2019.

https://en.wikipedia.org/wiki/2019_Indian_general_election

Namita Bajpai, SP-BSP Gathbandhan Faces Existential Crisis in U.P., *Ibid.*
Neera Chandhoke, The Making of the 2019 Verdict, *The Hindu*, 27.05.2019.
Neerja Chowdhury, Modi all the Way, *Ibid.*
Panner Selvan, Electoral Outcomes Don't Alter the Purpose of Journalism, *The Hindu*, 27.05.2019.
Parthasarathy, G, BJP's Pakistan Conundrum, *Ibid.*
Poornima Joshi, After Modi Meets the President, *Ibid.*
Poornima Joshi, Modi 2.0: Bigger and Broader, *Ibid.*
Pushkar Banakar, Microscopic Calculations Work, *The New Indian Express*, 24.05.2019.
Pushkar Banakar, Saffron Brigade Blurs Rural Urban Divide, *Ibid.*
Quraishi, It's Time to take Stock of Electoral Process, 25.05.2019.
Rajeev Bhargava, How to Rescue Genuine Secularism, *The Hindu*, 28.05.2019.
Ramakrishan S., A Reflection of People's Trust in Modi, *Ibid.*
Ramesh, M., India and the Perils of being an Outlier, *Business Line*, 25.02.2019.
Richa Sharma, No Progress for Congress, *The New Sunday Express*, 26.05.2019.
Ritwika Mitra, The Rise and Rise in Saffron Party's Vote Share, *The New Indian Express*, 25.05.2019.
Ruchir Sharma, Modi vs Modi, *The Times of India*, 24.05.2019.
Sandeep Shastri *et. al*; Explaining the Modi Sweep Across Regions, *Ibid.*
Sanjay Kumar, A Clear Vote for Nationalism and Signalling an End to Caste Politics, *Ibid.*
Shashi Sekhar, Global Implications of the Mandate, *Ibid.*
Shiv Visvanathan, What the Thumbing Mandate for Modi Means, *Ibid.*
Singh, K.C., Time for Rise of Modi the Statesman, *Ibid.*
Suhas Palshikar, Turning Social Consolidation on its Head, *The Hindu*, 26.05.2019.
The Editorial, *Business Line*, 25.02.2019.
The Editorial, *Deccan Chronicle*, 25.05.2019.
The Editorial, *The Hindu, Ibid.*
The Editorial, *The Hindu, Ibid.*
The Editorial, *The Times of India*, 24.05.2019.
The Hindu, For A Rediscovery of India, Editorial, 24 May, 2019.
Valsan Thampu, Will the Congress Panic and Commit Harakiri?, *Ibid.*
Vidya Subramanyam, The Leader who is Bigger than his Party, *Ibid.*
Zoya Hasan, No Easy Solutions for the Congress, *The Hindu*, 25.05.2019.

3

Lok Sabha Polls (2019) in Kerala

A Decisive Political Vote—Not a Minority Consolidation

M.R. Biju and *M.R.B. Anantha Padmanabha*

Prelude

When the Congress suffered drubbing in most parts of the country, Kerala bucked the trend and stood firmly with it, handing the party-led United Democratic Front a landslide. While the UDF won 19 of the 20 seats on offer, the Communists suffered a humiliating defeat, winning only one seat in their only remaining bastion. The verdict was almost a repeat of 1977 when the UDF won all 20 seats. The Sabarimala factor made its impact, but not as predicted. While the CPM-led Left Democratic Front suffered a debacle, the BJP-led NDA failed to win even a single seat. The BJP, riding on Sabarimala sentiments, had entertained hopes of winning at least two seats, but the best the party could achieve was a runner-up position in Thiruvananthapuram. In all other seats, the NDA finished third. However, the BJP was able to bag close to 3 lakh votes in Pathanamthitta and Thrissur.

Alappuzha turned out to be a face-saver for the Left as A.M. Ariff, the CPM's sitting MLA from Aroor, managed to wrest the seat from the Congress. In the UDF tally of 19, the Congress has 15, Muslim League two, and Kerala Congress (M) and RSP one each. Nine of these seats were won by a margin of more than one lakh votes, with Congress chief Rahul Gandhi breezing past his nearest rival P.P. Suneer of the CPM by a record 4.31 lakh votes in Wayanad. The ignominious defeat the Left suffered will have far-reaching repercussions in state politics. Chief Minister Pinarayi Vijayan will have too many questions to answer, especially on the Sabarimala front. It could even go a long way in redefining his political ambitions. State Congress president Mullappally Ramachandran and senior leader Ramesh Chennithala have demanded Pinarayi's resignation, terming the verdict a fitting reply to his "arrogance and the Left Government's anti-people policies."

While the LDF suffered shock-defeats in its traditional strong-holds, including in north Kerala, the victory of underdogs Remya Haridas (Alathur) and V.K. Sreekandan (Palakkad) over sitting MPs P.K. Biju and M.B. Rajesh respectively should further demoralise the front. Chief Minister Vijayan, who termed the verdict unexpected, said the party would look into the factors that led to the debacle. In a statement, he said there was a strong anti-BJP sentiment in Kerala following the widespread campaigning by the Left which led to the verdict. The exit polls about the state came true as far as the UDF landslide is concerned. BJP state chief P.S. Sreedharan Pillai blamed the party's failure to win a seat on UDF's minority appeasement tactics, but said the NDA would soon emerge as an alternative in the state. The failure is sure to trigger conflicts in the party's state unit in the coming days. But it would not be surprising if a state leader finds a place in the new Narendra Modi cabinet.

The huge victory of the UDF in the state trouncing the Left Front by a margin of 19-1 seems to be surprisingly owing to the consolidation of minority and majority votes in favour of the front, obviously for different reasons. While the candidature of Rahul Gandhi from Wayanad, who was projected as the Prime Minister candidate of the UPA, led to the minority consolidation in favour of the UDF and the Congress, the Sabarimala issue was considered one of the major factors which looked to the majority consolidating.

Surprisingly, the Congress reaped the benefits of the Sabarimala issue in which the BJP was vociferous and fought it out on the streets resulting in several party workers being jailed. However, the BJP could not get any seat in the state even after all the struggles it had undertaken for the cause. The Congress stand all through the issue was that the party has always been with the devotees and that the UDF Government led by Oommen Chandy had given an affidavit in the Supreme Court opposing the entry of women in Sabarimala. KPCC president Mullappally Ramachandran while speaking to Express said, "I am jubilant and the party has done exceedingly well and this victory against the arrogance of the Chief Minister and the anti-people policies of the LDF Government. Pinarayi Vijayan should put in his papers taking responsibility for this huge drubbing the people have given the Left Front."

Keeping this in background, this chapter examines the political significance of the Seventeenth Lok Sabha Polls in Kerala and its aftermath. It has been categorized under four heads. Part-I presents the regionwise Analysis of the Results, Part-II unforce the role played by BJP and its allies,

Part-III on the electoral performance of the LDF in General and the CPI (M) in particular. The role of SDPI, BDJS and Religious and Caste based Organisations are also unfolded in Part-III. Part-IV presents the findings of the Study.

PART-I
PEOPLE'S VERDICT– REGIONWISE ANALYSIS

A. Central Kerala

Central Kerala is traditionally pro-UDF, but the alliance was imbued with the force of a juggernaut as it demolished the strongholds of the Left in the Thrissur and Idukki Lok Sabha constituencies in the general election this time. In Alappuzha, where CPI (M)'s A.M. Ariff bucked the trend to post a win by over 9,000 votes, he trailed in all Assembly segments except Cherthala, which gave him a lead of 17,000, and Kayamkulam, where he led by some 4,000 votes. The jolt suffered by the Left front in the region could be gauged from the fact that of the 42 Assembly segments in the Thrissur, Chalakudy, Ernakulam, Idukki, Alappuzha and Kottayam Lok Sabha constituencies, the alliance could garner a lead in just three segments, with CPI (M)'s V.N. Vasavan also managing to lead the Vaikom assembly segment of the Kottayam seat by about 9,000 votes. In the Assembly election in 2016, the Left had secured 26 of the 42 segments in these Lok Sabha constituencies.

Four of the UDF candidates from the region posted victory margins of over one lakh, while it was over 93,000 votes for T.N. Prathapan in Thrissur, where NDA candidate and film star Suresh Gopi managed to clinch the second position in the Thrissur assembly segment, relegating CPI's Rajaji Mathew Thomas to the third spot. The Thrissur Assembly segment is held by CPI leader and Agriculture Minister V.S. Sunil Kumar. In Ernakulam where Hibi Eden, MLA, posted a record victory by margin of 1.69 lakh votes, the Left could not come anywhere close to him in any of the Assembly segments. In the Thripunithura, Vypeen, Kochi and Paravur segments where the Left was hoping to clinch a lead, it suffered a rout.

In Chalakudy, actor and sitting MP Innocent put up a close fight only in the Kaipamangalam Assembly segment (held by the CPI). Idukki, which was won by Congress's Dean Kuriakose by a margin of 1.71 lakh votes, bestowed on him the biggest lead from the Thodupuzha segment (37,000 votes) followed by Muvattupuzha (30,000 votes), which is held by the CPI in the Assembly. Kottayam sprang no surprises, as Thomas Chazhikkadan won comfortably. But NDA candidate P.C. Thomas was able to garner 1.55

lakh votes, thrice over the votes polled by the NDA candidate in 2014. Alappuzha too witnessed a similar trend, with NDA candidate K.S. Radhakrishnan polling 1.86 lakh votes, thereby spoiling Congress's prospects.

B. Southern Kerala

Riding on the crest of a high wave of anti-Central and State government sentiment, the United Democratic Front (UDF) surfed to victory in five Lok Sabha constituencies in south Kerala on Thursday. The UDF win in Thiruvananthapuram, Attingal, Kollam, Pathanamthitta and Mavelikara also stymied a total rightward shift in votes to the National Democratic Alliance (NDA), which presumed to reap dividends from the deeply polarising Sabarimala issue. The front's emphatic win in the south signalled a consolidation of minority votes in its favour in the face of the Sangh Parivar's attempt to assault secular values and arbitrate on issues such as the consumption of beef, Babri Masjid, Triple Talaq Bill and the proposed Church Act. It also indicated a general reluctance among voters hurt by the State government's handling of the temple issue to bet entirely on the untested Bharatiya Janata Party (BJP). The UDF wins also suggested that a majority of the voters had decided to stay the course with the Congress to express their grievances.

Notably, the UDF's star candidate Shashi Tharoor trumped his nearest rival Kummanam Rajasekharan of the BJP by a positive 99,989 votes in Thiruvananthapuram. He bulldozed C. Divakaran of the LDF to the third position and upped his lead. In Attingal, widely reckoned as a Left bastion, Adoor Prakash of the UDF dashed the hopes of incumbent A. Sampath of the CPI(M) by a whopping 38,247 votes. In a surprise, Sobha Surendran of the NDA bagged 2,48,081 votes in the segment.

Upending poll predictions, Anto Antony of the UDF won by 44,613 votes in the hotly contested Pathanamthitta constituency. The Parliamentary segment was the epicentre of the rancorous Sabarimala debate which pitted the government against the Congress and the BJP. Mr. Antony pushed Veena George of the LDF and K. Surendran of the NDA to second and third place respectively. In Kollam, N.K. Premachandran of the UDF won by a wide margin of 1,49,772 votes over his rival K.N. Balagopal of the CPI(M). Mr. Premachandran, who was personally vilified by the LDF for deserting it in 2014, leaned on his appeal and Parliamentary prowess to beat his rivals. In Mavelikara, Kodikunnil Suresh of the Congress handily defeated Chittayam Gopakumar of the LDF by a lead of 61,500 votes. The NDA has claimed that is has improved its vote share in all the four constituencies.

C. Northern Kerala

A mind-boggling 4.31 lakh vote victory for Rahul Gandhi in Wayanad has given the UDF the highest victory margin in the Malabar region, apart from the largest number of votes polled in the State. From Kasaragod to Alathur, all the nine constituencies in the region stood firmly behind the UDF seven for the Congress and two for the Indian Union Muslim League (IUML). The most exciting victory in the State this time of the greenhorn Ramya Haridas with a 1.58 lakh vote margin at Alathur is also from the region.

But for Palakkad and Kasaragod, Malabar gave huge majorities to the UDF candidates. Most exit polls had discounted UDF fortunes in Kasaragod [which is part of the CPI(M) heartland in Malabar] and Palakkad [where the CPI(M)'s sitting MP M.B. Rajesh had built up reputation for being a good legislator]. But Rajmohan Unnithan and Sreekantan could swim along with the UDF wave, though their margins were not as impressive as others. That Gandhi would secure an impressive victory was a foregone conclusion. Senior Congress and IUML leaders had earlier expressed the hope that his margin would be between 2 lakh and 2.5 lakh. But they are all now mesmerised by the 4.31-lakh margin Gandhi has won. UDF leaders concede gleefully that the untiring grassroots-level work by the IUML workers and some of the tiny Muslim parties had a big role in Mr. Gandhi's spectacular win.

Gandhi's triumph is even more outstanding considering the fact that he had campaigned in the constituency just for a day. He is among the big-ticket winners in the country and is not very far behind BJP president Amit Shah, who has mopped up a margin of over five lakh votes. Gandhi has lost his sitting seat of Amethi to Smriti Irani and hence he will now be forced to keep Wayanad. Earlier, it was believed that Mr. Gandhi, after winning Wayanad, would opt to retain Amethi. P.K. Kunhalikutty's victory margin of 2.60 lakh in Malappuram is the second largest in the State, after Gandhi. If Gandhi is reckoned as an 'outsider,' Kunhalikutty's is the largest victory margin in Kerala of a Malayali candidate.

E.T. Mohammed Basheer's victory margin of 1.93 lakh in Ponnani is spectacular when viewed against the background that at one time it had seemed that his contest against P.V. Anvar was a close one. In Kozhikode, Vadakara and Kannur, the Congress had run a strong campaign and their candidates were strong too. In Vadakara, fielding of K. Muraleedharan was a very tactical move.

D. Political Violence in Kasaragod and its Aftermath

The issue of political violence has played a decisive role in shaping the electoral outcome in the parliamentary constituencies of north Malabar as it was the United Democratic Front's (UDF) key campaign theme in the aftermath of the twin murders of Youth Congress workers Kripesh and Sharath Lal at Kalloytt in Kasaragod in February. The electoral debacle of the Communist Party of India (Marxist) in the Kannur, Kasaragod, and Vadakara constituencies, parts of which have seen incidents of political violence and murders, is a clear indication that the UDF's concerted efforts during the campaign to keep the issue live yielded results. Congress candidates in the constituencies left no stone unturned to train the spotlight on what it called the CPI (M)'s culture of eliminating its rivals. UDF circles say that its campaign salvo targeting the CPI (M)'s alleged culture of political violence struck a chord with the electorate in the region.

"The outcome was also the people's mandate against political violence perpetrated by the CPI(M) in Kannur and neighbouring areas," said K. Sudhakaran, who romped home from Kannur with a thumping margin. People were fed up with political violence in the region, he added. Mr. Sudhakaran polled 5,29,741 votes in the Kannur Lok Sabha constituency while his rival candidate polled 4,35,182. The Bharatiya Janata Party's C.K. Padmanabhan came a distant third with 68,509 votes. The UDF had also invoked during the electioneering the murder of S.P. Shuhaib near Mattannur last year. The appeal of the UDF candidates to the outrage of people against the youth's murders gave a poignant touch to the electioneering of the UDF.

The candidature of CPI(M) leader P. Jayarajan, who is an accused in the cases of murders of Rashtriya Swayamsevak Sangh worker K. Manoj and Indian Union Muslim League worker Abdul Shukkoor, both investigated by the CBI, was utilised by the UDF during the campaign to portray the CPI(M) as a party that sheltered the accused if cases of political violence. The CPI(M) will be left to do some serious introspection in the coming days on the situation that led to its rout in north Malabar, which it treated as its invincible fortresses. The party's major cause of concern will be erosion of votes even in its stronghold Assembly segments such as Dharmadam, Mattannur, and Taliparamba, where Mr. Sudhakaran could garner substantial number of votes.

People's Verdict 2019

Sl. No.	Constituency	Total Votes	Votes Polled	UDF	LDF	NDAs	Victory Margin	Name of Candidates won/ Party
1.	Kasaragod	1360827	1100099	174961	434523	176049	40438	Rajmohan Unnithan (Congress)
2.	Kannur	1262144	1048171	529741	434523	68509	94559	K. Sudhakaran (Congress)
3.	Vadakara	1266250	1060923	526755	435182	80128	84663	K. Muraleedharan (Congress)
4.	Wayanad	1352819	1090403	706367	442092	431770	78816	Rahul Gandhi (Congress)
5.	Kozhikode	1315355	1071572	493444	408219	161216	85225	M.K. Raghavan (Congress)
6.	Malappuram	1369878	1033302	589873	329720	82332	260153	P.K. Kunjalikutty (Muslim League)
7.	Ponnani	1356408	1016815	521824	328637	110603	193273	E.T. Mohammed Basheer (Muslim League)
8.	Palakkad	1320680	1025825	399274	387617	218550	11637	V.K. Sreekantan (Congress)
9.	Alathur	1264471	1015693	533815	374847	89837	158968	Remya Haridas (Congress)
10.	Thrissur	1336399	1040579	415089	321456	293822	93633	T.R. Prathapan (Congress)
11.	Chalakudy	1229476	880044	473444	341170	154159	132274	Benny Behnan (Congress)
12.	Ernakulam	1245334	965665	491263	322110	137749	169153	Hibi Eaden (Congress)
13.	Idukki	1203258	917563	498493	327440	78648	171053	Dean Kuriakose (Congress)
14.	Kottayam	1205376	807562	421046	314797	155135	106259	Thomas Chazhikadan (Congress)
15.	Alappuzha	1351405	1082304	443003	433790	186278	9213	A.M. Ariff [CPI(M)]
16.	Mavelikkara	1301067	963984	437997	376497	132323	61500	Kodikunnil Suresh (Congress)
17.	Pathanamthitta	1378587	1022763	380089	335476	295627	44613	Anto Antony (Congress)
18.	Kollam	1292636	861212	497264	347492	102319	149772	N.K. Premachandran (Congress)
19.	Attingal	1346641	961212	380995	342348	248081	38247	Adoor Prakash (Congress)
20.	Thiruvananthapuram	1367523	1004429	416131	316142	258556	99989	Sashi Tharoor (Congress)

Source: Compiled by the Authors.

PART-II
BJP NEED FRESH STRATEGIES

Despite its aggressive poll campaign exploiting the discontent among the Ayyappa devotees against the CPM stand on Sabarimala issue the BJP failed miserably to open its account in the state yet again. But the NDA could increase its vote share from 19,44,204 in 2014 Lok Sabha Polls to 31,34,213 in 2019, an increase of 11,88,909 votes.

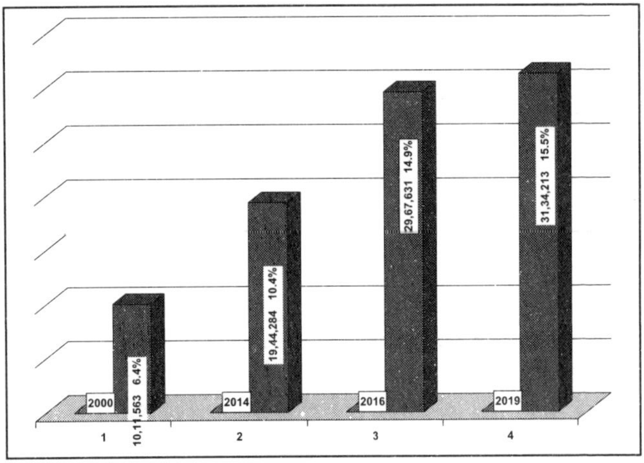

Source: Data compiled and illustrated by authors

Has the BJP reached a stagnation point in its growth trajectory in Kerala? The results of the Lok Sabha election, where the party failed to raise its vote share, points to the need for the party to look beyond its traditional vote base in Kerala. The party's vote base grew from 6.4 per cent in 2009 to 14.9 in 2014. However, despite the Sabarimala issue, the party's vote share grew only by 0.5 per cent, which was worrying. The BJP was hoping to raise its vote share beyond the 20 per cent mark and win Thiruvananthapuram and Pathanamthitta seats exploiting the sentiments of the Ayyappa devotees who were hurt by the incidents at Sabarimala. Though the role of the BJP-RSS workers in foiling attempts to facilitate entry of young women to the hill shrine was appreciated by the devotees, it failed to convert the support into votes. According to a senior leader, a section of the Hindus, who vowed support to the efforts to protect the traditions and practices voted for the Congress candidates to ensure the defeat of the CPM.

Based on a directive from BJP president Amit Shah, the BJP in Kerala had initiated steps to win the confidence of the Christian community in Kerala much before the elections. Though the leaders held talks with the Church representatives and Minister of State for Tourism Alphons Kannanthanam sanctioned funds for certain churches, they failed to win the confidence of the community.

"There are some apprehensions among the Christian community, which we need to address. The party has been trying to reach out to them and the Orthodox community had indicated their willingness to support us. However, it did not happen. There are issues like blocking of NGO funding and the request to facilitate the visit of Pope Francis to India. Even Kannanthanam did not get the support of the community. Some of the demands of the community will be met by the new government to dispel the misgivings," said BJP spokesperson.

"Many Hindu families had parted ways with the CPM after the Sabarimala incident. They decided to teach the Pinarayi government a lesson and voted for the UDF to ensure the defeat of LDF candidates. Though BJP candidates could not win, we are happy to see the rout of the LDF cases were slapped on around 35,000 devotees for participating in the Sabarimala agitation. Around 10,000 people were arrested and more than 100 people were put in jail for more than a month. We are happy that the electorate in Kerala has given a befitting reply to the LDF for the atrocities against devotees," said Sabarimala Karma Samithi general convenor.

Aggressive Campaign Failed

Despite its aggressive campaigning exploiting the discontent among the Ayyappa devotees against the CPM stand on Sabarimala issue, the BJP failed miserably to open its account in the state yet again. In 2014, the BJP had lost Thiruvananthapuram constituency by a slender margin of 15,530 votes. With the Sabarimala sentiments triggering a Hindu vote consolidation in south and central Kerala, BJP had fielded: former Mizoram Governor Kummanam Rajasekharan here, hoping to win the seat: with a comfortable majority. Though the party's vote share increased from 2,82,336 in 2014 to 3,13,925 this time, the percentage of votes plummeted from 32.45 per cent to 31.28 per cent. Congress candidate Shashi Tharoor's victory with a margin of one lakh votes has in fact shocked the BJP leadership in the state. In Pathanamthitta, where BJP candidate M.T. Ramesh had secured 1,38,954 votes in 2014, the party polled 2,97,396 votes.

Though there was an increase of 112 per cent in vote share it was not sufficient to win the seat. The party was hoping to win Pathanamthitta, riding on the strong sentiments among the Hindu community, who were hurt by the Sabarimala incident. Congress candidate Anto Antony was polled 37.11 per cent votes to win the seat, while CPM candidate Veena George secured 32.8 per cent votes. BJP candidate K. Surendran finished a distant third with 28.97 per cent vote.

BDJS helped NDA to Increase its Vote Share

The support of the Bharath Dharma Jana Sena (BDJS), which represents the prominent Ezhava community, has helped the NDA to improve its vote share in the State. BJP president P.S. Sreedharan Pillai himself had appreciated the BDJS workers' dedicated support during campaigning. Now, the steep rise in the NDA's vote share in Alappuzha, Attingal, Thrissur 'and Wayanad constituencies, where the Ezhava community has a strong presence, points to 'the shift in its allegiance'.

The NDA, which had secured 90,528 votes in 2014, almost tripled the tally this time—2,46,502. In Varkala, Attingal, Chirayinkeezhu and Aruvikkara Assembly constituencies, the alliance polled 34,343, 42,389, 32,829 and 30,151 votes in that order. In Alappuzha, where former Public Service Commission chairman K.S. Radhakrishnan contested, NDA increased its vote share from 43,051 to 1,86,092. BJP leaders had lauded the campaigning by BDJS activists at Manalur, Nattika, Thrissur, Irinjalakkuda and Puthukkad. Though actor Suresh Gopi won sizable votes on his own, the role of BDJS cannot be ignored as the the NDA's vote share increased from 1,02,681 to 2,93,405. "The increase in votes points to the NDA's growth as a third front in Kerala. The people of the state have cast their votes against murder politics," said BDJS president Thushar Vellappally.

BJP Votes Fell in UDF Kitty

Did the BJP supporters cast their votes in favour of UDF candidates in key constituencies to ensure the defeat of their, bête noire CPM? A close look at the voting pattern in CPM bastions reveals at steep decline in BJP votes which points to a possible transfer of votes. It may be noted that Sabarimala Karma Samithi patron Swami Chidanandapuri had given a call to Ayyappa devotees to cast their votes for UDF candidates in constituencies where the BJP was not strong to ensure the defeat of the CPM candidates. However, other leaders of the Sabarimala Karma Samithi and the BJP had objected to the suggestion.

However, it seems, there is a steep decline in BJP votes in constituencies like Kasaragod, Kannur, Adakara, Alathur and few others where the opinion polls suggested a victory for the LDF candidates. The Sabarimala issue, that hurt the sentiments of the devotees had created discontent among the Hindu majority, which was considered the vote base of the CPM. According to Sabarimala Karma Samithi leaders, many families, who were staunch supporters of the CPM parted ways with the party after the Sabarimala agitation. The BJP was expecting a steep increase in its vote share in view, of the positive polarisation of majority votes. However, the party's vote share increased only marginally, leaving the leaders disenchanted.

According to BJP leaders, the devotees who were annoyed by the CPM stand on Sabarimala issue cast their votes in favour of the UDF candidates to ensure the defeat of the CPM. This shift in votes has poured cold water on the poll prospects of the BJP at least in Thiruvananthapuram and Pathanamthitta. "Discontent was brewing among the traditional vote base of the CPM over the handling of the Sabarimala issue. We hoped this will help us cross the 20 per cent mark in vote share. But a major chunk of the votes went to the UDF as they thought only the UDF can spoil the chances of the CPM," said a senior BJP leader.

Constituencies where NDA's vote share declined as compared to 2016 Assembly Polls

Constituency	*2016 Assembly Polls*	*2019 LS Polls*
Kasaragod	197574	176049
Kannur	88949	68509
Vadakara	120363	80128
Alathur	150273	89832
Kozhikode	158885	161216
Wayanad	93291	78818
Idukki	185160	133545
Mavelikkara	185160	133546
Kollam	130300	103339

Source: Data compiled by the Author.

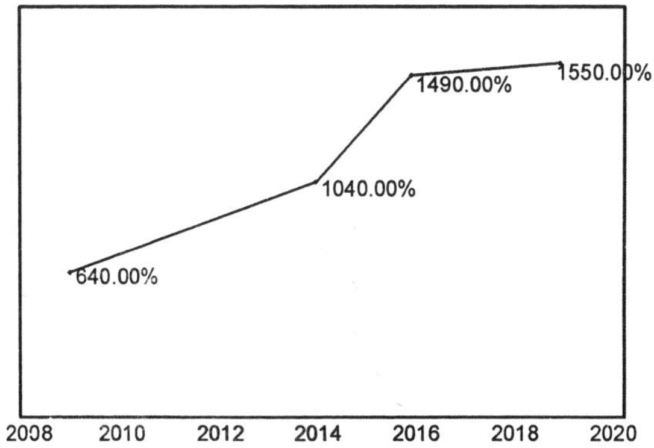

Source: Data Comilation and Graphic Illustration by Authors.

A look into the rise in vote share of the NDA/BJP over the LS elections

Constituencies where NDA's vo.. share increased

Constituency	*2016*	*2019*
Attingal	176535	748081s
Thiruvananthapuram	267303	316142
Pathanamthitta	190872	297396
Kottayam	165409	155135
Thrissur	205041	293822
Ponnani	83228	110003
Palakkad	190288	218556

Source: Data compiled by authors.

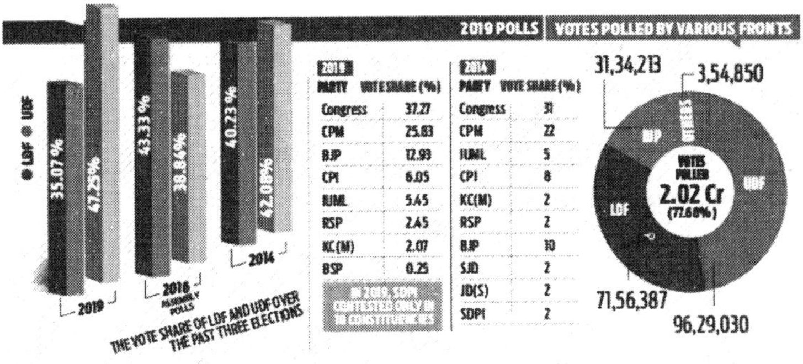

Source: *The New Sunday Express,* 26.05.2019.

In Dharmadom, the constituency of the Chief Minister, CPM's vote share declined from 87,329 in 2016 to 74,730, says a BJP leader. "It is not our votes that got drained. A section of the traditional voters of the CPM voted for the UDF to ensure the defeat of the CPM leaders. There was an anti-Pinarayi wave in the state and the UDF benefited from it. In Palakkad, the discontent among the supporters of the CPM over the Sabarimala issue was evident," said BJP spokesperson B. Gopalakrishnan.

The RSS attempt to micro-manage the campaign and resources by deploying its cadre had forced to hibernation hardcore BJP workers who could gauge the trends at the grassroots. This had slackened the campaign machinery, sources said. Flags in assigning senior BJP leaders for managing the campaign have drawn flak at a preliminary post-poll review. For, instance, leaders familiar with the trends and preferences of the voters in Thiruvananthapuram were compelled to move to other districts. The pattern was replicated elsewhere too: The resource management mode has come in for criticism." A reported attempt to place the blame for the reversal squarely on the BJP State "leadership" is being pointed out as a conscious effort of the Sangh Parivar to cloak its slips in candidate selection and campaign 'Management'. Critics of the Sangh Parivar are citing the face-losing defeat Kummanam Rajasekharan and Surendran suffered in the Capital and Pathanamthitta as a case in point.

PART-III
SEVERE SETBACK FOR THE LEFT PARTIES: LOST 8 PER CENT OF ITS VOTE SHARE

The UDF tsunami that decimated the Left Front in the Lok Sabha polls is proving to be more cause for worry to the LDF. Apart from being reduced to just one seat, the LDF also lost around 8 per cent of its vote share, compared to the 2016 Assembly elections when it won 91 seats. In an obvious indication of traditional voters having swayed away from the Left Front this time, the difference in vote percentage between the LDF and the UDF—which was just 2 per cent in the 2014 LS polls—turned out to be around 12 per cent. this time. The LDF which had polled around 40.23 per cent in the 2014 Lok Sabha polls, had increased its vote share to around 43.33 per cent in the 2016 Assembly elections. But this time, the vote share went down to just around 35.07 per cent, thereby recording a drastic dip of around 8 per cent.

On the other hand, the UDF had polled around 42.08 per cent in the 2014 LS polls, which had dipped to around 38.84 per cent in the 2016 Assembly elections. But, the Congress-led front was able to significantly improve its vote share by around 9 per cent to touch 47.25 per cent during this Lok Sabha elections. The BJP-led NDA too was able to improve its status to 15.20 per cent this time from 10.85 per cent in the 2014 LS polls. The LDF, which bagged the upper hand in 91 Assembly constituencies in 2016, managed a majority in only 16 Assembly segments of the parliamentary constituencies in the state. In constituencies like Attingal and Alathur, the difference in vote share was very evident. In Thiruvananthapuram, where the Sabarimala issue had created major ripples, the Congress candidate Shashi Tharoor won a majority in CPM's sitting Assembly segments like Kazhakoottam, Neyyattinkara and Parassala. In Kazhakoottam the sitting seat of CPM Minister Kadakampally Surendran—Left candidate C. Divakaran was pushed to a pathetic third spot.

Similarly, in the Attingal Lok Sabha constituency, considered to be a Left stronghold from where the LDF had won six of the seven Assembly segments in 2016, Left candidate A. Sampath was pushed to the second position in six Assembly segments. Only in Nedumangad—the sitting seat of C. Divakaran—Sampath could come first, that too with a meagre margin of around 700 votes. The UDF's foray into Left bastions like Palakkad and Alathur has caused shock waves in the Left camp. In Palakkad's Pattambi Assembly segment, which is the CPI's sitting seat, UDF's V.K. Sreekandan polled 67,644 votes while LDF's M.B. Rajesh could win only 50,465 votes. In 2016, CPI's Muhammed Muhassin had won around 45.84 per cent of the votes here.

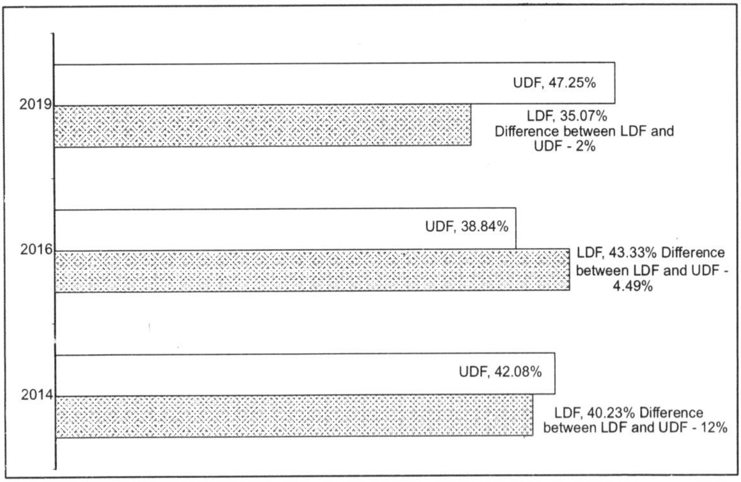

Vote Share of the UDF and LDF

Source: Data compilation and illustration by authors.

A. LDF failed to Secure Majority in 80 per cent Seats

Now after the poll rout, the LDF is in for another shocker. An analysis of the election results reveals the LDF candidates failed to secure a lead in 80 per cent of the sitting seats. Compounding the CPM-led alliance's worry, by polls are due to be held in the six seats from where the sitting MLAs have been elected to the Lok Sabha. Further worsening matters, four of these seats are held by the UDF. Of the total 140 assembly constituencies spread across 20 Lok Sabha constituencies in Kerala, the LDF was able to secure lead only in 16 sitting assembly seats in the Lok Sabha polls. However, the margin of lead has considerably diminished in all these 16 assembly constituencies. The front has a total tally of 91 seats in the Assembly. In Southern Kerala, the LDF was able to maintain a lead of 759 votes in Nedumangad assembly constituency. It is the sitting seat of C. Divakaran of the CPI who won the 2016 polls by a margin of

3,621 votes. In the capital city, the front was pushed to the third position in Kazhakkoottam, Thiruvananthapuram and Vattiyoorkkavu. Meanwhile, the BJP has secured a lead of 12,041 votes in Nemom assembly constituency in Thiruvananthapuram. Sitting MLA O. Rajagopal of BJP won the seat by a margin of 8,671 votes in 2016. This is also the only assembly seat in which BJP secured a majority in this year's LS polls.

The other assembly constituencies in which LDF was able to secure lead are Adoor, Kayamkulam, Cherthala, Vaikom, Shoranur, Ottappalam, Kongad, Malampuzha, Thalassery, Dharmadam, Mattannur, Kanhangad, Thrikkaripur, Payyannur and Kalliyasseri. Among the list, Dharmadam in Kannur LS constituency is the sitting seat of Chief Minister Pinarayi Vijayan, from where he was elected in 2016 with a majority of 37,905 votes. However, in the Lok Sabha polls this year, the CPM candidate was able to manage a lead of 4,000 votes only. CPM's lone winner in the Lok Sabha polls is A.M. Ariff who is the sitting MLA of Aroor. However, he also trailed by a margin of 648 votes in the Lok Sabha polls in his own constituency. Among the other constituencies where the bypolls will be conducted, in Manjeswaram, the LDF is at the third position in the LS polls behind UDF and BJP. In Ernakulam, sitting MLA Hibi Eden who emerged victorious secured a healthy lead of 31,176 votes over his opponent P. Rajeev in the LS polls. In Pala, where the bypolls will be held, the UDF is well ahead of LDF with a lead of 33,472 votes. Meanwhile, in Konni assembly constituency, where bypolls will be held after sitting MLA Adoor Prakash winning the LS election from Attingal, the UDF got a slight edge over LDF with a margin of 2,721 votes.

B. CPM Admits Sabarimala Factor

Amid rumblings of dissent within following its debacle in the Lok Sabha elections, the CPM admitted that the Sabarimala factor played a major role in its drubbing. Observing that there was an erosion of its traditional vote base, the party decided to probe the reasons that led to the defeat. In a statement issued after the party state secretariat meeting on Friday, the CPM said, "Statistics show that right wing forces were successful in misleading a section of the faithful." The statement, however, didn't mention the word 'Sabarimala'. While the admission indicated a rethink within the party as its leaders had repeatedly assured during electioneering that the Sabarimala issue will not have any impact on the election outcome, it comes at a time when the CPM leadership is facing severe criticism and calls for introspection after the party-led LDF won only one of the

20 Lok Sabha seats in Kerala. The party leadership felt that minority consolidation in favour of the UDF was not the only reason for the defeat. "Not only the minorities, a section of women and upper class Hindus also voted against the Left. That is why there was a substantial decrease in CPM's vote share," pointed out a senior Left leader.

C. SDPI's Rising Clout

SDPI's claim that they had supported Congress-led UDF in Lok Sabha polls has strong validity if one analyses the result in constituencies where the party decided not to field their candidates and support the UDF. The SDPI votes plummeted to just 80,000 votes this time from 2.73 lakh votes secured in 2014 indicating that the party has transferred all votes in favour of the UDF candidates in Kasaragod, Pathanamthitta, Thiruvananthapuram, Kollam, Idukki, Kottayam and Thrissur. SDPI Kerala state president Abdul Majeed Faizi has also announced that their party cadre supported the UDF candidates. The SDPI decided to support UDF after its relationship turned sore with the CPM leadership which came down heavily on the SDPI for its alleged terrorist activities.

The SDPI, which contested only in 10 seats in 2019 elections, has come fourth in five constituencies. In Malappuram, they secured 19,106 votes followed by 18,124 in Ponnani, 8,142 in Kannur, 5,544 in Vadakara and 5,426 in Wayanad. An analysis of the 2014 election results shows that the SDPI had secured 2.73 lakh votes with majority of the votes from Kasaragod (9,713), Pathanamthitta (11,353), Kollam (12,812), Idukki (10,401) and Thrissur (6,894). This elections, the SDPI leadership chose not to field candidates in these constituencies and the UDF managed to come out with thumping victory in Kasaragod, Idukki and Thrissur which were sitting seats of the CPM, most importantly Kasaragod constituency which was held by LDF for the last 30 years. In fact, the relation between SDPI and the CPM worsened in 2018 when Students Federation of India (SFI) leader Abhimanyu of Maharaja College was allegedly murdered by SDPI workers on the college campus on July 1.

D. Religion and Caste-based Organisations

With the UDF winning the elections in the state with a huge margin, the role played by religion and caste-based organisations has to be taken into account. SNDP the prominent organisation of the powerful Ezhava community, was not clear in its position, oscillating between the BJP and the Left Front. NSS, as always openly took an equidistant stand in the elections. But it had taken an open stand regarding the Sabarimala issue with both the BJP and the Congress expecting the NSS vote to be in their kitty. Ultimately it seems the NSS support has worked in favour of the Congress as both Kummanam Rajasekharan in Thiruvananthapuram and K. Surendran in Pathanamthitta lost with huge margins.

The CPM and the Left Front fielded Veena George, MLA from Pathanamthitta Lok Sabha seat expecting the outright support of the Orthodox Church as was during the last Assembly elections. In the 2016 Assembly elections, the Orthodox church had openly stated Veena was the 'daughter of the Church', which worked in her favour as she trounced Sivadasan Nair. However, the Orthodox Church did not extend its support wholeheartedly to Veena this time, resulting in her drubbing. The Catholic community seem to have voted extensively in support of the UDF. In constituencies like Ernakulam, Chalakkudy and Thrissur which have a sizeable Catholic population, the UDF candidates won with good margins.

Muslim consolidation in favour of the UDF was another phenomenon witnessed in this election and the community voted extensively for the UDF. The presence of Rahul Gandhi from Wayanad helped in the consolidation of Muslim votes as he was projected as the Prime Minister candidate of the UPA. A faction of the Keerala Pulayar Mahasabha (KPMS) led by Punnala Sreekumar was extending its support to the LDF and Pinarayi Vijayan as it was in the forefront of the Women's Wall. However, this did not help the prospects of CPM and LDF.

E. NOTA Votes Dip by One Lakh

Votes under NOTA (None of the Above) option saw a considerable dip in this year's General elections than the 2014 Lok Sabha polls. While 2,10,563 NOTA votes were cast in 2014, it reduced to 1,02,436 votes this year, a difference of 1,08,127 votes. In this election, Alathur had the highest number of NOTA votes at 7,722, followed by Chalakkudy at 7,578 and Kottayam at 7,191. Wayanad had the lowest number of NOTA votes at 2,155.

At no constituency did NOTA votes exceed the winning margin this year. The only constituency where NOTA votes came close to the victory margin was in Alappuzha, where the LDF and UDF were in a neck and neck fight. Here, 6,057 NOTA votes were polled, while the victory margin of LDF's A.M. Ariff was 9,069 votes. In 2014, most NOTA votes were cast in Malappuram at 21,829, followed by Alathur at 21,417 and

Pathanamthitta at 16,538. NOTA votes had also played a decisive role in the Kannur and Vadakara constituencies in 2014, as they exceeded the winning margin in the two seats.

F. LDF got Maximum Postal Votes

Postal vote was big topic of discussion this elections after there were complaints from various quarters that Kerala Police Association (KPA) has rigged postal votes of police personnel in favour of LDF candidates. Of the valid 73,575 postal votes cast this elections, LDF secured 32,051 votes while UDF won 24,704 votes, NDA 15,465 votes and others 1,354 votes. It was in Kollam constituency that the maximum number of postal votes was cast (6,835) followed by Mavelikkara (6,746), Thiruvananthapuram (6,445), Alappuzha (6,206) and Kannur (5,917). Surprisingly, the Election Commission also declared 11,952 postal votes across the state as invalid citing various errors and faults in the forms submitted by the voters. Highest number of invalid votes was in Alappuzha (1,384) followed by Mavelikkara (1,325), Attingal (1,160) and Thiruvananthapuram (1,088).

The LDF got maximum postal votes of 3,329 in Kollam while it was 2,967 votes in Alappuzha, 2,900 votes in Kannur and 2,780 votes in

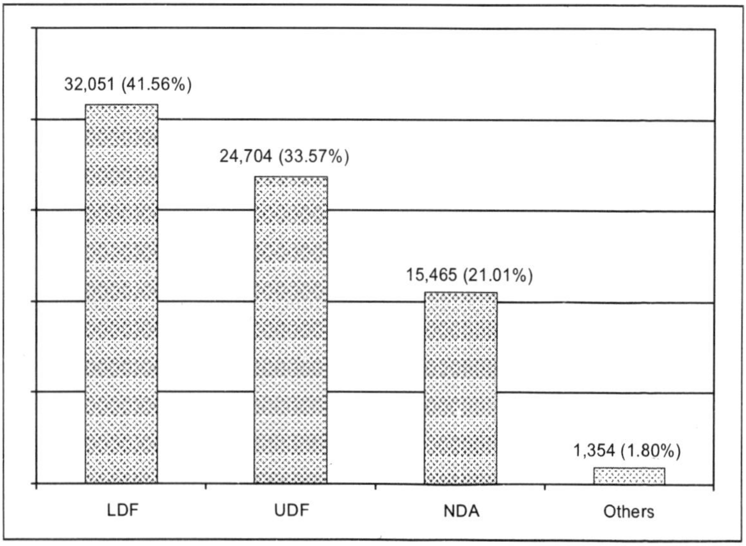

Vote Share of the LDF, UDF, NDA and others

Source: Compiled by the authors.

Mavelikkara. As far as NDA is concerned, maximum postal votes was in Thiruvananthapuram (2,217) followed by Pathanamthitta (1,769), Attingal (1,579) and Alappuzha (1,451).

Postal votes secured by different fronts. Total valid postal votes—73,575, invalid postal votes—11,952. 6,835 votes in Kollam constituency are the maximum number of postal votes cast in a constituency.

"Many postal votes were declared invalid as they did not have proper signature of the gazetted officer approving the validity of the vote. All postal votes were thoroughly verified 'for discrepancies," said Additional Chief Electoral Officer B. Surendran Pillai.

G. Challenges Ahead for the Congress

The Congress and UDF which gained tremendously in the elections have to face the uphill task of rising up to the aspirations of the people who had given a landslide mandate to the party and the front. KPCC president Mullappally Ramachandran had recently said it is a 'fearsome result,' clearly hinting at the responsibility the people of the state have vested in the Congress and its affiliates in the UDF. The Congress knows the votes polled by its candidates were mostly anti-incumbency ones against Pinarayi and Modi. The party leadership feels majority and minority consolidation has taken place in its favour. While the majority voted in protest against the political stand of the Chief Minister on the Sabarimala issue, the minority votes went in favour of Rahul Gandhi, against the Narendra Modi Government and its policies. Party think-tanks were surprised that around 10 lakh votes were removed from the voters list and that the Left front had meticulously planned electioneering by posting mostly Left-leaning officers for election duty. The non-functioning of the party machinery is the major reason the party leadership found behind such a large number of votes being removed from the list.

The immediate challenge before the front is the local body polls in 2020. The front knows it has to rise up to the level of the present mandate and for that the organisational machinery has to be intact and proper. The Congress leadership knows the performance of the elected party MPs will be a major barometer for the public to vote in its favour in the local body polls as well as the 2021 assembly polls. Mullappally, who said priority will be given to a total revamp of the organisation from top to booth level, is seeking the support of the AICC president and his team for the same. With the party machinery in place, the Congress knows it can take on the challenge posed by the Left and the NDA in the next local body and assembly polls. The major contention the party and the front have to face will be the performance of the MPs. The leadership knows with a proper organisational machinery in place and the MP's performing according to the wishes of the people, then a repeat of the present success is not a difficult proposition. One can only keep one's fingers crossed.

H. Challenges Ahead for the Left

The Left parties in the state should realize that society has changed, people have changed, their outlook and aspirations too have changed. In such a scenario the left has to reinvent itself. Further the left parties have to reframe their party programmes in accordance with the changes that has taken place in the polity, society and economy. Moreover state-society relations have undergone drastic changes. Individuals who are/were moved by political theories and ideologies and theories is almost vanished or disappeared. How effectively and how soon the left will address this reality is most important. Another important question before the left parties is what political alternative they can present before the common masses. Such a political alternative should be able to carry the convictions of the people. Also they should explore new avenues and opportunities in tune with changing time and needs. Unless the left leadership in general and the CPI(M) leadership in particular makes an honest introspection and takes urgent remedial measures, the left parties in Kerala may find the sands under its feet running out as happened in West Bengal and Tripura.

PART-IV
CONCLUDING OBSERVATIONS

A. Vote Share

The vote share of the UDF, which won 19 out of 20 seats, has jumped from 42.08 per cent in the 2014 elections to 47.25 per cent in the 2019 elections. The LDF's share dipped from 40.23 per cent in 2014 to 35.2 per cent this time. While the BJP-led NDA failed to win even a single seat, its vote share has gone up. In 2014, the NDA had bagged 10.85 per cent of the votes. In 2019, the front's share has risen to 15.20 per cent, with the BJP accounting for 12.93 per cent of the votes, as per EC data. Partywise, the Congress took home 37.27 per cent of the votes in 2019. Five years ago, the grand old party's Kerala unit had managed 31 per cent. 'The CPI(M) which contested in 16 seats in 2019 as against the 15 in 2014, also increased its individual vote share from 22 per cent to 25.83 per cent, as per EC data. The Communist Party of India, which failed to score a single victory, saw its vote share dipping from 8 per cent in 2014 to 6.05 per cent.

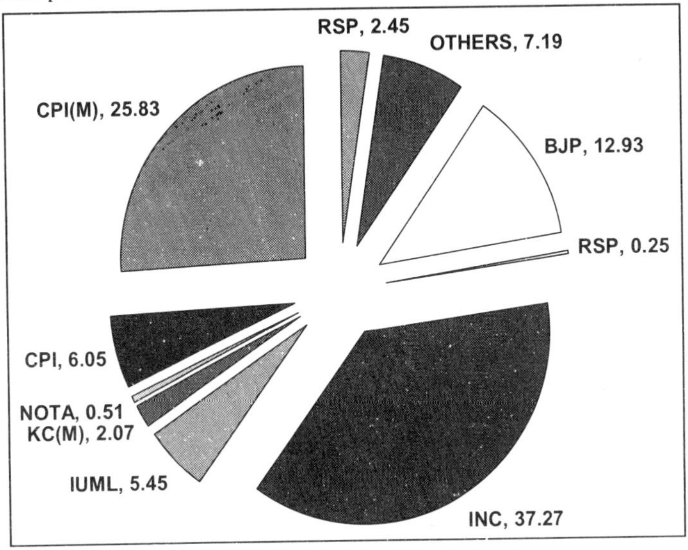

Source: Illustration by the authors

B. Position of the Left Parties

For the Left parties in Kerala it is the time for a clear introspection. Unless they adopt stringent corrective measures, they may soon be on the road to elimination. Arrogance of some top most leaders of the left parties and violence promoted by a section are primarily responsible for the party's decline in the state. While the Kannur model of violence practiced by party workers across the state has had a drastic impact, even other factors cannot be neglected. While instances of apparent double speak led to a loss of credibility, a sour lack of connect with the masses too may have contributed to the rout. The authoritarian style of functioning of the state Chief Minister also contributed a lot. For example, on issues like Sabarimala, the stand of the CM was not in tune with the ground realities prevailed in the state. The Hindus comprising the Ezhavas and Nairs have been main supporters of the CPM. The way the order of the Apex Court on Sabarimala was handled by the state government forced a large section of the Hindu women to desert the party. Further, the Left parties unlike the past are unable to convince the people outside the party and take them into confidence. The leadership even refused to listen the pulse of the commonman, naturally the sympathizers began dwindling.

C. Position of the IUML

The IUML's share remained constant with the party taking home 5.45 per cent of the votes. Kerala Congress (Mani) and the RSP accounted for 2.07 per cent and 2.45 per cent respectively this time, a slight increase from 2014. In Vadakara, one of the keenly watched constituencies, K. Muraleedharan cornered over 5.26 lakh votes, increasing the UDF share from 43.48 per cent (Mullapally Ramachandran in 2014) to 49.6 per cent.

D. Wayanad, Alathur and Trivandrum

In high-profile Wayanad; the candidature of 'Rahul Gandhi ensured that the—UDF share climbed to a whopping 64 per cent from 41.2 per cent. Ramya Haridas of the UDF wrested Alathur from the LDF by claiming over 50 per cent of the votes. The BJP, despite ending up third in Pathanamthitta, managed to bag almost 30 per cent of the votes. Same went for Thrissur where actor Suresh Gopi increased the saffron party's share to around 28 per cent. In Thiruvananthapuram, Shashi Tharoor, performing a hat-trick, increased his share from 34.2 per cent to around 41 per cent in the process.

E. Theory of Minority Consolidation

The popular narrative was that it was a 'minority consolidation' which facilitated the dream like run of the Congress-led United Democratic Front and the rout of the Left Democratic Front in the Lok Sabha election in Kerala. 'This reductionist view seems to be a gross under-reading of a very decisive political vote and a devaluation of a significant democratic resistance by a sizeable chunk of the electorate.

The "minority consolidation theory" gained traction during the unending TV debates that followed exit poll results. It says that one of the two major reasons for the spectacular victory of the UDF with a success rate of 95 per cent was the consolidation of the 'Muslim vote in Malabar and the Christian vote in the central Kerala and coastal regions of the state.

F. Other Solid Reasons

The other reason, according to this line of thinking is the Sabarimala effect, which forced a substantial section of the Hindu faithful to vote for Congress. This, the claim goes was to teach the LDF a lesson for tinkering with a Hindu religious practice. In effect, the UDF wave was triggered by the "majority consolidation" originating from a religious cause and the 'minority consolidation originating from fear. However, in the popular narrative the minority consolidation is communal and other is not. True, Muslims and Christians, who made up 45 per cent of the electorate, did vote for the UDF in higher numbers this time than any other recent elections. Dubbing this as communal would be unfair. Rather, it was a decisive political vote which carried a clear political message that a majority of the minority communities in Kerala did not want Modi as their Prime Minister, moreover elections in a democracy is exactly for this to choose your government and your ruler. More than a pro-UDF or anti-LDF vote, this was anti-Modi vote. It was a decisive political act aimed to unseat the BJP governance at the National Level.

REFERENCES

Anand, G., UDF makes a clean Sweep in South Kerala, *Ibid.*

Anandan, S., Left on the Mat in Central Kerala, *The Hindu*, 24.05.2019

Anil S. and Rajesh Abraham, Last Fort, Last Chance, *Ibid.*

Anil S., Post-Defeat Rumblings in LDF Camps. *Ibid.*

Arun Lakshman, Minority, Majority Consolidation worked in favour of UDF, *The New Indian Express*, 24.05.2019.

Arun Lakshmanan, Congress Tall Task, *Ibid.*

Arun Lakshmanan, How Caste and Religion played a Part in Elections in State, *Ibid.*

Basheer, K.P.M., Malabar gives huge Margins to UDF, *Ibid.*

Dhinesh Kallungal, A Repeat of David *vs.* Goliath in Alathoor, *Ibid.*

Dileep Kumar, NOTA Votes dip by 1 Lakh, *Ibid.*

John Mary, Congress needs Kerala Style Coalition in India, *Deccan Chronicle*, 25.05.2019.

Majoj Viswanathan, Aggressive Campaigning Fails to Yield Results for NDA, *Ibid.*

Manoj Vishwanathan, For Growth BJP needs to look Beyond, *Ibid.*

Prabhash, J., In the changing Scenario there is need for the Left to Reinvent, *The New Sunday Express*, 26.05.2019.

Ramdas P., BDJS aids NDA increase Vote Share, *Ibid.*

4

General Elections 2019

Performance of Maharashtra—Analytical Study

Mrudul Nile

Genesis of Maharashtra Politics—Ideology and Social Reforms

Maharashtra has a legacy of progressive social movements which are deep rooted in its social and political history. The state of Maharashtra has been one of the leading states contributing immensely to the social policies of the nation. A state that boasts of Gokhale, Agarkar, Lokmanya Tilak who contributed to the freedom struggle in India, to Mahatma Jyotirao Phule, Savitri Bai Phule and Dr. B.R. Ambedkar, who are the founders of the social thought of not only Maharashtra but also of the entire country, left great impact on politics of today.

The formation of the state of Maharashtra was a result of the Samyukta Maharashtra Movement, which was led by the Leftist stalwarts like Shreedhar Mahadev Joshi, Shripad Amrit Dange, Narayan Ganesh Gore. Other leaders included Maina Gawankar, Walchand Kothari, Pralhad Keshav Atre, Keshav Sitaram Thackeray, Pandurang Mahadev Bapat, Bhausaheb Raut, and Amar Shaikh. This political culture was carried by the Congress system in Maharashtra all throughout.

Maharashtra has been an important bastion of Indian National Congress. In fact, a closer look at the performance of Indian National Congress in Maharashtra, replicates with the trends in the Centre. Maharashtra is the second largest state with 48 seats in Lok Sabha. Hence, for any political party Maharashtra, is an important state for the Lok Sabha Election. Though the Rashtriya Swayamsevak Sangh headquarters is situated in Maharashtra, it was very difficult for the Bharatiya Janata Party to make its inroads in Maharashtra's political space.

Maharashtra is divided into five regions, namely Konkan, Western Maharashtra, Marathwada, Khandesh (North Maharashtra) and Vidarbha. Each region has its peculiar political and social history which is generally not deviated during the elections.

Konkan comprises Mumbai, Raigad, Ratnagiri and Sindhudurg districts. These areas have influenced the political process of Maharashtra to a great extent. In fact seven Bharat Ratnas are from this region. Mumbai being the epicentre of almost all the political and social activities since pre-Independence, it has its own identity. Though the Congress has its stronghold on this region, since the emergence of Shiv Sena, the urban Marathi speaking middle class mostly migrated from Raigadh, Ratnagiri and Sindhudurg districts forms its clientele. This region is also the centre for the *Dalit* movement of Maharashtra. The movement of assertion under Dr. B.R. Ambedkar began from Mahad and later occupied Mumbai and other parts of the state and country.

Western Maharashtra is the fertile and mostly agrarian region. Political economy of Maharashtra largely depends upon western Maharashtra. This region has a dominance of the Maratha community. The Maharashtra's political leadership largely is determined by this region. One of the most important reasons for the economic development this region has achieved, is attributed to one the most distinct model of cooperatives, which influences political process in the state. As most of the farmers are a part of the cooperative for their economic interdependence, it is difficult for them to dissociate from the political patronage of the local leader in the region. Education, and local self-government institutions are also intrinsically linked is these political personalities. This region also sees the dominance of the dynastic politics and many families continue to represent people in the region. The most important intermediate caste which dominates Maharashtra politics is from this region. There is also a close relationship between land-caste-politics, which emerges as one of the most important factors of political process in the state.

Marathwada is rather the most underdeveloped regions of the state. It is a part of the erstwhile Nizam state and therefore, the cultural continuity of Hyderabad state can be observed in the region. One of the reasons for the underdevelopment may be attributed to the fact that political leadership in the region cannot compete with the leaders of Western Maharashtra due to the weak economy in the region. The region is drought-prone and the Human Development Index is very low. Land holdings are small and industries are not well developed. Educationally, too the region does not compete with the rest of Maharashtra. Manifest *dalit* assertion can be seen in this region. Renaming of Marathwada University to Dr. Babasaheb Ambedkar Marathwada University was a long drawn struggle where the members of Scheduled Caste especially the neo-Buddhists actually participated in large numbers. Dr. Ambedkar, made Aurangabad the centre of educational activities. Milind College and Nagsen Van always remained the epicentre of *dalit* ideology and struggle in this region. This region also has a large Muslim population due to both, being the part of Hyderabad state and the Mughals actually had converted Aurangabad as its capital.

Vidarbha comprises eleven districts on the eastern end of Maharashtra. There is a popular feeling in Vidarbha that this underdevelopment is a result of deliberate neglect on the part of the state government and has often led to the repeated demands for a separate statehood for Vidharba.

Vidarbha too was once a very important region of dominance of Congress. Even during emergency, Vidarbha stood with Congress (Rasam, 2014). However, due to its negligence of the local issues and its comparative underdevelopment, where Vidarbha issue was not taken up in Delhi during the Congress regime, Congress continuously faces the erosion of its dominance in the region. Further, the BJP which did not have enough political space in the state was always in favour of a separate state to be carved out of Maharashtra. This demand is supported by the BJP for the fact that they can assert their dominance in the region. The top leaders of the state like the former Chief Minister, Devendra Fadnavis, Nitin Gadkari and Sudhir Mungatiwar have always favoured the status of separate state for Vidarbha. With the presence of RSS headquarter in Nagpur, it is most likely that they can give develop a distinct political culture in the region which may/can be beneficial to the BJP.

The social composition of the region determines the political participation and the changing contours of the electoral performance of the party. Unlike western Maharashtra, Marathas do not form a dominant political class. The sense of identity is not strong among the poor and rich Marathas in the region. Neither the *Koshti* (weavers), *Telis* (oilmen), and *Komti* (traders) who form a significantly large population do not identify with the Marathas, and they in turn do not have much contact with the Kunbi peasants. The influence of non-Brahmin and non-Maratha caste is considerable in this region (Sirsikar, 1995). The Scheduled Caste in the region have attained equal social space due to their educational attainment and employment in government sector. Educationally, the Scheduled Caste in the region have kept a mark in the state with a very strong assertive *dalit* base.

The region also faces a problem of farmer suicide due to vagaries of nature and mostly an arid climate. The landholdings are comparatively small. Industrially, the region is backward.

There are eleven Parliamentary constituencies in the region, namely Nagpur, Ramtek, Bhandara-Gondia, Gadchiroli-Chimur, Chandrapur, Akola, Amravati, Buldhana, Yavatmal-Washim, Raver and Wardha.

Khandesh, i.e. North Maharashtra, includes the districts of Nashik, Jalgaon, Dhule and Nandurbar. All the four districts have considerable tribal population. Political leadership in the region saw a shift of Maratha youth towards the BJP (Rasam, 2014). This region barring Nashik and Jalgoan, did not get enough attention from the government thus the anti-incumbency developed which gave away the region to BJP, which was contested by the new (youth) Maratha leadership in the region.

Setting the Background for the 17th General Election, Maharashtra

Elections in Maharashtra in 2019 are seen in the context of the age old rivalry between the dominance of Marathas and the superiority of the Brahmins (Peshwa).

Maharashtra has a long history of a bitter struggle between the Marathas and the Brahmins. The Brahmins under the Peshwa had rendered the actual rulers to merely pensioners of the Peshwa. The 17th General Elections in Maharashtra draws a direct corollary to the historical events, when the Marathas were ousted from the throne by the Brahmins.

This old rivalry was first erupted immediately after the partition and assassination of Mahatma Gandhi. The Marathas who dominated the Congress system in India and particularly the Maharashtra had inflicted violence against the Brahmins as Nathuram Godse was identified with the Brahmin community. Many Brahmins fled their homes in rural Maharashtra and settled in urban places of Maharashtra. Probably, this can be attributed to the reason why the Brahmins could not make a mark in the politics of Maharashtra. Even when Manohar Joshi became the Chief Minister in 1995, he was called as the 'First Brahmin Chief Minister' of the state.

Since 1925, a Hindu 'cultural' outfit was established by Dr. K.B. Hegdewar, a medical doctor in Nagpur. Since then it is observed that the organisation aims at consolidation of the social and political aspirations of the Brahmins in Maharashtra and later the same has spread to the other parts of the country. Though, Nagpur emerges as one of the most important centres, it was Pune in western Maharashtra which actually was recognised as a seat of the Brahmin politics in Maharashtra. Pune invariably is recognised with the Peshwas and thus the Marathas identified it as its rival. The Brahmins since then pledge their allegiance to the Bharatiya Jana Sangh and later the Bharatiya Janata Party.

Marathas dominated the state politics since its inception (with one term in 1995 to Shiv Sena-BJP coalition). Thereafter, the Congress-NCP has been in power, more so for the last fifteen years before the 2014 elections. For the Congress-NCP, 2014 General Elections was not a much of a worry because of its strong rural background and the institutions (both social and economic) developed by the leaders of both the parties.

BJP, in Maharashtra, exploited the MADHAV formula to a great extent. In fact the entire edifice of the clientele base of BJP rests on this formula. MADHAV essentially means the Mali, Dhangar and Vanjari, these are the dominant communities in Marathwada region. This formula was designed by the then Maharashtra leaders, Pramod Mahajan and Gopinath Mundhe. This formula played an important role in expanding the electoral base of BJP. However, this is merely an electoral formula but largely the party is known as a Brahmin party.

However, both the parties failed to gauge the new model of propaganda and polarisation in the state. The state was no doubt influenced by the 'India Against Corruption' movement lead by people without political backgrounds like Arvind Kejriwal, Anna Hazare, Kiran Bedi, Baba Ramdev and others. People were swayed with the new group which initially emerged as a social group to raise its voice against the corruption in Congress. Though the movement was essentially carried out in New Delhi against the ruling Congress government, the movement spread to the large parts of the country.

As Anna Hazare was known for his social work and earlier crusader for the Right to Information Movement in Maharashtra, volunteers of Aam Admi left no opportunity to criticise the ruling dispensation of Congress-NCP in the state. Activities like flash mobs and common people wearing the the Gandhi Cap with slogans like *Main Bhi Anna* (I am also Anna) not only became popular but also were identified as political symbol. It then becomes very interesting to note that the *Gandhi Topi* (cap) came to be recognised with Anna Hazare and Nehru Jacket is now called as Modi Jacket. Hence, it can be inferred that the way the entire political discourse and the objects with parties are identified were hijacked by the new emerging political outfits.

Another factor that the Congress and NCP did not take into consideration was that of the Narendra Modi's candidature as Prime Ministerial candidate. A Parliamentary election model was converted to the Presidential model. In the Parliamentary system, the majority party decides on the leader or the Prime Minister, was totally violated and the Congress too fell to the trap. Further, Narendra Modi did not carry a national leader image, the Congress-NCP took time to understand the impact of BJP campaign and the charisma Narendra Modi could develop over the time. Hence, before the 2014 elections, the leaders in Maharashtra were well confident that they could hold the state. However, the Modi Wave completely devastated their understanding.

Since the Prime Ministerial candidate of BJP came from Gujarat, this model was much talked about in the whole country. Though, it was difficult to clearly identify the model in terms of development in the areas of roads, electricity and the ease of doing business, more important issues of governance like the RTI, HDI and the situation of Dalits and Minorities did not form the part of the campaign from the Congress and NCP, whereas they carry the image of good governance and secularism.

Further, the basic issues of poverty, education, poor health did not form the part of this election. The entire election was fought on one issue of corruption. It must be noted here that since then the people-centric approach of governance was diverted to general principles of governance where no party could be held responsible for not delivering the resources generated by the state. The illusionary discourse of '*Vikas*' (development) was developed for the purpose of electoral gains. The basic issues were given a back seat.

Though a very well educated and an intelligent Chief Minister with experience of national politics and Prime Minister's Office was at the helm of affairs in the state, its was practically difficult to articulate public aspirations. Both BJP and AAP through the India Against Corruption was responsible for a defeat of Congress-NCP in Maharashtra. One must also note that BJP portrayed themselves as a modern party.

Followed by the defeat in the Lok Sabha Elections in 2014, the state assembly elections which were due in few months was the last blow on the Congress-NCP in Maharashtra. Thus, the dominance of Congress-NCP or the Marathas in Maharashtra was completely demolished.

With the emergence of the BJP and their penetration in the local self-government institutions, it became pertinent for the predominantly Maratha parties that the Maratha politics and its pride had to be consolidated during the upcoming elections in the 2019. With its policies in Maharashtra, especially the beef ban, the Muslims considered it to be not only a blow on their food habit, but also livelihood. The *dalits* too who are not the traditional voters of BJP were kept at bay in all the policies and the financial benefits they could earlier draw from the state. Though the BJP attempted to play a Maratha Card by setting up of the Commission for the Economically Weaker Sections (Marathas) it could not stand the test in the court and the recommendations for reservations was set aside. The tribals too showed their discontent with the government and thousands of tribals and farmers marched from Nashik to Mumbai to protest against the government. Just prior to the farmers march, the state witnessed farmers protest to register the agrarian distress in Maharashtra. The protest began in Yeola, in Nashik district.

The Maratha leadership could consolidate the agrarian community, as most of them had an experience and expertise of dealing with agrarian distress and drought mitigation. The problem of Minimum Support Price and procurement of agricultural produce were the issues which the BJP failed to address.

Between 2015 to 2017 Maharashtra witnessed worst drought in Maharashtra. The state government failed in various fronts to control the drought. There was rampant disorientation of people towards the government. Though the state government came with some important schemes like "Jal Yukta Shivar", these schemes were not successful to give immediate relief to the farmer. However, the scheme did not go well with the people and could not win the trust of the people as it could not bring the people out of the misery of shortages.

One of the most important impact drought has, on the ruling dispensation is that generally the government in power is voted out. The Bharitya Janata Party tried it hard to deflect peoples attention from the issues of unemployment, drought and inflation. The only narrative that could counter this was that of Nationalism. When it looked that the people in Maharashtra will outvote the BJP, Pulwama incident gave a new life to the BJP-SS combine. Hence, it could not really make an impact and the seats were not affected much.

Campaign, Manifesto and Issues

Just before the general elections in 2019, it looked like the Congress-NCP was gaining ground due to wrong economic policies, a fairly sound narrative was created against the government. This was the time when the Marathas leadership too realised that the Maratha hegemony was challenged and if they were not able to arrest/control the BJP, it would be practically impossible for the Marathas to 'rule' the state again. Therefore, a very rigorous electoral campaign was designed against the BJP-SS combine.

NCP was the only party who could effectively 'fight' the elections in Maharashtra. NCP managed to bring on board Raj Thackrey, the estranged cousin of Uddhav Thackrey, the party chief of Shiv Sena. Though the founder of the Maharashtra Navnirman Sena, Raj Thackrey did not field any candidate in the General Elections 2019, he took many public meetings and attempted to expose the Central Government. Raj Thackrey toured the entire state in a attempt to educate the public about not only the wrong policies but also the propaganda politics that BJP was engaged in. A new way of campaign was introduced by his party wherein the advertisements that the party came with were exposed by bringing them to the campaign and asking them to speak for themselves. A new phrase '*laav re te*' meaning 'play that one' became very popular. This was looked as one of the major attempt to counter the IT Cell of BJP.

It was also presumed that Raj Thackery was hired by the Congress-NCP for a parallel campaign in Maharashtra. The Election Commission of India went to an extent to bar him from holding such campaigns as his party was not contesting the general election in Maharashtra. However, one must also look at the fact that Raj Thackrey was well aware that due to his party Maharshtra Navnirman Sena strength was inadequate to contest the general elections, he was rather making a ground for his party in the ensuing state assembly elections in Maharashtra. It may not be assumed that he did not get an indirect support from both the parties. The fact that later, a meeting between Raj Thackrey and Sonia Gandhi took place, is self-evident that the campaign was programmed and if not both, at least the Congress favoured and gave all the support for such campaign.

A closer look at the manifestos, it appears that the manifestos were made just for the sake of having a manifesto. The BJP manifesto was designed in such a way that it looked more like organisation building and not really had anything to do with the electoral promises. Though some areas such as kisan credit card or small merchants credit cards schemes were announced, it also discusses organisation building in terms of 10,000 Farmer producers organisations to be set up all over the country. Amendment of Article 370 was used to generate the national sentiments among the people. There was a mention about a 360 degree reform in higher learning and the universities with excellence. Domain based universities would be set up and thus the entire discourse of education would undergo a new change. Set up five regional centres of excellence on urban issues. These centres will provide support to states and local bodies on issues of urban governance and growth. This appears to be an extension of NITI Aayog and though it appears to be decentralised, a closer look gives a picture of emerging centralising tendencies.

The Congress too laid a lot of emphasis on the farmers, it appears from the manifesto that the policies were rooted more through institutional perspective. Present a separate **"Kisan Budget"** to ensure priority to the issues affecting the agriculture sector

Establish a permanent **National Commission on Agricultural Development and Planning** to examine and advise the government on how to make agriculture viable, competitive and remunerative (will subsume the existing Commission for Agricultural Costs and Prices and recommend appropriate minimum support prices).

Establish a Commission on Marginal Farmers and Agricultural Labour

Distortions in Land Acquisition, Rehabilitation and Resettlement Act, 2013 and the Forest Rights Act, 2006 will be removed and the original purposes of the Acts restored and enforced.

As against the 'Make in India' policy of the BJP, the Congress came with the 'Make for the World' policy. In terms of labour and employment too, more programmed policies and experience was seen the manifesto. In the health care sector, the Congress stressed on Government expenditure on healthcare will be doubled to 3 per cent of GDP by the year 2023-24.

Enact the Right to Healthcare Act that will guarantee to every citizen the right to healthcare services, including free diagnostics, out-patient care, medicines and hospitalisation through a network of public hospitals and enlisted private hospitals.

While the manifestos of both the parties look exhaustive, an objective assessment of the manifestos tilts towards the Congress. While Congress manifesto attempts to balance between social indicators and the nationalist sentiments, BJP's manifesto is more nationalist.

Given the fact that the parties design their manifestos, it must be noted that they are not discussed by the general public when they vote. The manifestos of the both the parties did not percolate in the public. People believed in the social media, and this was the most important medium of awareness and education, which determined the voting preferences among people.

Tough Alliances

The Vanchit Bahujan Aghadi

A year before the election or less than that, a new alliance of All India Majlis-E-Ittehadul Muslimeen and Bharip Bahujan Mahasangh (BBMS) where Barrister Assauddin Owasi and Advocate Prakash Ambedkar, grandson of Dr. B.R. Ambedkar came together to form the Vanchit Bahujan Aghadi. This coalition was essentially the Muslims and *Dalits* coalition. This alliance was the most important factor in the whole election as the *dalits* who were looking for the alternate after Ramdas Athawale joined the BJP, could bestow their trust in this alliance. Both the Muslims and the *dalits* were marginalised in last five years and there was no political platform who could take up their issues. Earlier, Congress was the only party who could, to some extent cater to the *dalits* and the Muslims. But as the party was thrown to fourth position in Maharashtra in the period between 2014 to 2019, a political vent was necessary for these communities.

The Muslims were denied their social, political and economic space in the state was very much evident from the policies that were brought by the BJP government in the state. The Muslim population was reduced to a second class citizenship in the state. Moreover, the corollary drawn between Muslims and Pakistan was exploited more by the Shiv Sena. With the new labels of terrorists discourse was focused more on the Muslims.

The Scheduled Caste community or the *dalits* (erstwhile Mahars) were leading the protests in Maharashtra. The massive protest against the Una flogging in Gujarat was a major protest in Mumbai which was led by the *dalit* leaders including Prakash Ambedkar. The *dalit* community in Maharasthra was always weary of the BJP and was not a natural ally to Bharitya Janata Party. In 2014, Ramdas Athawale parted the ways with Sharad Pawar and decided to join the NDA. This has invariably affected the dalit and more importantly the Mahar community's political future. It seemed as if the political aspirations of the Scheduled Caste were to depend on Advocate Prakash Ambedkar alone.

Advocate Prakash Ambedkar, carries the legacy of the Dr. Ambedkar and is seen to be a most important leader of the neo-Buddhist community or the erstwhile Mahars. The *dalits* in Maharashtra are identified with the neo-Buddhist community or the Mahars in Maharashtra. There were certain very important incidents in Maharashtra which could consolidate the *dalit* population; some of them being the razing of the Ambedkar Press in Dadar, Una Flogging and the Yalgar Parishad in Pune and finally the Bhima Koregoan incident. Many youth who participated in the Bhim-Koregoan homage (which ever year takes place) were arrested with serious charges against them, whereas the Bhide and Ekbote were left scott free. Social media also carried photographs of the Prime Minister meeting with Bhide. It is alleged that the violence was carried out at the behest of the two.

As the Muslims are labeled as terrorists, the *dalits* are labelled as Naxals by the parties like the BJP and SS. The portrayal of dalits as naxals is generally due to their allegiance to a more liberal-leftist ideology with emphasis on social indicators of development. Dr. Babasaheb Ambedkar's ideas on religion, either through the 'Riddles', 'Who Were *Shudras*', 'The Genesis of Caste' and others have always remained a matter of disagreement to both the Hindu parties and therefore, the acceptance level of the *Dalit-Bahujan* has always remained rather low among these parties. The fear of losing the reservation and the indirect moves by the ruling party was essentially taken up seriously by the community. The sudden change in the structure of education in terms of privatisation and sudden fee hike with reducing budget in social welfare schemes, were some of the main reasons for the increasing discontent among the *dalits* in Maharashtra. Therefore, the *dalit* community welcomed the move by Advocate Prakash Ambedkar for an alliance with MIM.

The duo launched the alliance which was called as the Vanchit Bahujan Aghadi. Prakash Ambedkar gave a call for public funding of the party and could collect enough fund for them to contest the election. People not only gave cash, but also gave their ornaments to fund the party. This was the peak of the aspirational politics amongst the Scheduled Caste in Maharashtra. The community was convinced and took to history, that Dr. B.R. Ambekar never went with Congress and BJP was out of question to be supported. The Vanchit Bahujan Aghadi they felt represented the aspirations of the *Dalits* and is a *dalit* party with a more expanse. All educated youth, women, social activists, businessmen, academicians, workers, labourers, women and children participated in rallies and campaigns of the party.

The Vanchit Bahujan Aghadi was also asked to be a part of the Congress-NCP alliance. However, Advocate Prakash Ambedkar, it is alleged that turned down the Congress offer. The version of the Vanchit Bahujan Aghadi is that, they asked for those seats where Congress is on number two to be given to the VBA, however, the Congress did not agree to the same and therefore the alliance could not be done. Following, the failure of talks, the Vanchit Bahujan Aghadi decided to contest all 48 seats. Advocate Prakash Ambedkar contested from two constituencies of Akola and Solapur. Solapur constituency was contested against the former Defence Minister, Sushil Kumar Shinde.

During the campaign the secular groups were quite unhappy with the Vanchit Bahujan Aghadi as it fielded the candidates in such a way that it was clear that the advantage would go to BJP. They were also criticised as being the B-Team of BJP. There was no rocket science needed to understand that Vanchit Bahujan Aghadi was playing a spoiler in the whole election in Maharashtra. Finally, it was evident from the results that the VBA could get only one seat in Aurangabad where a MIM candidate, Imtiyaz Jaleel won the seat for the VBA. Ten out of 48 seats were affected by the Vanchit Bahujan Aghadi. The statistics of the same are as follows:

Sl. No	Parliamentary Constituency	Votes Secured by VBA	Party affected	Difference to winning candidate	Difference	Percentage of Votes Secured by VBA
1.	Gadchiroli-Chimur	1,11,468	Congress	77,523	33,942	9.8
2.	Nanded	1,66,196	Congress	40,148	1,26,048	14.7
3.	Solapur	1,70,060	Congress	1,58,608	11,399	15.7
4.	Chandrapur	1,12,079	BJP	44,764	76,316	9.0
5.	Buldhana	1,72,627	NCP	1,33,287	39,340	15.4
6.	Parbhani	1,49,946	NCP	42,199	1,07,747	12.0
7.	Amravati	65,135	Shiv Sena	36,951	28,184	5.9
8.	Aurangabad	3,89,042	Shiv Sena	4,492	3,84,550	32.5
9.	Hathkarangle	1,23,419	Swabhimani	96,039	27,380	9.9
10.	Sangli	3,00234	Swabhimani	1,64,352	1,35,882	25.2

Source: Data compiled by Dr. Sangharatna Sonawane for a special issue of Vanchit Bahujan Aghadi: Apekshaani Vastavata.

It is critical to note that for the first time in the history of elections, the candidates were not fielded as per the population percentage but were randomly fielded. It may also be a possibility that in order to make an impact and to please the new entrants, it was essential to field the candidates in every parliamentary constituency. Another way for party funding was to contest the elections, it was essential to give a ticket to the political aspirants.

The alliance between the MIM and BBM that is the Vanchit Bahujan Aghadi was short lived and could not even contest together, the elections to the Legislative Assembly of the State in 2019.

Bhartiya Janata Party and Shiv Sena

Within a year of the securing power in the Centre and Legislative Assembly in Maharashtra in 2014 Shiv Sena and the Bhartiya Janata Party developed a rift. As both the parties contested the elections as a part of the NDA, with the rise of Narendra Modi, Shiv Sena was reduced to a junior partner. It was Shiv Sena who had given a hand holding to the BJP first when they entered into Maharashtra. The Bharatiya Janata Party thrived on Shiv Sena in the initial years. With a negligible presence in Maharashtra, and a complete opposite political culture *vis-à-vis* the political ideology of the Maharashtra, it was the help rendered by the Shiv Sena because of which the party could hold itself in the State. However, BJP being a national party always wanted to have an equal say in the politics of Maharashtra. While the Shiv Sena had a purely an OBC, native working class base, could initially help the alliance to the fullest. The BJP cannot be considered as a party with the native Maharashtrian identity, but it maintained its political agenda in a most programmed and systematic manner. This scientific manoeuvrability was missing and the party relied more on the physical strength in its formative years. Hence, the Shiv Sena too developed and attempted to scientifically produce identity factors among the youth and the poor and migrant OBC population in Maharashtra. The first success that the alliance got was in the year 1995, where BJP was a junior partner in the government.

While the BJP is not essentially Maharashtra political party, it could develop because the Sena supported BJP for almost 25 years, during the 2019 elections, Sena could sense that its dominance was gradually eroding within the alliance. Shiv Sena right from the day one has been in a critical mode with the BJP. This alliance was so affected, that at times it has seen that both the parties contesting separately for the local self-government institutions. Within a year of its existence in the state, Shiv Sena was ready to withdraw from the government. Hence, Uddhav Thackeray had gone up to call the BJP-SS a 'Rotten Alliance'.

Shiv Sena's status as a junior partner was much evident during its campaign to the General Elections. Right from the beginning Shiv Sena used the local issues to come to prominence. Being largely a local party, the issues of national importance never appeared within the campaign and manifesto of the party. Further, the major success to Shiv Sena was due to the Modi wave in 2014. Shiv Sena formed its alliance with BJP in 1984 and could achieve its victory in 1989 with one seat in Lok Sabha.

Shiv Sena hardly had any issues which they could talk about which were of national importance. BJP, with its national presence and the government in the Centre reiterated the policies that their National leaders were talking about. The 'Dussherra Melava' is an annual event that Shiv Sena has been organising for years now, is an opportunity to connect to the people and activists. The 2019 Dussherra Melava which was just before the Lok Sabha elections, Uddhav Thackrey hardly had any issues. Hence, the centre stage of the coalition was occupied by the BJP.

Shiv Sena, in order to have its standing and an equal partner in the coalition started talking about national issues of Article 370, Uniform Civil Code, Savarkar and Saffron.

The relationship between both the parties became so sour that neither the BJP nor the SS wanted to contest together. SS emerged as one of the biggest critique of BJP after demonetisation. Series of editorials against demonetisation were carried by '*Saamna*' the Shiv Sena mouthpiece. In the state too, though Shiv Sena was in power, it behaved more like a opposition party.

Statistics, Performance and Contest

This section attempts to look at the voting percentage and actual voters in each constituency. What were the factors that contributed to the performance of the party with some important Parliamentary constituencies.

We have already discussed the regions of Maharashtra in the earlier part. This part shall assess the voter turnout constituency-wise in each region and some of the major trends which affected the result.

Western Maharashtra

There are eleven parliamentary constituencies in the region, namely Maval, Pune, Baramati, Shirur, Ahmadnagar, Kolhapur, Satara, Sangli, Madha, Solapur and Hathkanangle.

One of the most important constituencies in this region was Solapur. Former Chief Minister of Maharashtra and the Defence Minister, Shri Sushil Kumar has developed Solapur Parliamentary constituency. The entry of Vanchit Bahujan Aghadi and the candidature of Advocate Prakash

Western Maharashtra

Sl. No.	Parliamentary Constituency and Number of Electors	2019				2014			
		Male Voters	*Female Voters*	*Total Voters*	*% Voters*	*Male Voters*	*Female Voters*	*Total Voters*	*% Voters*
1.	Mawal	7,43,584	6,21,926	13,65515	61.70	6,46,904	5,27,044	1173984	60.11
2.	Pune	5,50,415	4,83,397	10,33,824	49.82	5,33,792	4,59,588	9,93,380	54.14
3.	Baramati	711970	587269	12,99,242	61.51	602117	463496	1065613	58.83
4.	Shirur	717962	572428	1290395	59.37	613290	475412	1088702	59.73
5.	Ahmednagar	6,52,845	5,39,052	11,91,905	64.28	5,94,749	4,65,801	1060550	62.33
6.	Kolhapur	6,93,774	631630	1325408	70.71	663565	595421	12,58,986	71.72
7.	Satara	578908	530358	11,09,260	60.32	519148	456561	9,75,709	56.79
8.	Sangli	625668	553139	1178823	65.38	556695	486169	1042864	63.52
9.	Madha	657104	553625	12,10,732	63.56	594868	483305	1,07,8173	62.53
10.	Solapur	586,352	494896	10,81,254	58.62	5,26,695	423356	956651	55.88
11.	Hathkanangle	659957	586281	1246256	70.31	630470	556249	1186719	73.00

Source: Data Compiled by the Author.

Ambedkar in this constituency was the most talked about contest. Both the leaders wielded enough support in the region and therefore, it was certain that the fight will be between both of them however, the bastion of Congress was lost to Bharatiya Janata Party's Dr. Jai Siddheshwar Shivacharya Mahaswamiji. Total votes secured 5,24,985, which was 48.41 per cent. In fact the Scheduled Caste reserved constituency was won by a 'Swamiji' in the bitter fight amongst the two known *dalit* leaders, who have been challenging the ritualism and have a clear identity of being a *dalit*. Further, it must also be taken into consideration that Advocate Prakash Ambedkar had organised a huge rally in Solapur, where large number of people supported him. The vote share of VBA was almost 15.5 per cent which is quite high. This certainly raised the ambition of the Vanchit Bahujan Aghadi.

Hathkanangle was another major constituency which was important for the general elections in Maharashtra. Mr. Raju Shetti, who was once a member of Shetkari Sangathan, and worked for farmers of Maharashtra, launched his own party the Swabhimani Paksha. He had an alliance with the BJP during the 2014 general elections but disillusioned by the policies of the government towards the farmers and particularly in Maharashtra.

In a close contest between Raju Shetti and Dharyasheel Mane of the Shiv Sena (NDA) secured 585776 votes with 46.78 per cent vote share to win the seat.

Kolhapur had the maximum voting percentage of 71.72. Sanjay Mandlik of Shiv Sena contested the important seat in the politically strong Kolhapur seat. The dividends of the local leader, Chandrakant Dada Patil of BJP, Minister for Agriculture and Gurdian Minister of Kolhapur could amass huge support for their NDA candidate. Though the relationship between BJP and Shiv Sena was estranged one, they contested Lok Sabha together and the general support went to Sanjay Mandlik. The runner up candidate was NCP's Dhananjay Mahadik. Dhananjay Mahadik has a strong political background and also is a major player in cooperative movement. As cooperative banks were in serious trouble after the demonetisation, common people lost faith in the cooperatives. Thus, these institutions could not pay the dividend as expected.

Mawal and Baramati Parliamentary constituencies were again one of the most important constituencies for the Nationalist Congress Party. Sharad Pawar who has left a mark on Maharashtra politics, had fielded his grandson, Parth Pawar and his daughter, Ms. Supriya Sule. Both the constituencies were of utmost importance to the NCP. BJP tried hard to defeat Supriya Sule in Baramati with the top leaders, Narendra Modi and

Uddhav Thackeray addressed the election rally in Baramati. Amit Shah also challenged 'capturing' Baramati from Sharad Pawar. However, the results suggest that BJP could not do much damage in Baramati. Whereas in Mawal, Barne, the sitting MP defeated Parth Pawar.

Sangli is considered to be a part of the Congress bastion. Grand children of Vasantdada Patil are local influential in the constituency. Cooperative movement is very strong in the region. Social composition of this region has a good representation of Dhangar, Scheduled Caste and the Muslims. Gopichand Padalkar had contested on BJP ticket for the Legislative Assembly in 2014. However, he later claimed to have left BJP on the issue of classifying the Dhangars from Nomadic tribes to Scheduled Tribes, which the BJP government in Maharashtra failed to do. He then started to mobilise the Dhangar community against the BJP all across the state of Maharashtra. This in a way was to break the MADHAV formula of BJP.

He later shifted his loyalties to Vanchit Bahujan Aghadi. The first meeting between Owasi, Prakash Ambedkar and Padalkar took place in Aurangabd. Padalkar, was looked as a most important candidate of VBA. His close contestant was Sanjay Kaka Patil. Sanjay Kaka Patil was known for his arrogance and not so people friendly. Padalkar's entire campaign was centred around the nature of governance in the areas and the way Sanjay Kaka Patil dealt with things. Vishal Patil contested from Swabhimani Paksha. He was not willing to contest in the beginning, however, he declared his candidature only towards the end and began his campaign. Padalkar secured 3,00,234 votes and Vishal Patil secured 1,64,352 votes. The winning candidate Sanjay Kaka Patil 5,08,995 votes with 42.77 per cent votes. Thus, this was directly beneficial to the BJP candidate.

This constituency becomes important as the same Gopichand Padalkar later contested against Ajit Pawar for the state assembly elections. This was a clear strategy either of the BJP or that of VBA to give a safe passage to the BJP candidate in the constituency. However, Padalkar could not even save his deposit in the assembly polls on 2019.

Shirur constituency was an important constituency for the NCP. They had fielded Amol Kolhe, a television actor, whose very popular serial on Sambhaji Maharaj played great dividends to the NCP. As mentioned above the direct correlation of the Peshwa *versus* Maratha was well exploited by the party.

Vidarbha

There are eleven Parliamentary constituencies in the region, namely Nagpur, Ramtek, Bhandara-Gondia, Gadchiroli-Chimur, Chandrapur, Akola, Amravati, Buldhana, Yavatmal-Washim, Raver and Wardha.

Nagpur, a headquarters of Rashtriya Swayamsevak Sangh, is the most important seat for the BJP. The veteran leader Nitin Gadkari and the most closest competitor of Narendra Modi, contests from this Parliamentary constituency. RSS for Nitin Gadkari and Nitin Gadkari for RSS is almost synonymous. Just before the elections, Gadkari had also criticised the top leadership that the top leadership should take credit for the setbacks in the party. Gadkari was more vocal and this showed his disagreements with the top leadership.

The second most important candidate contesting from this constituency was Nana Patole. Nana Patole a sitting MP from Bhandara-Gondia, resigned from the Lok Sabha citing rising agrarian distress. He claimed that both the Centre as well as the State governments have failed to address the agrarian crisis. He had earlier quit Congress in 2014 and defeated Praful Patel in the general elections. Nana Patole contested against Nitin Gadkari. Gadkari secured 55.67 per cent votes whereas Nana Patole secured 37.45 per cent votes from the constituency. The voters in rural Nagpur voted for Patole, whereas largely the urban voters, voted for Gadkari. The Kunbi agrarian community strongly supported Patole, but the RSS network could do enough damage to Patole to an extent that he lost by almost two lakh votes.

Ramtek, which is adjoining Nagpur is a parliamentary constituency reserved for Scheduled Caste candidate. The Scheduled Caste population in Vidarbha is most conscious community. Though the SC population is generally non-BJP voters, for quite some time, there has been enough ground work by the BJP-RSS to lure the voters.

Congress was facing a tussle between the senior leader Mukul Wasnik and Nitin Raut. Nitin Raut was heading All India Scheduled Caste and Scheduled Tribes front of Congress party. However, the Congress denied the ticket to both of them, but intermittently Nitin Raut suggested Kishore Gajbhiye, a retired bureaucrat as the Congress candidate. Krupal Tuamane has been winning this seat since two terms. Kishore Gajbhiye though contested, Congress could have fielded more seasoned candidate to fight the election. Though the image of Kishore Gajbhiye as a former Municipal Commissioner enhanced the image of Congress but the winability of the candidate was low.

Vidarbha Region

Sl. No.	Parliamentary Constituency Name	2019				2014			
		Male Voters	Female Voters	Total Voters	% Voters	Male Voters	Female Voters	Total Voters	% Voters
1.	Nagpur	620371	561330	1181715	54.70	578754	504850	1083604	57.12
2.	Ramtek	638891	553537	1192429	62.07	576271	473007	1049278	62.64
3.	Bhandara-Gondia	627086	608474	1235560	68.31	615597	580693	1196290	72.31
4.	Gadchiroli-Chimur	580321	557036	1137358	71.98	537674	489980	1027654	70.04
5.	Chandrapur	652431	581550	1233786	64.65	602269	506480	1108749	63.29
6.	Akola	607024	509871	1116902	59.99	543956	433633	977589	58.51
7.	Amravati	602099	502841	1104947	60.36	554649	446414	1001063	62.29
8.	Buldhana	601170	516898	1118069	63.56	535827	442565	978392	61.25
9.	Yavatmal-Washim	622515	547460	1169977	61.10	564176	467163	1031339	58.87
10.	Raver	583456	505236	1088692	61.40	555229	455617	1010846	63.48
11.	Wardha	573135	494017	1067152	61.26	553504	458574	1012178	64.79

Source: Data Compiled by the Author.

Marathwada

There are eight Parliamentary constituencies in the region, namely Aurangabad, Jalna, Beed, Nanded, Hingoli, Latur, Osmanabad and Parbhani.

One of the most important Parliamentary constituencies in Marathawada region is Nanded. Nanded is again a stronghold of Congress. Ashok Chavan former Chief Minister and sitting MP in 2014 contested from this constituency. During the Modi Wave of 2014, only two Congress candidates were elected to the Lok Sabha, one was Ashok Chavan and the other was Raju Satav. The Congress initially was sceptical to give ticket to Ashok Chavan due to the allegations of Adarsh scam. However, he was given the ticket only on the condition that he shall help Raju Satav, former President of Youth Congress. BJP started its campaign for the elections since 2017, during the Nanded Waghala Municipal Corporations. BJP portrayed Prataprao Chiklikar as their candidate.

In fact the subcaste politics of Maratha also played against Ashok Chavan. Further, it was brought to the fore that Ashok Chavan supported only the Maratha *karyakartas* and did not actually help the other communities went against him. The constituency is also dominated by the Dhangar community and the influence of Padalkar was seen in this region too. Also all the non-Marathas came against Ashok Chavan. Professor Yashpal Bhinge of VBA secured close to 1,40,000 votes where Ashok Chavan lost by 56,000. The margin of loss was just 3.55 per cent.

Vanchit Bahujan Aghadi's one of the first and most important meeting between Advocate Prakash Ambedkar, Owaisi and Sanjay Padalkar took place in Aurangabad to form the VBA. Chandrakan Khaire a political heavy weight and a four times MP was contesting on SS ticket from NDA. Jadhav Harshawardhan, son-in-law of Raosaheb Danve could not get the BJP ticket as it was in alliance with SS, he contested as an independent candidate. It went in favour of Imtiaz Jaleel. The margin percentage is just .37 per cent. Jadhav cut the votes of Shiv Sena candidate Chandrakant Khaire. He then accused Danve of back stabbing him. As a slogan of *"jiski jitni sankhya bhari uski utni hissedari"* was given, which appealed o the people. Further, as mentioned earlier, the demography of urangabad is such that people from Muslim community, Scheduled Caste pulation is quite large. The scheduled caste population is well aware nd assertive in the region.

Marathwada

Sl. No.	Parliamentary Constituency Name	2019				2014			
		Male Voters	Female Voters	Total Voters	% Voters	Male Voters	Female Voters	Total Voters	% Voters
1.	Aurangabad	659019	537423	1196449	63.48	554458	428022	982480	61.85
2.	Jalna	657947	545873	1203821	64.55	595979	469547	1065526	66.15
3.	Beed	732331	616806	1349138	66.10	680369	551091	1231460	68.75
4.	Nanded	594848	524395	1119255	65.16	548032	462233	1010265	60.11
5.	Hingoli	617420	534774	1152195	66.50	575663	473420	1049083	66.29
6.	Latur	525060	545401	1170464	62.14	576599	477934	1054533	62.69
7.	Osmanabad	640975	553782	1194768	63.34	611537	505020	1116557	63.65
8.	Parbhani	676532	574979	1251511	63.08	637377	523946	1161323	64.44

Source: Data Compiled by the author.

North Maharashtra

There are in all six Parliamentary constituencies, namely Dhule, Jalgaon, Nandurbar, Nashik, Dindori and Shirdi in the region.

Nandurbar, which is a Scheduled Tribe constituency, has a 95 per cent of its population from the communities like the Bhils. This is one of the most undeveloped areas of the State with generally hilly terrain. The human development index is very low. Manikrao Gavit since 1981 had represented the people of Nandurbar. However, with the changing discourse of governance that he brought in 2014, the Congress lost this stronghold to Dr. Heena Gavit.

2019 Election saw the infighting between both Dr. Heena Gavit and Dr. Suhas Natavadkar. Initially, the BJP was not clear about the candidature of Dr. Gavit. However, the same was finalised just before the elections. Meanwhile, the Congress had unanimously decided upon the candidature of Advocate K.C. Padavi. Congress also began its campaign well before time and raised the issues of agricultural distress, issues of irrigation and low industrial pace.

Dr. Heena Gavit secured 6,39,136 votes out of 12,77,991 voters which accounts to 49.86 per cent.

Konkan Region

This region comprises the following parliamentary constituencies; Mumbai North, Mumbai North-West, Mumbai North-East, Mumbai North-Central, Mumbai South-Central, Mumbai South, Raigad, Thane, Kalyan, Bhiwandi, Ratnagiri-Sindhudurg and Palghar.

Mumbai region is generally accounted as a completely separate constituency for the entire state. There are six constituencies in Mumbai and is considered as the voice of the urban-dwellers in the state. All the top leaders of both NDA and UPA campaigned in Mumbai. In a way one can say that the campaign in Maharashtra began from Mumbai.

One of the most sought electoral battle was seen between Gopal Shetty and Urmila Matondkar actress-turned politician. Gopal Shetty, a veteran of BJP had actually developed the constituency since 2014. He is known for his work amongst the people. There was no coordination of Congress during the elections. There was a sudden change of guards of Mumbai Congress President from Sanjay Nirupam to Milind Devra. There was an issue of planning of the entire elections in Mumbai. In Mumbai North, Gopal Shetty won by four lakh votes. None of the Congress

North Maharashtra

Sl. No.	Parliamentary Constituency Name	2019				2014			
		Male Voters	*Female Voters*	*Total Voters*	*% Voters*	*Male Voters*	*Fesmale Voters*	*Total Voters*	*% Voters*
1.	Dhule	590256	489593	1079856	56.69	540775	438455	979230	58.68
2.	Jalgoan	584620	495943	1080576	56.12	550503	439312	989815	58.00
3.	Nandurbar	663475	614513	1277991	68.34	583431	530953	1114384	66.61
4.	Nashik	615905	502643	1118553	59.43	523318	412087	935405	58.83
5.	Dindori	628124	506627	1134754	65.64	546617	422882	969499	63.41
6.	Shirdi	559147	463259	1022439	64.54	519824	412130	931954	63.80

Source: Data compiled by the authors.

Konkan Region

Sl. No.	Parliamentary Constituency Name	2019				2014			
		Male Voters	Female Voters	Total Voters	% Voters	Male Voters	Female Voters	Total Voters	% Voters
1.	Mumbai North	542095	445794	988056	59.98	527247	418394	945641	53.07
2.	Mumbai North-West	521777	418350	940131	54.28	504202	393043	897245	50.57
3.	Mumbai North-East	503965	403222	907228	57.12	485677	375903	861550	51.70
4.	Mumbai North-Central	495920	404526	900451	53.60	472010	372857	844867	48.67
5.	Mumbai South-Central	432252	363195	795478	55.23	424310	343790	768100	53.09
6.	Mumbai South	438484	361012	799501	51.45	436292	342366	778658	52.49
7.	Thane	647401	519722	1167138	49.24	590956	462684	1053640	50.87
8.	Kalyan	507075	380808	887955	45.19	472077	352517	824594	42.94
9.	Bhivandi	569800	432947	1002763	53.06	572705	372339	875044	51.62
10.	Palghar	641041	560121	1201186	63.71	531904	460337	992241	62.91
11.	Raigad	505067	515102	1020169	61.77	485550	502232	987782	64.47
12.	Ratnagiri-Sindhudurg	447639	449716	897355	61.69	444269	451748	896017	65.56

Source: Data compiled by the author.

candidates be it Priya Dutt, Eknath Gaikwad, Milind Deora, really 'fought' the elections. Sanjay Niprupam was the only one who could give a tough fight to this rival Gajanan Kirtikar. Sanjay Dina Patil of NCP tried make his mark in the election but as NCP has more rural-agrarian clientele and only one seat in Mumbai, he too could not appeal to the people.

Mumbai General Elections 2019

Sl. No.	*Candidate*	*Party*	*Votes Secured*
Mumbai South			
1.	Arvind Ganpat Sawant	Shiv Sena	4,21,937
2.	Milind Murli Deora	INC	3,21,870
Mumbai North-East			
1.	Manoj Kotak	BJP	5,14,599
2.	Sanjay Dina Patil	NCP	2,88,113
Mumbai North-Central			
1.	Poonam Mahajan	BJP	4,86,672
2.	Priya Sunil Dutt	INC	3,56,667
Mumbai North-Central			
1.	Gajanan Chandrakant Kirtikar	Shiv Sena	5,70,063
2.	Sanjay Brijkishorlal Nirupam	INC	3,09,735
Mumbai South-Central			
1.	Rahul Ramesh Shewale	Shiv Sena	4,24,913
2.	Eknath Mahadeo Gaikwad	Congress	2,72,774
Mumbai North			
1.	Gopal Chinayya Shetty	BJP	7,06,678
2.	Urmila Matondkar	Congress	2,41,431

Source: Data compiled by the author.

The results in Mumbai are well evident that the performance of Congress was alarmingly down in the Mumbai region. Mumbai being a metropolis and densely populated, most voters were exposed new media. For the entire campaign, electronic media was used the most. Further, the Shiv Sena had its beginning from Mumbai and therefore, the swing in favour of NDA was clear. The issues of Mumbai are different and these issues are to be dealt differently. The manifestos did not catch the attention of the people, but the daily struggles of the people were some of the issues in Mumbai election.

Conclusion

Maharashtra as mentioned above replicates the voting pattern which affects the central government was seen in 2019 elections too. Earlier, the Congress used to replicate the pattern but now since 2014, BJP too has been successful to replicate the pattern.

BJP exploited every opportunity to win the election. Pulwama was a life saving incident for the BJP.

Congress's strategy to lure the people failed. Rahul Gandhi, the then Congress President, came with a slogan *'Chowkidar Chor Hai'* and tried to expose the issue of Rafael deal. But with the Pulwama attack, BJP stressed the need for it. Congress could not actually muster the support of the public sector undertakings which were being considered for privatisation, the bank employees strike, the farmers march, the *dalits* and Muslims.

The Vanchit Bahujan Aghadi was one of the most important factor which influenced the results in almost ten out of forty eight constituencies. In many places, VBA occupied third position.

The Shiv Sena completely bread on BJP's campaign and more importantly derived the benefits of the Pulwama attack. Shiv Sena could not take up local issues effectively during the entire campaign of general elections 2019.

REFERENCES

1. Manifesto of Bharatiya Janata Party
2. Manifesto of Indian National Congress
3. Rasam, V. (2014), Changing Politics of Maharashtra: An Analysis of Maharashtra Elections, 2014, *Social Science Perspective*, Vol. 6, p. 384.

5

The Citizenship (Amendment) Act, 2019

Constitutional and Legal Dimensions

M.R. Biju and *M.R.B. Anantha Padmanabha*

The Citizenship (Amendment) Act, 2019 (CAA) is an Act passed by the Indian Parliament, amending the Citizenship Act of 1955. This new legislation gives an opportunity to illegal migrants who entered India on or before 31 December, 2014 for Indian Citizenship. The Act also specified that illegal migrant category include Hindus, Sikhs, Buddhists, Jains, Parsis and Christians who came from Afghanistan, Pakistan and Bangladesh. It also seeks to relax the requirement of residence in India for citizenship by naturalisation from 11 years to 5 years for these migrants. The Act excludes Muslims from such eligibility. The Union Cabinet cleared the Bill on 4th December, 2019. It was passed by Lok Sabha on 10 December, 2019 and subsequently in the Rajya Sabha on 11 December, 2019. Keeping this in background this chapter attempts to examine the constitutional, legal and political implications of this legislation. The study has been classified under six broad heads—introduction, background of CAA provisions of granting citizenship, argument for and against CAA, its impact on north-east and finally views of various political parties on it.

No doubt, the CAA is a very serious move with far-reaching consequences and deeper impact on the basic character of the Constitution and therefore, it needs a closer look. It seeks to give shelter and protection to persecuted minorities in Bangladesh, Pakistan and Afghanistan. This ushers in a fundamental change in country's process of citizenship by naturalisation which allows foreigners to become Indians. Under the current legal dispensation, illegal immigrants cannot apply for Indian citizenship. Current law bars Hindu migrants from Bangladesh, who have entered India without papers to become citizens. It also excludes anyone who has entered using a legal document but has overstayed visa. At the same time, the CAA also shortens the waiting period for naturalisation for these chosen communities who would now require a six-year residence instead of the previous condition of having been a resident of India for at least 11 out of the last 14 years. Thus, once again creating two kinds of citizens that is a serious violation of fundamental rights granted to Indian citizens by the Constitution.

The stated objective of the CAA sounds logical but going through its text is stunningly shocking as it not only seriously questions its own stated objective but also negates the fundamental character of the Constitution. It also tears apart the plural fabric of Indian society. The present legislation, with its careful listing of protected communities, has explicitly and deliberately left out Muslims which is nothing but discriminatory. It excludes creating different categories of citizenship in which one is superior to the other where in religious faith is the sole determining criteria.

In other words, the CAA paves way for Indian citizenship to lakhs of immigrants, who identify themselves with any of the given religions, even if they lacked any document to prove their residency. It also means that any immigrant who does not belong to the said communities would not be eligible for Indian citizenship. Also, as per the Citizenship (Amendment) Act, any illegal immigrant from Afghanistan, Pakistan and Bangladesh who belongs to these said communities will not be deported or imprisoned if they are not carrying any valid documents for their residency in India.

Earlier, the duration of the immigrants' residency was 11 years. The amended Bill has reduced it to five years. This means that immigrants from the three countries and from the mentioned religions, who have entered India before December 31, 2014, would not be treated as illegal immigrants.

Background of the CAA

During the 2014 elections, the Bharatiya Janata Party had promised to grant citizenship to Hindu refugees from Bangladesh and Pakistan. In the party's election manifesto in 2014, the BJP had promised to welcome Hindu refugees and give shelter to them. The Citizenship (Amendment) Bill, 2016 was introduced and passed in Lok Sabha but there was widespread political opposition and protests in the North East India. Their chief concern was that the demography of North East India will change with the influx of migrants from Bangladesh. In the 2019 election campaign, the BJP's manifesto reiterated its commitment to bring in the Bill. The National Register of Citizens (NRC) was updated in Assam state in 2019, leaving out 1.9 million residents, a majority of whom were Hindus, without citizenship. This matter brought urgency to bring in the Bill.

The Bill was introduced in Lok Sabha on 19 July, 2016 as the Citizenship (Amendment) Bill, 2016. It was referred to the Joint Parliamentary Committee on 12 August, 2016. The Committee submitted its report on 7 January, 2019. In January 2016, the Citizenship (Amendment) Bill was introduced to amend the Citizenship Act, 1955. It was introduced in Lok Sabha on 19 July, 2016 and was referred to a Joint Parliamentary Committee on 12 August, 2016, which submitted its report on 7 January, 2019. It was passed by Lok Sabha on 8 January, 2019. It lapsed with the dissolution of the 16th Lok Sabha. Subsequently, the Union Cabinet cleared the Citizenship (Amendment) Bill, 2019 on 4 December, 2019 for introduction in the parliament. The Bill was introduced in 17th Lok Sabha by the Minister of Home Affairs Amit Shah on 9 December 2019 and was passed on 10 December, 2019 at 12:11 A.M. (IST) with 311 MPs voting in favour and 80 against the Bill.

The Bill was subsequently passed by the Rajya Sabha on 11 December, 2019 with 125 votes in favour and 99 votes against it. Those voted in favour included BJP allies such as Janata Dal (United), AIADMK, Biju Janata Dal, TDP and YSR-Congress, apart from BJP. After receiving assent from the President of India on 12 December 2019, the Bill assumed the status of an Act. However, the Act will come into force on a date of Government of India's choosing and will be notified as such.

The Bill amends the Citizenship Act of 1955 to give eligibility for Indian citizenship to illegal migrants who are Hindus, Sikhs, Buddhists, Jains, Parsis and Christians from Afghanistan, Bangladesh and Pakistan, and who entered India on or before 31 December, 2014. The Bill does not include Muslims. Immediate beneficiaries of the Bill, according to IB records, will be just over 30,000 people. India's previous citizenship law, Citizenship Act, 1955, did not consider religious affiliation to be a criterion for eligibility.

Under the Act, one of the requirements for citizenship by naturalisation is that the applicant must have resided in India during the last 12 months, and for 11 of the previous 14 years. The Bill relaxes this

11-year requirement to five years for persons belonging to the same six religions and three countries. The bill exempts the tribal areas of Assam, Meghalaya, Mizoram, and Tripura, included in the Sixth Schedule to the Constitution from its applicability. These tribal areas include Karbi Anglong in Assam, Garo Hills in Meghalaya, Chakma district in Mizoram, and Tribal Areas district in Tripura. It also exempted the areas regulated through the Inner Line Permit which includes Arunachal Pradesh, Mizoram and Nagaland. The inclusion of Manipur in Inner Line Permit is also announced on 10 December, 2019. The Bill includes new provisions for cancellation of the registration of Overseas Citizenship of India (OCI) such as registration through fraud, in case of OCI holder sentenced to imprisonment for two or more years within five years of registration and in necessity in the interest of sovereignty and security of India. It also includes a provision on violation of any law notified by the Central Government. It also adds the opportunity for the OCI holder to be heard before the cancellation.

Provisions of Granting Citizenship in India

Persons domiciled in the territory of India as on 26 November, 1949 automatically became Indian citizens by virtue of operation of the relevant provisions of the Indian Constitution coming into force, and most of these constitutional provisions came into force on 26 January, 1950. The Constitution of India also made provision regarding citizenship for migrants from the territories of Pakistan which had been part of India before partition.

Citizenship by Birth

Any person born in India on or after 26 January, 1950, but prior to the commencement of the 1986 Act on 1 July 1987, is a citizen of India by birth. A person born in India on or after 1 July, 1987 but before 3 December, 2004 is a citizen of India if one of parents was a citizen of India at the time of the birth. Those born in India on or after 3 December, 2004 are considered citizens of India only if both of their parents are citizens of India or if one parent is a citizen of India and the other is not an illegal migrant at the time of their birth. In September 2013, Bombay High Court gave a judgment that a birth certificate, passport or even an Aadhaar card alone may not be enough to prove Indian citizenship, unless the parents are Indian citizens.

Citizenship by Descent

Persons born outside India on or after 26 January, 1950 but before 10 December, 1992 are citizens of India by descent if their father was a citizen of India at the time of their birth. Persons born outside India on or after 10 December, 1992 are considered citizens of India if either of their parents is a citizen of India at the time of their birth. From 3rd December, 2004 onwards, persons born outside of India shall not be considered citizens of India unless their birth is registered at an Indian diplomatic mission within one year of the date of birth. In certain circumstances it is possible to register after one year with the permission of the Central Government. The application for registration of the birth of a child must be made to an Indian diplomatic mission and must be accompanied by an undertaking in writing from the parents of the child that he or she does not hold the passport of another country.

Citizenship by Registration

The Central Government may, on an application, register as a citizen of India under Section 5 of the Citizenship Act, 1955 any person (not being an illegal migrant) if s/he belongs to any of the following categories:

- a person of Indian origin who is ordinarily resident in India for seven years before making application under Section 5(1)(a) (throughout the period of twelve months immediately before making application and for six years in the aggregate in the eight years preceding the 12 months).
- a person of Indian origin who is ordinarily resident in any country or place outside undivided India.
- a person who is married to a citizen of India and is ordinarily resident in India for seven years before making an application for registration.
- minor children of persons who are citizens of India.
- a person of full age and capacity whose parents are registered as citizens of India.
- a person of full age and capacity who, or either of his parents, was earlier citizen of independent India, and has been residing in India for one year immediately before making an application for registration.

- a person of full age and capacity who has been registered as an overseas citizen of India for five years, and who has been residing in India for one year before making an application for registration.

Citizenship by Naturalization

Citizenship of India by naturalization can be acquired by a foreigner who is ordinarily resident in India for 12 years (throughout the period of 12 months immediately preceding the date of application and for 11 years in the aggregate of 14 years preceding the 12 months) and other qualifications as specified in Section 6 (1) of the Citizen Act, 1955.

Arguments in Favour of CAA

- The government has clarified that Pakistan, Afghanistan and Bangladesh are Islamic republics where Muslims are in majority hence they cannot be treated as persecuted minorities. It has assured that the government will examine the application from any other community on a case to case basis.
- This Bill will come as a big boon to all those people who have been the victims of Partition and the subsequent conversion of the three countries into theocratic Islamic republics.
- Citing partition between India and Pakistan on religious lines in 1947, the government has argued that millions of citizens of undivided India belonging to various faiths were staying in Pakistan and Bangladesh from 1947.
- The constitutions of Pakistan, Afghanistan and Bangladesh provide for a specific state religion. As a result, many persons belonging to Hindu, Sikh, Buddhist, Jain, Parsi and Christian communities have faced persecution on grounds of religion in those countries.
- Many such persons have fled to India to seek shelter and continued to stay in India even if their travel documents have expired or they have incomplete or no documents.
- After Independence, not once but twice, India conceded that the minorities in its neighbourhood is its responsibility. First, immediately after Partition and again during the Indira-Mujib Pact in 1972 when India had agreed to absorb over 1.2 million refugees. It is a historical fact that on both occasions, it was

only the Hindus, Sikhs, Buddhists and Christians who had come over to Indian side.

Arguments Against the CAA

- The fundamental criticism of the Bill has been that it specifically targets Muslims. Critics argue that it is violative of Article 14 of the Constitution (which guarantees the right to equality) and the principle of secularism.
- India has several other refugees that include Tamils from Sri Lanka and Hindu Rohingya from Myanmar. They are not covered under the Act.
- Despite exemption granted to some regions in the North-eastern states, the prospect of citizenship for massive numbers of illegal Bangladeshi migrants has triggered deep anxieties in the states.
- It will be difficult for the government to differentiate between illegal migrants and those persecuted.

Exemption of Certain Areas of North-East

The Citizenship (Amendment) Act, exempts certain areas in the North-East from this provision. The Citizenship (Amendment) Bill would not apply to tribal areas of Assam, Meghalaya, Mizoram and Tripura as included in Sixth Schedule to the Constitution and the area covered under the Inner Limit notified under the Bengal Eastern Frontier Regulation, 1873.

This effectively means that Arunachal Pradesh, Nagaland and Mizoram along with almost whole of Meghalaya and parts of Assam and Tripura would stay out of the purview of the Citizenship (Amendment) Act. Besides, the Citizenship Act also makes amendments to provisions related to the Overseas Citizens of India (OCI) cardholders. As per the Citizenship Act, a foreigner may register as an OCI under the 1955 Act if they are of Indian origin (e.g. former citizen of India or their descendants) or the spouse of a person of Indian origin. The Citizenship (Amendment) Act entitles the OCI cardholders to benefits such as the right to travel to India, and to work and study in the country. The Citizenship Bill, which was passed in the Rajya Sabha, amends the Act to allow cancellation of OCI registration if the person has violated any law notified by the Central Government.

Criticisms of the Opposition

The Opposition parties severely criticised the passage of the Citizenship (Amendment) Bill by the Parliament, with Congress interim president Sonia Gandhi saying it marks a "dark day" in the constitutional history of India and is a "victory of narrow-minded and bigoted forces" over the country's pluralism. According to her "the legislation fundamentally challenges the idea of India that our forefathers fought for and, in its place, creates a disturbed, distorted and divided India where religion will become a determinant of nationhood." She further added that, this legislation is not just an affront to the eternal principles of quality and religious non-discrimination that have been enshrined in our Constitution, but represence a rejection of an India that would be a free nation for all her people, irrespective of religion, region, caste, language and ethnicity. To her, it was ironic that the government pushed through the Bill when the country and the world was celebrating 150th birth anniversary of Mahatma Gandhi.

Several senior Congress leaders indicated that the party may move the Supreme Court against the Citizenship Bill with Abhishek Singhvi saying that the legislation will be legally challenged in the near future as it is "highly suspect" in terms of constitutionality. Hitting out at Home Minister Amit Shah over his remarks in support of the Bill, senior Congress leader P. Chidambaram told reporters, "The Home Minister says 130 crore people are supporting us, obviously he does not count Assam, Northeast and all other protesters as part of the 130 crore." "No one in the government would take responsibility for the content of the CAA or its constitutionality. The intent of the Bill is to tell the Muslims 'you are not equal human beings with equal rights', P. Chidambaram said on Twitter.

Apprehensions of North East and Response of Home Minister

Amid protest in their home states, MPs from North East raised serious concerns in the parliament over the potential flow of immigrants into the region and a threat to the indigenous communities, during the debate on this Bill. Rejecting the apprehensions of the members of the house Home Minister Amit Shah said Muslims from other countries have the right to apply for Indian citizenship as per existing rules. As many as 566 Muslims have been given citizenship, he said. He attacked opposition the Congress saying statements by the party's leaders match those of Pakistani leaders on not just the Citizenship Bill but also on scrapping of Article 370. Amit

Shah said the Bill seeks to correct the wrong done by the partition of the country on religious lines. He went on to attack the Congress for alleged doublespeak on the issue, saying the party had during its rule given Indian citizenship to 13,000 Hindus and Sikhs from Pakistan without raising a word about the same for other communities. He also said the legislation does not violate Article 14 of the Constitution as it does not prohibit laws based on reasonable classification. Amit Shah further argued that the 20 per cent decline in the religious minority population of both Pakistan and Bangladesh necessitated such a Bill, adding that the Indian Muslim community will not be affected by the legislation.

The Cases of Assam, Tripura, Meghalaya

Sub-Section 6B of the Citizenship (Amendment) Act, 2019 (CAA) listed out the provisions to grant Citizenship rights to Hindu and Non-Muslim minorities of Pakistan, Bangladesh and Afghanistan. The Act also states that nothing in sub-section 6B shall apply to tribal area(s) of Assam, Meghalaya, Mizoram or Tripura as included in the Sixth Schedule to the Constitution and the area covered under The Inner Line notified under the Bengal Eastern Frontier Regulation of 1873. The Sixth Schedule allows constitution of autonomous district councils in tribal areas. As per the Schedule in Meghalaya, Assam and Mizoram there can be three councils and in Tripura one council. In total there will be ten district councils for the whole North East.

The Case of Assam and Manipur

According to 2011 Census, Assam has a population of 3.12 crore. Out of it 61.47 per cent are Hindus, 34.22 per cent are Muslims and around 12.44 per cent are Tribals comprising Bodos and others. But unfortunately unlike Assam all the tribal states of the North East have got protection from both CAA and ILP (Inner Line Permit) system. The ILP system regulates the visit of outsiders to states under the Bengal Eastern Frontier Regulations 1873. Earlier it was in force in three states of North eastern parts—Arunachal Pradesh, Mizoram and Nagaland. But very recently Manipur too came under the ILP system. In fact ILP was withdrawn from Manipur 1950. Later attempts of the state to reintroduce it has not succeeded due to the protest by tribals in 1950. In 2018 the Chief Minister of Manipur mooted the idea once again and Manipur People's Protection Bill was passed after a series of political consultations with the concerned. Now it is waiting for the approval of the President. Manipur has a population of 28.56 lakh. Out of it 41.39 per cent are Hindus and 41.29 are Christians. A sizeable number of tribals are also living in Manipur. Most of them belonged to the category of Tangkhul Nagas and Kukis.

With regard to Assam is concerned in between 1979 to 1985 the state witnessed a mass movement against illegal migrations under the All Assam Gana Sangram Parishad. After thousands of lives were lost, the Assam Accord was signed in 1985 that aimed to address two key concerns of the Assamese peoples—'stop foreigners from Bangladesh and provide some constitutional safeguards for Assamese citizens'. First, the cut-off date for foreigners to gain Citizenship was fixed as 25 March, 1971, though initially, leaders of the movement wanted illegal migrants to be expelled as per the National Register of Citizens 1951 of Assam; agitation leaders had also spoken of a 1967 cut-off and Clause six of the Accord which stated that 'constitutional, legislative and administrative safeguards,' as may be appropriate, shall be provided to protect, preserve and promote the cultural, social, linguistic identity and heritage of the Assamese people.

Cases of Tripura and Meghalaya

In Tripura around 32 per cent of the people (around 36 lakh) are tribals. In 2015 after insurgency appeared to have waned, the Tripura government revoked the Armed Forces (Special Powers) Act (AFSPA). It had been in force in the state since 1997 was repealed after elections to the Tripura Tribal Areas Autonomous District Council. It had been a long standing demanding of the tribal parties such as the Indigenous Nationalist Party of Tripura and the Indigenous Peoples Front of Tripura. After the CAA Bill was passed, protests broke out in four districts of the state shattering years of peace.

With regard to the state of Meghalaya is concerned, it is protected from CAA because of the existence of Sixth Schedule—some areas of capital Shillong, however fall outside of its purview. But there is a strong demand to extend ILP to the State. Protesters want the Governor to give his nod to a proposed ordinance that seeks mandatory registration of outsiders entering the State.

Conclusion

In conclusion, it can be stated that the CAA aims to provide Citizenship to those who had been forced to seek shelter in India because of religious persecution or fear of persecution in their home countries – Afghanistan, Pakistan and Bangladesh. It is primarily meant Hindus, Sikhs, Jains, Buddhists, Parsis and Christians. This is a drastic shift from the provisions of the Citizenship Act of 1955 that labels a person as an 'illegal immigrant' if he or she has entered India without travel documents or has overstayed the date specified in the documents. It therefore amends the 1955 Act to grant exemptions to illegal migrants from the above mentioned countries, who reached India on or before December 2014. Further, according to this new Act, the Amendment will not be applicable to the tribal areas of Meghalaya, Mizoram or Tripura as included in the 6th Schedule to the Constitution and in the areas covered under the 'inner line' notified under the Bengal Eastern Frontier Regulation of 1873. Finally, it also proposes to incorporate a Subsection (D) Section 7, providing for cancellation of Overseas Citizen of India (OCI) registration where the OCI card holder has violated any provision of the Citizenship Act of any other law in force.

REFERENCES

CAB, 2019 Bill Summary" (PDF), *PRS India*, 9 December 2019.

Roshini Sinha, Explainer the Citizenship Amendment Bill, 2019 http://prsindia.org/theprsblog/explainer-citizenship-amendment-bill-2019 https://www.indiatoday.in/india/story/citizenship-amendment-bill-all-you-need-to- know-about-cab-1627516-2019-12-11

Shadan Farasat, A Patently Unconstitutional Piece of Legislation, *The Hindu*, December 11, 2019.

"Satish Misra, taking a close look at Citizenship Amendment Bill" https://www.orfonline.org/expert-speak/taking-a-close-look-at-citizenship-amendment-bill-58676/ https://en.wikipedia.org/wiki/ Citizenship_(Amendment)_Act,_2019 http://prsindia.org/theprsblog/explainer-citizenship-amendment-bill-2019

"The Citizenship (Amendment) Bill, 2019", *PRS India*, Retrieved 11 December, 2019.

"The Citizenship (Amendment) Act, 2019", *The Gazette of India*, 12 December 2019. Retrieved 14 December 2019.

6

The Right to Information (Amendment) Bill, 2019

An Overview

M.R. Biju and *M.R.B. Anantha Padmanabha*

Right to Information (RTI) is Act of the Parliament of India to provide for setting out the practical regime of the right to information for citizens and replaces the erstwhile Freedom of Information Act, 2002. Under the provisions of the Act, any citizen of India may request information from a "public authority" (a body of Government or "instrumentality of State") which is required to reply expeditiously or within thirty days. The Act also requires every public authority to computerise their records for wide dissemination and to proactively certain categories of information so that the citizens need minimum recourse to request for information formally. This law was passed by Parliament on 15 June 2005 and came fully into force on 12 October, 2005. Everyday, over 4800 RTI applications are filed. In the first ten years of the commencement of the Act over 17,500,000 applications had been filed.

In India, the organisation called Mazdoor Kisan Shakti Sangathan was instrumental in the passage of RTI Act. Aruna Roy is the mastermind behind the RTI Act, 2005. RTI is a legal right for every citizen of India. The authorities under RTI Act, 2005 are called quasi-judicial authorities. This act was enacted in order to consolidate the fundamental right in the Constitution of India 'freedom of speech'. Information disclosure in India is restricted by the Official Secrets Act, 1923 and various other special laws, which the new RTI Act relaxes. Right to Information codifies a fundamental right of the citizens of India. RTI has proven to be very useful, but is counteracted by the Whistleblowers Act.

Transparency seems to be the only means for sustaining democratic governance. That is why the right to information has been legislated in about 70 countries of the world, and another 30 countries are in the process of legislation. It was in this context that the RTI was enacted in India in 2005. The experience of 5 years shows that the response to this Act has been very positive and optimistic. It has also been widely welcomed by the people at all levels. They have been seeking various types of Information from different authorities. The RTI Act confers on all citizens the right to seek information and makes it the duty of the public authorities to disseminate the same for better governance and accountability. It covers the central, state and local governments and recipients of Government Grants but does not apply to the intelligence and security organisations except if the information released to the allegations of corruption. Against this backdrop, an attempt has been made here to examine the fundamental linkages and differences between RTI Act, 2005 with the Right to Information Amendment Bill, 2019. This chapter has been categorized under five major heads. Part-I examines the legislating right to information in Indian context, Part-II makes an indepth critical enquiry on the features as well as working of the RTI Act, 2005. Part-III unearths the salient features of the Right to Information (Amendment) Bill, 2019. This part also makes a comparative appraisal of these two historic legislations and Part-IV presents the concluding observations.

PART-I
LEGISLATING THE RIGHT TO INFORMATION IN INDIA

Objections to the Official Secrets Act have been raised ever since 1948, when the Press Laws Enquiry Committee recommended certain amendments. In fact, the Act has been used time and again to suit the purposes of the government. In 1977, a Working Group was formed by the Janata Party government to look into the possibilities of amending the Official Secrets Act. Unfortunately, the Working Group did not recommend changes, as it felt that Act related to the protection of national safety and did not prevent the release of information in the public interest; despite overwhelming evidence to the contrary, Official Secrets Act remained unaltered. In early 1989, V.P. Singh's National Front Government came to power and declared its decision to make Right to Information a fundamental right. Later a Committee set up in 1989 by the National Front Government recommended limiting the areas where government information could be hidden and opening up of all other spheres of information. As most of the members of the Committee were bureaucrats, something different was not expected, so no legislation followed from these recommendations.

Finally, the focus of citizens' groups shifted from demanding merely an amendment to the Official Secrets Act, to its replacement by a comprehensive legislation towards the Right to Information. The initiative for the Right to Information was taken by a mass based organisation, the Mazdoor Kisan Shakti Sangathan (MKSS) in early nineties in a very backward region of Rajasthan—Bhim Tehsil. This agitation for transparency was started by asking for copies of bills and vouchers and names of persons who have been paid wages mentioned in the muster rolls for the construction of school, dispensaries, small dams and community centres in the Block Development & Panchayat Officer office. After years of knocking at officials' doors and despite the usual apathy of the State Government, MKSS succeeded in getting photocopies of certain relevant documents. Misappropriation of funds was clearly obvious. MKSS organised several Jan Sunwai (People's hearing), between December 1994 and April 1995, in Rajasthan. This grassroot movement spread very fast to other areas of Rajasthan and to other States establishing firmly that information is power and people should have the right to official information.

Subsequently, the National Campaign for People's Right to Information (NCPRI) formed in the late-1990s became a broad-based platform for action. As the campaign gathered momentum, it became clear that the right to information had to be legally enforceable. It was demanded that information that cannot be denied to Parliament or state legislatures cannot be denied to a citizen either. In 1996, Justice P.B. Sawant, the Chairman of the Press Council of India, drafted the Bill keeping in view the dire need of the day and the observations made by eminent persons that in a democracy, it is the people who are the masters and those utilising public resources and excercising public power are their agents.

The Press Council of India and the 1998 Resolution

The Press Council of India, the Press Institute of India, the National Campaign for People's Right to Information and the Forum for Right to Information unanimously submitted the Resolution on February 20, 1998 to Government of India for amending the proposed Bill.

Main points of the 1998 Resolution are as follows:

(i) The Right to Information should also be extended with respect of companies, NGOs and international agencies whose activities are of a public nature and have a direct bearing on public interest;
(ii) The law must contain strong, penal provisions against wilful and wanton withholding or delay in supplying information or deliberately supplying misleading or inaccurate information;
(iii) The law must contain an appeal mechanism of an independent nature to provide reliable redress to any citizen dissatisfied with any decision of a public authority under this law;
(iv) The categories of information, which can be restricted are—withheld by the Government, are too wide in the draft Bill. In particular, the restriction on disclosing internal notings and official correspondence between public officials and offices has no justification whatsoever;
(v) Similarly the restriction on confidential communications between the State and Centre and their agencies have no justification, unless they harm public interest; and
(vi) The restriction on disclosure of the record of discussions of Secretaries and other public servants also needs to be removed. However, this draft also went into cold storage due to the fall of two United Front Governments.

Freedom of Information Bill, 2000

The BJP-led National Democratic Alliance reworked on the Shourie's draft to finalise the Freedom of Information Bill, 2000. It was introduced in the Lok Sabha on July 25, 2000. However, after the president's signature this Act could not be notified in the Government Gazette.

This Freedom of Information Bill included some provisions that were not in the Shourie draft, such as the requirement that urgent requests in cases involving life and liberty should get a response within 48 hours. Various provisions of the Act were similar to that of the RTI Act except on the points on which it has been criticized.

The Act has been criticised on the following main points: It reinforces the controlling role of the government official, who retains wide discretionary powers to withhold information. For example, requests for information involving "disproportionate diversion of the resources of a public authority" can be shot down by the public information officer.

This leaves open the danger that government officials might be transformed from gatekeepers of the Official Secrets Act to gatekeepers of the Freedom of Information Act.

The most scathing indictment of the Act has come from the critics who focus on the sweeping exemptions it permits, viz. restrictions on information relating to security, foreign policy, defence, law enforcement and public safety. The Act also excludes Cabinet papers, including records of the Council of Ministers, secretaries and other officials. Information shared between the Centre and States were not subject to disclosure. These exemptions effectively shielded the whole process of decision-making from mandatory disclosure.

PART-II
THE RIGHT TO INFORMATION ACT, 2005

The Parliament of India passed legislation on Right to Information in 2005. It is a landmark legislation in Indian context. It is in consonance with provisions of International Covenants on the issue and has brought India in line with other developed democracies of the world. Right to Information Act, 2005 was passed by both the Houses in the Summer Session of the Parliament and received assent of President on June 15, 2005. Around 150 amendments were introduced in the original draft. The Act replaces relatively weak and ineffective legislation, the Freedom of Information Act, 2002.

Salient Features

- The Act provides all citizens the right to information, subject to the provisions of the Act.
- It covers all the three tiers, i.e. central, state and local government and also the three branches, i.e. legislative, executive and judiciary of the government.
- It applies to "Public Authorities" established or constituted by or under the Constitution; by any law made by the appropriate Government or, any other body owned, controlled or substantially financed directly or indirectly by the appropriate Government and includes non-government organisation substantially financed by the government.
- The ambit, covers even the private bodies and their information can be accessed through the controlling public authority.

- The Act provides that information of the third party can be accessed after giving ten days notice to the third party.
- It casts an obligation on Public Authorities to grant access to information and to publish certain categories of information. Public Authorities are also supposed to maintain their record in the indexed and catalogued manner. The responsibilities about *suo motu* disclosure/publication by public authorities have been considerably enlarged.
- The Act lays down the machinery for the grant of access to information. The Public Authorities are required to designate Public Information Officers and Assistant Public Information Officers for dealing with requests for information and also to assist persons' seeking information.
- Provision has been made for transfer of a request by a public authority to another public authority, wherein the subject' matter/information is held by the latter.
- A time limit has been prescribed for compliance with requests for information under the Act, viz. 30 days for normal information; 40 days for third party information; life and liberty information in 48 hours and information relating to human rights violation in 45 days.
- The Act provides that in case PIO rejects the application, he/she is bound to give reasons of such rejection; the period within which can appeal against such rejection may be referred as well as the particulars of the appellate authority.
- The Act excludes the time taken for calculation and intimation of fees from the time frame.
- The Act prescribes for reasonable fee for providing information. Also, no fee to be charged from persons who are below poverty line. Further, information to be provided free of charge where the response time limit is not adhered to.
- Certain categories of information have been exempted from disclosure. The categories, by way of illustration, include, information likely to affect security of the State, strategic, scientific or economic interests of the State, detection and investigation of offences, public order, conduct of international relations and Cabinet papers. Trade or commercial secrets, information the disclosure of which would cause breach of privilege of Parliament or State Legislature and personal information which has no relationship with public activity and

could cause unwarranted invasion of the privacy of any person are also exempted from disclosure. However, exemptions provided are not absolute and withholding of information must be balanced against disclosure in the public interest. Information is to be released even if harm is shown to the public authority if the public benefit in knowing the information outweighs the harm that may be caused by disclosure.

- The Act contains a provision for reveal of certain information, which is otherwise, exempted from disclosure on completion of 20 years after the incident.
- The Act also incorporates the principle of severability.
- It envisages creation of an independent non-judicial machinery, viz. Central Information Commission and State Information Commissions comprising a Chief Information Commissioner and Information Commissioners to decide 2nd stage appeals. At the same time, there is no hierarchy of Commissions.
- Legal framework for exercise of powers by the Commission defined in the Act.
- The Commission while inquiring into any matter has the same powers as are vested in a civil court while trying a suit under the Code of Civil Procedure.
- The Act provides a two-tier Appellate Forum. First appeal to the departmental officer assigned the responsibility of the Public Information Officer. The second appeal to be made to the Commission.
- On a request for information being refused, the applicant can prefer an appeal to the prescribed authority within 30 days of the decision; the time limit for disposal of appeal being also 30 days extendable to 45 days. The second appeal can be made within 90 days of the decision of the first appellate authority.
- In case of a grievance at PIO level, there is a provision for making a complaint directly to the Commission.
- Intelligence and security agencies specified in Schedule II to the Act have been exempted from being covered within the ambit of the Act. However, the exemption is not absolute; agencies shall have the obligation to provide information in matters relating to corruption and human rights violations.
- The decisions of the Commission are binding.
- The jurisdiction of subordinate courts has been barred.

- The provisions of the proposed Act have been made overriding in character, so that the scheme is not subverted through the operation of other minor Acts.
- Under the provision of the Act CIC/SIC can impose a penalty of Rs. 250 per day on PIO. This penalty can go up to a maximum of Rs. 25000.
- There is a provision of disciplinary action against PIO for any contravention of the Act. A disciplinary action can be recommended as per the service rules applicable to the PIO.
- The Act provides that there is no criminal liability of the PIO and the PIO is immune from the actions done in good faith.
- Central Information Commission and State Information Commissions to monitor the implementation of the Act and prepare an Annual Report to be laid before Parliament/State Legislature.
- Rule making power for effective operationalisation of the Act is with the competent authority, i.e. Central/State Government subject to the approval of Parliament and Assembly respectively.
- The Act repeals the Freedom of Information Act, 2002.

Deficiencies in the RTI Act

In spite of being very exhaustive and with all its positive features, the RTI Act suffers from some weaknesses which has impeded its uniform and effective implementation during the last three years. These deficiencies are discussed below:

1. Substantial Financing

The Act does not define the word "substantially financed". Though some Information Commissioners both at the Centre and the State level are of the view that since the word control is there in the definition of public authority so why the need of the definition of substantial financing has not aroused as one can have the information of public authority even if it has not been financed because it is controlled by some agency or department under certain existing Act. However, the substantial financing has created a lot of confusion for the user and providers of information under the Act. Therefore, it should have been amplified by way of an explanation. This omission will result in different interpretations of the term by different states and public authorities.

2. NGOs

There is another dimension to this issue. The expression Non-Governmental Organisations as used in the Act is ambiguous. The NGOs are a class and category apart from the other private sector organisations. The use of the phrase 'Non-Governmental Organisations' creates an illusion that the Act is applicable only to NGOs because they receive funds under various projects and schemes of the Government as partners in implementation. There are many other private institutions specially the Government aided private schools and colleges who believe that they should not be designated as public authority on the spurious argument that they belong to the private sector.

3. Lack of Clarity on Public Authorities

The Act also imposes certain obligations on public authorities in Section 4. Primarily, these relate to (a) proper maintenance and upkeep of records, and (b) *suo motu* dissemination of information through publication of information directories about the functions and functioning of each public authority. But, the public authorities have generally been treating this provision as optional rather than compulsory. The dictionary meaning of obligation is binding power, written bond, duty, something that obligates one to a course of action etc. But it appears that in the absence of any penalty clause, the task is not viewed as an obligation, this raises a question: What option the Information Commission has if the Public Authority does not comply with this provision? Unless enforced, these obligations will remain only on paper.

4. On Life and Liberty

The Act does not define the information falling under life and liberty. Sikkim has defined life and liberty in its RTI rule as if the information requested relates to a person's confinement, internment, arbitrary detention, imminent death at the hands of the State or another individual, torture or violation of due process rights. Moreover, there is no provision for relatively speedier disposal of appeals/complaints regarding information pertaining to 'Life and Liberty' unlike 48 hours time stipulated for providing such information. The Act should be amended to include such provisions.

5. On First Appellate Authority

The Section 19(1) provides for the designation of an appellate authority at the Public Authority level who is an officer senior in rank to the Public Information Officer (PIO). However, the Act is silent about the powers and functions of the first appellate authority. As a result, there is confusion about the role and responsibility of the first appellate authorities. Moreover, the Act does not in a way, make the first appeal mandatory when it says that any person aggrieved by the decision of the PIO may prefer an appeal to such officer who is senior in rank to her/him. In general perception, an applicant is supposed to appeal with the Information Commission only after she/he has exhausted all options. The Act does not support this perception. It is not clear whether the Information Commission can entertain an appeal when the first appeal has not been preferred by the appellant.

6. On Appeals and Complaints

The grounds of a complaint under Section 18 and for an appeal under Section 19 are overlapping. Separate grounds should be there for appeals and complaints. Three clauses of Section 18(1), i.e. Clause (b) relating to refusal of access to information; (c) relating to no response to the request for information within the stipulated time; and (e) relating to give incomplete, misleading or false information may be deleted as these ground's are basically for exercising appellate powers under Section 19.

7. Contempt Provisions

Section 19(7) of the Act states that the decision of the Information Commission shall be binding. But it is not supported by 'Contempt of Court' provision to enforce compliance of its decision by the public authority. Due to the absence of such a provision there are instances of non-compliance of orders passed by the Commission.

8. On the Powers of Civil Courts

Information Commissions have been conferred powers of a civil court under Section 18(3) under the Civil Procedure Code, 1908. The powers of civil court under Sections 18(3) have been given only for limited purposes. These do not cover powers concerning execution of decrees and recovery of fine etc. The ICs powers of civil courts may be incorporated into a separate section within the same Chapter V so that it becomes applicable to all proceedings (including enquiry, appeal and penalty proceedings). Similarly, the provisions under Section 19 (7) and 19(8) may be incorporated in separate sections in Chapter V so that these powers can be applied in case of all proceedings before the Commission. Similarly, there is no uniformity of procedure of enquiry, the procedure for hearing under Section 19 and for conducting enquiry under Section 18 which points should be clearly outlined.

9. Time Frame for the Information Commissioners

Unlike the time limit for the First Appellate Authority for giving decisions on appeals, the Act does not provide any time limit to decide the appeal. Due to the absence of this provision, ICs are very often not giving the decisions on appeals on time and not only this the disposal rate is also not very good. To avoid any delay in disposal of appeals, there should be a provision regarding the time limit in the Act.

PART-III
THE RIGHT TO INFORMATION (AMENDMENT) BILL, 2019

Parliament adopted the RTI Act to give effect to people's right to access information from governments which is a deemed fundamental right within the meaning and scope of Article 19(1)(a) of the Constitution. This is Government of India's third attempt to amend this seminal law since its enforcement in October 2005. First, in August 2006, the Union Cabinet approved proposals to amend the law in order to keep "file notings" or opinion and advice recorded on file by officers involved in a decision-making chain on issues other than those relating to development and social issues. Thanks to the very vocal and widespread opposition from the citizenry, the government was compelled to shelve the proposal without ever introducing it in Parliament. Second, in 2013, Government of India tabled a Bill to amend the RTI Act in order to insulate from public scrutiny, all political parties and information that regulatory authorities hold about them. The Department-related Parliamentary Standing Committee on Personnel, Public Grievances, Law and Justice approved the amendment proposals despite widespread criticism from the citizenry. However that Bill lapsed with the dissolution of the 14th Lok Sabha.

In both instances, in the past, Government of India's proposals to amend the RTI Act were in reaction to the progressive and pro-transparency decisions issued by Information Commissions, particularly, the Central Information Commission (CIC) on crucial matters such as the disclosure of file notings (between 2005 and 2006) and declaring the six national political parties as public authorities under the RTI Act (in June 2013). The justification for the current round of amendments to the RTI Act which seeks to give Government of India near absolute power over all Information Commissions (Centre and State-level), mentioned in the Statement of Objects and Reasons attached to the Bill is not sufficiently convincing as will be argued below. In the absence of any disclosure of other pertinent reasons for amending the RTI Act, this critique is limited to examine the justification publicly declared by Government of India apart from the amendment proposals themselves. This critique of the Amendment Bill is based on the following core themes:

1. the absence of any consultation with the citizenry on the amendment proposals despite Government of India being required to so do under its own Pre-Legislative Consultation Policy of 2014;
2. the amendment proposals may violate the right to equality before the law guaranteed under Article 14 of the Constitution;
3. the amendment proposals contradict Government of India's 2017 policy of upgrading and harmonising the remuneration packages offered to other Tribunals and Adjudicating Authorities established under various Central laws;
4. the amendment proposals are contrary to the rationale informing the October 2017 recommendations of the Law Commission of India for harmonising the salaries and terms and conditions of service of other statutory tribunals established under Central laws (even though it did not cover Information Commissions); and
5. Parliament is being moved to confer excessive powers of delegated legislation on Government of India—so that the proposals are a blow to the federal scheme of the RTI Act (Venkatesh Nayak, 2018).

Lack of Consultation with Stakeholders

In the past, when the text of the RTI Bill was drafted in 2004, and the RTI Rules were drafted in 2005 and replaced in 2012 and more recently when they were sought to be amended in April 2017 the draft proposals were placed in the public domain for consultation. Government of India has worked on the latest amendment proposals without consulting any stakeholder. This despite the adoption of the Pre-Legislative Consultation

Policy in 2014 which requires every Department piloting new legislation or amendments to an existing one to place the draft Bill in the public domain through print or electronic media for enabling affected people to send their views and comments. This policy itself was the outcome of civil society advocacy for institutionalising a mechanism to involve people in the exercise of law-making in a timely and meaningful manner. The concerned Department is required to hold consultations with all stakeholders who are likely to be impacted by the proposed legislation and provide feedback from this exercise, first to the Union Cabinet which approves the legislative proposals for tabling in Parliament and next to the Department-related Parliamentary Standing Committee which vets the Bill and makes recommendations for changes where appropriate.

None of these steps of pre-legislative consultation seem to have been complied with in the current exercise to amend the RTI Act. There is no report of the Department of Personnel and Training—the nodal department for the implementation of the RTI Act, having consulted the Information Commissions who stand directly affected by the proposed amendments, let alone discussions with civil society or the citizenry, lakhs of whom have used the RTI Act in strategic ways to make public authorities more transparent and accountable.

Further, the RTI Act is the Government's own tool for combating corruption. This is made explicit in the Preamble of the Act itself where "containing corruption" and making the government and its instrumentalities accountable to the governed, namely the citizenry are mentioned among the core public interests that the law seeks to promote by establishing a regime of transparency. The law seeks to empower citizens to bring to light instances of corruption by demanding transparency of governmental action and the spending of public funds. Information Commissions are the mediators who ensure that public authorities do not withhold access to information regarding allegations of corruption and wrongdoing of their functionaries simply because it may cause some embarrassment or inconvenience.

Key Elements in the Proposed Legislation

The Amendment Bill seeks to incorporate the following changes in the existing RTI Act:

1. remove the stipulation regarding the remuneration payable to Chief Information Commissioner and the Information Commissioners of the CIC and place discretionary power in the

hands of GoI to vary it at will through the exercise of rule-making powers;

2. remove the stipulation regarding the remuneration payable to the State Chief Information Commissioner and the Information Commissioners of the State Information Commissions (SICs) and place discretionary power in the hands of Government of India to vary it at will through the exercise of rule-making powers;
3. remove the fixity of tenure for the Chief Information and Information Commissioners at both the Central and State levels (one term of five years maximum, and superannuation at the age of 65 years) provided in the law and place discretionary power in the hands of GoI to vary it at will through the exercise of rule-making powers; and
4. empower GoI to make rules on the aforementioned subject matters.

Rationale for the Amendment

The justification that GoI has provided for these proposals in the Statement of Objects and Reasons attached to the Amendment Bill may be summarised as follows:

1. The Election Commission of India (ECI) is a constitutional authority performing its appointed functions under the Constitution whereas the Information Commissions are statutory authorities established under the RTI Act;
2. The ECI is "responsible for the superintendence, direction and control of the preparation of the electoral rolls for and the conduct of all elections to Parliament and to the Legislature of every State and of elections to the offices of the President and Vice-President";
3. The Chief Election Commissioner and the Election Commissioners are entitled to salaries and allowances equal to that of a Judge of the Supreme Court; and
4. The salaries and allowances and other terms and conditions of service that the Information Commissioners are entitled to are equal to that of the members of the ECI (except in the case of State Information Commissioners whose salary and allowances are equal to that of the Chief Secretary of the State); and as the respective mandates of the ECI and the Information

Commissions are different, the latter's status and service condmitions need to be rationalised accordingly.

Table 6.1: Comparison of the provisions of the Right to Information Act, 2005 and the Right to Information (Amendment) Bill, 2019.

Provision	*RTI Act, 2005*	*RTI (Amendment) Bill, 2019*
Term	The Chief Information Commissioner (CIC) and Information Commissioners (ICs) (at the central and state level) will hold office for a term of five years.	The Bill removes this provision and states that the Central government will notify the term of office for the CIC and the ICs.
Quantum of Salary	The salary of the CIC and ICs (at the central level) will be equivalent to the salary paid to the Chief Election Commissioner and Election Commissioners, respectively. Similarly, the salary of the CIC and ICs (at the state level) will be equivalent to the salary paid to the Election Commissioners and the Chief Secretary to the state government, respectively.	The Bill removes these provisions and states that the salaries, allowances, and other terms and conditions of service of the central and state CIC and ICs will be determined by the Central Government.
Deductions in Salary	The Act states that at the time of the appointment of the CIC and ICs (at the central and state level), if they are receiving pension or any other retirement benefits for previous government service, their salaries will be reduced by an amount equal to the pension. Previous government service includes service under: (i) the Central Government, (ii) state government, (iii) corporation established under a Central or State law, and (iv) company owned or controlled by the Central or State government.	The Bill removes these provisions.

Source: http://www.prsindia.org/

TI Amendment Bill (2019) in India's Federal Context

It has already been shown above, that the amendment proposals adversely affect the legislative scheme of the RTI Act which is essentially federal in character. The salaries and allowances of the State Information Commissioners are paid up from the Consolidated Fund of the respective States over which Government of India has no control under ordinary circumstances. Similarly, the information access disputes that State Information Commissions are called upon to hear and decide through appeals and complaints procedure under the RTI Act pertain to information or official records held by or under the control of State Governments or public authorities under their jurisdiction. This is clear from a combined reading of the definition of the phrase—"appropriate government" contained in Section 2(a) of the RTI Act read with the rule-making power given to them under Section 27 of the Act. How can an SIC which is constituted and whose salaries and tenure are determined by Government of India effectively function in the State is a question that the Statement of Objects and Reasons attached to the Amendment Bill fails to answer.

Under Section 15(1) of the RTI Act it is the responsibility of the State Government to establish and constitute the State Information Commission. Under Section 15(3) of the Act it is the Governor of the State who is empowered to appoint the State Chief Information Commissioner and the State Information Commissioners upon the recommendation of the Selection Committee headed by the State's Chief Minister, a Cabinet Minister from that very State chosen by such Chief Minister and the Leader of the Opposition of the Legislative Assembly of that State. The power to remove them on grounds of proved misbehaviour or incapacity are vested with the Governor of the concerned State who shall act on the findings of the Supreme Court of India which is empowered to conduct an inquiry on such matters. Additionally, the Governor may remove any Member of the State Information Commission on grounds of adjudged insolvency, conviction for an offence of moral turpitude, engaging in paid employment outside the duties of one's office, has become infirm of body or mind so as to affect his duties or has acquired any financial or other interests that are likely to prejudicially affect his or her performance or functions as a member of the Information Commission. The decisions of an SIC cannot be challenged before the CIC. In other words, the federal character of the legislative scheme of the RTI Act is unequivocal. The jurisdictional limits of the Central and State level are distinguished sharply and with adequate clarity. Government of India has no role to play at all in the establishment and the functioning of the SICs. The Amendment Bill seeks to obliterate this federal character of the legislative scheme which is unwarranted.

Further, Section 27(2) empowers the State Governments to make rules for the manner in which appeals procedure will be conducted before the SICs. They are also empowered to make rules for fixing the salaries and allowances payable to the officials and employees of the SICs in addition to determining their terms and conditions of service. If the Amendment Bill was to become law, then two sets of Rules would govern the SICs—one made by the Central Government for the tenure and remuneration package for the Information Commissioners and the other made by the State Government for the officials and employees of the SIC. This "diarchy" itself will create major problems in the functioning of the SICs.

Further, all annual reports of the State Information Commission are required to be tabled in the concerned State Legislature through the State Government. Although hardly any instance of the SIC reports being debated in the State Legislature has been reported in the media so far, in theory, the State Legislatures may examine the performance of the respective SICs using their annual report as a basis. However, if Government of India is given the power to make rules for their salaries and tenure, they may no longer be accountable to the State Legislatures. Further, according to the Rules of Procedure and Conduct of Business adopted by the Lok Sabha and the Rajya Sabha, a matter falling within the exclusive jurisdiction of the State Government may not be raised in Parliament because there is no representative of such Government to submit a reply or defend governmental action on the floor of the House. So if the Amendment Bill becomes law, the SICs may not be held accountable in Parliament either. In short, in our humble opinion the amendment proposals will end up creating a mess as regards the accountability of SICs to people's elected representatives is concerned. The Amendment proposals seek to obliterate the federal character of the legislative scheme of the RTI Act.

Government of India's justification for the amendment proposals is berthed on the issue of rationalising the status of the Information Commissions. In fact this is not an issue of stature at all. The current scheme of the RTI Act is designed to ensure the autonomy of the Information Commissions so that they may work under conditions free from government influence. Measures for ensuring operational and financial autonomy for the Information Commissions were incorporated in the Act because the government and other public authorities would be the principal respondents in a majority of information access disputes. Therefore, Parliament and civil society advocates agreed on the current mechanism which permits the Information Commission to perform their appointed functions without fear or favour. The Amendment proposals seek to alter this very basic feature of the RTI Act.

In its 272nd Report assessing the statutory framework of tribunals, the Law Commission recalled the observation of a seventh Judge Constitution Bench of the Supreme Court in L. Chandra Kumar where the Court called for an independent supervisory body to be appointed to oversee the functioning of statutory tribunals. Until such a mechanism is established, the tribunals should be under a nodal Ministry, it opined. The Court recommended that the Union Ministry of Law and Justice play this role until the independent supervisory mechanism is established. The Law Commission has also recommended the establishment of such a nodal agency under the Union Ministry of Law and Justice. This recommendation needs widespread debate in order to insulate bodies such as the Information Commissions from interference by Government of India as is being contemplated under the Amendment Bill.

In light of the very serious problems highlighted above with regard to the amendment proposals and the justification underlying them, it is advisable that the Amendment Bill be dropped without introduction in Parliament. Instead the requisite orders may be issued to upgrade the salaries of the Information Commissioners at all levels in accordance with the provisions of the RTI Act as they exist today and initiate measures to improve their functioning by providing them with an adequate number of staff of high calibre for quickly disposing appeals and complaints.

PART-IV
CONCLUDING OBSERVATIONS

Every citizen has the right to know how the government is functioning. Right to Information empowers every citizen to obtain information from the government. It is duty of public authorities to maintain records for the easy access and to publish within 120 days the name of the particular officers who should give information and in regard to the framing of the rules and regulations. All information shall be disseminated widely and in such form and manner which is easily accessible to the public. It has been provided that it is required that the request to be disposed of within 30 days provided that where information sought for concerns life or liberty of a person, the same shall be provided within 48 hours. If a request is rejected it shall be communicated giving reasons and specifying the procedure for appeal and the designation of the appellate authority. The Act also exempts granting information where it would disproportionately divert the resources of the public authority or would be detrimental to the safety and preservation of the record in question.

Knowledge and information is the prerequisite for the enjoyment of this right because the lack of authentic information on matters of public interest leads to the wild rumours. Freedom of speech and expression includes the right to receive and collect information. Since the democracy is the government of the people who are the sovereign masters. There can be no government by the people if they are ignorant of the issues to be resolved, the argument for and against different solutions and the facts underlying those arguments. The taxes collected by the government belong to the people. They have the right to know in what manner they are being governed and how their money is being spent. The business of the government should be a participatory process. The fact should be made public. Only a fully informed citizenry can be better equipped for the performance of these duties.

The Right to Information Act enables the citizens to get the required information for the redressal of the grievances within a specified time from the date of filing application. Any citizen can ask for information under this law by applying in writing or through electronic means to the Public Information Officer (PIO), specifying the particulars of the information sought for. The Right to Information has been judicially recognized as a part of the fundamental right to speech and expression. Information is *sine qua non* for the efficient functioning of democracy. It keeps the people informed about the socio-political and economic affairs and issues. In a developing country like India, the availability of the information is required to be assured to the people in a simple and speedy manner because the development process depends on it.

Over the past few years, RTI has gained increasing importance in the human rights discourse as well as the larger democratic discourse. Since a democratic government must be sensitive to the public opinion for which information must be made available by it to the people. Effective accountability rests on the peoples' acquaintance with the information. A system that operates in secrecy tends to loose the faith of the people as much as its own legitimacy and credibility. Openness and full access to the information are the two pillars of the democratic state. It will equip the citizens to participate meaningfully in the democratic and political process. Governance is undoubtedly strengthened by the RTI. That is why the RTI has been recognized as an essential requirements of the good governance. The enactment of the RTI Act, 2005 is a bold step. The Act covers not only the public sector but also the NGOs and the private sector to some extent. In addition to this, it has various other positive features like provision of First and Second Appellate Authorities. It is also one of the toughest legislations in the world, as it is the only RTI Act imposing penalty for any contravention of the provisions of the Act.

However, mere conferment of the right is not enough. Its successful implementation in the true spirit is needed. The revision and review of legislations contrary to this right is required. Suitable amendments in the conduct of rules for public servants, attitudinal change in the behaviour of the bureaucracy, creation of efficient information management system, more frequent use of this right by press and will of the citizens are also required. Many loopholes need to be plucked. However, despite the weaknesses, it is a *Magna Carta* for introducing reforms in the governance in the country and will go a long way in strengthening the roots of democracy by introducing transparency and accountability in governance.

In conclusion with regard to the Right to Information Amendment Bill, 2019 is concerned, serious problems highlighted above with regard to the amendment proposals and the justification underlying them, it is advisable that the Amendment Bill has to be redrafted and recasted thoroughly. Instead the requisite orders may be issued to upgrade the salaries of the Information Commissioners at all levels in accordance with the provisions of the RTI Act as they exist today and initiate measures to improve their functioning by providing them with an adequate number of staff of high calibre for quickly disposing appeals and complaints.

REFERENCES

B.L. Fadia and K. Fadia, *Public Administration*, Sahitya Bhavan, 2004.

Harinderjit Kaur, Right to Information, *South Asia Politics*, Vol. 8, No. 12, April 2010.

https://www.humanrightsinitiative.org/download/CHRI-RTIABill2018-critique-Jul18.

https://indianexpress.com/article/india/no-trust-debate-today-government-holds-back-rtichanges-bill-narendra-modi-rahul-gandhi-5266801.

http://www.legislative.gov.in/documents/pre-legislative-consultation-policy

https://indiacode.nic.in/bitstream/123456789/1965/1/199111., accessed on 30, July, 2018

http://eci.nic.in/eci_main/right-toinformation/RTI17062015

http://egazette.nic.in/WriteReadData/2018/182326

http://lawcommissionofindia.nic.in/reports/Report272

http://www.newindianexpress.com/thesundaystandard/2018/jul/22/rti-amendment-will-promote—patronage-says-former-chief-information-commissioner-wajahat-habibullah-1846678.html

J.G Roy, *Right to Information Initiatives and Impact*, IIPA, New Delhi, March 2006.

M.R. Biju, *Democratic Political Process.* (Ed.) Mittal, New Delhi, 2008.

M.R. Biju, *Democracy in the Modern World: The Indian Experience,* Two Volumes Kanishka, New Delhi, 2009.

M.R. Biju, *Strategic Management, Social Security and Banking Sector Reforms: Issues and Concerns*, AuthorsPress, New Delhi, 2010.

M.R. Biju, *Development Issues in Contemporary India*, Concept Publishing Company Pvt. Ltd., New Delhi, 2010.

M.M. Semwal and Sunil K., Right to information and Judiciary, *IJPS*, Volume LXIX, No. 4, December 2008.

R.S. Dhaka, *Right to Information and Good Governance*, Concept Publishing Co. Pvt. Ltd., New Delhi, 2010.

S. Pande and S. Singh, *Right to Information Act 2005*, NBT, New Delhi, 2008.

Sapna Chadah, Right to Information Regime in India, IJPA, March 2006.

Venkatesh Nayak, *Access to Information Programme*, Commonwealth Human Rights Initiative, New Delhi, July 2018.

7

RTI Amendment, 2019: A Threat to Participatory Democracy

Tanvi Yadav and *Nagendra Ambedkar Sole*

Introduction

Knowledge and Information are the backbones of a democratic state. People with proper Information can contribute to establishing good governance and better society. Active participation is the need for thriving democracy. People through their knowledge make a country as welfare state by keeping eyes on transparency and accountability of Government. Thomas Jefferson in 1789 said that "whenever the people are well informed; they can be trusted with their own government that whenever things get so far wrong as to attract their notice, they may be relied on to set them to rights." Jefferson often recognized that "information is the currency of democracy".

After the establishment of the UNO, the international community adhered to practice, freedom of Information as a basic Human Right. In Article 19 of the Universal Declaration of Human Rights (UDHR) laid down that, "Everyone has the right to freedom of opinion and expression; this right includes freedom to hold opinions without interference and to seek, receive and impart information and ideas through any media and regardless of frontiers" (UDHR, 1948). Right to Information is the part of freedom of expression; it described in the International Covenant on Civil and Political Rights (ICCPR), 1966.

Almost all the developed countries have the law on the Right to Information. In India, the Right to Information (RTI) Act recognised in 2005, which played a significant role in increasing accountability and transparency by giving rights to citizens of check and balance through questioning. Every year around six million RTIs filed from its inception (Engage, 2019). RTI Act of 2005 considered as robust and fortified, it consist Central Information Commission (CIC), an institution which governs the Act and is equal to Election Commission of India in terms of power. Government officials sentenced to a fine for delays in providing Information or falsifying or destroying the data.

Right to Information raised the expectations in India as it is considered as the democratic weapon to empower the common man concerning the Government. The objects of the RTI Act itself is the reflection of the intention of the Act as it lays down as "An Act, to provide for setting out the practical regime of right to information for citizens to secure access to information and to promote transparency, and accountability in the working of every public authority" (RTI Act, 2005). The RTI, 2019 Amendment Act raised so many doubts about the honesty and intention of the Government. RTI changed the scenario of participation in democracy in India; however, the latest amendment can deteriorate the roots of participatory democracy. This chapter will explore the journey of RTI in India and the current threat to it.

Evolution of RTI in India

In the colonial rule, India adopted the Official Secrecy, where the legislature intended to keep the government functioning in secret. The Act restricts leakage of any information. The objective was to help the colonial administration to a safe and secure position. After Independence, the circumstances drastically changed in India. India adopted its new Constitution and incorporated most of the excellent features in the Constitution of India borrowed from Constitutions of other countries of the world. The preamble of the Constitution declares India a democratic state to attain equal justice for everybody. The chapter on fundamental rights covers most of the unique humanitarian principles, including freedom of the press, expressions, etc.

In the 1990s, Aruna Roy started the Right to Information movement in the state of Rajasthan and said: "Right to know is the right to live". In June 1994 an organisation which works for issues of labours and farmers named as the Mazdoor Kisan Shakti Sangathan (MKSS) highlighted gram panchayat of Rajsamand district in Rajasthan about the corruption in a public development scheme (Engage, 2019). They asked Information about accounts from the local government officials and through their continuous struggle, got success in accessing the data, and use it to end to corruption and exploitation. Several other NGOs, civil societies and activists also joined the MKSS movement of Information and Transparency.

A long battle for Information finally culminated in RTI Act, and the enactment of Act took place in 2005 came into force in October 2005 and signed by the then President A.P.J. Abdul Kalam and replaced the Freedom of Information Act, 2002. RTI Act overruled most of the provisions of Official Secrets Act and strengthened the rights of general people to questions the authorities. RTI Act empowered every citizen to seek information regarding the government and its officials except exceptions regarding sensitive information to the national security. The RTI Act was proved across the country as a significant landmark in the country's march towards strengthening of democracy (Misra, 2019). RTI Act's objective was to consolidate with the fundamental rights of Freedom of Speech as enshrined in the Constitution of India. RTI was a part of check and balances as autonomous structures set up to regulate and monitor the government and are essential to a democratic state committed to delivering justice and constitutional guarantees (Roy & Dey, 2019).

For NGOs, Media and Activist RTI, high power recognised to reveal the truth and strengthen themselves to make democracy more vibrant. Many Activists, in the field of Government services, monetary schemes, environment issues, criminal matters even at the local level, did excellent work and made justice available even to the socio-economic and political backward people. More than 80 RTI activists lost their life as by courage and determination they were using the RTI to challenge to unaccountable power (Roy & Dey, 2019), many Activists faced harassment and assault, confronted the threats from politicians and mafias, but still, RTI has become a hope for peace and harmony and brought to light dubious practices (Regidi, 2017).

RTI helped to expose corruption in Government (Sharma, 2015) and been used to uncover secret truths covered by the Government. However, it does not mean that everything was right in the enforcement of the Act. In many cases, the public information officers (PIOs) continue to deny access to information held by them. The misuse of Section 8(1)(j) of the RTI Act, 2005 which codified privacy exception, by PIOs is rampant and most times reduced this Act into a mockery (Sridhar, 2017). But the amendment of 2019 brings a threat to information purpose. On the announcement of RTI Amendment 2019, Opposition leaders and activists claimed that the proposed amendment would destroy the object and independence of RTI Act.

Indian Judiciary on RTI

The constitutional mandates of freedom of speech and expression have gained its momentum by the successive judicial interpretations on different occasions. *Romesh Thappar* vs. *State of Madras* (AIR 1950 SC 594) was the first case when the Supreme Court discussed the people's right to know. Right to Information, the Supreme Court declared, is part of Article 19 (1) (a) of the Constitution of India, in *Hamdard Dawakhana* vs. *Union of India* (AIR 1960 SC 554). In the *State of Punjab* vs. *Sodhi Sukhdev Singh* (AIR 1961 SC 493), while discussing the Official Secrets Act, the Court initiated the discourse of Right to Information as a legal right.

In *Amar Chand Butail* vs. *Union of India* (AIR 1964 SC 1658), Supreme Court laid down that public interest doctrine should apply to the freedom of information. In *Bennett Coleman* vs. *Union of India* (AIR 1973 SC 106), Chief Justice Ray states that freedom of the press includes the Right of all citizens to speak, publish and express their views and Right of the people to read which refers to Right of the readers to get Information. In the *State of U.P.* vs. *Raj Narain* (AIR 1975 SC 885). Supreme Court opined that "citizens of country have a right to know every public act, everything that is done in a public way by the public functionaries."

In *S.P. Gupta* vs. *Union of India* (1981 Supp. SCC 87) a seven-Judge Bench of the Supreme Court observed thus: "Where a society has chosen to accept democracy as its creedal faith, it is elementary that the citizens ought to know what their Government is doing. No democratic Government can survive without accountability, and the basic postulate of accountability is that the people should have information about the functioning of the Government. If people know how Government is functioning, they can fulfil the role which democracy assigns to them and make democracy an effective participatory Democracy."

In *Indian Express Newspapers (Bombay) (P) Ltd.* vs. *Union of India* (1985 1 SCC 641), the Supreme Court observed, "The public interest in freedom of debate and dialogue, can be successful when the citizens of democratic country get information and use it in their decisions." In *Sheela Barse* vs. *Union of India* (AIR 1986 SC 1773), Supreme Court issued directions for release of Information to her relating to under trials kept in different parts of the country. *Reliance Petrochemicals Ltd.* vs. *Indian Express Newspapers, Bombay (P) Ltd.* (1988 4 SCC 592) recognised the Right to know as emanating from the Right to life.

Tata Press Ltd. vs. *MTNL* (1995 5 SCC 139) observed while considering the scope of Article 19(1) (a) in the context of advertising or commercial speech, held that the public has a right to receive Information. The Supreme Court in *Secretary, Ministry of Information and Broadcasting* vs. *Cricket Association of Bengal* (1995 2 SCC 161), laid down that by ensuring the Right of speech and expression, citizens of India must have a plurality of view and an extensive range of opinions on public issues. "A successful democracy posits an aware citizenry. Diversity of opinions, ideas, views and ideologies is an essential requirement which enables the citizens to arrive at informal judgments on all issues concerning them."

The *Dinesh Trivedi* vs. *Union of India* (1996 4 SCC 306) case concerned the questions of the disclosure of the Vohra Committee Report; the Supreme Court acknowledged the importance of open Government in a participative democracy. The Court observed: "In modern constitutional democracies, it is axiomatic that citizens have a right to know about the affairs of the Government which, having been elected by them, seeks to formulate sound policies of governance aimed at their welfare." It went on to serve that "democracy expects openness and openness is concomitant of a free society, and the sunlight is a disinfectant."

In *D.K. Basu* vs. *State of West Bengal* (AIR 1997 SC 610), Supreme Court held that the detainees have right to know the charges framed or reasons for arrest, place of detention, Right to get the relatives informed about the arrest. In *UOI* vs. *Association for Democratic Reforms* (AIR 2002 SC 2112), the scope of Article 19 (1) (a) was extended and laid down that the Right to know of the candidate contesting election to a House of Parliament or a state legislature or a panchayat or a municipal corporation is a precondition to the exercise of a citizen's right to vote.

In *Peoples Union for Civil Liberties* vs. *Union of India* (AIR 2003 SC 2363), held that real democracy could not exist unless the citizens have a right to participate in the affairs of the policy of the country. The Supreme Court held in *State of Andhra Pradesh* vs. *Canara Bank* (AIR 2005 SC 186) that the Right to Information is not absolute, but it is a part of Right to freedom of speech and expression. Section 8 of the RTI Act, 2005 balances the right to privacy and Right to Information and recognises that both provisions are essential and require protection, and in case of conflict between two rights, the test of overriding public interest can apply to decide whether Information should be withheld or disclosed.

The Supreme Court evolved the principle of community participation in *Research Foundation for Science Technology and Natural Resource*

Policy vs. *Union of India* [JT 2007 (11) SC 49], and held that the Right to Information and community participation for protection of the environment and human health is the part of Article 21 of the Constitution. *Secretary-General Supreme Court of India* vs. *Subash Chandra Agrawal* (AIR 2010 Del 159) held that Right to Information is not the emergence of RTI Act, 2005, it emerged from the constitutional guarantee under Article 19 (1).

In *Central Board of Secondary Education (CBSE)* vs. *Aditya Bandopadhyay* (2011 SCC 497) it held that the examining bodies—Universities, Examination Boards etc., are bound to provide access to Information, and any applicant can either inspect the document/record, take notes, absracts or obtain certified copies thereof. In *Anjali Bhardwaj* vs. *Union of India* [Writ Petition (Civil) No. 436 of 2018], the Supreme Court gave significant judgment on timely and transparent appointments of Information Commissioners. The Court directed that the government must specify the terms and conditions of appointment in the advertisement when inviting applications to the post of Information Commissioners.

In September 2019, Supreme Court Bench of Justices Deepak Gupta and Aniruddha Bose held that Non-Government Organisations which are being paid by the Government, have to provide information to the seekers under the RTI Act. Five-judge bench of the Supreme Court of India consisting of Chief Justice Ranjan Gogoi, Justice N.V. Ramana, Justice D.Y. Chandrachud, Justice Deepak Gupta and Justice Sanjiv Khanna with a 3:2 majority laid down that "the Chief Justice of India's office will also be covered by the Right to Information Act" in November 2019.

The Supreme Court bench comprising Justices D.Y. Chandrachud and K.M. Joseph in January 2020 accepted the plea challenging RTI 2019 amendment and issued notice to present the case. The plea was filed by Member of Parliament Jairam Ramesh challenging the amendments in the Right to Information Act, 2005 on the ground of violation of Article 14, 19, and 21 of the Constitution. Sridhar Acharyulu, ex-CIC said that the RTI (Amendment) Bill is not just a hit on the RTI Act but also on the freedom of speech from where RTI emanates. He highlighted, the Supreme Court repeatedly declared the Right to Information is a fundamental right enshrined in the Constitution of India (Sangathan, 2019).

RTI Act and Amendments

RTI Act, 2005 was enacted with three motives of transparency, accountability and empowerment and provided autonomous Information

Commission to regulate and enforce the Act. The RTI 2005 Act laid down that "the public authorities are required to make disclosures of their "organisation, functions and structure", "powers and duties of its officers and employees", and "financial information" (Dutta, 2019). Failing of Public authorities to provide such information, gives the right to citizens to demand the related data. Under the Act, Public authorities include all official institutions of the Central and State Governments and non-governmental organisations that are controlled or substantially financed by the Government.

The object of RTI Act laid down that "democracy requires an informed citizenry and transparency of information which are vital to its functioning and also to contain corruption and to hold Governments and their instrumentalities accountable to the governed" (RTI Act, 2005). Section 8, sub-section (1) (j) of the RTI Act states that "information which relates to personal information the disclosure of which has no relationship to any public activity or interest, or which would cause unwarranted invasion of the privacy of the individual unless the Central Public Information Officer or the State Public Information Officer or the appellate authority, as the case may be, is satisfied that the larger public interest justifies the disclosure of such information" (RTI Act, 2005).

Under RTI Act 2005, the head of the Central Information Commission will be a Chief Information Commissioner along with ten other Information Commissioners and their appointment will be done by the President of India for a fixed tenure of five years. Their salary will be of the rank of the Chief Election Commissioner and Election Commissioners respectively. These provisions give the Central Information Commission autonomy, and protection from government interference and 2019 amendment is changing these provisions.

The Central Government introduced the Right to Information (Amendment) Bill, 2019 in the Lok Sabha without any public debate on the contents of the Bill on 19th July, 2019. The Bill became public only on 18th July, 2019, when it circulated to MP's of Lok Sabha. Various Members of Parliament asked to refer the Bill to a Standing Committee and objected the bill as a threat to democracy. However, their request was ignored with 117 MPs voted against referring them to a Select Committee and 75 voting for it (Misra, 2019).

From 2011 to 2013, India was at 2nd position in the functioning of accession laws of information among the 123 countries. But its place is continuously slipping down since 2014 for that the first reason was the non-appointment of the CIC. In 2014, the position for the CIC was left vacant for ten months first time since the enactment of the law. Since 2014 the government has repeatedly tried to dilute the RTI Act, first through proposed changes to rules in 2017 and then through proposed amendments to the Act in 2018.

The government also failed to fill vacancies in the Central Information Commission on time, when activists went to the Supreme Court to demand fulfilment of vacant posts in the Commission. A study based on RTI laid down despite a Supreme Court directive in February 2019, the Centre could not make timely appointments to Commissions (Bhatnagar, 2019). Vacancies for prolonged periods have the effect of increasing the already high number of pending applications for timely Information (Engage, 2019).

During the first tenure of NDA, the Government already tried to amend the Act but could not table the amendment in parliament. However, Lok Sabha was not a problem for NDA in the first tenure, but their position was weak in Rajya Sabha where they were not in the majority. In the present tenure of NDA, they have the full majority in 17th Lok Sabha and Rajya Sabha is not be a problem any longer as NDA along with some other parties has the strength of 127 members which helped it in passing in Rajya Sabha (TOI, 2019), which make easy for them to bring out the change in RTI Act in the form of RTI (Amendment) Act, 2019.

The amendment reduces the independence of CIC, which dangers the transparency of RTI from the political influence. The Bill, however, faced severe criticism from the opposition, media, activists and the ordinary citizens—who alleged the Government of sabotaging the citizens' Right to Information. An RTI application revealed that even "the Central Information Commission was not consulted regarding the Right to Information Amendment Act, 2019" (Jebaraj, 2019).

On 22nd July and 25th July, 2019, the Lok Sabha and Rajya Sabha passed the RTI (Amendment) Bill, 2019 respectively—passed with 218 members voting in its favour and 79 against in Lok Sabha (TOI, 2019). The 2019 amendments are regressive, which will undermine the most reliable law of transparency in India and dilute the independence of Information Commissions. Significant changes of 2019 RTI Act are as follows:

Amendment in Section 13

By amending clause (a) of Sub-section (1) of Section 13, clause (b) of Sub section (2) of Section 13 and clause (c) of Sub-section (5) of

Section 13, The Amendment is removing the statutory protection of tenure, salaries, allowances and conditions of service of Chief Information Commissioner and Information Commissioners of Central Information Commission and making it with the prescription of Central Government. In RTI Act, 2005, the tenure of CIC and ICs was fixed as five years but now under RTI Amendment Act 2019, the tenure will be decided by the Central Government, and it can vary as per the government will. In 2019 rules, the tenure is put as three years, and there is a provision for reappointment also.

Amendment in Section 16

By amending clause (a) of Sub-section (1) of Section 16, clause (b) of Sub-section (2) of Section 16 and clause (c) of Sub-section (5) of Section 16, Amendment is removing the statutory protection of tenure, salaries, allowances and conditions of service of Chief Information Commissioner and Information Commissioners of State Information Commission and making it with the prescription of Central Government. In RTI Act, 2005, the tenure of State's CIC and ICs was fixed as five years but now under RTI Amendment Act, 2019, the Central Government will decide the tenure, and it can vary as per the government will. In 2019 rules, the tenure is put as three years, and there is a provision for reappointment. Salary and allowances will also be decided time to time by the Central Government.

Dangers of Amendment

The RTI Amendment bill was passed and converted into Act without the consultation of Central Information Commission, without the opinion of public and without referring to the Select Committee. Even the opposition in parliament was ignored, Congress leader Adhir Ranjan Chowdhury named such amendment as "dangerous", and former Union Minister A. Raja termed passing of the RTI Amendment Bill as a "dark day for democracy" (Dutta, 2019). The Government's honesty is not apparent in bringing these amendments in RTI as the Bill severely dilutes the provisions of RTI Act, 2005. Pertinent dangers to right to information are as follows:

(a) Irrational Reasons

The Minister Mr. Jitendra Singh, while introducing the Bill in the Lok

Sabha, named the amendment a benevolent and minor mechanism of rule-making, not a significant change in Law (Roy & Dey, 2019). The Central Government justified that the Election Commission is a constitutional body, but the Information Commission is not; it is a statutory body; hence both cannot be treated on the same parlance. It is the Government's justification through objects of Act that Election Commission of India (ECI)'s functions are very different from the Central Information Commission and State Information Commissions, and therefore the same need to be "rationalised."

The simply reading objects and reasons of amendment act, the "reason" for this amendment does not make sense. The Government offers no justification as to why CIC should no longer enjoy the same status as ECs. In 2017, the 272nd Report of the Law Commission of India recommended that the salaries and allowances of many of the Statutory Tribunals must be revised. Under Finance Act, 2017, NDA government upgrades the wages, benefits and other facilities of chairman, members and officers of almost all the tribunals, which are also not constitutional bodies, but government treated them like Election Commissioners. The CIC and ICs also perform quasi-judicial functions and must be treated equally like other Statutory Tribunals and Authorities. However, the RTI 2019 Amendment is violating the right of equality and equal protection under Article 14 of the Constitution.

The reasons of amendment of RTI Act are very irrational, maybe debate and discourse in public domain by activists and academicians could have reached on a better understanding, but even opposition in parliament was not listened and adamantly act was passed. NDA government in many irrational decisions reasoned that it would be beneficial in the long term, same intentions appeared but as economist John Maynard Keynes said, "In the long term we are all dead"; hence such long time planning with no consistent output is worthless and weaken the present and future of the country as well.

The Government has drastically changed the character of the Information Commissions by scheming the tenure and acquiring the power to fix salaries, allowances and other terms of service (Misra, 2019). Many statutory bodies have given status and protection equating to constitutional bodies such as Lok Pal, Vigilance and other tribunals. In the last 14 years of the implementation of the RTI Act, this provision has not hindered the functioning of the institutional framework of the country. Therefore, there is no rationale for amending the Right to Information.

(b) Fears of Accountability

During the UPA government regime, Right to Information was extensively used by the BJP party to expose the scams, scandals and various omissions and commissions (Misra, 2019). Hence, the amendment in RTI during its regime is doubtful. Amendment clearly shows that Government by taking command in its hand can threaten or entice the CIC and ICs by removal, the extension of tenure, increase or curtailment in salary as per their suitability to for the ruling dispensation (Dutta, 2019).

On 24th July 2019, seven former Information Commissioners of the Central Information Commission addressed a press conference in Delhi and termed the amendment as an apparent attack on peoples' fundamental Right to know and the autonomy of Information Commissions and requested the Government to withdraw the regressive changes. There is a suspicion that amendment comes in the backdrop of a few orders of the Information Commission that were considered uncomfortable for the Modi government in recent times such as on PM Modi's degree row and the status of non-performing assets in public sector banks (Dutta, 2019).

RTI has been used to override the traditional structures of secrecy and exclusive control. RTI can also be used to cross-verification of the affidavits of compelling electoral candidates with official documents and individual Information Commissioners having ruled in favour of disclosure. Recently, Subhankar Sarkar filed an RTI in Prime Minister Office and asked the citizenship certificate of Prime Minister Narendra Modi, on which PMO replied PM do not need certificate because he is an Indian citizen by birth (Quint, 2020). This RTI is the slap on government face who are trying to force citizens to prove their citizenships by certificates which are not available. The amendment would have been done to avoid such questions which take government's accountability before suppressing the citizens by regressive rules and regulations and take full control over CIC.

Yashovardhan Azad, ex-CIC said that "the amendment bill was an apparent attempt to control the tenure and salary of information commissioners by the Government, most of the applications under RTI Act are registered by the marginalised sections of society in a proposition to secure their rights from the Government. In the majority of the cases, the respondent is the Government and therefore, to ensure that Commissions can function independently, their sovereignty must be safeguarded. He believed instead of strengthening the RTI Act by proper implementation of proactive disclosure and greater transparency in the appointment of commissioners; the Government is amending the law (Sangathan, 2019).

In the RTI Act, there was no provision of reappointment, but this provision in amendment can create problems in accountability. The RTI Amendment disempower the ordinary person while empowering the Central Government (Misra, 2019). M.M. Ansari highlighted that the Government had discontinued the weekly show on DD news about RTI Act known as "*Janane ka Haq*" (Sangathan, 2019). From closing the show, it is clear that the government wants people not to be so aware of their rights. The concerns of activists and ex-CIC's about unsatisfactory justifications of Government lead to the conclusion that there will be no independence and transparency in RTI authorities which is an apparent threat to the aims and objectives of Right to Information of accountability.

(c) Abuse of Federalism

RTI Act, 2005 empower state governments for the constitution of the State Information Commission where SCIC and SICs are appointed by the Governor based on the recommendations of the committee consisting of the Chief Minister, Leader of Opposition of the Legislative Assembly and a cabinet minister of that state. The state government is also empowered to provides employees to the commission and salary and allowances of SCIC and SCIs.

By amending Section 16 of RTI Act, Central Government is taking control to decide tenure, salaries and allowances of SCIC and SCIs, and discouraging the independence of SICs which raises the critical issues of the federal system of our country. The amendment is an apparent attempt of the government to militates against the spirit of federalism and disempowering the state Information Commission is obviously against the principles of cooperative federalism about which Prime Minister Narendra Modi himself spoke about eloquently (Misra, 2019).

RTI pioneers in India, Aruna Roy and Nikhil Dey said that through amendment the control on Commissioners of the States is an assault on the idea of federalism (Roy & Dey, 2019). The consolidated fund of concerned state pays the State Information Commissioners salary and allowances; Amendment gives power to the central government to decide salary and allowances is arbitrary and weaken the federal system of the country. The amendment is unreasonable as the Central Government has no control over the consolidated fund of state unless there is President rule in the state under Article 356 of the Constitution of India.

(d) Threat to Independence

The 2019 Amendment Act is brought to exactly change sections 13, 16 and 27 of RTI Act, 2005, which equates the status of the Central Information Commissioners and the State Information Commissioners with the Election Commissioners and the Chief Secretary in the States respectively, so that they can function independently and effectively (Roy & Dey, 2019). The Amendment undermines the independence of Information Commissions, and thereby significantly dilute the widely used framework for transparency in India. The short tenure of CICs and ICs is an advantage for the government to see their performance as per their orders, their people also have the chance for reappointment to safeguard the secret truths of government.

Information Commissions are the final authorities to decide on claims of access to information which is a deemed fundamental right under the Constitution. Statutory guarantee of tenure and status is crucial to ensure that the Information Commissioners function independently and without political interference. Enabling the Central Government to determine the tenure and salaries of the Commissions will fundamentally weaken the institution of the information commissions and bound them to work under political pressure. Commissioners will be wary of passing directions to information that the Central Government does not wish to provide.

Conclusion

"If liberty and equality, as is thought by some are chiefly to be found in democracy, they will be best attained when all persons alike share in the Government to the utmost" (Aristotle). Spirit of any democracy can be justified by the Right of the people to inspect those in power. Without discussion and dispute, the establishment of democracy will be empty at its Centre. After Independence, among the progressive laws of India, RTI Act is accepted and considered as dynamic law in the nation. It is the most sincere hope to survive the dying democracy of India.

Now when the time has come to make Information Commission as a constitutional body, the government is trying to destroy its soul by threatening the independent position of Chief Information Commissioner and Information Commissioners by taking advantage of Information Commission not being a constitutional body. However, the Government cannot "punish" an independent-minded IC by removing them. The provision of the RTI Act governing the removal of ICs is not affected by this amendment, and the rules cannot be changed to cut short the tenure of anyone IC without falling afoul of the principal RTI Act. Though, the steps of government make it clear that there is a threat to the government in revealing Information to the people.

Right to Information promotes the public interest by promoting openness in administration, discouraging arbitrariness in decision-making and making administration responsible towards ordinary people. It can be used as a tool of corruption check and prevent arbitrary state actions. Aruna Roy and Nikhil Dey rightly pointed out that the RTI has been and will be used for transparency and accountability in India and government will realise that they can amend a law but cannot stop a movement.

Right to information with the upliftment of judiciary can be a great check and balance of governance in India. As Abraham Lincoln said in 1861, "Let the people know the facts, and the country will be safe", it is necessary to the development and security of the country to make the people aware. However, the present RTI amendment is not only a threat to RTI but also to the notion of participatory democracy.

REFERENCES

Bhatnagar, G.V. (2019). RTI "Report Card" Laments Pending Cases, Vacancies in Information Commissions. Retrieved February 2, 2020, from *The Wire* website: https://thewire.in/government/rti-information-commissions-vacancies-pending-cases

Dutta, P.K. (2019, July 23). What makes RTI Amendment Bill so controversial? *India Today*. Retrieved from https://www.indiatoday.in/news-analysis/story/what-makes-rti-amendment-bill-so-controversial-1572596-2019-07-23

Engage. (2019). Right to Information : The Promise of Participatory. *EPW*, (July).

Jebaraj, P. (2019, November 28). CIC was not consulted on RTI amendment Act. *The Hindu*. Retrieved from https://www.thehindu.com/news/national/cic-was-not-consulted-on-rti-amendment-act/article30099380.ece

Misra, S. (2019). Amended RTI Act: What is at stake? Retrieved February 3, 2020, from *Observer Research Foundation* website: https://www.orfonline.org/expert-speak/amended-rti-act-what-at-stake-53573/

Quint. (2020). In RTI Reply, PMO Says PM Modi Needs No Citizenship Certificate. Retrieved March 2, 2020, from *The Quint* website: https://www.thequint.com/news/politics/caa-narendra-modi-needs-no-citizenship-certificate-pmo-response-to-rti

Regidi, A. (2017). RTI Reveal of Aadhaar Disclosure by Govt. Websites Highlights Privacy Risks with Aadhaar Data Collection. Retrieved from Firstpost website: https://www.firstpost.com/india/rti-reveal-of-aadhaar-data-breach-by-govt-websites-highlights-the-privacy-risks-posed-by-unsupervised-data-collection-4218981.html

Roy, A., & Dey, N. (2019, July 22). The tremor of unwelcome amendments to the RTI Act. *The Hindu*. Retrieved from https://www.thehindu.com/opinion/lead/the-tremor-of-unwelcome-amendments/article28628537.ece

Sangathan, S N. (2019). Amendment to the RTI. *Economic and Political Weekly*, *54*(30), 5.

Sharma, B. (2015). 5 Scams The RTI Act Helped Bust In Its First 10 Years. Retrieved from *Huffington Post* website: https://www.huffingtonpost.in/2015/10/12/5-most-critical-scams-exp_n_8263302.html

Sridhar, M. (2017). Right To Privacy and RTI Act. *Economic and Political Weekly*, *52*(38), 29–31.

TOI. (2019, July 23). RTI Amendment Bill: Explained. *Times of India*. Retrieved from https://timesofindia.indiatimes.com/india/rti-amendment-bill-explained/articleshow/70341996.cms

8

Addressing the Three Threats of Indian Democracy

Power of Money, Media and Corporates

P. Lazarus Samraj, Gothanda Moorthy C. and *Vineeth Thomas*

Introduction

From the dawn of Independence in 1947, Indian Democracy is marching towards positive direction in spite of so many ups and downs. It is well known for its robust electoral politics and conducting periodical elections for the smooth transfer of power by involving large number of electorates and along the way it is breaking its own records in conducting elections in which more and more number of political parties as well as candidates are contesting from diverse backgrounds. Strong constitutional foundations, socio-political culture of tolerance, living philosophy of salvation through good deeds and humanism along with its inherent ability to withstand so many intermittent negative factors are helping Indian Democracy to move in a right direction. Even though proactive political participation of more and more people and groups with bare minimum political education are a welcome sign, there are so many forces which are trying to manipulate the ignorant, semi-literates and needy voters for their political dividends. Consequently manipulative and manoeuvring tactics are dominating people-centric growth-oriented real issues.

In this chapter, the scholars have identified three factors—-Money, Media and Corporate which are competing with each other in manipulating the voters by hook or crook for the sake of winning elections. Great Indian Democratic Experiment which was started by Mahatma Gandhi and his followers based on the high principles of truth, non-violence, moral values, transparency, self-denial, humanism, inclusiveness are greatly harmed by the aforesaid evil trios.

In this context, this chapter analyses the role and influence of the above said trios along with their ulterior motives.

Money

Multiparty democracies are known for their electoral politics in which every party and candidate contests with the objective of winning the support of maximum number of voters by giving tall promises and building the image of the leaders/parties by the sweet eloquent speeches about their capacity and deeds and at the same time tarnishing the image of opposition leaders/parties by genuine as well as manufactured allegations.[1,2] However, in transitional democracies like India, some special factors come into play. Affluent political parties with money power often uses all tricks from their books to woo the voters. Consequently, most of the prominent candidates raise bulk chunk of monetary resources for election related expenditure through so many wrong ways including getting funds with strings attached from corporates, government contractors, liquor barons, bootleggers, real estate moguls and others who have succeeded in accumulating huge wealth by wrong means.[3, 4, 5, 6]

One of the most powerful instruments used by the strong candidates/ political parties to win the support of the neutral/non-card holders with little educational background is alluring them with the gift of money. Consequently, without knowing the value of their votes, most of the voters belonging to above marginalised, political aparthiest are ready to sell their votes.[7, 8]

Voter purchase is carried out in two methods such as Open Cash Purchase and Promise of freebies in case of winning the elections.

Open Cash Purchase is so rampant in contemporary Indian polity. In most of the elections in general and by-elections in particular, the ruling as well as wealthy opposition parties systematically formulate their strategies to corrupt the voters.[9, 10] The most spectacular instance of this sort is an event that occurred during the Thirumangalam Assembly Constituency by-election in 2009. Thirumangalam lies in Madurai district, Tamil Nadu State. According to the media reports, M.K. Azhagiri, one of the sons of M. Karunanidhi, the then Chief Minister of Tamil Nadu, introduced a new novel voter bribing method, named as *Thirumangalam Formula*[11] for scientifically planning and distributing money to all the voters as well as getting pledge from them about their vote to his party candidate in the name of deity or other.[12] Since then this *Thirumangalam formula* is followed in almost all the byelections in Tamil Nadu by the ruling parties irrespective of whoever is in state power.[13] The latest interesting example is R.K. Nagar by-election (2017) in Chennai, Tamil Nadu. It is alleged that AIADMK rebel candidate T.T.V. Dinakaran gave Rs. 10,000 before voting and promised to give Rs. 10,000 after voting. Consequently except the ruling party of the state, all the opposing candidates lost their security deposits.)[14]

However, it is wrong to form a sweeping conclusion that money is everything in an election. The so-called hero of Thirumangalam by-election lost the subsequent assembly election in Thirumangalam and even his ward in the subsequent panchayat election.[15] This shows that voters are fooling the political leaders in the subsequent elections without making fuss. Both voters and the political parties are simultaneously fooling each other. This establishes that the Indian voters are not dumb fools but becoming cunningly clever in manipulating the parties. In one way it is a rewarding experiment for a transitional democracy. Hopefully, once the crook politicians realise that giving money won't ensure their electoral victories, they will stop giving money for votes.

Promise of freebies in case of coming to power after election becomes a stable feature in the contemporary Indian polity. Apart from alluring voters with money, prospective winning parties are promising a lot of freebies before elections. For instance, during Bihar Assembly Election (2015), Nitish Kumar-led Mahagathbandhan parties [JD(U) + RJD + Congress Alliance] promised free Wi-Fi to College and Universities, farm loan waiver to farmers, reservation in government jobs for women, free electricity connection to every house etc.[16]

Besides vote purchase, money power flexes its muscle in other aspects also. It is used for creating Shock and Awe Effect in voters psyche. To create Shock and Awe Effect in the hearts and minds of voters and supporters, almost all the political parties invest bulk chunk of money for organizing colourful rallies, conducting massive public meetings, hoarding large banners, advertising and addressing the people through TV, Radio, Internet etc.[17, 18]

One of the most pertinent question being asked in every democratic forum is how these guys get money for disposal. But the answer is that it is complicated. We can delineate a few resources.

The first one is, reallocation of welfare funds. In order to fulfil their uneconomic, unrealistic election eve promises, the ruling parties raise funds by reallocating or reducing the funds available for welfare measures like education, health and infrastructure.[19]

The second one is, indulging in immoral practices as state policy. Legalising drugs, selling alcohol, stealthily allowing prostitution are some of the facets. Due to state-run liquor shops, each and every nook and corner of the towns and the villages, liquor becomes available even to children. They have sales target too. This liquor causes various ailments for the people that they suffer from failure of body organs and loss of balanced minds. In general, India is known for its strong family foundations which is built upon the principles of love and care. But consumption of liquor disintegrates families and also causes stress which is reflected in the form of domestic violence, rebellious and directionless children, divorce rates, suicides and so many other problems are on the rise.[20, 21, 22]

The third one is indulging in Unfettered Corruption. For instance, since 1967, Tamil Nadu Politics is dominated by two major Dravidian parties—DMK & AIADMK, claiming the same political legacy of social justice oriented, rationalistic, Self-Respected and Anti-brahminical ideology of Dravidian Movement.[23, 24] But they sold their soul to devil and morphed into neo-capitalistic parties. Now they are indulging in things which are completely opposite to what they are claiming. Now they have become pseudo-Dravidians and become infamous for their repeated corrupt practices.[25, 26]

The fourth one is, Sales of Political Office. The political parties, in order to get some financial *quid pro quo*, nominate industrialists and billionaires for safer seats and positions in Rajya Sabha (Upper House of Indian Parliament). It is nothing but blatantly selling the seats. For instance, in 2004, Mr. M.A.M. Ramaswamy, a sparsely spoken, horse baron and industrialist, hailing from Tamil Nadu, was nominated by Janata Dal (Secular) Party in Karnataka,[27] a neighbour state, who was well known for downgrading the once highly reputed Annamalai University as the most corrupt University of India by appointing ineligible candidates as faculty members.[28]

As long as the voters are ignorant of the value of their votes, having the culture of justifying the mentality of accepting money for votes, eradication of the abuse of money in Indian election in general and by-election in particular is next to impossibility. However, allowing this menace will corrode democracy in the long run. In most of the transitional democracies, people with high moral order cannot mobilize money to contest even in municipal elections. This forces them to take back foot.

When most of the straightforward, genuinely concerned people are not ready to enter public life, ordinary voters who are having the intention of making positive impact in politics through ballot are left hapless.[29]

It is high time for the indifferent and silent egg heads of India to come out of their ivory tower arm chair to formulate strategies to address the issues of the ills of money power. First the higher educational institutions which are located in different parts of India should initiate serious research to study the causes and remedies to address this menace. Indian Democracy is known for its unique nature from regions to regions, from constituencies to constituencies. Therefore, it is necessary to carry out in-depth, multi-dimensional case studies with updated data and advanced statistical tools.

Election Commission, an autonomous body, which is expected to conduct free and fair elections should use its authority to act against the parties and the candidates who distribute money for vote. Not knowing one's strength and responsibility is a self-defeating exercise. When T.N. Seshan was the Chief Election Commissioner, he was known for implementing the toughest, strict and successful elections by exercising his powers. Even though he had attracted the admiration of many people he won the displeasure of corrupt political leaders.[30]

Apart from the above it is necessary to educate the politically ignorant, politically illiterate and first generation as well as first time voters the importance of voting. Without knowing the value of the vote which can change the destiny of many generations, they throw it like biscuits to dogs. Both primary and secondary school teachers of every constituency should be trained for democracy and encouraged to conduct voter outreach programmes to create voters awareness in every nook and corner of all the towns and villages. This may generate long term dividends.

As a young democracy, Indian Democracy should conduct Studentsl Union elections in universities and colleges to train the young leaders. The young voters should be taught at the institutional level about the election process and democratic credentials and values of transparency, accountability and other leadership qualities so that the young leaders in due course would play positive and productive role in future. If positive and regulated political activism culture develops in India, it will cause the genesis of a new culture in India in the long run and it may put an end to selecting their leaders in cinema theatres, in communal riots, and in caste violence.

Finally, the committed NGOs, social activists and sacrificial hearted youth may join together to organise campaigns for propagating ethics in politics, injecting the high ideals of not accepting money or freebies, voting with self-respect, importance of hard work and value judgement.

Media

It is a well-known fact that there is a close relationship between capitalist economic structure, multi-party political system and the growth of so many electronic and print media. It is universal in almost all types of democratic countries.[31] In multiparty democracy, Independent media is considered as one of the guardians of democratic values and processes. Independent and unbiased media is called as 24×7 Opposition for keeping its eye on day-to-day political developments and transmitting them to wider public for making informed political decisions.[32] Media is expected to be informative, educative, critical, analytical, problem-solving and creating awareness among the public and also help them to express and mobilise public opinion.[33]

Due to capitalist economics' inherent structure, most of the media are having some level of affiliations or totally working as the radio box of their sponsors. Hence it is not possible to expect fair, free and unbiased reports from most of the media.[34, 35, 36] As mentioned elsewhere most of the political leaders in their mission to win the support of their voters are very keen in using, misusing and abusing the media power. These things with their inbuilt ulterior motives are systematically carried out in many ways.

First of all, building up the image of their own party and party leaders. They depict him as a demigod/only saviour available and popularise his policies and programmes. For praising/popularising him, the Media conduct debates with invited flatterers, paid intellectuals and sycophants and regularly tarnish the image of the opposition leaders/leaders. They hide the failures and negative characteristics of their paid masters.[37, 38]

Secondly, Diversionary Tactics. There is a mad rat-race going on among the political parties to shape the political deliberations of the society according to their design. They try to manipulate the political environment by propagating their views through their own media.[39, 40, 41] They adopt so many tricks to achieve their agenda. They make them addicted to unique type of news as well as programmes primarily by producing sensational news and emotional mega serials in order to enslave them inspiring them to give priority to entertainment rather than political affairs.[42, 43]

Thirdly, Targeted Audience Specific News. The leaders invest a lot of money and tricks to appear in the prime time programmes in neutral media to reach out maximum number of people. Along the way, they convert popular democracy into a media-centric and manipulative galacracy.[44, 45] Many leaders have dedicated captive PR office to boost up their reach.[46] Through propaganda, the leaders try to colonize the minds of the people so as to justify right as wrong and vice versa or something else.[47] Their influence on media is ubiquitous. Their cob-web is spread in all levels of politics—International, national, state and municipal. They want to make the people think in a way which is desired/designed by them, i.e. Tailor-made Thinking Process.[48, 49, 50]

In India, the legacy of Media is rich in content as well as description. Media was effectively used by both the ruling as well as opposition party leaders even in pre-Independence era. During Indian Independence Movement (c. 1900-1947), Indian Media had played decisive role in bringing out and rallying the ordinary Indians against the brutal mighty British Indian Empire, by advocating and popularizing democratic values, ideals of Swadeshi movement and the merits of Home rule.[51] During National Internal Emergency (1975-77), it is the media which brought the atrocities of the police and lawless behaviour of the bureaucrats to the attention of the inattentive Indian populace and planted them in their moral consciousness.[52] During Global Economic Meltdown (2008), it is the Indian media which stabilised the Indian markets by propagating the story of strong economic fundamentals of Indian economy to the world as well as to the domestic investors.[53] During Jallikattu Movement (2017) in Tamil Nadu, in the name of Tamil Culture and Pride, multitude of Tamils were systematically organised all over the world and caused amendment to the Central Act by an unorganised, invisible youth through social media is an exemplary example of political mobilisation through social media for a committed cause.[54]

It has its own negative history also. The one-sided, fact free, contradictory stories created by the media are really creating lots of confusion among the indecisive, uninformed citizens. For instance, during 2014 General Elections campaign, BJP campaign Leader Narendra Modi promised to deposit Rs. 15 lakh in the bank account of each Indian after coming to power.[55] BJP leaders used it as proxy for the corrupt practices of the previous government. They developed Black Money theory and aggressively promoted it to win the support of the fence sitters. After the election, BJP National President Amit Shah said that it is "Jumla".[56] These types of somersaults have become new norms in Indian Democracy as the attention of the media moves to another popping up saleable issue instead of reminding the people about this type of false promises.

However, it is a fallacy to conclude that the manipulative power of the media alone can make/break political decisions. A few instances can throw light on this aspect. The then Prime Minister Smt. Indira Gandhi was unable to win the 1977 General Election, despite the strong support of the media during and after emergency.[57] Similarly the then Prime Minister Rajiv Gandhi was defeated in the 1989 General Election, despite his charisma, youthfulness and lust for scientific empowerment, because of his complexities in Bofors scandal.[58] Atal Bihari Vajpayee led NDA government lost the 2004 General Election despite projecting and popularising the advertisement "India Shining."[59]

This shows that the media's manipulative ability in Indian politics is waning day by day for most of the neutral and educated citizens are developing the habit of either not watching the manipulative media or cross-checking the news with multiple sources. The advent of social media and the growth of smart phone usage as a two-edged sword are playing a balancing role in most of the democracies. For instance, in the last presidential election in America (2016), the electronic and print media strongly supported Hillary Clinton which was systematically countered by Republican controlled social media. Consequently the person with the support of social media won the election.[60]

Similarly in India most of the growing educated population is addicted to smart phone and social media. Social media is known for systematically tarnishing the image of so many political leaders. For instance recently in Tamil Nadu which is well known for Dravidian culture of Anti-Brahmanical movement, Tamilians were systematically ridiculing and tarnishing the image of the BJP leaders, though most of the print media were systematically building the image of Modi and BJP and it was reflected in the recently held R.K. Nagar by-elections (2017) where the BJP got lesser number of votes than even NOTA.[61]

In spite of the partisan role of media in general, the media is playing positive role also. However, it is necessary to create accountability, regularity, fairness and transparency in media also. Any democracy or organisation/enterprise which is promoting secrecy rather than transparency is a self-defeating enterprise. It is applicable to media also. In the name of secrecy, business ethics and profits, most of the media are not ready to reveal their financial transactions to the public domain. While most of the media in democracy is fighting for more and more transparency, they continue to maintain secrecy of their own financial transactions. It is pure hypocrisy. Consequently it may reduce the credibility of the media and soon the people will start boycotting it.

Secondly, all the higher educational institutions which are offering degrees on Media and Communication should go for a paradigm shift by restructuring their curriculum. They should educate the new media graduates with media ethics, problem solving techniques, and probing the issues with problem solving solutions. They should educate the masses and empower the youth with futuristic goals, promoting integrity and humanism. Further the emergence of the social media as an effective force and the opening up of Indian economy give opportunities for the young educated media persons to start their own media outlets.

Above all the popular media should be liberated from the colonial mindset of the bureaucrats as well as century old repressive laws of rigidity and censorship. The proposed new laws should empower not only freedom of expression but also protect the citizens as it is necessary to protect the innocent people from the organised harassment of the state.

Corporates

Private property and democracy are two sides of the same coin. Multiplying wealth, adopting the latest technologies and inventions and the consumerist mentality of the people are the backbone of corporates controlled economy.[62] Modern phase of capitalism was popularised by American puritan (WWW—working, worshipping, and witnessing) founding fathers by sharing and caring created the philanthropist mentality among the American capitalist class.[63] However, the greed of capitalists and the crony capitalism with its inbuilt evil designs made them indulge in manipulating and manoeuvring trade practices, products and prices. They are extending their practices in purchasing the power centres by hook or crook. They are eliminating each other by adopting all means including price war, hostile takeover, trust breach, intellectual theft etc. Above all, they are cheating the customers by selling sub-standard products which makes mockery of capitalist model of economy.

In this modern high tech world, democratic elections are mainly won by the manipulative power of the political parties. Almost all the political parties are hiring professional managers to organise mega events to convince the voters with their money power. This trend is very obvious in most of the transitional democracies like India. In America almost all the main Presidential candidates are mainly depending upon the corporate donations. Corporates consider the elections as a type of investment to get their benefits through their candidates in short term or long term.

However, the setback faced by the communist model due to the collapse of the Soviet Union and the emergence of USA as the sole super power compelled most of the Third World countries including India to go for a paradigm shift in their economic policy by adopting capitalist free market economy.

After Economic Liberalisation in India (1991), the newly emerged business class replaced the erstwhile socio-political elites. The phenomenal forces of Liberalisation, Privatisation and Globalisation (LPG) have unleashed the profit seeking of business class. They are indulging in manoeuvring and manipulating politics through their money power and managerial power. With their insatiable appetite for profit, they try to influence and co-opt each and every force of society to increase their profit.

This unprecedented unholy alliance of greedy corporates and power hanker politicians started to play joint and proactive role with the agenda of exploiting people in a subtle legal way. Election tickets are collaboratively decided between the parties and the corporates and then distributed to the representatives/point persons of the corporates.[64, 65] Election expenditures are meted out with corporate money. Then the Corporates start influencing/pressurising the public decision-making mechanisms.[66] The spectacular incident of this practise is the story of Vijay Mallya from Karnataka, the most controversial liquor baron. He entered the Parliament (Upper House) and occupied membership in a policy-making board which was related with his business interests.[67] He is a Text Book Case of Conflict of Interests in public life, but No one had worried and even the authorities are not ready to acknowledge this.[68]

Corporates are demanding their money back with high margin profit. For that, the corporates are creating laws, rules and regulations according to their needs, whims and fancies in their board rooms and feed the parliament/state assembly to pass it as public law. They are converting law making process as a farce. They alchemise their business interest as the legitimate public interest and demand unflinching government support for its successful execution. This money-centric politics result into all forms of corruptions at all levels such as infamous corruption stories of 2G Spectrum Auction, PNB Bank Scam etc.[69, 70, 71]

Furthermore, the Governments execute corporate agenda as government agenda and demand unwavering popular support for its success.[72, 73] They have the audacity of calling it as a national mission but hiding all relevant information/statistics to the wider public.[74, 75] They even deride the people who oppose these as anti-national and naxalism.[76, 77, 78, 79]

At the behest of corporates, they weaken the public sectors by huge disinvestment processes.[80] Even they do not spare important profit making PSUs.[81, 82] It is a paradox that all the bright minds of India are joining IAS service and the IAS Officers are managing the PSUs. But PSUs had fallen sick as per Government statistics and the Government sold it to less endowed minds claiming that they would make profit out of it. Here the question raised is whether these IAS officers are incompetent when compared with greedy corporate investors and their CEOs?

Corporate controlled democracy with the help of power-centric political leaders is systematically crippling the values of well-established constitutional institutions and vital economic fundamentals of the society.[83, 84, 85] This scenario is reflected in government policies like Low Corporate Tax, Tax Cut to Millionaires, Uncollected taxes, non-persecution of tax defaulters, unscientific allocation of scarce natural resources, abusing the cover of national interest/security etc.[86, 87, 88]

Authors like to bring some of these details to the readers. Every year the uncollected Tax in India amounts to the tune of few lakh crore rupees, a whooping amount for a developing country.[89, 90] In Coal Block allocation during the UPA-II Government (2009-2014), the then Coal Secretary was convicted by a Law Court.[91] In the name of national security, Indian Armed Forces bought Tatra trucks, Bofors howitzer, Augusta Westland, VVIP helicopters for arbitrary prices and mired in controversy.[92] Buying of Nuclear Powered Submarines, Next-generation Fighter Jets, outdated Nuclear Reactors from foreign companies are nothing but scam in making.[93, 94, 95] Even a portion of the total money which is being spent on these deals can make world class Universities and R&D centres in India.[96] Central/State Governments are deliberately underfeeding the PSUs and their R&D facilities to make them sick and kill them eventually.[97] Buying of Metro Rail coaches from foreign private companies instead of Indian Railway factories,[98] Bullet trains from Ahmedabad to Mumbai which costs Rs. 98000 crore are at the cost of under/unconnected far-flung parts of India.[99] Compulsorily buying costly commercial software instead of strictly enforcing the use of freely available spy proof Open Software is making fun of India's IT Super Power status.[100, 101] Commodity market trading of agricultural produces,[102, 103] allowing Genetically Modified (GM) crops without alleviating people's genuine fear,[104, 105] systematically and ruthlessly exterminating the native breeds of livestock[106] are pure betrayal of innocent, hapless Indian farmers.[107, 108]

We should not leave these malaises unattended. We have to develop cure and preventive mechanism to safeguard our political system. This society is not made for the luxurious lifestyle of few at the cost of others. Everyone should get adequate opportunity to lead a good, prosperous, happy, peaceful life.

Most of the intellectuals as well as social activists strongly believe that the corporates are emerging as an untameable aggressive beast with the ulterior motive of greed at the destruction of all ethical and moral foundations. However, it is the responsibility of the people to initiate discussions to formulate problem solving strategies as opinionated mentality is negative and destructive.

Firstly, the transitional societies like India in general and all the higher educational institutions in particular should deepen the democratic culture by popularising human rights education, positive humanism and moral and ethical values within their campus as well as at village levels. A self-disciplined, self-content, educated and well-connected society is a backbone of any country. This well organised and autonomous society should be encouraged to create consumer forums to identify goods and services with credibility by educating the people about the manipulative designs of the corporates. If all these small village units are integrated, they can put a check on the ulterior motives of the corporates. Further, the corporates should be forced to invest some percentage of their profit for the development of the locality in a transparent manner as the existing Corporate Social Responsibility (CSR) did not rise up to the expectation. John F. Kennedy once said that consumer forums are the greatest representatives of people. They can decide and dictate the corporates if they are organised systematically.

Secondly, meticulously designed and built public enterprises should be strengthened. Nehru called India's PSUs as the Temples of Modern India. However due to the poor leadership corruption prevailing at all levels, lack of commitment by the employees, leaders lack vision, too much of fake unionism have converted most of the PSUs as white elephants, a great liability to the exchequer. Consequently, 1991 onwards the successive governments are competing with each other in selling the national assets to the greedy corporates instead of formulating ways and means to restore the status of highly valuable PSUs as commander of economy. Both the Central and State Government owned enterprises are having huge properties with outdated infrastructure and workforce. Most of them were profit making companies in initial stages. In Tamil Nadu the various transport corporations were competing with each other in providing the best service to the passengers and also making huge profit by giving good incentives to the workers in 1970s. But the successive administrations with their corrupt and greedy mentality have shown huge losses and at present the buses are not maintained properly and are in poor conditions. Hence the government can initiate steps to strengthen the PSUs by involving the local higher educational institutions. They can also establish research institutions to create work culture and to apply latest tools and techniques for converting PSUs as profit making enterprises. There should be a complete change from top to bottom in spirit and practice.

Thirdly public nature of laws should be ensured. For that, each and every bill should be introduced to the public forums for discussion before being submitted to the appropriate law making houses through the mechanism of Law Impact Assessment Hearings (L.I.A.) on the line of Environment Impact Assessment Hearings (E.I.A). The existing method of select/joint committee hearing is highly inadequate and unproductive.

Fourthly, conflict of interest phenomena of elected representatives should be eliminated. For that, the Parliament should enact generic Act and each and every committee of parliament/state assembly should develop foolproof mechanism to filter out the questionable personalities and punish them for wilful suppression of data and violations of regulations, besides throwing them away from law making bodies.

Finally, to protect the farmers from corporate greed, Governments should establish Agricultural Universities in each and every district and create Agricultural Extension Centres where cultivation is more. Through these institutions each and every farmer should be given adequate exposure and training about modern agricultural practices adopted all over the world. Farmers must be encouraged and motivated to use the R&D facilities of these institutes to compete at world level.

Conclusion

In any democratic election, leaders and political parties are formulating multiple strategies to win the support of maximum number of voters even by forming opportunistic, election-oriented alliances. The emergence of so many multinational corporations with money power and media power in both the developed and developing democracies is creating evidently effective impacts in democratic elections as well as policy formulations. Obviously, the corporates are aiding, assisting, and projecting the image of their compatible leaders for utilising them as their pawn to get things done. With their media power they know the art of manipulating the innocent as well as neutral voters.

In developed democracies like America, the event managers and election strategists are formulating astute techniques to build the image of their customer-leader as well as to damage the reputation of the targeted opposition in electronic and print media with the support of corporates' money. However, in the transitional democracies like India the ever increasing role of corporates controlled media and the money power is growing day by day making mockery of the election. The unholy alliances lead to so many compromising tactics. Consequently a sizeable number of voters are losing their faith on their democratic elections.

In this context, this chapter suggests that it is necessary to formulate humanistic and holy alliances to address the issue in order to save the basic values of democracy. Otherwise the corporates and money-centric democracy may lead the society to anarchy. It is high time for intelligentsia to save the democratic movement from decay.

NOTES

1. Joseph M. Colomer (ed.), *Handbook of Electoral System Choice* (New York: Palgrave Macmillan, 2004).
2. Waldemar Wojtasik, "Functions of Elections in Democratic Systems," *Political Preferences*, no. 4 (2013): 25–38, doi:10. 6084/m9. figshare. 729054.
3. Robert Williams (ed.), *Party Finance and Political Corruption* (New York: St. Martin's Press, LLC, 2000).
4. Devesh Kapur and Milan Vaishnav, "Quid Pro Quo: Builders, Politicians, and Election Finance in India," *CGD Working Paper 276* (Washington, DC, 2011), http://dx. doi. org/10. 2139/ssrn. 1972987.
5. *Electoral Statistics Pocket Book 2017* (New Delhi: Election Commission of India, 2017), http://eci.nic.in/eci_main1/current/Electoral_Statistics_Pocket_Book2017_18052017. pdf.
6. *General Elections 2014- Reference Handbook* (New Delhi: Government of India, 2014), http://pib.nic.in/elections2014/Tree.aspx.
7. Vernon Hewitt, *Political Mobilisation and Democracy in India: States of Emergency* (New York: Routledge, 2008).
8. D.L. Sheth, "Political Development of Indian Electorate," *Economic and Political Weekly* 5, No. 3 (2012): 137–48.
9. R.K. Radhakrishnan, "We Pay You Vote," *Frontline* (Chennai, July 2016).
10. Anirban Mitra, Shabana Mitra, and Arnab Mukherji, "Cash for Votes: Evidence from India," *School of Economics Discussion Papers* (Kent, 2017), https://www.kent.ac.uk/economics/documents/research/papers/2017/1711.pdf
11. A.S. Nazir Ahamed, "Cash-for-Vote: Genesis of the 'Thirumangalam Formula,'" *The Hindu*, May 14, 2016, http://www.thehindu.com/elections/

tamilnadu2016/cashforvote-genesis-of-the-thirumangalam-formula/article8601057.ece.

12. "DMK Wins Thirumangalam Bypoll," January 13, 2009, http://indianexpress.com/article/news-archive/web/dmk-wins-thirumangalam-bypoll/.
13. Ajit Prakash Shah, "Law Commission of India: Report No. 255," *Electoral Reforms* (New Delhi: Law Commission of India, 2015).
14. "4 Dhinakaran Supporters Arrested for 'bribing' Voters," *The Hindu*, December 17, 2017, http://www.thehindu.com/news/national/tamil-nadu/4-dhinakaran-supporters-arrested-for-bribing-voters/article22282879.ece.
15. "Statistical Report on General Election, 2011 to the Legislative Assembly of Tamil Nadu" (New Delhi: Election Commission of India, 2011), http://eci.nic. in/eci_main/StatisticalReports/AE2011/stat_TN_May2011. pdf.
16. "Mahagathbandhan Manifesto Sings Nitish Tune," *The Times of India*, October 10, 2015, http://timesofindia.indiatimes.com/city/patna/Mahagathbandhan-manifesto-sings-Nitish-tune/articleshow/49294369.cms.
17. "BJP Spent Rs. 60 Crore on Narendra Modi's 3D Rallies during Lok Sabha Polls," *The Times of India*, January 21, 2015, http://timesofindia.indiatimes.com/india/BJP-spent-Rs-60-crore-on-Narendra-Modis-3D-rallies-during-Lok-Sabha-polls/articleshow/45959849. cms.
18. K.V. Lakshmana, "Two Dead, 15 Injured in Stampede at Jayalalithaa Rally," *Hindustan Times*, April 16, 2016, http://www.hindustantimes.com/assembly-elections/two-dead-15-injured-in-stampede-at-jayalalithaa-rally/story-TORludm9N3FZg6Ie8r73OO. html.
19. "State Finances—A Study of Budgets of 2015-16" (New Delhi: Reserve Bank of India, 2016).
20. Gururaj, G. et al., *Alcohol Related Harm-Implications for Public Health and Policy in India,* Publication No. 73 (Bangalore: National Institute of Mental Health & Neuro Sciences, 2011).
21. "Global Status Report on Alcohol and Health 2014" (Geneva: WHO Press, 2014), doi:/entity/substance_abuse/publications/global_alcohol_report/en/index. html.
22. "Public Health Problems Caused by Harmful Use of Alcohol: Gaining or Losing More?," *Alcohol Control Series*, vol. 2 (New Delhi: WHO Regional Office for South-East Asia, 2006), doi:10. 1017/CBO9781107415324.004. s
23. G. Premakumar, "Genesis of the Dravidian Movement in the Madras Presidency, 1852-1917" (Ph.D. Dissertation, Manonmaniam Sundaranar University, 2001).
24. B. Kolappan, "It's Been 50 Years since the Dravidian Juggernaut Started Rolling," *The Hindu*, February 25, 2017, http://www.thehindu.com/todays-paper/tp-national/tp-tamilnadu/fifty-years-on-the-dravidian-juggernaut-continues-to-roll/article17364330.ece.
25. Arun Janardhanan, "Tainted by Graft, Ex-DMK Ministers Struggle," *The Indian Express*, May 12, 2016, http://indianexpress.com/article/elections-2016/india/india-news-india/tamil-nadu-elections-tainted-by-graft-ex-dmk-ministers-struggle-2796014/.

26. "Anger against Jayalalithaa's Conviction Continues, " *The Hindu*, October 4, 2014, http://www. thehindu.com/news/national/tamil-nadu/anger-against-jayalalithaas-conviction-continues/article6469382.ece.
27. "Venkaiah, Ramaswamy Elected to Rajya Sabha," *The Hindu*, June 28, 2004, http://www.thehindu.com/2004/06/29/stories/2004062904690600.htm.
28. "Annamalai University VC Suspended over Irregularities," *The Times of India*, April 7, 2013, http://timesofindia.indiatimes.com/home/education/news/Annamalai-university-VC-suspended-over-irregularities/articleshowprint/19422271.cms.
29. V.R. Vachana and Maya Roy, "NOTA and the Indian Voter," *The Hindu*, February 28, 2017, http://www.thehindu.com/todays-paper/tp-opinion/nota-and-the-indian-voter/article17379880.ece.
30. David Gilmartin, "One Day's Sultan: T.N. Seshan and Indian Democracy," *Contributions to Indian Sociology* 43, no. 2 (2009): 247–84, doi:10. 1177/006996670904300203.
31. Eli M. Noam and The International Media Concentration Collaboration, *Who Owns the World's Media* (Oxford: Oxford University Press, 2016).
32. Julianne Schultz, *Reviving the Fourth Estate—Democracy, Accountability and the Media* (Cambridge: Cambridge University Press, 1998).
33. Adam F. Simon, *Mass Informed Consent—Evidence on Upgrading Democracy with Polls and New Media* (Plymouth, UK: Rowman & Littlefield Publishers, 2011).
34. Saifuddin Ahmed, "The Role of the Media during Communal Riots in India: A Study of the 1984 Sikh Riots and the 2002 Gujarat Riots," *Media Asia* 37, no. 2 (2010): 103–11, doi:10. 1080/01296612. 2010. 11771982.
35. Soumya Dutta, "Social Responsibility of Media and Indian Democracy," *Global Media Journal-Indian Edition*, no. Summer Issue/June (2011): 1-8.
36. Maitrayee Chaudhuri, "Indian Media and Its Transformed Public," *Contributions to Indian Sociology* 44, no. 1–2 (2010): 57–78, doi:10. 1177/006996671004400204.
37. Glen Halbrooks, "How Politicians Use Media to Win Elections," *The Balance*, 2017, https://www. thebalance.com/how-politicians-use-media-to-win-elections-2315204.
38. Stefaan Walgrave and Peter Van Aelst, "Political Agenda Setting and the Mass Media," *Oxford*, 2016, http://politics. oxfordre.com/view/10. 1093/acrefore/9780190228637. 001. 0001/acrefore-9780190228637-e-46.
39. Robinson Meyer, "Who Owns Your Media?," *Newslaundry*, 2015, https://www. newslaundry.com/2014/02/05/who-owns-your-media-4.
40. Gayatri Wani and Nilesh Alone, "A Survey on Impact of Social Media on Election System," *International Journal of Computer Science and Information Technologies* 5, no. 6 (2014): 7363–66, http://www. ijcsit.com/docs/Volume 5/vol5issue06/ijcsit20140506100. pdf.
41. K. Asha and N. Usha Rani, "Usage of Social Media in the 2014 Indian General Elections—A Review of Modi Factor and IT Czar's Digital Trail," *Journal of Media and Social Development* 2, no. 2 (2014): 4–32. D

42. Chandan Nandy, "Arnab's Sunanda Death 'Story': Rich on Sensation, Poor on Evidence Tapes Don't Constitute Evidence," *The Quint*, 2017, https:// www. thequint.com/news/india/republic-tv-sunanda-pushkar-report-little-evidence.
43. Salil Desai, "Brand Modi: Created, Marketed by Media," *The Tribune*, 2018, http://www. tribuneindia.com/news/comment/brand-modi-created-marketed-by-media/517385. html.
44. "PM Modi's 'Mann Ki Baat' a 'one-Sided' Communication: Congress," *The Indian Express*, September 24, 2017, http://indianexpress.com/article/india/pm-narendra-modis-mann-ki-baat-a-one-sided-communication-congress-bhu-violence-fuel-price-unemployment-4859330/.
45. "Award Wapsi to Defame India: Anupam Kher Leads March against Intolerance Protests," *FIRSTPOST*, 2017, http://www. firstpost.com/india/award-wapsi-to-defame-india-anupam-kher-leads-march-against-intolerance-protests-2498828. html.
46. "Is Political PR the next Big Thing in India's PR Business?," *PRmoment India*, 2014, http://www. prmoment. in/category/pr-insight/is-political-pr-the-next-big-thing-in-indias-pr-business.
47. Garth S. Jowett and Victoria O'Donnell, *Propaganda and Persuasion*, 5th ed. (New Delhi: SAGE Publications, 2012).
48. Philip M. Taylor, *Munitions of the Mind*, 3rd ed. (Manchester: Manchester University Press, 2003).
49. Sucheta Nair, "Agenda-Setting Function of the Indian Press with Specific Relevance to the Press in Kerala" (PhD Dissertation, University of Calicut, 2008).
50. Bogdan Pătruþ and Monica Pătruþ, eds., *Social Media in Politics: Case Studies on the Political Power of Social Media* (London: Springer, 2014).
51. Navneet Anand, "Role of the Press in Political Mobilisation: A Comparative Analysis of Colonial and Independent India" (PhD Dissertation, Jawaharlal Nehru University, 1999).
52. Chandrakanta K. Mathur, "Mass Media and Democracy in India: A Political Study of Their Relationship in Post-Emergency Period" (PhD Dissertation, University of Delhi, 2013).
53. Mohan J. Dutta and Soumitro Sen, "Coverage of the Financial Crisis in English Language Print Media in India/ : Ideologies of Neoliberalism," *Journal of Creative Communications* 9, no. 3 (2014): 199–213, doi:10. 1177/0973258614545015.
54. Ilangovan Rajasekaran and R. Vijaya Sankar, "The Marina Moment," *Frontline* (Chennai, February 2017).
55. *Reality of 15 Lakh Promise by Narendra Modi*, Video, (2015), https://www. youtube.com/watch?v=rHPcapJqbQk.
56. "Modiji on Rs. 15 Lakh Returning to Accounts Was a Political 'jumla': Amit Shah to ABP News," *ABP News*, 2015, http://www.abplive.in/http:// m.abplive.in/india-news/modiji-on-rs-15-lakh-returning-to-accounts-was-a-political-jumla-amit-shah-to-abp-news-150752.
57. Kuldip Nayar, *The Judgement* (New Delhi: Vikas Publishing House Pvt. Ltd., 1977).

58. Chitra Subramaniam-duella, "The Bofors Story, 25 Years after," *The Hoot*, 2012, http://www.thehoot.org/media-watch/media-practice/the-bofors-story-25-years-after-5884.
59. Ramashray Roy and Paul Wallace, (eds.), *India's 2004 Elections: Grass-Roots and National Perspectives* (New Delhi: SAGE Publications, 2007).
60. Chris Baynes, "Donald Trump Says He Would Not Be President without Twitter | The Independent," *The Independent*, 2017, http://www. independent. co. uk/news/world/americas/us-politics/donald-trump-tweets-twitter-social-media-facebook-instagram-fox-business-network-would-not-be-a8013491. html.
61. "R.K. Nagar Bypoll Result Updates: T.T.V. Dhinakaran Wins by over 40,000 Votes; Supporters Celebrate Victory," *FIRSTPOST*, 2017, http://www. firstpost.com/politics/rk-nagar-by-election-results-2017-live-updates-high-profile-jayalalithaa-seat-to-get-new-mla-today-dmk-aiadmk-and-rebel-leader-ttv-dhinakaran-in-fray-elections-4273155. html.
62. James Fulcher, *Capitalism: A Very Short Introduction* (New York: Oxford University Press, 2000).
63. Charles Post, *The American Road to Capitalism* (Boston: Brill, 2011).
64. "96% of Newly-Elected Rajya Sabha MPs Are Crorepatis," *Hindustan Times*, June 29, 2016, http://www. hindustantimes.com/india-news/96-of-newly-elected-rajya-sabha-mps-are-crorepatis/story-omOmVPydw2Chlv1 xFTdxRM. html.
65. "Lok Sabha Election Watch 2014" (New Delhi: Association for Democratic Reforms, 2014), https://adrindia.org/sites/default files Lok_Sabha_Report_ 2014_compressed. pdf.
66. "FICCI for Substantial Slash in Policy Rates by RBI," *Outlook* (New Delhi, August 2017), https://www. outlookindia.com/newsscroll/ficci-for-substantial-slash-in-policy-rates-by-rbi/1121859.
67. "Detailed Profile: Dr. Vijay Mallya," *Government of India*, accessed June 26, 2017, http://www. archive.india.gov.in/govt/rajyasabhampbiodata. php?mpcode=1892.
68. "Rajya Sabha Ethics Committee Recommends Expulsion of Vijay Mallya," *The Indian Express*, May 4, 2016, http://indianexpress.com/article/india/ india-news-india/rajya-sabha-ethics-committee-recommends-expulsion-of-vijay-mallya-2783856/.
69. "India's Corruption Scandals," *BBC*, 2012, http://www. bbc.com/news/ world-south-asia-12769214.
70. Mohit M. Rao, "No Scam in Rafale Deal, Says Nirmala Sitharaman," *The Hindu*, 2018, http://www. thehindu.com/news/national/no-scam-in-rafale-deal-says-nirmala-sitharaman/article22791670.ece.
71. "Explained: How Did the Alleged Rs. 11,000 Crore Nirav Modi, Punjab National Bank Scam Go Unnoticed?," *Scroll*, 2018, https://scroll.in/article/ 868825/explained-how-did-the-alleged-rs-11000-crore-nirav-modi-punjab-national-bank-scam-go-unnoticed.
72. "Stir against GAIL Pipeline Turns Violent in Kozhikode; 10 in Police Custody | Video," *Manorama Online*, 2017, http://english.

manoramaonline.com/news/kerala/2017/11/01/gail-lng-pipeline-protest-kozhikode-police-lathicharge. html.

73. "Hill of Resistance," *Frontline* (Chennai, March 2015), http://www.frontline.in/the-nation/hill-of-resistance/article6951423. ece?css=print.
74. "RBI to Reveal Data of Total Deposits Post-Demonetisation after 30 June," *Livemint*, 2017, http://www. livemint.com/Politics/BHGtYscQGN2A9OrpDChpuO/RBI-to-reveal-data-of-total-deposits-post-demonetisation-aft. html.
75. "Villagers Protest against INO Project," *The Hindu*, March 29, 2015, http://www. thehindu.com/news/cities/Madurai/villagers-protest-against-ino-project/article7044565.ece.
76. Rajnath Singh Says 'Anti-National' Forces Not Able to Appreciate India's Economic Progress," *FIRSTPOST*, 2017, http://www.firstpost.com/world/rajnath-singh-says-anti-national-forces-not-able-to-appreciate-indias-economic-progress-4124569.html
77. Jecmon Jacob, "Intelligence Agencies Identify Maoist, Islamic Radical Support behind People's Protests in Kerala," *India Today*, 2017, http://indiatoday.intoday.in/story/kerala-intelligence-agencies-maoist-islamic-radical/1/982868. html.
78. S. Sharma, "Guns and Protests: Media Coverage of the Conflicts in the Indian State of Chhattisgarh" (Oxford: Reuters Institute for the study of Journalism, University of Oxford, 2012), http://reutersinstitute.politics.ox.ac.uk/fileadmin/documents/Publications/fellows__papers/2011-2012/Guns_and_Protests. pdf.
79. G Sampath, "Who Is Anti-National?," *The Hindu*, February 17, 2016, http://www. thehindu.com/opinion/op-ed/Who-is-an-anti-national/article14082785.ece.
80. P.K. Jain, Seema Gupta, and Surendra S. Yadav, *Public Sector Enterprises in India: The Impact of Disinvestment and Self Obligation on Financial Performance* (New Delhi: Springer, 2014).
81. "Master Database of All Past CPSE Disinvestments," *BSEPSU*, 2017, http://www. bsepsu.com/master_disinvestment1.asp?ord=fin_year, mnth_year.
82. "Public Enterprises Survey 2015-16" (New Delhi: Ministry of Heavy Industries and Public Enterprises, Government of India, 2016).
83. Amiya Kumar Bagchi, ed., *Democracy and Development: Proceedings of the IEA Conference Held in Barcelona, Spain* (New York, 1995).
84. Lisa Anderson, "Demystifying the Arab Spring Parsing the Differences Between Tunisia, Egypt, and Libya," *Foreign Affairs* 90, no. 3 (2011): 2-7.
85. Ethan B. Kapstein and Nathan Converse, "Why Democracies Fail," *Journal of Democracy* 19, no. 4 (2008): 57–68, doi:10. 1353/jod. 0. 0031.
86. Dexter Whitfield, *Public Services or Corporate Welfare: Rethinking the Nation State in the Global Economy* (London: Pluto Press, 2001).
87. J. Angresano, *A Corporate Welfare Economy* (New York: Routledge, 2016), https://books.google.co. in/books?id=bXePCwAAQBAJ.
88. Tasha Fairfield, *Private Wealth and Public Revenue in Latin America: Business Power and Tax Politics* (Cambridge: Cambridge University Press, 2015).

89. "Report of the Comptroller and Auditor General of India for the Year Ended March 2016," vol. 2 of 2017 (New Delhi: Comptroller and Auditor General of India, 2017).
90. "Govt Has Forgone Rs. 17.15 Lakh Crore Revenue due to Tax Incentives in the Last Three Financial Years," *The Indian Express*, July 19, 2016, http://indianexpress.com/article/business/economy/govt-forgoes-rs-17-15-lakh-crore-revenue-due-to-tax-incentives-in-the-last-three-financial-years-2923820/.
91. "Ex-Coal Secretary Gupta Convicted for Block Allocation Fraud," *The Hindu*, May 19, 2017, http://www. thehindu.com/news/national/coal-scam-case-special-court-convicts-gupta-others/article18502212. ece.
92. "Corruption in Armed Forces: How Extensive Is the Rot?," *FIRSTPOST*, 2012, http://www. firstpost.com/india/corruption-in-armed-forces-how-extensive-is-the-rot-388808. html.
93. "India to Acquire $2 Billion Nuclear Attack Submarine from Russia," *The Economic Times*, October 19, 2016, https://economictimes. indiatimes.com/news/defence/india-to-acquire-2-billion-nuclear-attack-submarine-from-russia/articleshow/54937354.cms.
94. "India Signs $8.8bn Deal to Buy 36 French Rafale Fighter Jets," *DAWN*, September 23, 2016, https://www. dawn.com/news/1285605.
95. "India, France Sign MoU for Construction of Six Nuclear Reactors at Jaitapur," *The Economic Times*, May 23, 2016, https://economictimes. indiatimes.com/industry/energy/power/india-france-sign-mou-for-construction-of-six-nuclear-reactors-at-jaitapur/articleshow/51529708. cms.
96. Nivedita Rao, "Demand for Grants 2017-18 Analysis: Human Resource Development" (New Delhi: PRS Legislative Research, 2017), http://www. prsindia. org/administrator/uploads/general/1488296976~~DfG 2017-18 Education. pdf.
97. "Public Enterprises Survey 2015-16.
98. "Alstom Delivers Its First Two Metro Train Sets to Chennai Metro in India," *Alstom*, 2014, http://www. alstom.com/press-centre/2014/2/alstom-delivers-its-first-two-metro-train-sets-to-chennai-metro-in-india/.
99. D. Raghunandan, "Does India Need a Bullet Train?," *The Hindu*, October 6, 2017, http://www. thehindu.com/opinion/op-ed/does-india-need-a-bullet-train/article19803252.ece.
100. "Policy on Adoption of Open Source Software for Government of India" (New Delhi: Ministry of Communication & Information Technology, Government of India, 2015), http://meity.gov. in/writereaddata/files/policy_on_adoption_of_oss.pdf.
101. "Indian Government Promoting Monopoly in Software Industry," *Free Software Foundation of India*, accessed November 11, 2017, http://fsf. org. in/news/indian-government-promoting-monopoly-in-software.
102. Neeraj Mahajan and Kavaljit Singh, *A Beginner's Guide to Indian Commodity Futures Markets* (New Delhi: Madhyam, 2015), http://www. madhyam.org.in/wp-content/uploads/2015/04/Commodity-Guide. pdf.
103. "Commodity-wise, Market-wise Daily Report on 10112017," *Government*

of India, 2017, http://www. agmarknet.nic.in/agnew/NationalBEnglish/CommodityWiseDailyReport2.aspx.

104. "Impact Evaluation & Socio-Economic Study of Bt Cotton" (New Delhi: Ministry of Agriculture, Government of India, 2016), http://www.nfsm.gov.in/Publicity/2016-17/Final Report-BT Cotton.pdf.

105. "National Consultations on Bt Brinjal A Primer on Concerns, Issues and Prospects" (Ministry of Environment & Forest, Government of India, n.d.), http://www.moef.nic.in/downloads/public-information/Bt Brinjal Primer.pdf.

106. Himakiran Anugula, "Banning Jallikattu Will Undermine Tamil Nadu's Indigenous Cattle Breeds," *The Wire*, 2017, https://thewire. in/19157/banning-jallikattu-will-decimate-indias-indigenous-cattle-breeds/.

107. Tanvi Deshpande, "State of Agriculture in India" (New Delhi: PRS Legislative Research, 2017).

108. Dhananjay Mahapatra, "Over 12,000 Farmer Suicides per Year, Centre Tells Supreme Court," *The Times of India*, May 3, 2017, https://timesofindia.indiatimes.com/india/over-12000-farmer-suicides-per-year-centre-tells-supreme-court/articleshow/58486441.cms.

9

Role of State Administration in Accelerating Farmers' Income in Odisha

Soumya Sagarika Sahoo and *Padmalaya Mahapatra*

Introduction

Odisha is largely a rural and an agrarian economy. Close to 83 per cent of its people live in rural areas and about 61.8 per cent of its 17.5 million workforce is employed in agriculture.[1] The sector contributes about 18 per cent to the state's GDP. The state has a gross cropped area of about 8 million hectares, 46 per cent of which is double-cropped.[2] The state is divided into 10 agro-climatic zones and it suffers from frequent droughts and floods and sometimes both in the same year.

The State is not only striving for increasing farm incomes, but it is also committed to secure the health and well-being of its farmers. A State Plan scheme "Biju Krushak Kalyan Yojana (BKKY)" was, accordingly launched in the year 2013 to provide health and accident insurance coverage of up to Rupees One Lakh to 55.00 lakh farmer families. While ensuring greater resources are provided to the agriculture sector, the State has also made sure greater transparency and accountability in implementation of schemes and programmes through several e-Governance projects and and web-based monitoring programmes.

State of Agriculture in Odisha

Odisha is largely a rural and an agrarian economy. Close to 83 per cent of its people live in rural areas and about 61.8 per cent of its 17.5 million workforce is employed in agriculture. The sector contributes about 18 per cent to the state's GDP. The state has a gross cropped area of about 8 million hectares, 46 per cent of which is double-cropped. Paddy is the main crop and covers about 3.89 million hectares (for the triennium ending 2017-18). The state is divided into 10 agro-climatic zones and it suffers from frequent droughts and floods, and sometimes both, in the same year inflicting colossal damage to the Agri-sector. Despite this, agriculture has proven to be one of the most resilient sectors of the state.

Agricultural GDP

In 16 years since the beginning of this century (2000-01 to 2016-17), Odisha's agricultural GDP nearly doubled in real terms, clocking an average annual growth rate of about 4.5 per cent, higher than the all-India average of 3.1 per cent. The state accounts for 3 per cent of India's agricultural GDP.

Table 9.1: Contribution of Different Sectors to GDP of India

Sl. No.	*Sector*	*%*
1	*Primary Sector*	18.57
1.1	Agriculture, forestry and fishing	15.87
1.2	Mining and quarrying	2.70
2	*Secondary Sector*	27.03
2.1	Manufacturing	16.83
2.2	Electricity, gas, water supply and other utility services	2.67
2.3	Construction	7.54
3	*Tertiary Sector*	54.40
3.1	Trade, hotels, transport, communication and services related to broadcasting	18.62
3.2	Financial, real estate and professional services	20.96
3.3	Public Administration, defence and other services	14.82
	GVA at basic prices	**100.00**

Theoretical Perspective

Bhupinder and Santosh (2010) analysed the diversification of agriculture in Haryana. Primary data was collected from a total of 420 respondents covering three districts, six blocks and six villages. They have chosen variables for the study based on the problems expressed by sample farmers. Farmers have reported problems like price, number of regulated markets, transport, finance, literacy, irrigation, etc. The major problems faced by the farmers were price fluctuation and finance related aspects.

Bhat and Shah (2011) studied the Land Use and Cropping Pattern in Jammu and Kashmir. The State depends on subsistence farming without any surplus, but from the last few decades a great change has taken place in the variety of crops. The cropping pattern is influenced by physical, technological and institutional factors like land reformation, consolidation of holdings and credit facilities, price structure, procurement policies and storage facilities.

Joydeep Saha (2013) studied the crop diversification in Indian agriculture with Special Reference to Emerging Crops. He revealed that crop diversification is found to be continuing over the time period and most of the states are associated with this process. He also proposed that although food crop dependency persists strongly, commercial and horticultural crops are emerging significantly.

Mishra and Pankaj (2015) studied the agricultural land resource utilization in Trans-Yamuna region in Allahabad District, Uttar Pradesh. They proposed that, Indian agriculture occupies a prominent place not only because it supplies food to the people, raw materials to the industries and various items of export trade, but also because it constitutes an integral part of our culture and tradition and the general fabric of life in the country.

Objectives of the Study

- To find out the role of the State or Central Government in accelerating farmers' income.
- To analyse the strategies to accelerate farmers' income in agriculture sector.
- To find out main obstacles in growth of agriculture sector.

Research Questions

1. Is the State Government capable enough to accelerate farmers' income?
2. Are Government Policies or Strategies successful in reaching farmers?

Method of the Study

This chapter is based on both primary and secondary data.

Primary Data: A total of around 1000 farmers of Harichandanpur block of Keonjhar district of Odisha are selected and their involvement in agricultural activities, their income out of their agricultural activities and through marketing of their produces or Government assistances for different agricultural activities will be examined through questionnaire/survey method.

Secondary Data: Data has been collected from different Government reports like Economic Survey, Agricultural Policy, Policy Visions etc., journals, newspapers, publications, books and websites.

Farmers' Income

An average Odisha farmer earned about Rs. 7,731 per month, i.e. about Rs. 92,772 per year.[3] In 2002-03, the average monthly income was Rs.10,627, which means that in 13 years between 2002-03 and 2015-16, Odisha farmer's incomes grew more than seven times or at a compound annual growth rate (CAGR) of 16.5 per cent in nominal terms and 8.4 per cent in real terms. During the same period, the all-India average income of farmers grew from Rs.2,115 to Rs.8,931, i.e. at a CAGR of 11.7 per cent in nominal and 3.7 per cent in real terms.

Even though the absolute level of Odisha farmer incomes (in 2015-16) is lower than all-India average, the rate at which these incomes grew between 2002-03 and 2015-16 is more than double India's average growth rate. In fact, a state-wise comparison of these growth rates reveal that Odisha farmer incomes grew the fastest in this period in the entire country.

In addition to this, farmers' incomes in Odisha increased much faster than even the rate at which its own agricultural GDP increased. Between 2002-03 and 2015-16, its agricultural GDP increased at a CAGR of 3.7 per cent and its farmers' incomes grew at more than double that rate at 8.4 per cent.

These are encouraging signs. It is evident that the state is placed on a high growth path in agriculture and it is important that the Odisha government builds on these successes, recognises the constraints and formulates a policy to overcome the challenges and harness the potential and opportunities that fast-emerging markets within the state and outside provide while keeping the policy focus steadfast on farmers' well-being.

The average annual growth rate in real terms in agriculture as well as its allied sectors has remained static in the last six years, in turn impacting farmers' income, the Economic Survey 2019-20, released on January 31, 2020, has said.

The annual growth rate in real terms in agriculture and its allied sectors was 2.88 per cent from 2014-15 to 2018-19, according to the Survey. The estimated growth rate in 2019-20 is 2.9 per cent.

Farmers should be incentivised to adopt water-efficient practices in order to avert a looming water crisis, the Survey said. It called for shifting the focus in agriculture to 'irrigation water productivity' from 'land productivity'.[4]

Sources of Growth in Farmers' Income

Doubling of farmers' income till 2022-23 over the base year of 2015-16, requires annual growth of 10.41 per cent in farmers' income.[5] This implies that the on-going and previously achieved rate of growth in farm income has to be sharply accelerated. Therefore, strong measures will be needed to harness all possible sources of growth in farmers' income within as well as outside the agriculture sector. The major sources of growth operating within agriculture sector are:

- Improvement in productivity;
- Resource use efficiency or saving in cost of production;
- Increase in cropping intensity; and
- Diversification towards high value crops.

The sources outside the agriculture include:

- Shifting cultivators from farm to non-farm occupations; and
- Improvement in terms of trade for farmers or real prices received by farmers.

The possibilities of doubling farmers' income in real terms from above sources are explored in the following sections.

(i) Increase in Agricultural Productivity

There are two sources to increase in agricultural output, viz. area and productivity. Due to rising demand for land for non-agricultural uses and already high share or arable land in total geographical area of the country, further expansion in area under cultivation is not feasible. Rather there is a decline of about 10 lakh hectare, as agricultural land has been diverted to non-agricultural uses since the year 2004-05. Therefore, agricultural output has to be increased through improvement in productivity per unit of land. Productivity of most of the crops in the country is low and there is considerable scope to raise it.

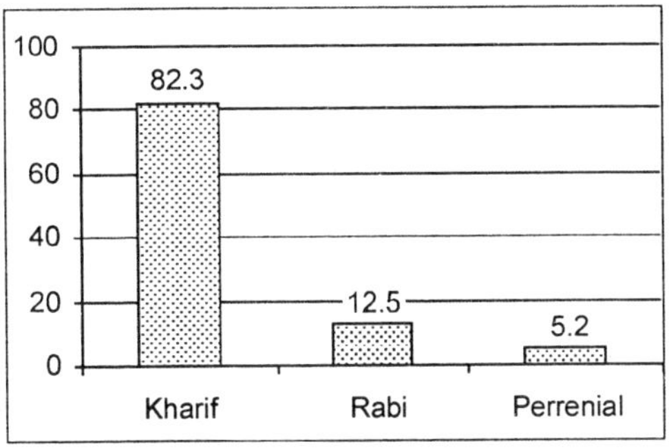

Season-wise Area Coverage

(ii) Improvement in Total Factor Productivity

The improvement in Total Factor Productivity (TFP) is an important source of output growth which directly contributes to cost saving and thus increase in income. TFP is the portion of output not explained by the amount of inputs used in the production.

(iii) Increase in Crop Intensity

India has two main crop growing seasons namely, Kharif and Rabi, which make it possible to cultivate two crops a year on the same land. With availability of irrigation and new technology it has become possible to raise short duration crops after the main kharif and main rabi season.[6]

Strategy for Improving Farmers' Income

The sources of growth in output and income can be put in four categories:

1. Development initiatives including infrastructure;
2. Technology;
3. Policies; and
4. Institutional mechanism.

Development Initiatives

Some recent development initiatives of the Central Government aiming to raise output and reduce cost include *Pradhan Mantri Krishi Sinchai*

Yojana, *Soil Health Card* and *Paramparagat Krishi Vikash Yojana*. These programmes need to be implemented in time to get the desired effect of farmers' income.

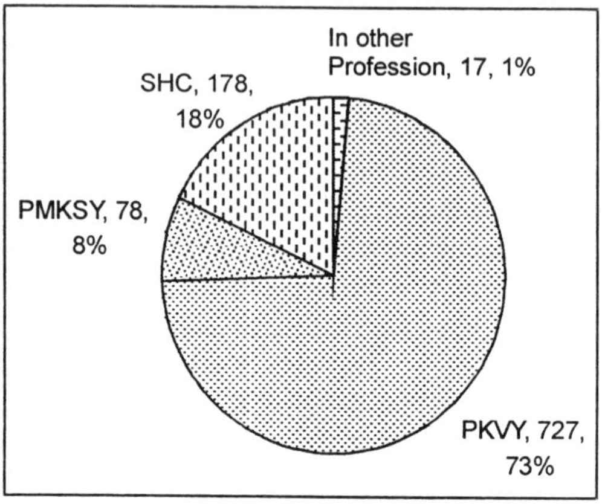

Central Government Project Beneficiary

Odisha is the largest producer of sweet potato in India. It generates the largest Value Of Output (VOO)[5] in India in the case of cowpea, sunhemp and pumpkin. Its VOO ranks second in India in the case of brinjal, sunflower, cabbage, jujube (ber), bitter gourd, lemon and pointed gourd (parmal). It also ranks high in the production of okra, cauliflower, and cashew.

The hard work of the entrepreneurial Odisha farmer, complemented with progressive interventions by government, and its visionary leadership, has catapulted Odisha agriculture to its present stature.

Some of the pioneering steps taken by Government of Odisha include the following:

1. *Consistent growth in funding for agriculture*: In 2018-19, Rs.17,937 crore was allocated for the sector.
2. *Exclusive budget for agriculture and setting up of an agriculture cabinet*: The state has an exclusive budget for agriculture and an independent agricultural cabinet that oversees programme implementation and inter-department co-ordination.
3. *Reformed agricultural input delivery systems*: The Department of Agriculture and Farmers' Empowerment undertook a multi-pronged approach to reform the agricultural input delivery system in the state. From direct benefit transfer (DBT) in seeds (over 3.5

lakh farmers benefited in 2017-18), to subsidisation of farm machinery (about 40,000 farmers received subsidies for farm mechanisation), innovations in delivering irrigation access through the Jalanidhi-I scheme (due to which the state's irrigation coverage increased to 43 per cent); to harnessing technology to improve input delivery, the department undertook to reform input management and delivery system.

4. *Real-time monitoring of all the key operational areas and schemes of the department*: Institutionalisation of a decision support system has helped officials monitor real-time progress and deliver on key operational areas like seed supply, fertilizer supply, PMFBY coverage, rainfall, schemes etc. *via* fast, data-backed decision-making.
5. *Developing inter-departmental convergence at the block level:* This was done through Farm Information and Advisory Centre (FIAC) meetings where officials meet every fortnight and resolve problems faced by farmers.
6. Innovation awards, called the "Mukhya Mantri Abhinav Krushi Jantrapati Samman Yojana" for farmers who innovate in the use of farm implements have been instituted at the district and state level.
7. Mukhyamantri Krushi Udyog Yojana (MKUY) has been launched to support entrepreneurs in setting up their own industrial units.
8. The department has started a customized Agro-advisory service under the name of "**AMA KRUSHI**". More than 4 lakh farmers across Odisha have been profiled under the service and received the weekly advisory over IVRS. The service currently provides agro-advisory service on 11 crops and answer questions for 40+ crops. It also supplements the IVR service with platforms like Community Radio, WhatsApp, SMS to reach the last mile.

In addition, initiatives in extension such as making Village Agricultural Workers (VAW)/Agriculture Overseers (AO)/Horticulture Extension Workers (HEW)/Soil Conservation Extension Workers (SCEW)/Livestock Inspector (LI) available at farmer counselling centres at GP/Panchayati Raj Institution (PRI) office on designated days to provide counselling to farmers, organisation of Krushak Sampark Mela at the block level, district level Krishi Mahotsav and state level exhibitions-*cum*-farmers' fairs and Krushak Sachetanata Karyakrama for exposure visits of farmers etc., have helped in building community-led initiatives.

Women farmers have also received special attention. Efforts were made to reduce drudgery and promote efficiency by involving institutions like ICAR's Central Institute for Women in Agriculture (CIWA) and Odisha University of Agriculture and Technology (OUAT) among others.

Focus on traditional and mega schemes aimed at farmers' welfare and knowledge development for better agricultural practices also gained momentum since 2013. Schemes like KALIA, credit guarantee schemes etc., are innovative schemes that have successfully provided financial stability to farmers. MoUs with seven international agencies and five national agencies, setting up of research institutes (high altitude research station of OUAT in Koraput, Jute Research Station in Kendrapara and a Sugarcane Research Station in Nayagarh) and agriculture polytechnics (10) have provided crucial improvement in technical manpower for agriculture, availability of quality seeds and cultivation practices.

In addition, the department undertook new initiatives to promote monetisation of farm produce. The department's five-pronged approach in that regard included:

1. *Diversification of the production basket*: Incentivising non-paddy crops (pulses, oilseeds, maize, cotton and horticultural crops) under the state plan, seed reserve policy for non-paddy crops, assured procurement for pulses and oilseeds and millets under the price support scheme (PSS);
2. *Promoting post-harvest management through infrastructure investment*: Key initiatives included setting up of international standard assaying facility by NABL, the availability of a food safety officer at Paradip port and the creation of 10 assaying laboratories;
3. *Launching the Farmer Producer Organization (FPO) Policy* for linking all farmers, mainly ones sowing high value crops like fruits, vegetables, flowers, spice, etc., to the markets.
4. *Promotion of tribal regions by creating agriculture production clusters (APCs):* About 1 lakh farmers in 20-25 production groups are being created to practice market-linked production of identified crops, especially horticulture crops; SAFAL in co-ordination with Odisha Livelihood Mission (OLM) workers worked to deliver better price discovery in mango; and gram unnati promoted demand-driven production in coconut.
5. *Launching the Organic Farming Policy* to promote organic farming and provide a market for the products.

Policy/Scheme	Objective	Progress
KALIA 2018: The scheme aims to accelerate agricultural prosperity and reduce poverty in State and covers 92 per cent of cultivators, loanee as well as non-loanee farmers, share-croppers and landless agricultural labourers: • Support provided through grant of INR 5,000 per family per season. • Vulnerable cultivators to receive a lump-sum financial assistance of INR 10,000 per family. • Life insurance support: cover of INR 2 lakh with a nominal premium. • Interest free crop loans up to INR 50,000.	KALIA 2018: The scheme aims to accelerate agricultural prosperity and reduce poverty in State and covers 92 per cent of cultivators, loanee as well as non-loanee farmers, share croppers and landless agricultural labourers: • Support provided through grant of INR 5,000 per family per season. • Vulnerable cultivators to receive a lump-sum financial assistance of INR 10,000 per family. • Life insurance support: cover of INR 2 lakh with a nominal premium. • Interest free crop loans up to INR 50,000.	KALIA 2018: The scheme aims to accelerate agricultural prosperity and reduce poverty in State and covers 92 per cent of cultivators, loanee as well as non-loanee farmers, share-croppers and landless agricultural labourers: • Support provided through grant of INR 5,000 per family per season. • Vulnerable cultivators to receive a lump-sum financial assistance of INR 10,000 per family Life insurance support: cover of INR 2 lakh with a nominal premium. • Interest free crop loans up to INR 50,000.
Organic Farming Policy, 2018	Policy aims to promote organic farming to improve soil fertility and productivity, judicious use of water resources and to encourage farming with use of local resources.	• Default organic areas to be targeted to intensify agro-ecological approaches. • State intends to bring 2 lakh hectares of agricultural area under organic farming State interventions through knowledge dissemination, soil health management, promotion of seed sovereignty, among others.
Odisha Farmer Producer Organisations (FPOs) Policy, 2018	Objective of the policy is to generate higher returns to farming communities by establishment of FPOs; and make Odisha the most sought after investment	• Farmers will be eligible for financial and capacity building assistance for limited purpose of implementation of product-specific cluster/commercial crop cycles.

	destination for agribusiness and food processing.	• FPOs will be given priority for access to markets and linking to market aggregators. • Single Window Clearance System to be made applicable to FPOs for issue of licenses. • Land will be made available to FPOs at a concessional rate or free.
Agriculture Production Cluster Project, 2018	Project for promotion of Agriculture production cluster to trigger growth in farm sector with the objective of sustainable doubling of income of small and marginal farmers. Total 30 APCs will be promoted involving around 650 micro APCs covering 1 lakh farmers.	• Groups will be facilitated to practice synchronized market linked production of identified crops (especially horticulture), covering around 40 acres in a contiguous manner. • Livestock rearing is also planned with around 40 of the families in these clusters. • Depending upon the commodity, aggregation centres will be developed for grading, sorting, packaging and temporary storage before transporting.
State Agriculture Policy, 2013	Bring in a shift from subsistence agriculture to profitable, commercial, agriculture. Enhance productivity of crops through seed replacement, water management, farm mechanisation. Encourage crop substitution, focus on organic farming.	• Produce 12 lakh ha quintal of certified seeds through promotion of private seed entrepreneurs. Promotion of participatory irrigation management through Pani Panchayat system; assured irrigation for at least 35 of cultivable land in each block. Emphasis on 'balanced fertilization' through Integrated Nutrient Management. Development of suitable farm machinery, technical know-how training for farmers

Source: Odisha Economic Survey 2018-19.

Odisha's Agriculture and Farmers' Empowerment Department, in line with the vision outlined in the Odisha Agriculture Policy, 2013, ensured the holistic development and progress of all aspects of the state's agriculture. SAMRUDHI—Agricultural Policy, 2020, Odisha builds on these achievements. But to harness the complete potential of the state's resources in an inclusive and sustainable manner, necessitates identifying challenges and constraints.

The major constraints in Odisha's agriculture have been identified as follows:

1. *Shrinking land and landholding size*: Increasing pressure on land has led to fragmentation resulting in the average land holding size falling to 0.95 ha in 2015-16 from 1.89 ha in 1970-71. The impact of natural calamities additionally has expanded fallow lands in the state. In 2015-16, about 1.7 million hectares of land was classified as fallow of which 0.7 million hectares are permanent fallows.
2. *Falling number of cultivators and growing landless*: With increasing fragmentation of land, the total number of cultivators has shrunk in the state. Between Census 2001 and 2011, Odisha's agricultural labour force increased from 9.2 million to 10.8 million. While the number of people who are cultivators (or the number of people who own land) fell from 4.2 million to 4.1 million, the number of labourers who are landless increased from 5 million to 6.7 million. From 46 per cent, the share of cultivators in state's total agricultural workforce fell to 38 per cent.
3. *Huge intra-state disparity in farmers' incomes*: Among Odisha's 30 districts, farmers in 17 districts earned lower incomes than the state average. For example, a Jharsuguda farmer earned five times more than a Keonjhar farmer.
4. *Gap between irrigation coverage and cropping intensities*: There is a gap between irrigation coverage and level of cropping intensities (proportion of area taking more than one crop) reported in the state. Higher irrigation coverage is expected to result in higher cropping intensities. But despite high levels of irrigation coverage (as a percentage of gross cropped area), cropping intensities in districts like Bargarh, Malkangiri, Koraput, Sambalpur and Bhadrak are low. Then there are districts like Nayagarh, Angul and Deogarh, where despite low levels of irrigation coverage, cropping intensity is high.

5. *High but volatile agricultural GDP growth*: Between 2000-01 and 2016-17, Odisha's agricultural GDP grew at an average annual rate of 4.5 per cent compared to India's average of 3.1 per cent during the period. Analysis reveals that Odisha's growth rate is more volatile than the all-India rate.[7] The high volatility is partially explained by the impact of weather and climatic variability on agricultural growth.
6. *Low productivity per hectare*: While Odisha's productivity in major crops like paddy, groundnut, gram, lentils, etc., have improved over time, it is still below those of some of the best states in India. There is also a large yield gap between the different districts in the state, indicating a gap in resources, diffusion of technology and sharing of knowledge.
7. *Highly labour-intensive production processes*: Shrinking landholding sizes and low levels of absolute incomes restrict the investment capability of a farmer; consequently, the dominant role of labour in the cultivation process in the state for most crops has continued over the years. Subsidising the purchase of farm machines and equipment has also not resulted in higher sales. The custom hiring centres (CHC) too have not been able to drastically improve farmer's access to farm machinery and equipment.
8. *High dependence on weather and climate*: During the last five years, variability in production (mainly of paddy) points to the need for more effective climate resilient strategies. While the importance of paddy to farmers in the state cannot be overlooked, the productivity of large areas under paddy cultivation is low, resulting in very low returns to the farmers. Some districts cultivate paddy during the rabi season as well, depending on the availability of irrigation, but productivity is low, implying sub-optimal benefits from irrigation due to improper choice of crops.
9. *Growing gap between Odisha's demand (consumption basket) and supply (production basket)*: The state's economy is growing fast and, as is the trend elsewhere, the consumption basket is changing. Consumers are increasingly demanding more pulses, vegetables, dairy, eggs, fish and meat. This should ideally have resulted in changing the composition of the state's production basket; however, a large part of the eggs, pulses and meat that are consumed by the state are imported from neighbouring states.
10. *Low seed replacement ratio*: The SRR for most crops grown in

the state, barring paddy, are lower than the national average as well as below the desired level of 33 per cent, especially in the case of self-pollinated crops.

To build on the strengths, while addressing the concerns and keeping farmers' welfare as its central theme, the SAMRUDHI—Agricultural Policy 2020, Odisha vision is presented next.

Vision

To harness the potential of Odisha's agricultural sector in a sustainable manner, aimed at continuously raising farmers' incomes and welfare while ensuring nutritional security.

Objective

This policy will focus on farmers' well-being and aim is to achieve the following objectives:

1. Ensuring continuous growth in farmers' income.
2. Making the growth process inclusive of small and marginal farmers, and landless farmers.
3. Ensuring sustainable, stable and scalable agricultural growth.

Building on KALIA

In a pioneering effort to improve farmer's income and welfare, Odisha undertook the implementation of its flagship scheme for farmers called Krushak Assistance for Livelihood and Income Augmentation (KALIA). The scheme was launched in December 2018 and was designed to deliver an unconditional cash transfer directly to small and marginal farmers, sharecroppers and landless agricultural households. Up to a total of 75 lakh farmer families will directly benefit from this scheme.

Under the scheme, there are three types of beneficiaries/benefits:

1. *Small and marginal farmers, including sharecroppers*, are entitled to receive financial assistance as per KALIA scheme. This is an unconditional payment and the farmer gets it just before each cropping season to support his agricultural activities.
2. *Landless agricultural households*: To handhold landless

agricultural households to help create sustainable livelihoods, the state government, under the KALIA scheme, has committed to giving financial assistance to the selected agricultural landless agricultural household. The payment will be made in three instalments. While the first instalment is unconditional, the subsequent two instalments are conditional upon the progress made by the landless in livelihood activity. The government also undertakes training and monitoring through its network of VAWs/Aos/HEWs/SCEWs/LIs to ensure that the landless are genuinely helped to develop the livelihood activities they choose to pursue.

3. *Insurance cover*: The component will provide the following insurance cover to cultivators and landless agricultural labourers, who are primarily dependent on agriculture as the main activity:
   a. Life insurance cover of Rs. 2.00 lakh will be provided to all savings bank account holders between 18 and 50 years. The Government of Odisha will bear the farmers' share of the annual premium.
   b. Personal accident cover of Rs.2.00 lakh for all savings bank account holders aged between 18 and 50 years. The Government of Odisha will bear the farmer's share of premium.
   c. In respect of beneficiaries whose age is between 51 and 70 years, the entire amount towards annual premium will be borne by the Government of Odisha.

Organic Agriculture

To respond to challenges from climate change and to enhance farmer incomes, Department of Agriculture and Farmers' Empowerment released the Odisha Organic Farming Policy, 2018. The aim is to undertake 360-degree development of organic farming in the state and increase the acreage from 20,800 hectares currently to at least 200,000 hectares in the next five years.

Sizable parts of the state, particularly those located in rain-fed, dryland and hilly areas, are prone to weather and climate vagaries. Increasing agricultural productivity and farmers' income in these areas has always been a daunting challenge for policy-makers. Due to various factors including geographical location and the use of traditional cultivation practices, the existing level of fertilizer and pesticide use is low in these areas, i.e. they are 'naturally organic' areas. These areas are amenable to a quick shift to 'organic agriculture' and will be identified as clusters to promote organic farming. Soil health cards will help identify these areas.

Under the scheme PKVY, by the Government of Odisha, 80 per cent of our study are a are covered and farmers are being trained Organic Cultivation, Process of Low On-Farm Input Preparation, by experts, like scientists from KVKs and RRTTS, Agriculturists, Organic Experts etc.

Farmers are getting assistance under the scheme to prepare inputs, purchase of seeds etc. Assistance is also to hire other agricultural implements under the component Custom Hiring Centre (CHC). Government is also promoting formation of Farmer Producer Company (FPO/FPC) by providing assistance to the farmers, by which farmers can get market linkages through these FPOs/FPCs. Farmer awareness programmes and Exposure visits are being arranged under such schemes.

Component	*Assistance Per Acre*
Input Assistance	Rs. 3300/Ac.
Preparation of Vermi Compost Unit	Rs. 2500/Ac.
Remuneration of Lead Resource Person	Rs. 4000/Month
Formation of FPO/FPC	Rs. 20000/Group
Transportation of Organic Produces	Rs. 6200/Group

Other such assistance is being provided to farmers directly through Direct Beneficiary Transfer (DBT) to their account so that farmers can be beneficial.

While encouraging a shift to organic farming, the emphasis will be on market driven production programmes where the produce can be sold at premium prices. Systems will be put in place to ensure easy certification of such organic produce.

Integrated Farming

A large number of farmers do integrated farming in a traditional way. Farmers, who are able to combine agriculture with dairying, animal husbandry, poultry, fishery etc., are able to generate more income for themselves. However, most programmes of the government are crop or activity specific.

Markets, Infrastructure, Value-chains and Processing

Ensuring timely and sufficient access to transparent and deep markets and to supporting infrastructure to all farmers will be a guiding goalpost of this Policy. Policy's thrust to produce higher quality and higher quantity per hectare will be concurrently supported by policy incentives that will deliver deeper, and efficient markets. Efforts will be made to deepen access to fair and remunerative markets and to bring transparency in the system. Supporting infrastructure that involves storages, warehouses, logistical support will be ensured while creating a conducive and a stable policy environment to encourage private participation wherever possible.

Research, Development and Extension

The Odisha University of Agriculture and Technology (OUAT) will focus on more applied and adaptive research in agriculture and allied field, and develop new knowledge for improving productivity, nutritional security and income of farmers under climatic change while taking care of the natural resources and its sustenance. It will also focus on producing quality technical manpower.

With the focus of enhancing farmer incomes, this Policy aims to redesign and reorient the State's Research and Development (R&D) machinery. In that regard, the Policy recommends following changes.

To drive this vision, following interventions are envisaged:

1. Research priority areas for each block will be identified by OUAT in consultation with various ICAR agencies and the state's extension machinery together with farmers.
2. It will be ensured that all new knowledge is relevant and sensitive particularly to needs of state's small and marginal farmers and women farmers.
3. Paddy is the main crop of the state and is a water guzzler, research will focus on bringing the water consumption per kilogram of paddy to half its current level in the next five years.
4. Suitable agro-ecological agronomic innovations such as System of Rice Intensification (SRI), Non-pesticidal Management (NPM), Integrated Pest Management (IPM), Zero Budget Natural Farming (ZBNF), biodynamic farming, organic agriculture, conservation agriculture, intercropping, poly-cropping etc., will be studied and evaluated for adoption particularly in rain-fed areas.

5. Role of Krishi Vigyan Kendras (KVK) will be reoriented to support local needs.
6. OUAT students will be required to spend a prescribed minimum period in farmers' fields as part of the curriculum with support from the government.

Women in Agriculture

Nearly 48 per cent of all labourers in Odisha are female, i.e. 9 lakhs out of 21 lakh agricultural labourers and 18 per cent of all cultivators are women. Women are engaged heavily in all phases of the agricultural cycle, i.e. sowing, intercultural activities, harvesting and post-harvest management. Women-owned landholdings are limited and uneconomical, resulting in their higher involvement as agricultural labourers.[8] There are an estimated 500,000 single landless women in Odisha. They will be treated as a special target group for development intervention.

Concluding Observations

Farmers' income is increased when productivity goes up, cost of production comes down, risk is reduced, post-harvest loss is minimized and commodities produced get a remunerative price.[9] It should also improve income from allied activities to agriculture. Aiming to boost Indian Agriculture, the Government of India has set a goal to double the farmers' income by the year 2022.

Average agricultural productivity and farmers income of Odisha is low as compared to other states in the country.

- To increase crop productivity, quality and judicious use of inputs such as water, seeds, fertilizer and pesticides need to be improved with efficient use of modern technology and diversification of enterprises.
- To increase income of farmers, a range of strategies (Economic, Technological, Infrastructural/Information, Political/Policy and Social) need to be adopted to transform the current production-driven cropping system to income-driven farming system and reduce the disparity among farmers of different regions of India.
- Agricultural research should be re-oriented with farmers' participatory approach to unshackle the vicious circle of poverty and drudgery and fulfil the aspirations of resource-poor, smallholder farmers.

- The state should enhance its investments on agricultural research and development to achieve the target of doubling farmers' income and address the growing challenges of resources degradation, escalating input crisis and costs with overarching effects of climate change.
- The State Government should take steps to lessen middlemen so that farmer can get better price for their marketable produces.
- Doubling farmers' income is quite challenging but it is attainable. Three-pronged strategy focused on: (i) development initiatives, (ii) technological, and (iii) policy reforms in agriculture is needed to double farmers' income.

NOTES

1. Census 2011.
2. Cropping intensity estimated from state government data.
3. NABARD NAFIS 2015-16.
4. Economic Survey 2019-20.
5. NITI Ayog (2017), Doubling Farmers' Income, Rationale, Strategy, Prospects, and Action Plan.
6. Some crops like sugarcane, apple, mango etc., are perennial and they occupy land throughout the year. Their share in net cultivated area remains small.
7. Between 2000-01 and 2016-17, the coefficient of variation of Odisha's agricultural GDP growth was estimated at 2.42 against a coefficient of 1.33 at the all-India level.
8. S.S. Sahoo (2019), Feminization of Agriculture: Changing Trends In Indian Agriculture, presented in 2nd South Asia Conference on Multidisciplinary Research (SAMR'19), at Sri Lanka.
9. Indian Council of Agricultural Research (2018), *Doubling Farmers' Income by 2022.*

REFERENCES

Birthal, P.S., Negi, D.S. and Roy, D. (2017), Enhancing Farmers' Income: Who to Target and How?, *Policy Paper No. 30*, ICAR-National Institute of Agricultural Economics and Policy Research, New Delhi.

Chand, Ramesh, NITI Ayog, (2017), *Doubling Farmers' Income, Rationale, Strategy, Prospects, and Action Plan.*

Directorate of Agriculture & Food Production, Government of Odisha, (2014-15), Status of Agriculture In Odisha.

Draft Agriculture Policy 2019.

Odisha Organic Agriculture Policy 2018.

Paroda, R.S. (2017) Strategy paper on "Indian Agriculture for Achieving Sustainable Development Goals". *Trust for Advancement of Agricultural Sciences*, New Delhi, p. 28.

Paroda, R.S., (2017), "Strategy for Doubling Farmers' Income".

Puspalak, S., Pathak, H., Indian Council of Agricultural Research, (2018), *Doubling Farmers' Income by 2022.*

S.S. Sahoo, (2019), Feminization of Agriculture: Changing Trends in Indian Agriculture, presented in 2nd South Asia Conference on Multidisciplinary Research (SAMR'19), at Sri Lanka.

SAMRUDHI-Agriculture Policy 2020.

PART 2

Governance, Gender and Subaltern Resistance

10

Economic Status and Living Standards of Agricultural Women Workers in Visakhapatnam District of Andhra Pradesh

D. Pulla Rao

In the lower socio-economic level of the society, women do more hazardous manual labour than men. Women do more than half of the agricultural works in India. Still men are considered to be the bread winners. This sense of women being inferior is passed on from one generation through psychological conditionings. The most widespread and de-humanizing discriminations and assault against women are on the psychological level. The female psyche is being crushed at the very childhood. The female psyche is brutalized long before bodily violence is inflicted on her. They are conditioned to accept inferior positions in society. Women from childhood undergo a slow unconscious process of destructive or denial of their self-worth. Society, through a process of conditioning, creates in girls at home and in school certain thinking patterns, which ascribed to the female sex an inferior status.

Besides, society gradually trains them to make this value system their own. Usually baby girls are given bangles, anklets etc. thus communicating a sense of fragility. Another result of the social conditioning is that man either as father; brother or husband considers women as socio-economic gift of his household. A woman's value judged, not so much in terms of her worth as a person with rights and dignity as in terms of her utility to man. Expression of this mentality is found in different language and society. For example, in national language Hindi, girl is called '*paraya dhan*' and boy '*apana dhan*'. Any assessment of the status of women has to start from the social framework, social structures, cultural norms and value systems that influence social expectations regarding the behaviour of both men and women and determine women's roles and their position in the society.

The condition of women is more miserable in the rural India with respect to various socio-economic aspects.

Rural poverty is one of the important characteristics of India and nearly 45 per cent of rural people are below poverty line. Most of them are just surviving with day-to-day earnings. If we take International poverty line (1994) into consideration in India there were 47 per cent of the population at below $1 a day category and 87.5 per cent at below $2 at a day category. Under such circumstances, within the family, the worst sufferers are needless to say women and girl children. For this category of women, neither credit nor skill training is accessible. Better health care and higher educational opportunities are far reaching dreams for their children and there is no need to say about the status of girl child in such families. She (girl child) is treated as a "silent lamb" born to suffer all evils in the male dominated society. So far much has not been done for this vulnerable sub culture of the society.

Indian society has been bound by culture and tradition since ancient times. The patriarchal system and the gender stereotypes in the family and society have always showed a preference for the male child. Sons were regarded as a means of social security and women remained under male domination. Due to her subordinated position, she has suffered years of discrimination, exploitation and subjugation. She became the victim of several evils like child marriage, Sati, polygamy, Purdah system, female infanticide, forced pregnancy, rape etc. In such incidents/recorded cases surprisingly mother-in-law are also taking active part (forgetting the fact that they are also women and some time back they also played daughter-in-law role).

The population for 2011 Census information shows that Visakhapatnam district had a population of 42.8 lakh and the sex ratio (Females for 1000 males) was found to be 1003 in 2011 as against 990 in 1981 and 1010 in 1971 respectively. Density of population is very high in Visakhapatnam district which is 384 and Andhra Pradesh whereas it is low as compared to 1971, 1981, 1991, and 2001 censuses respectively. The literacy rate in Visakhapatnam district has increased from 18.58 per cent in 1971 to 60.0 per cent in 1991. In the state as a whole the literacy has increased from 24.57 per cent in 1971 to 60.47 per cent in 2011. The decennial growth rate of population during 1991-01 in Visakhapatnam district is 15.36 per cent as against 27.50 per cent during 1981-1991 and 11.89 per cent during 2001-2011. As a whole Andhra Pradesh, the decennial growth rate is 11.10 per cent during 1991-2001.

The literacy levels in the selected Visakhapatnam district is very nearer to the state average. This is due to number of different categories of educational institutions are more available in the Visakhapatnam district. Even the indicators explaining the extent of health facilities are available more in the Visakhapatnam district.

The main focus of the study is laid on analysing the different issues relating to economic status and living standards of the agriculture women workers and to examine the inter-area variations in the selected agriculture women worker households in the relatively advanced Pendurthi mandal and relatively interior Devarapalli mandals in the Visakhapatnam district in Andhra Pradesh.

The Visakhapatnam district is selected for the study due to the fact that the district has higher proportion of rural population. The relatively advanced Pendurthi mandal and relatively interior Devarapalli mandals are selected from the Visakhapatnam district purposively to examine the inter-mandal variations. Also these two mandals are selected for the study because they are the rural mandals that are having a high proportion of rural population.

Four villages are randomly selected from each selected mandal depending upon the higher concentration of rural population and a total of eight villages are selected for the study. From the relatively interior Devarapalli mandal the villages Raiwada, Nagayyapeta, Thenugupudi and Kasipuram are selected from the interior parts of the mandal. Similarly from the Pendurthi mandal another four villages Rampuram, Pinagadi, Pedagadi and Saripalli are selected from the semi urban areas of the mandal. From each village a number of 50 agriculture women households are selected on random basis. From each mandal 200 households and from the selected eight villages from the two selected mandals as a whole a number of 400 sample agriculture women workers are selected for in-depth of the study. The total of 400 selected agriculture women worker households from the eight villages of the two selected mandals are equally proportioned in the selected mandals. To examine the inter-area variations in the socio-economic conditions of women households are selected from the villages based on the random sampling procedure.

Regarding data collection and techniques used in the analysis are concerned, information relating to the socio-economic status of the selected agriculture women households is collected while canvassing a predesigned and structured household schedule in the selected villages during December 2016 to October 2017 in different visits. The secondary data has been obtained from Annual Reports of the district authorities, District handbook of statistics of different years published by the Chief Planning Officer, Visakhapatnam, Thasidar and M.P.D.O. offices of Pendurthi and Devarapalli Mandals. Census data are used to collect population data. In analysing the data apart from tabular analysis with averages and percentages, different statistical techniques are used at appropriate places. Tabular analysis with averages and percentages are used to explain the general profile and their different economic patterns.

I. Indicators Relating to Economic Status of the Selected Agriculture Women Workers

(a) Land Particulars of the Sample Agriculture Women Workers

The land particulars of the selected sample agriculture women workers are presented in the following Table 10.1.

Table 10.1: Land Particulars of the Selected Sample

Sl. No.	*Acres*	*No. of the Respondents*		
		Pendurthi	*Devarapalli*	*Grand Total*
1.	<1	13 (8.67)	26 (17.33)	39 (13.00)
2.	1-3	44 (29.33)	52 (34.67)	96 (32.00)
3.	3-5	61 (40.67)	44 (29.33)	105 (35.00)
4.	5-8	21 (14.00)	19 (12.67)	40 (13.33)
5.	8 above	11 (7.33)	9 (6.00)	20 (6.67)
	Total	**200 (100.00)**	**200 (100.00)**	**400 (100.00)**

Source: Field Survey.

The above Table 10.1 shows that the particulars of land owned by different categories of selected agriculture women workers. The data given in Table 10.1 reveal that in case of agriculture women workers selected from Pendurthi mandal reveal that, 8.67 per cent of respondents have less than 1 acre.

29.33 per cent have 1 to 3 acres of land. Similarly 40.67 per cent have 3 to 5 acres of land. 14.00 percentage of respondents have 5 to 8 acres of land and 7.33 per cent of them have 8 and above acres of land. In case of the respondents selected from Devarapalli mandal, 17.33 per cent have less than one acre of land. 34.67 per cent of them have 1 to 3 acres of land.

29.33 per cent of them have 3 to 5 acres of land. Similarly 12.67 per cent of them have 5 to 8 acres of land and 6.00 per cent of them have above 8 acres of land. In the present study most of the respondents are small and marginal farmers. 13 per cent of them have less than one acre of land.

32.00 per cent of them have 1 to 3 acres of land. 35.00 per cent of them have 3 to 5 acres of land. Similarly 13.33 per cent of them have 5 to 8 acres of land and 6.67 per cent of them have above 8 acres of land.

Irrigation plays a very important role in agriculture. Irrigation is said to be the oldest applied science in the world. In ordinary sense, irrigation means artificial application of water to soil to assist in the growth of plants. Thus, it means of making up deficiencies in the moisture content of soil. If there is no definite and permanent irrigation source, the farmers face many problems and also more loss. The farmers should have a proper and suitable plan about their crops. Because certain crops like paddy and cotton require more water and some crops like maize, groundnut require less water, so the farmers have to select their crops not only on the basis of nature of soil but also on the basis of irrigation facilities available. A farmer cannot totally depend on rain water. Generally the permanent sources of irrigation are canals, tanks, wells etc.

(b) Occupational Patterns

The information relating to the occupational patterns of the selected sample agriculture women workers are presented in the following Table 10.2.

Table 10.2: Occupation Pattern of the Sample Households

Sl. No.	*Occupation*	*No. of Respondents*		*Grand Total*
		Pendurthi	*Devarapalli*	
1.	Agriculture Labour	127 (84.67)	119 (79.33)	246 (82.00)
2.	Allied Activities	23 (15.33)	32 (21.33)	55 (18.00)
	Total	**200 (100.00)**	**200 (100.00)**	**400 (100.00)**

Source: Field Study.

Table 10.2 reveals the occupational particulars of respondents. In case of Pendurthi mandal majority of women respondent's main occupation is agricultural works. 84.67 per cent stated that their main occupation is agricultural works and only 15.33 per cent are allied activities. In the same manner in case of Devarapalli mandal 79.33 per cent women workers' main occupation is agricultural works and 21.33 per cent are in the allied activities. Totally we can say that 82.00 per cent respondents' main occupation is agriculture and other respondents 18.00 per cent belong to allied activities.

Table 10.3: Subsidiary Occupations of the Sample Households

Sl. No.	*Occupation*	*No. of Respondents*		*Grand Total*
		Pendurthi	*Devarapalli*	
1.	Non-Agricultural Labourers	21 (30.43)	23 (40.35)	44 (34.92)
2.	Traders	13 (18.84)	9 (15.79)	22 (17.46)
3.	Artisans	15 (21.74)	11 (19.30)	26 (20.63)
4.	Services	13 (18.84)	11 (19.30)	24 (19.05)
5.	Other	07 (10.14)	3 (5.26)	10 (7.94)
	Total	**69 (100.00)**	**57 (100.00)**	**126 (100.00)**

Source: Field Study.

The employment in agriculture is largely seasonal in character. Therefore, majority of the households stated that they are also depending on subsidiary occupations. As per the above Table 10.3 in case of Pendurthi mandal 69 women members are working as non-agricultural labourers, shop owners, artisans, and other services. In Devarapalli mandal 57 women member respondents having subsidiary occupations like artisans, shop owner, non-agricultural labourers and other services. It is clear from the data that compared to Pendurthi mandal women workers, in case of the Devarapalli mandal women workers, majority of the households are depending on subsidiary occupations.

The statistical information relating to the working days of the sample agriculture women workers are presented in Table 10.4.

From Table 10.4 it can be noticed that out of 400 sample agriculture women workers 85.67 per cent are able to get the work about 100 man-days in a year and 14.33 per cent from 100-200 man-days. If we look into the monthly availability of working days, the selected agriculture women workers from Pendurthi mandal women still in forefront in getting more number of working days in a month. 43.33 per cent of them are able to get 16-30 days working day and 56.67 per cent of their income is

Table 10.4: Working Days Particulars of the Sample Agriculture Women Workers

Selected Mandals	Weekly in Days			Monthly in Days			Yearly in Days		
	1-3	4-7	Total	1-15	16-30	Total	1-100	100-200	Total
Pendurthi	55 (36.67)	95 (63.33)	150 (100)	55 (36.67)	95 (63.33)	150 (100)	115 (76.67)	35 (23.33)	200 (100)
Devarapalli	101 (67.33)	49 (32.67)	150 (100)	115 (76.67)	35 (23.33)	150 (100)	142 (94.67)	08 (5.33)	200 (100)
Total	**156 (52.00)**	**144 (48.00)**	**300 (100)**	**170 (56.67)**	**130 (43.33)**	**300 (100)**	**257 (85.67)**	**43 (14.33)**	**400 (100)**

Note: Figures in parentheses are percentages to total.
Source: Field Survey.

confined with working days of 15 days only. Further it is classified that the working days are on weekly basis. 48.00 per cent selected agriculture women workers are getting work assignment between 4-7 man-days and 52.00 per cent are in the range of 1-3 working days. The working days which are available on weekly, month and annual basis are not sufficient. Majority of the agriculture women workers from the Devarapalli mandal women are unable to get maximum number of working days. Still the poverty exists in the interior hill tract villages in spite of implementing a number of welfare and developmental programme by central and state Governments.

(c) Income Levels of the Selected Households

The income particulars earned by the selected sample from different sources are presented in Table 10.5.

Table 10.5 explains the particulars of the income of the respondents. In case of Pendurthi mandal women out of 150 respondents, majority of the respondents, i.e. 29.33% are earning Rs. 5,000 to 10,000 from agriculture. Only 3.33 per cent are earning less than Rs. 5000 from agriculture. 11.33 per cent are earning above Rs. 40,000 from agriculture. In case of Pendurthi mandal out of 150 respondents only 69 respondents are earning non-agriculture income also. In this mandal majority of the respondents, i.e. 30.43 per cent are earning below Rs. 5000. Very less percentage of respondents only 8.70 per cent are earning Rs. 20,000 to 30,000.

In case of Devarapalli mandal women majority of the respondents 39.33 per cent are earning in between of Rs. 10,000 to 20,000. Very less

Table 10.5: Income Particulars of the Agriculture Women Workers Households

Income Level	No. of Respondents				Grand Total	
	Pendurthi mandal		Devarapalli mandal			
	Agri. Income	Non-Agri. Income	Agri. Income	Non-Agri. Income	Agri. Income	Non-Agri. Income
5000	5 (3.33)	21 (30.43)	8 (5.33)	23 (40.35)	13 (4.33)	44 (34.92)
5000-10000	44 (29.33)	31 (44.93)	42 (28.00)	24 (42.11)	86 (28.67)	55 (43.65)
10000-20000	43 (28.67)	11 (15.94)	59 (39.33)	7 (12.28)	102 (34.00)	18 (14.29)
20000-30000	25 (16.67)	06 (8.70)	21 (14.00)	3 (5.26)	46 (15.33)	09 (7.14)
30000-40000	16 (10.67)	—	11 (7.33)	—	27 (9.00)	—
40000 above	17 (11.33)	—	09 (6.00)	—	26 (8.67)	—
Total	150 (100.00)	69 (100.00)	150 (100.00)	57 (100.00)	300 (100.00)	126 (100.00)

Source: Field Survey.

number of respondents (only 5.33%) are earning below Rs. 5,000. 6 per cent are earning Rs. 40,000 from agriculture. In case of this mandal out of 150 respondents nearly 57 respondents are earning non-agriculture income also. Majority of ..e respondents 42.11 per cent are earning in between of Rs. 5,000 to 10,000. Very less respondents 5.26 per cent are getting Rs. 20,000 to 30,000 from non-agriculture income. From the total respondents, majority of the respondents 34 per cent are earning in between of Rs. 10,000 to 20,000. Very less respondents only 4.33 per cent are earning below Rs. 5,000 from agriculture. Majority of the respondents 43.65 per cent are getting below Rs. 5,000-10,000 from non-agriculture. Very less respondents 7.14 per cent are earning above Rs. 20,000-30,000.

The particulars relating to the improven in the saving levels of the sample agriculture women workers are presented in Table 10.6.

Table 10.6 depicts the particulars of improvement in savings level of the sample agriculture women workers. Whatever the additional income is gained may be spent on consumption and remaining amount will be saved for further needs of the family members. Out of 400 sample agriculture women workers, 37.67 per cent opined that there is an improvement in saving level due to the government programmes,

Table 10.6: Particulars of Savings of the Sample Agriculture Women Workers

Sl. No.	*Selected Mandals*	*Yes*	*No*	*Total*
1.	Pendurthi	70 (46.67)	80 (53.33)	200 (100)
2.	Devarapalli	43 (28.67)	107 (71.33)	200 (100)
	Total	**113 (37.67)**	**187 (62.33)**	**400 (100)**

Note: Figures in parentheses are percentages to total.
Source: Field Survey.

62.33 per cent of the sample agriculture women workers opined that there is no improvement in their saving in spite of gaining additional employment through government programmes in recent times.

(d) Assets Structure of the Agriculture Women Workers

The details about profits, buying assets and durable goods by the selected agriculture women workers from the two selected mandals are presented in Table 10.7. Out of the total sample agriculture women workers, the proportion of women selected from Pendurthi mandal who, bought assets and durable goods is much higher than the women selected from the Devarapalli mandal.

From Table 10.7 it can be noticed that among women selected from Pendurthi mandal 42.67 per cent of sample agriculture women workers are reported that they have assets. In case of Devarapalli mandal, 34.00 per cent of sample agriculture women workers bought small assets like field or ground for various purposes, and 64 per cent bought durable goods, it is important to note that during the same period, the women selected from the Devarapalli mandal also have bought small assets and durable goods. The particulars relating to the distribution of selected agriculture women workers in terms of value of assets possessed is given in Table 10.8.

From Table 10.8 it can be observed that as high as 93.33 per cent of women selected from Pendurthi mandal are reported to own assets such as furniture, TV, fan etc. Around 89 per cent women selected from Devarapalli mandal reported to own livestock. Asset in the form of land are possessed by just 2 per cent and houses possessed by 7.33 per cent. In terms of value of assets, land topped Rs. 30,000, followed by houses (Rs. 25,000), in the distribution of agriculture women workers in terms of valuable assets possessed.

Table 10.7: Distribution of Sample Agriculture Women Workers who Owned Assets

Sl. No.	Items	*Pendurthi*			*Devarapalli*			*Total*		
		Yes	*No*	*Total*	*Yes*	*No*	*Total*	*Yes*	*No*	*Total*
1.	Bought assets	64 (42.67)	86 (57.33)	150 (100)	51 (34.00)	99 (66.00)	150 (100)	115 (38.33)	185 (61.67)	440 (100)
2.	Durable goods	96 (64.00)	54 (36.00)	150 (100)	85 (56.67)	65 (43.33)	150 (100)	181 (60.33)	119 (39.67)	440 (100)
3.	Not Applicable	—	—	200 (100)	—	—	200 (100)	—	—	400 (100)

Note: Figures in parentheses are percentages to total.
Source: Field Survey.

Table 10.8: Distribution of Agriculture Women Workers in Terms of Value of Assets Possessed

Sl. No.	*Economic Activity*	*Sample*	*Average Value*
1.	Land	14	30,000
2.	Livestock	134	5,000
3.	House	12	25,000
4.	Other assets	140	8,329
	Total	**300**	**38,359**

Source: Field Survey.

II. Living Standards of the Selected Agriculture Women Workers

In this section an attempt is made to examine the living standards of the selected sample agriculture women workers while taking into account the following indicators.

At the outset the durable goods used by the sample households is considered as an important indicator of living standards of the selected mandal women. In this context the data relating to the consumption patterns of the selected agriculture women workers are presented in the following Table 10.9.

Table 10.9: Type of Durable Goods

Sl. No.	*Types of Durable Goods*	*Pendurthi*	*Devarapalli*	*Total*
1.	Radio	29 (19.33)	18 (12.00)	47 (15.67)
2.	T.V.	18 (12.00)	10 (6.67)	28 (9.33)
3.	Furniture	45 (30.00)	33 (22.00)	78 (26.00)
4.	Gas Stove	12 (8.00)	7 (4.67)	19 (6.33)
5.	Tape Recorder	20 (13.33)	16 (10.67)	36 (12.00)
6.	Gold	11 (7.33)	3 (2.00)	14 (4.67)
7.	Any other	15 (10.00)	37 (24.67)	52 (17.33)
8.	Not Applicable	—	26 (17.33)	26 (8.67)
	Total	**200 (100)**	**200 (100)**	**400 (100)**

Note: Figures in parentheses are percentages to total.
Source: Field Survey.

From Table 10.9 it can be noticed that, out of the total sample agriculture women workers, the proportion of women selected from the Pendurthi mandal bought furniture (30%), Radio (19.33%) and other things (10%, television 12%). The selected members of Devarapalli mandal women also able to purchase durable items but the extent of purchasing the durables are very limited when compared to their counterparts of the Devarapalli mandal women. This indicates the life styles of the selected women in case of both the mandals.

Housing is one of the basic necessities of every human being, which constitute the protecting base for any individual and his family. An attempt is made to study the housing conditions of the selected mandal households and the data pertaining to it are presented in Table 10.10.

The mandal-wise distribution of houses of households indicate that all agriculture women workers put together 53.67 per cent possess their own houses and 46.67 per cent are living in the government colony houses. 2.33 per cent households are living in thatched houses, 85 (28.33 addition of tiled and RCC) per cent of the households are living in tiled and RCC roof houses. Among all the sample households the households selected from the Pendurthi mandal are relatively having more own tiled and RCC roof houses, the households selected from Devarapalli mandal are residing in the Government colony houses. More number of Devarapalli households are living in the RCC roof houses. As a whole the housing condition in the Pendurthi mandal women are relatively in good condition. However, more efforts of the governmental agencies are still required in a big way to build pucca houses in the remote hill tracts. Almost all the houses are electrified.

From Table 10.11 it can be noticed that the particulars of educational awareness in the sample households reveal that, of the selected 300 agriculture women workers, 26.67 per cent of Devarapalli women and 32 per cent of Pendurthi women are having awareness of education, whereas 68 per cent of Pendurthi women and 73.33 per cent of Devarapalli are not having awareness about education. In the field survey they expressed their view that did not created any sort of environment for the accumulation of knowledge through basic education. The particulars relating to decision-making relating to the selected sample agriculture women workers are presented in Table 10.12.

Table 10.12 explains the possibilities of decision-making by the selected agriculture women workers whether independently or they depend on some other sources. All these particulars presented in Table 10.2 reveal that more than 69.67 per cent of the sample agriculture women workers are unable to take decision on their own with regard to the business and other economic transactions and they are used to depend upon others for taking the final decision. The remaining 30.33 per cent of sample agriculture women workers are able to take wise decision

Table [illegible] [illegible]stribution of Households by Type of House and House Electrified

Mandal	*Own House*				*Government House*			*Grand Total*	*Houses Electrified*
	Thatched	*Tiled*	*RCC*	*Total*	*Tiled*	*RCC*	*Total*		
Pendurthi	2 (1.33)	41 (27.33)	36 (24.00)	79 (52.67)	42 (28.00)	29 (19.33)	71 (47.33)	200 (100)	100
Devarapalli	5 (3.33)	28 (18.67)	49 (32.67)	82 (54.67)	40 (26.67)	29 (19.33)	69 (46.00)	200 (100)	100
Total	**7 (2.33)**	**69 (23.00)**	**85 (28.33)**	**161 (53.67)**	**82 (27.33)**	**58 (19.33)**	**140 (46.67)**	**400 (100)**	**100**

Note: Figures in parentheses are percentages to total.
Source: Field Survey.

Table 10.11: Particulars of Educational Awareness of the Respondents

Sl. No.	Selected Mandal	Yes	No	Total
1.	Pendurthi	48 (32.00)	102 (68.00)	150 (100)
2.	Devarapalli	40 (26.67)	110 (73.33)	150 (100)
	Total	**88 (29.33)**	**212 (70.67)**	**300 (100)**

Note: Figures in brackets are percentages to total.
Source: Field Survey.

Table 10.12: Decision-making Particulars of the Selected Sample Agriculture Women Workers

Sl. No.	Selected Mandal	Yes	No	Total
1.	Pendurthi	56 (37.33)	94 (62.67)	150 (100)
2.	Devarapalli	35 (23.33)	115 (76.67)	150 (100)
	Total	**91 (30.33)**	**209 (69.67)**	**300 (100)**

Note: Figures in parentheses are percentages to total.
Source: Field Survey.

independently to improve the economic status. The agriculture women workers who are not able to take timely decisions are more in proportion in the case of the Devarapalli mandal women rather than their counterparts in the Pendurthi mandal. There is a need to organise certain awareness programmes particularly on decision-making issues in the interior rural areas of Devarapalli. The information relating to the decision-making process is presented in Table 10.13.

Table 10.13 explains the particulars of the decision-making process of the selected sample mandal women. The selected households are taking advice from their husband, parents, village elder and other sources. Majority of the members, i.e. 71.67 per cent of the sample agriculture women workers are taking advice from their husbands while taking a decision on any household economic activity. 13.33 per cent of sample agriculture women workers depending on their parents for taking a decision about the household economic activities. 8.67 per cent of agriculture women workers are taking advices from the village elders

Table 10.13: Particulars of the Decision-making Process of the Sample Agriculture Women Workers

Sl. No.	*Selected Mandals*	*Husband*	*Parents*	*Village Elder*	*Other*	*Total*
1.	Pendurthi	120 (80.00)	23 (15.33)	3 (2.00)	4 (2.67)	200 (100)
2.	Devarapalli	95 (63.33)	17 (11.33)	23 (15.33)	15 (10.00)	200 (100)
	Total	**215 (71.67)**	**40 (13.33)**	**26 (8.67)**	**19 (6.33)**	**400 (100)**

Note: Figures in parentheses are percentages to total.
Source: Field Survey.

that possess rich experiencc in different fields. There are 6.33 per cent of sample agriculture women workers normally depend on others while taking decision on household economic activity. Thus, it is evident from Table 10.13 that majority of the sample households seeking help and encouragement from their family members.

III. Summary of the Analysis

The prevailing conditions relating to economic status and living standards of the selected agriculture women worker households and their family members are in very poor state. The following are some of the major conclusions relating to the prevailing economic indicators of the selected agriculture women worker households.

The analysis relating to economic status and living standards of the selected agriculture women workers from the study area reveal that the occupation status of spouses of respective agriculture women worker is ascertained and analysed, the pattern of distribution by and large resembles the general pattern as is noticed in rural India. Agriculture and allied activities (animal rearing) are providing the livelihood to women workers' spouses. In case of both the selected mandals majority respondent's main occupation is agriculture works. The employment in agriculture is largely seasonal in character. Therefore, majority of the agriculture women worker households stated that they are also depending on subsidiary occupations like artisans, shop owner, non-agricultural labourers and other services. It is clear from the data that compared to Pendurthi mandal women, in case of the Devarapalli mandal majority of the households are depending on subsidiary occupations.

The analysis relating to working days shows that out of 400 sample women 85.67 per cent are able to get the work about 100 mandays in a year and 14.33 per cent from 100-200 man-days. If we look into the monthly availability of working days, the selected agriculture women worker from Pendurthi mandal still in forefront in getting more number of working days in a month. 43.33 per cent of them are able to get 16-30 day working day and 56.67 per cent of their income is confined with working days of 15 days only. The working days which are available on weekly, month and annual basis are not sufficient. Majority of the sample from the Devarapalli mandal are unable to get maximum number of working days. Still the poverty exits in the interior villages selected from Devarapalli mandal in spite of implementing a number of welfare and developmental programme by Central State and Governments.

The income patterns of the selected agriculture women worker households reveal that, in case of Pendurthi mandal agriculture women workers out of 200 respondents, majority of the respondents, nearly 30 per cent are earning Rs. 5,000 to 10,000 from agriculture. 3.33 per cent are earning less than Rs. 5000 from agriculture. 11.33 per cent are earning above Rs. 40,000 from agriculture. In case of Pendurthi mandal out of 200 respondents only 69 respondents are earning non-agriculture income also. In this mandal majority of the respondents per cent are earning below Rs. 5000. Very less percentage of respondents are earning Rs. 20,000 to 30,000. In case of Devarapalli mandal women majority of the respondents are earning in between of Rs. 10,000 to 20,000. Very less number of respondents are earning below Rs. 5,000.6 per cent are earning Rs. 40,000 from agriculture.

The information relating to details about buying assets and durable goods by the selected agriculture women workers from the two selected mandals reveal that, out of the total sample agriculture women workers, the proportion of women selected from Pendurthi mandal who bought assets and durable goods is much higher than the women selected from Devarapalli mandal. 42.67 per cent of sample agriculture women worker bought small asset like field or ground for various purposes, and nearly 64 per cent bought durable goods, it is important to note that during the same period, the agriculture women workers selected from Devarapalli mandal also bought small assets and durable goods.

The particulars of savings level of the sample agriculture women worker reveal that whatever the income they gained may be spent on consumption and remaining amount will be saved for further needs of the family members. Out of 400 sample agriculture women workers nearly

30 per cent opined that there is an improvement in saving level due to the government programmes, nearly 60 per cent of the sample agriculture women workers opined that there is no improvement in their saving in spite of gaining additional employment through government programmes in recent times.

The asset pattern of the households reveal that as high as 90 per cent of agriculture women workers selected from Pendurthi mandal are reported to own assets such as furniture, TV, fan, etc. Around 80 per cent agriculture women workers selected from Devarapalli mandal reported to own livestock. Asset in the form of land are possessed by just 2 per cent and houses possessed by 7 per cent. In terms of value of assets, land topped Rs. 30,000, followed by houses Rs. 25,000, in the distribution of agriculture women workers in terms of valuable assets possessed. The analysis pertaining to the use of durable goods used by the sample households is considered as an important indicator of living standards of the selected agriculture women worker. In this context, the asset pattern of the selected agriculture women worker households reveal that out of the total sample agriculture women worker, the proportion of agriculture women worker selected from the Pendurthi mandal bought furniture (30.00%) and other things 10 per cent, television (12%). The selected members of Devarapalli mandal women also able to purchase durable items but the extent of purchasing the durables are very limited when compared to their counterparts of the Devarapalli mandal. This indicates the life-styles of the selected agriculture women workers in case of both the mandals.

The mandal-wise distribution of housing conditions of households indicate that all the households put together 50 per cent possesses their own houses and 45 per cent are living in the government colony houses. 5 per cent households are living in thatched houses, 50 per cent of the households are living in tiled and RCC roof houses. Among all the sample households the households selected from the Pendurthi mandal are relatively having more in own tiled and RCC roof houses, the households selected from Devarapalli mandal are residing in the Government colony houses. More number of Devarapalli households are living in the RCC roof houses. As a whole the housing conditions in the Pendurthi mandal sample agriculture women workers are relatively in good condition. Almost all the houses are electrified.

The analysis of educational awareness among the sample households reveal that, in the selected 400 agriculture women workers, nearly 25 per cent of the agriculture women workers from Devarapalli mandal and 30 per cent of women workers from Pendurthi mandal are having awareness of education. And 68 per cent of selected Pendurthi sample women and 70 per cent of selected women workers from Devarapalli are not having awareness about education. In the field survey they expressed their view that did not created any sort of environment for the accumulation of knowledge through basic education.

The particulars relating to decision-making relating to the selected agriculture women worker households reveal the possibilities of decision-making by the selected agriculture women workers whether independently or they depend on some other sources shows that more than 70 per cent of the sample agriculture women workers are unable to take decision on their own with regard to economic transactions and they are dependent upon others for taking the final decision. The remaining 30 per cent of sample agriculture women workers are able to take wise decision independently to improve their economic status. The agriculture women workers who are not able to take timely decisions are more in proportion in the case of the Devarapalli mandal rather than their counterparts in the Pendurthi mandal. There is a need to organise certain awareness programmes particularly on decision-making issues in the interior rural villages.

The analysis relating to decision making process of the selected agriculture women worker households reveal that the selected agriculture women worker households are taking advice from their husband, parents, village elder and other sources. Majority of the members of the sample agriculture women workers are taking advice from their husband while taking a decision on any household economic activity. Nearly, 13.33 per cent of sample agriculture women workers depending on their parents for taking a decision about the household economic activities. Others are taking advices from the village elders that possess rich experience in different fields. Thus, it is evident that majority of the sample households seeking help and encouragement from their family members.

REFERENCES

Ajjarapu Alimelu Annapurna (2012). "Women Empowering through Microfinance (A Case Study of East Godavari District, Andhra Pradesh)", *International Research in Science & Advanced Technology*, Issue 1, Vol. 2, September-October, pp. 84-89.

Anupa Hazra (2013). "Adding New Dimensions to Sustainable Rural Growth", *Kurukshetra*, Vol. 61, No. 9, July, pp. 3-4.

Biju, M.R.M. (2006). *Women's Empowerment: Politics and Policies*, Mittal Publications, New Delhi.

Brinda Rani Doss (2013). "Socio-Economic Empowerment of Women through Self-Help Groups", *SELP Journal of Social Science*, Vol. IV, Issue 14, pp. 6-8.

Government of India (2011). "Faster, Sustainable and More Inclusive Growth: An Approach to the Twelfth Five Year Plan", Planning Commission, October, retrieved from http://planningcommission.gov.in/plans/planrel/12appdrft/appraoch_12plan.pdf.

Jugal Kishore Misra (2006). "Empowerment of Women in India", *The Indian Journal of Political Science*, Vol. 67, No. 4, October-December, pp. 867-878.

Meeta Krishna (2003). *Poverty Alleviation and Rural Poor*, Mittal Publications, New Delhi.

Mohapatra, P.C. (1989). "Employment of Women with Special Reference to Employment of Women-Heads of Households in Orissa", *Vision*, Vol. LX, No. 1 and 2, July-December, Institute of Economics and Social Studies, Bhubaneswar.

11

An Explorative Study on Gender Inequality and Women Empowerment through Various Indicators in India

Santhosh Mathew

Introduction

According to World Summit for Social Development, 1995, *"Empowerment requires the full participation of people in the formulation, implementation and evaluation of decisions determining the functioning and the well-being of our societies. Women empowerment refers to the creation of an environment for women where they can make decisions of their own for their personal benefits as well as for the society."*

Violence against women is a manifestation of historically unequal power relations between men and women. The Declaration on the Elimination of Violence against Women defines *"violence against women"* as *"any act of gender-based violence that results in, or is likely to result in, physical, sexual or psychological harm or suffering to women, including threats of such acts, coercion or arbitrary deprivation of liberty, whether occurring in public or in private life."* The Declaration requires States to *"exercise due diligence to prevent, investigate and, in accordance with national legislation, punish acts of violence against women, whether those acts are perpetrated by the State or by private persons."*

Global Perspective

Gender-based violence (GBV) or violence against women and girls (VAWG), is a global pandemic that affects 1 in 3 women in their lifetime. In figures says that, 35 per cent of women worldwide have experienced either physical and/or sexual intimate partner violence or non-partner sexual violence. Globally, 7 per cent of women have been sexually assaulted by someone other than a partner and as many as 38 per cent of murders of women are committed by an intimate partner. 200 million women have experienced female genital mutilation/cutting. This issue is not only devastating for survivors of violence and their families, but also entails significant social and economic costs. In some countries, violence against women is estimated to cost countries up to 3.7 per cent of their GDP – more than double what most governments spend on education. Failure to address this issue also entails a significant cost for the future. Numerous studies have shown that children growing up with violence are more likely to become survivors themselves or perpetrators of violence in the future. One characteristic of gender-based violence is that it knows no social or economic boundaries and affects women and girls of all socio-economic backgrounds. This issue needs to be addressed in both developing and developed countries. Decreasing violence against women and girls requires a community-based, multi-pronged approach, and sustained engagement with multiple stakeholders. The most effective initiatives address underlying risk factors for violence, including social norms regarding gender roles and the acceptability of violence.

Violence against Women in the Perspective of India

In India, the rural and urban divide also brings in differences in the enhancement of the lives of women. In our country, the educated and the urban population have realised the benefits of educating a girl child and financial freedom of women. More women from these groups are joining the workforce and are leading a better and stable life. However, discrimination, violence, and harassment at the workplace or in the closed walls of homes continue to exist. But, in rural and poor households, the situation is grim. Issues like female foeticide, dowry system, and child marriage are prevalent. The society is still committed to patriarchy. Irrespective of the laws, girls are not proffered the right to property and are considered as a burden. Even in well-to-do families, male children are often prioritised and have better access to fulfil their ambitions. Girls are often not educated and enlightened on the progress that humanity is making. They neither have health awareness nor financial awareness.The dimensions of women's empowerment are diverse across different states of India; they may differ indifferent cultural settings. Keeping in mind the diverse cultural practices in the different states of India, a series of questions was asked in the fourth round of the National Family Health Survey (NFHS-4). These questions are related to various aspects of women's empowerment, such as women's participation in household decision-making, their freedom of movement and access to money which they can spend as per their desire. NFHS-4 expanded the domain of women's empowerment by asking women new questions on whether they own a house and/or land alone or jointly with others and if they have a mobile phone that they themselves use.

Review of Literature

Tiwari and Shrestha (1996) identified the factors associated with intimate partner violence in Lekhnath Metropolitan city, Kaski, Nepal by using Logistic Regression Approach. Data was analysed using descriptive and inferential statistical methods for representing various influenced parameters of intimate partner violence. Shamita Das *et al.* (1996) examines the conditions of Asian Indian women immigrants facing obstacles and sacrifices their personal life and freedom in United States. In Indian customs and traditions, women treated as second grade in day-to-day life but taking spiritual example of women as Arundathi Devi's life who was the wise and learned wife of sage Vashistha. Krantz (2002) examines the violence against women in the perspective of global public health issues. Womden are facing financial burden due to health issues and quoted one of the reasons is that women are physically assaulted by their husbands in India. Rekha Datta (2003) describes self-employment can improve and empowers the women which increase the ability to take their own decision-making capacity and well-being. The self-employed women's associations are helping to grow women independently and equal priority with their counterparts in taking wise decisions. Bacchus *et al* (2004) explored the prevalence of domestic violence of pregnant women and it is associated with physical and psychological health on antenatal and postnatal wards. Peedicayil *et al.* (2004) found the women during pregnancy, how they were abused by spouse or violated them like hit, slap, kick, beat, use of weapon and harm in any other way. These are the major outcomes/factors violated women during pregnancy by their life partners. Farid (2006) examines that how women are facing problems during menstrual absorbents and how their life affected due to lack of poor hygiene leads to Reproductive Tract Infection (RTI). Because of unawareness of menstrual period they have been facing huge health problems. Babu and Kar (2009) reported the prevalence and issues related to domestic violence against women from across all socio-economic category of Eastern zone of India. This study identified the factors such as urban residences, older age, lower education and lower family income are associated with incidence of domestic violence. Devakunchari *et al.* (2019) presented the analysis of crimes against women from 2002 to 2011 by using

Regression model and also explained how different age groups of women facing violence against them.

Indicators of Women Empowerment in NFHS-4

Based on NFHS-4 (2015-16) rankings, poor performance States of India were considered for representing various Women's Empowerment and Gender Based Violence (age 15-49 years) indicators.

1. Participation in Household Decisions

Table 11.1: Participation in Household Decisions

India & States	*Urban*	*Rural*
India	85.8	83.0
Andhra Pradesh	78.8	80.4
Bihar	77.6	74.8
Delhi	74.1	0
Dadra & Nagar Haveli	79.4	77.7
Haryana	77.0	76.4
Kerala	91.7	92.4
Telangana	81.8	80.3
Uttar Pradesh	85.5	80.3

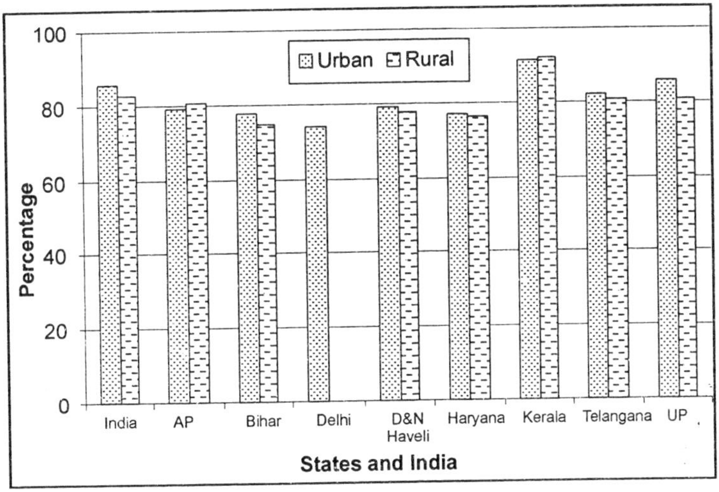

Fig. 11.1: Participation in Household Decisions

From Table 11.1, we observed that slight difference among rural and urban populations in participating the major household decisions of poor performing states and India represented in Figure 11.1.

2. *Women who worked in the last 12 Months who were paid in cash (%)*

Table 11.2: Women who worked in the last 12 Months who were paid in cash

India and States	*Urban*	*Rural*
India	23.2	25.4
Arunachal Pradesh	18.3	16.7
Assam	18.6	16.7
Bihar	11.6	12.6
Himachal Pradesh	27.2	15.5
Haryana	18.7	16.8
Jammu & Kashmir	15.2	11.0
Punjab	17.5	19.1
Uttar Pradesh	19.3	15.7
Uttarakhand	17.4	14.4

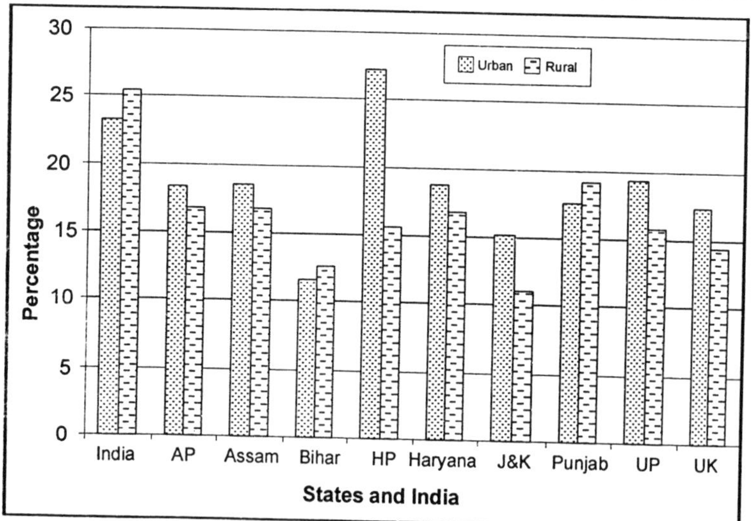

Fig. 11.2: Women who worked in the last 12 Months who were paid in cash

In Table 11.2, it is depicted that there is minor variation among low performance States except Himachal Pradesh women paid in cash for last 12 working months. Variations in India and other poor performance States were represented in Figure 11.2.

3. Ever Married Women who have ever Experienced Spousal Violence (%)

Table 11.3: Ever Married Women who have ever Experienced Spousal Violence

India and States	*Urban*	*Rural*
India	25.3	34.1
Andaman & Nicobar Islands	19.4	17.4
Bihar	40.2	43.7
Chhattisgarh	35.4	37.1
Jharkhand	19.7	38.8
Manipur	48.1	56.1
Odisha	24.8	37.9
Telangana	37.1	47.6
Tamil Nadu	37.2	44.2
Uttar Pradesh	29.6	39.3

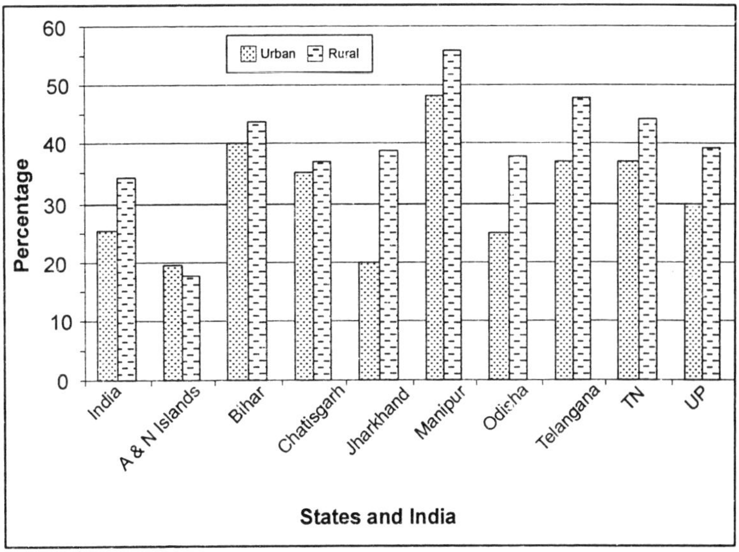

Fig. 11.3: Ever Married Women who have ever Experienced Spousal Violence

Table 11.3 represents that there is much difference in urban and rural populations of all over India of women who experienced spousal violence. There is much difference observed in poor performance states except Andaman & Nicobar Islands, Bihar and Chhattisgarh and represented in Fig. 11.3.

4. Ever Married Women who have Experiences Violence During any Pregnancy (%)

Table 11.4: Ever Married Women who have Experienced Violence During any Pregnancy

India and States	*Urban*	*Rural*
India	3.4	4.1
Andhra Pradesh	3.8	5.3
Bihar	6.8	4.5
Chhattisgarh	3.8	5.3
Daman & Diu	9.6	0
Haryana	3.0	6.3
Karnataka	8.7	4.5
Telangana	4.4	7.0
Tamil Nadu	5.0	7.5
West Bengal	5.4	4.8

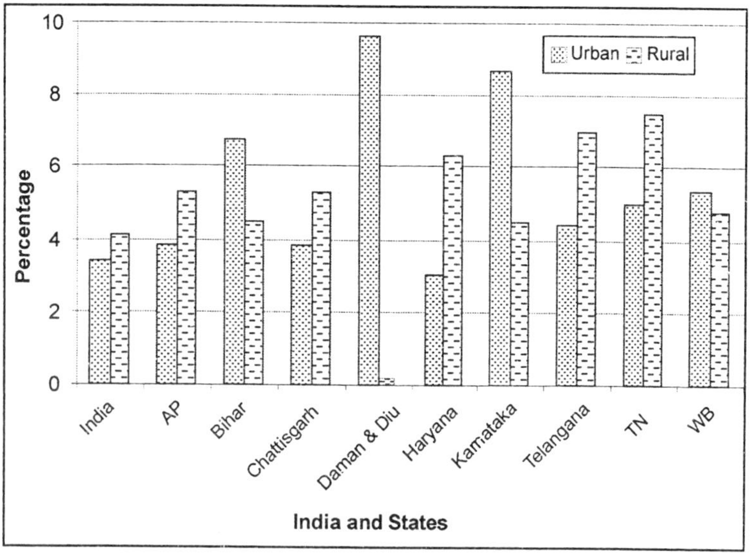

Fig. 11.4: Ever Married Women who have Experienced Violence during any Pregnancy

From Table 11.4, it is revealed that Daman and Diu is most vulnerable followed by Karnataka, Tamil Nadu and Telangana in spousal violence during pregnancy. Remaining States have less variation are observed in urban and rural populations.

5. Women Owning a House or Land (alone or jointly with others)

Table 11.5: Women Owning a House or Land (alone or jointly with others)

India and States	*Urban*	*Rural*
India	35.2	40.1
Chhattisgarh	23.8	27.3
Daman & Diu	30.9	19.2
D & N Haveli	41.7	3.9
Gujarat	29.7	25.2
Himachal Pradesh	9.2	11.6
Mizoram	14.9	27.2
Rajasthan	22.8	24.5
Sikkim	19.4	28.5
West Bengal	25.8	22.9

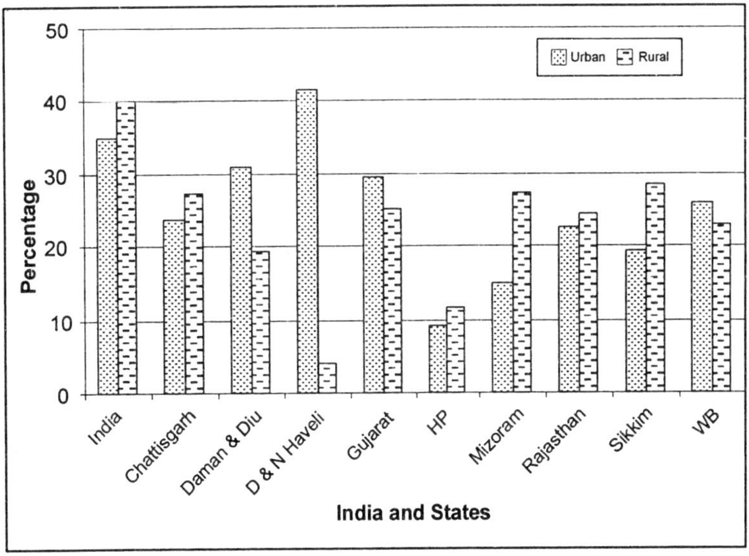

Fig. 11.5: Women Owning a House or Land (alone or jointly with others)

From Table 11.5, it represents women owning land or property of India and Poor Performed States. In this table, it is shown that D & N Haveli has least percentage in women having land or house in rural and observed high in urban women population. Chhattisgarh, Mizoram and Sikkim state women population in rural areas occupied much percentage than the urban population. A slight difference observed in remaining states as represented in Figure 11.5.

6. Women having a Bank or Savings Account that they themself Use (%)

Table 11.6: Women having a Bank or Savings Account that they themself Use

India and States	*Urban*	*Rural*
India	61.0	48.5
Assam	61.5	42.1
Bihar	36.9	24.6
D & N Haveli	47.5	27.4
Jharkhand	55.8	40.9
Maharashtra	52.0	38.7
Manipur	42.9	29.7
Madhya Pradesh	50.1	31.4
Nagaland	54.8	27.4
West Bengal	54.8	38.3

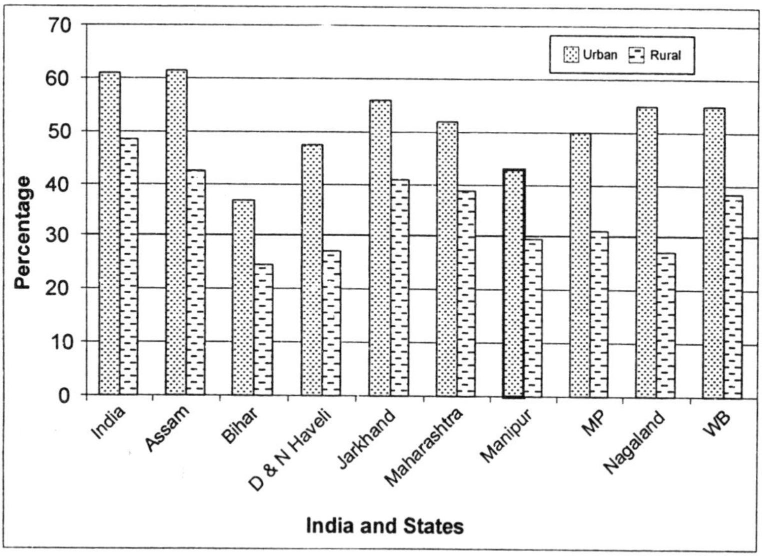

Figure 11.6: Women having a Bank or Savings Account that they themself Use

Table 11.6, presents that women having a Bank or savings account that they can use. In this table, it is observed that mostly urban women are having bank accounts than the rural population. That means urban women have freedom to maintain financial access by their own selves.

7. Women having a Mobile Phone that they themselves Use (%)

Table 11.7: Women having a Mobile Phone that themselves Use

India and States	*Urban*	*Rural*
India	61.8	36.9
Andhra Pradesh	54.1	27.8
Bihar	50.0	39.3
Chhattisgarh	54.7	22.9
D & N Haveli	57.8	18.1
Jharkhand	53.4	27.9
Madhya Pradesh	49.5	19.1
Odisha	64.7	32.5
Rajasthan	61.2	34.4
Uttar Pradesh	48.6	32.8

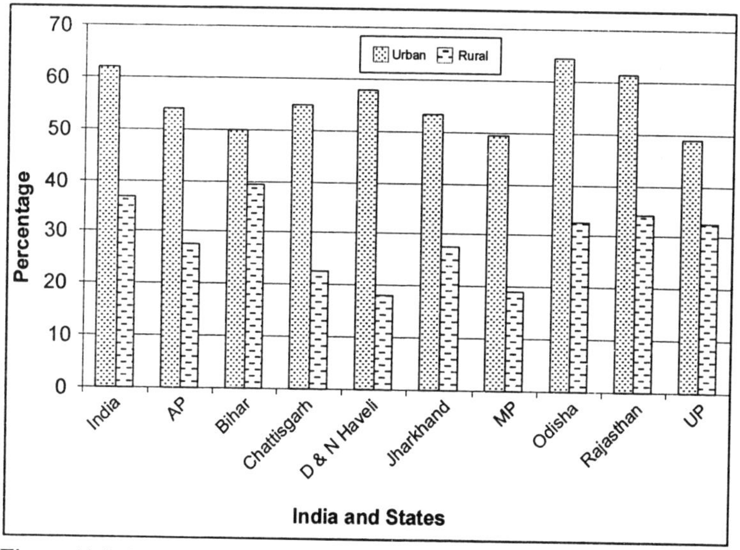

Figure 11.7: Women having a Mobile Phone that they themselves Use

Table 11.7 represents women having a mobile phone that they can use individually. Major difference is observed in urban women population than the rural areas in usage of mobile phones in India and poor performed states. Still women in rural areas lacking of awareness and unable to afford mobile phones on their own. The graphical representation of India and States are shown in Figure 11.7.

8. Women age 15-24 Years who use Hygienic Methods of Protection during their Menstrual Period (%)

Table 11.8: Women age 15-24 Years who use Hygienic Methods of Protection during their Menstrual Period

India and States	*Urban*	*Rural*
India	77.5	48.2
Assam	70.8	40.9
Bihar	55.6	27.3
Chhattisgarh	72.7	39.4
Jharkhand	77.2	39.4
Madhya Pradesh	65.4	26.4
Odisha	70.0	42.8
Tripura	56.5	38.6
Uttar Pradesh	68.6	39.9
West Bengal	72.9	47.6

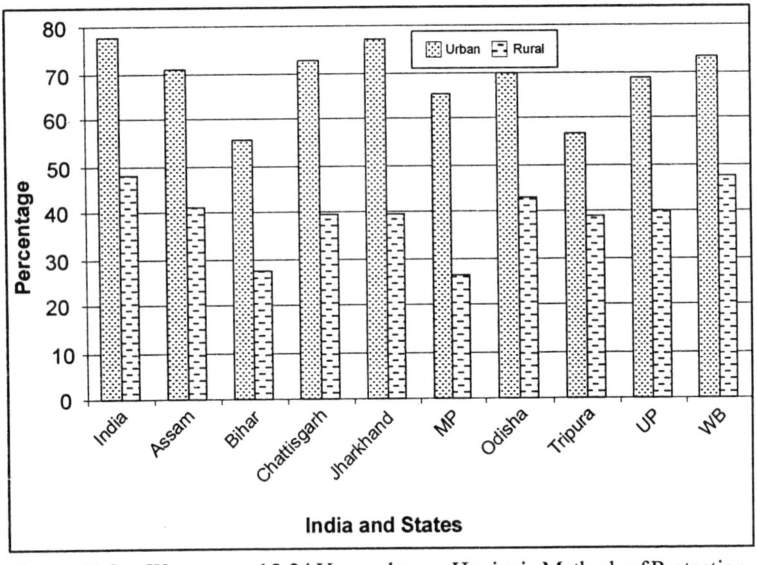

Figure 11.8: Women age 15-24 Years who use Hygienic Methods of Protection during their Menstrual Period

Table 11.8 depicts the women who are in age group of 15-24 use hygienic methods to protect their menstrual period. Overall observation from the table, women in urban areas has improved in usage of hygienic methods in their menstrual period than the rural population.

Cluster Analysis Results

From the cluster analysis, it is observed that all states and union territories clustered in five homogeneous groups based on their percentages of rural and urban women population. The visual representation of all states were displayed in the dendrogram for better understanding.

Rural

Cluster-1	*Cluster-2*	*Cluster-3*	*Cluster-4*	*Cluster-5*
J & K	Puducherry	Arunachal Pradesh	Odisha	Rajasthan
Uttarakhand	Tamil Nadu	Meghalaya	Tripura	U P
Daman & Diu	H P	Karnataka	Assam	Gujarat
Mizoram	Sikkim	A P	Jharkhand	Maharashtra
Punjab	Goa	Manipur	Madhya Pradesh	West Bengal
Haryana	Kerala	Telangana	Bihar	Chhattisgarh
Nagaland	A & N Islands			D & N Haveli

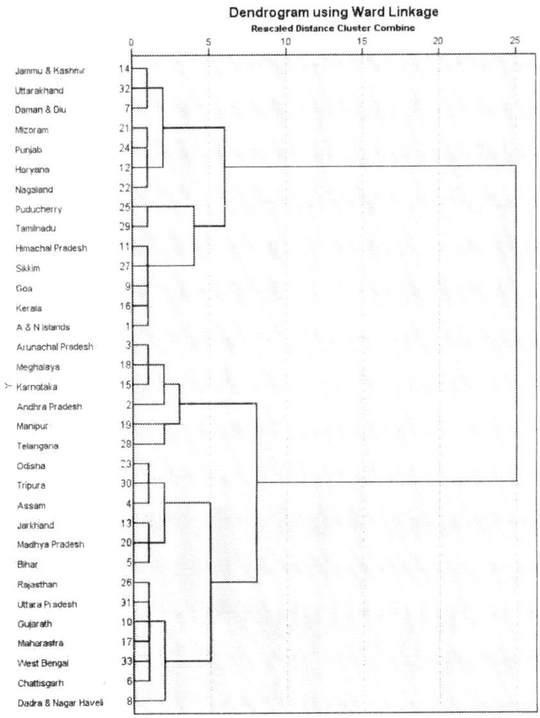

Urban:

Cluster-1	*Cluster-2*	*Cluster-3*	*Cluster-4*	*Cluster-5*
A & N Islands	Himachal Pradesh	Chhattisgarh	Assam	NCT Delhi
Goa	Mizoram	U P	Odisha	Haryana
Chandigarh	Sikkim	Rajasthan	Tripura	Daman & Diu
Kerala	Meghalaya	Uttarakhand	Jharkhand	Telangana
Punjab	Nagaland	Maharashtra	M P	Karnataka
Jammu & Kashmir		West Bengal	A P	Puducherry
Lakshadweep		Gujarat	D & N Haveli	Tamil Nadu
		Bihar		A P
				Manipur

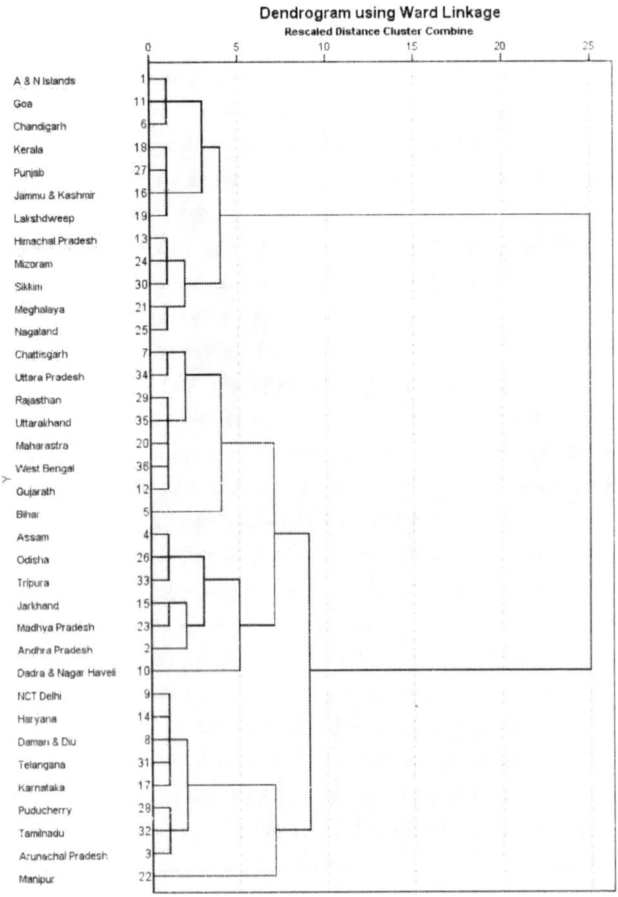

World Leaders, Words on Women Empowerment

"Not until the half of our population represented by women and girls can live free from fear, violence and everyday insecurity, can we truly say we live in a fair and equal world."

—*UN Secretary-General António Guterres*

"Around the world, women and girls are victims of countless acts of violence. The range of gender-based violence seems endless at times, occurring literally from womb to tomb."

—*Karl Kulessa, UNFPA Turkey Representative*

UN Women Turkey, Acting Head of the Office Sabine Freizer said in her speech that "violence against women has no boundaries of geography, culture or wealth. It doesn't only mean physical violence. It also includes sexual, verbal, emotional, psychological and financial abuse. For example, preventing women's economic participation in the society is a direct result of economic violence against women. Child and forced marriage is a form of violence. This year, together with thousands of women all around the world we say #hear me too. I am sure that young students like yourselves will be the powerhouse for ending violence against women."

REFERENCES

Abraham Peedicayil et al. (2004), Spousal physical violence against women during pregnancy, BJOG: *an International Journal of Obstetrics and Gynaecology*, Vol. 111, pp. 682–687, DOI: 10.1111/j.1471-0528.2004.00151.x

Afrose Fathima Farid (2006), Preferred menstrual absorbents, awareness and hygiene practices during mensuration amongst women in Chennai, India, *International Journal of Science, Engineering and Technology Research (IJSETR)*, Volume 5, Issue 5.

Bontha V. Babu and Shantanu K. Kar (2009), Domestic violence against women in eastern India: a population-based study on prevalence and related issues, *BMC Public Health* 2009, 9:129. doi: 10.1186/1471-2458-9-129.

Data from National Family Health Survey-4 (2015-2016), Government of India.

Devakunchari, Bhowmick S., Bhutada, S.P., Shishodia, Y. (2019), Analysis of Crimes against Women in India using Regression, *International Journal of Engineering and Advanced Technology (IJEAT)*, ISSN: 2249–8958, Volume 8, Issue 2S2, pp. 124-127.

G. Krantz (2002), Violence against Women: A Global Public Health Issue, *J Epidemiol Community Health*, 2002; 56: 242–243.

Loraine Bacchus (2004), Domestic violence: prevalence in pregnant women and associations with physical and psychological health, *European Journal of Obstetrics & Gynecology and Reproductive Biology*, Vol. 113, pp. 6–11.

Prativa Tiwari & Gauri Shrestha (2018), Factors Associated with Intimate Partner Violence: Logistic Regression Approach, *Nepalese Journal of Statistics*, Vol. 2, 37-52 DOI: http://dx.doi.org/10.3126/njs.v2i0.21154.

Rekha Datta (2003), From Development to Empowerment: The Self-Employed Women's Association in India, *International Journal of Politics, Culture and Society*, Vol. 16, No. 3, Spring.

Shamita Das Das Gupta, Sujatha Warrier (1996), In the Foot-steps of 'Arundhati'—Asian Indian Women's Experience of Domestic Violence in the United States, *Violence against Women*, Vol. 2, No. 3, pp. 238-259, Sage Publications, Inc.

12

Gender and Development

A Study of Maternal and Child Health Care Policies in Odisha

Padmalaya Mahapatra

Introduction

Gender discourse within the field of development has come a long way from building a case of 'inclusive' growth which prevents the marginalisation of women to questioning of the predominant notions of development itself. The body of feminist critique continues to traverse new terrains and posit new challenges. The neo-liberal vision of society with a strong undercurrent of economic determinism often celebrates the atomistic, unconnected, self-maximizing individual—a conception which largely inhibits the space of both culture and development. Women's limited access to and control of material resources and limited decision-making power within the household can produce high fertility rates, under-investment in aspects of family welfare such as child nutrition and education, and sub-optimal allocations of human capital in the economy. Maternal morbidity and mortality along with infant mortality rate is universally considered as human development indicators in a country and determines the health status of the people. In spite of very good plans and programmes, the reduction in MMR & IMR is much below the target set in Odisha. The present study is based on both primary and secondary sources of data. The paper attempts to analyse the impact of maternal health care policies on women's health status in Odisha. It mainly focuses on maternal mortality relating to socio-economic characteristics of deceased, status of ante-natal care, major causes that led to maternal death, major steps taken through various policies and programmes initiated by Government of India/Government of Odisha and their achievement.

Gender and Development

The Gender Related Development Index (GDI) is an index designed to measure gender equality. GDI together with the Gender Empowerment Measure (GEM) were introduced in 1995 in the Human Development Report written by the United Nations Development Programme. The GDI measures differences between male and female achievements in three basic dimensions of human development: health, education and command over economic resources. GDI is the ratio of female HDI to male HDI. To calculate it, the HDI is first calculated separately for females and for males. India ranks 130 in Gender Inequality Index: UN. According to the United Nations' Human Development Report, India is ranked 130 out of 155 countries on the Gender Inequality Index (GII). The gender index takes into account reproductive health, empowerment, and economic activity.

Maternal Health—Concept, Definition and Components

Maternal health refers to the health of women during pregnancy, childbirth and the postpartum period. While motherhood is often a positive and fulfilling experience, for too many women it is associated with suffering, ill-health and even death. Maternal health care is a concept that encompasses family planning, preconception, prenatal, and postnatal care. Goals of preconception care can include providing education, health promotion, screening and interventions for women of reproductive age to reduce risk factors that might affect future pregnancies. Prenatal care is the comprehensive care that women receive and provide for themselves throughout their pregnancy. Women who begin prenatal care early in their pregnancies have better birth outcomes than women who receive little or no care during their pregnancies. Postnatal care issues include recovery from childbirth, concerns about newborn care, nutrition, breastfeeding, and family planning.

Women constitute nearly half (49.5%) of the State's total population as per 2011 Census. As such their socio-economic development is a *sine qua non* for sustainable growth of the economy. Generally, women experience considerable disadvantage and discrimination in the society owing to gender differentiation. The gender bias propels disparities in terms of literacy, access to public health services and social development indicators. The female literacy of Odisha as per 2011 Census was 64 per cent which was at par with national averages. But gender gap in literacy as per 2011 Census was the highest in Nuapada district and lowest in Khordha district.

Infant Mortality in Odisha has made quantum leap with 56 points decline by reducing IMR from 96 (SRS 2000) to 40 in 2015-16 (NFHS-4) which is the highest point decline in the country far ahead of national average decline of 27 points and better than major States like Gujarat (28 points), Rajasthan (38 points), Chhattisgarh (25 points), Jharkhand (26 points), MP (36 points), UP (19 points). This translates into 51,000 more children being saved annually compared to the year 2000. IMR in rural Odisha was 43 as compared to 21 in urban areas in 2015-16. At the national level, IMR stood at 41 and varied from 46 in rural areas to 29 in urban areas in 2015-16.

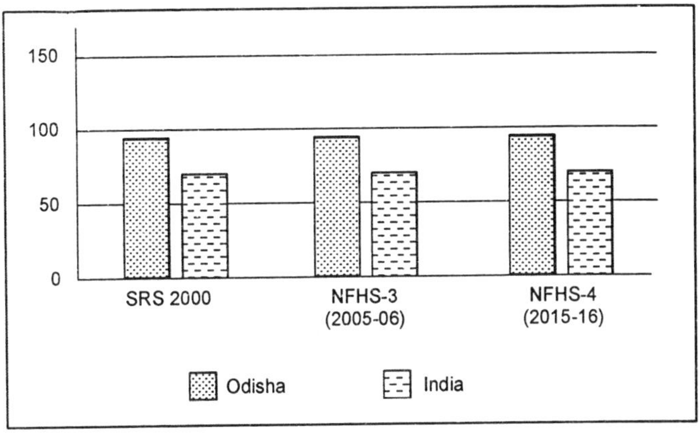

Fig. 12.1: Infant Mortality Rate Point decrease: Odisha-56, India-27

Source: National Family Health Survey.

Gender Inequality, Human Rights and its Effects on Maternal Health

Despite the country's growing economy and an ambitious rural health initiative, over 100,000 women die from pregnancy-related causes each year, more than anywhere else in the world. Many more suffer debilitating complications that they endure in silence due to impunity and lack of accountability in the health system. The medical causes of maternal mortality are well known and largely preventable, yet government policies have failed to have an impact.

Promotion of maternal and child health has been one of the most important objectives of the Family Welfare Programme in India. The current Reproductive and Child Health Programme (RCH) was launched in October 1997. In order to improve maternal health at the community level a cadre of community level skilled birth attendant who will attend to the pregnant women in the community is being considered.

Review of Literature

Miller (1989), Murthi, Anne and Dreze (1995), Gupta and Bhat (1997), George (1998), Bhat and Zavier (2003), Mishra, Roy and Rutherford (2004), Dyson and Moore (1983), Krishnaji (1987), Siddhanta, Nandy and Agnihotri (2003), Pandey (2003), Hill and Upchurch (1995) and Acharaya & Kumar (2004) explained the extent of gender differences in infant and child mortality in terms of gender differences in health status, disease incidence, preventive and curative treatment and social status.

"In many parts of the world, women receive less attention and health care than man do and particularly girls often receive very less support than boys. As a result of this gender bias, the mortality rates of females often exceed those of males in these countries. This is an important issue because gender discrimination that contributes to poorer health status for girls than for boys is likely to be the main pathway for excess female child mortality. Such discrimination occurs in a girl, receives less attention than would be bestowed upon a son. She is less warmly clad, she is probably not so well fed as a boy would be and when ill, her parents are not likely to make the same strenuous efforts to ensure her recovery."

Sugathan, Mishra and Retherford (2001), Kishor and Parasuraman (1998), Stephenson and Tusi (2002), Bourne & Walker (1991), McNay, Arokiasamy and Cassen (2003), Dyson and Moore (1983) and Rustagi (2004) evaluated the status of women in India with different indicators such as of women's work, education, health, survival, safety and participation in public/private decision-making.

Sudha, Rajan (1999), George (2002), Rutherford and Roy (2003), Bose (2007), Visaria (2007) examined the causes for eliminating the girl child. It indicates that they are rooted in rituals and perceptions that go back centuries: the fear of having to pay for a girl's dowry, the belief that for true salvation a son should perform the last rites, the conviction that lineage and inheritance run through the male line and that a son will look after his parents in their old age, whereas the daughters will belong to another family. Tied up to all this is the old perception of seeing only men as the bread earners.

Whatever our stance is on feminist economics, however, we need to be aware of these issues when analysing the effect of gender related issues on development at the macro level. Indeed, some of the newer fields in economics, such as behavioural economics, take some of these challenges more seriously. Another example of rising awareness of the need to consider changing social norms and culture is a recent book on economic growth by David Weil (2005), which gives considerable emphasis on culture and values.

During 50 years from 1950 to 2000, mortality in all age groups greatly improved. The infant mortality rate (IMR) was 90 per cent lower in 2000 than in 1950, making infants the age group that saw the greatest changes over time. Men experienced a decline of at least one-third across all age groups. Women's death rates at ages zero to 80 fell by at least 50 per cent, while improvements above age 80 constituted at least 30 per cent of the decline over the 50-year period. These sex specific differences in mortality declines were also reflected in life expectancy. Women's life expectancy increase was almost linear over time. Men, on the other hand, initially experienced a slower life expectancy increase. From the late 1970s onward, male mortality declined faster in relative terms than female mortality (Luy, 2004).

While at the beginning of the period, infant mortality contributed significantly to East-West differences, old age became much more important over time. Until the mid-1970s, the lower IMR and more rapid improvements in this rate in the GDR were responsible for part of the initial advantage of GDR in male life expectancy (Nolte *et al.*, 2000a). The first few years after reunification, the IMR fell in both the East and the West, and the rates converged in 1997 (Nolte *et al.*, 2000b, 2001).

In a cross-sectional study, under-5 mortality was found to be strongly associated with maternal and infant health programs. It was also strongly associated with the proportion of births attended by trained person. To raise the public health spending remains the main challenge in developing countries for improving the quality of maternal and child healthcare. (McGuire, J.W., 2006).

A study was conducted to describe the association between under-5 mortality and socio-economic, political, and healthcare factors between rich and poor children. In this study, higher incomes were associated with lower under-5 mortality rates (Houweling *et al.*, 2005).

Global under-5 mortality has dropped from 11.9 million in 1990 to 7.7 million deaths in 2010. 33 per cent of these deaths occurred in South Asia and 49.6 per cent in sub-Saharan Africa. Less than 1 per cent deaths occurred in developed countries. Compared to 1990 to 2000, there is accelerated decline in child mortality from 2000 to 2010 (Rajaratnam *et al.*, 2010).

In a study from India, under-5 mortality rate declined at a mean rate of 3.7 per cent per year between 2001 and 2012. According to this study, 222 districts were lagging in the process of achieving Millennium Development Goals. Female mortality rate was higher by 25 per cent in 303 districts (Ram *et al.*, 2013).

Objective

The main objective of the study is to ascertain the level and pattern of maternal mortality among the selected rural groups in Odisha. More specifically the study tries to:

- Determine the level of maternal mortality among the selected population groups in Rural Odisha.
- Identify the Risk Factors of Maternal mortality, know their operational mechanism and find out their related risks.
- Recommend appropriate intervention modes to prevent and control risk factors in order to reduce maternal and infant mortality.

Research Question

To what extent maternal and child health care policies influence to improve the health status of women in Odisha?

Method of Study

This study is based on both Primary and Secondary data. Data collected from empirical study in 2 Gram Panchayats of Cuttack district of Odisha. This study also involves personal interviews and discussions with several Women Leaders, Social Welfare Boards, and prominent members of NGOs etc.

- Field investigations, empirical surveys, direct interviews with villagers specially women, young mothers, traditional *dais*, Anganwadi workers, the Auxiliary nurse midwives, doctors and Self Help groups, Panchayat sarpanchs and members.
- Extensive scanning of published material on the subject.
- Scanning of a few previous and current Five Year Plan Provisions to reduce IMR and MMR. A special attention was given to the Midterm reviews not only of the Planning Commission but also of Reports of some Ministries, viz. Ministry of Health and Family Welfare, Ministry of Women and Child Development of the Centre and the States; National Rural Health Mission, selected local feedback from Panchayat Raj reviews and a few members of the Panchayats of the concerned States.

In any case, the problem of IMR and MMR is part of the Indian, "Social Complexity". To totally bring it down we need to take vigorous direct and indirect systemic reform steps. It is high time, we took not one but several, "first steps" some of them have been recommended here as we have to walk a thousand miles to bring down IMR/MMR in India.

Reduction of maternal and child deaths is one of the major challenges of the health system in Odisha. With several efforts from the State under the RMNCH+A campaign, it has been observed from the SRS reports, that there has been a decline in the State Maternal Mortality Ratio (MMR) and Infant Mortality Rate (IMR) over the years. (Odisha State strategy for accelerated reduction of Maternal and Infant Mortality—Odisha 2020).

The maternal mortality has been defined by WHO as death of a woman while pregnant or within 42 days of termination of pregnancy, irrespective of the cause of death (and) is intended for countries that wish to identify deaths occurring in pregnancy, child birth up to 6 weeks after the end of pregnancy but where the cause of death cannot be identified precisely (WHO cited in Royston, Mauldin, 1994).

For women and adolescent girls of reproductive age, the biological functions of pregnancy and childbirth intersect with gender inequalities and poverty to expose women to maternal health risks. A lack of autonomy to make decisions about one's own health care, low levels of education circumscribing the ability to make informed health care decisions, limited control over financial resources, restricted mobility to access health care services and power differentials between health care providers and recipients are all factors which may preclude women from receiving the quality of care essential for ensuring healthy pregnancies and deliveries.

Though the maternal mortality ratio declined by 37 per cent between 2000 – 2015, there were an estimated 303,000 maternal deaths worldwide in 2015 due to complications in pregnancy and childbirth. Almost all (99 per cent) occurred in developing regions, with the highest level (546 per 100,000 live births) in sub-Saharan Africa, followed by South Asia (182 per 100,000 live births).

Table 12.1: Maternal and New Born Health

Sl. No.	*Component*	*Rate*
1.	Proportion of women aged 15-49 who received post-natal care within 2 days after giving birth (%)	62
2.	Antenatal care coverage for at least four visits (%)	51
3.	Proportion of births attended by skilled health personnel (%)	81
4.	Caesarean section (%)	17
5.	Proportion of women 20-24 years old who gave birth before age of 18	22
6.	Number of women aged 15-49 years with a live birth delivered in a health facility	79
7.	Births who had their postnatal check-up within the first two days after birth (%)	24

Source: Other NS 2016.

Infant mortality is an indicator of the health status not only of infants, but also of the whole population and of their poverty ridden social and economic status in the country. They face excessive vulnerability, as underprivileged, to a hostile environment and suffer malnutrition and serious health problems; all this leads to high rates of infant mortality and morbidity. Infant mortality, i.e. deaths under one year of age in a year per 1000 live births, is an important indicator of child health and development. (*Source*: The Socio-economic determinants behind Infant Mortality and Maternal Mortality, sponsored by the Planning Commission of India, 2006.)

In 2015, the world began working towards a new global development agenda, seeking to achieve, by 2030, new targets set out in the Sustainable Development Goals (SDGs). The proposed SDG target for child mortality aims to end, by 2030, preventable deaths of newborn and children under 5 years of age, with all countries aiming to reduce neonatal mortality to at least as low as 12 deaths per 1,000 live births and under-5 mortality to at least as low as 25 deaths per 1,000 live births.

Table 12.2: Child Health

Sl No.	*Component*	*% Rate*
1.	Children under age 5 whose births are registered (%)	72
2.	Women aged 20-24 years who were first married on in union by age (%)	27
3.	Children aged 5-17 years engaged in Child Labour (%)	12
4.	Children aged 1 to 14 years who experienced any violent discipline (psychological aggression and/or physical punishment) in the past month (%)	Not Available
5.	Justification of Wife beating (female) (%)	47
6.	Justification of Wife beating (male) (%)	42
7.	Women aged 15-49 who have undergone female genital mutilation (%)	Not Available

Source: UNICEF/WHO 2017.

Table 12.3: Child Survival

Sl. No	*Component*	*Rate*
1.	Under-five mortality rate (U5MR), deaths per 1000 births	39
2.	Number of Under-five deaths	989,167
3.	Infant Mortality Rate (IMR), deaths per 1000 live births	32
4.	Neonatal Mortality rate (NMR), deaths per 1000 live births	24
5.	Under-five mortality rate (U5MR), deaths per 1000 live births (male)	39
6.	Under-five mortality rate (U5MR), deaths per 1000 live births (female)	40

Source: IGME 2018.

The world made remarkable progress in child survival in the past few decades, and millions of children have better survival chances than in 1990–95. 1 in 26 children died before reaching age five in 2018, compared to 1 in 11 in 1990. Moreover, progress in reducing child mortality has been accelerated in the 2000–2018 period compared with the 1990s, with the annual rate of reduction in the global under-five mortality rate increasing from 2.0 per cent in 1990–2000 to 3.8 per cent in 2000–2018. Despite the global progress in reducing child mortality over the past few decades, an estimated 5.3 million children under age five died in 2018–roughly half of those deaths occurred in sub-Saharan Africa.

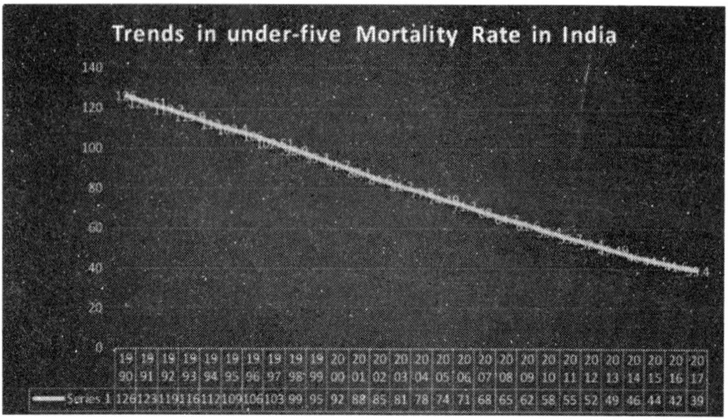

Fig. 12.2: Trends in under five Mortality Rate in India.

Source: IGME, 2018.

Existing Interventions for Reducing IMR and MMR in the State

State is continuing its consistent efforts for reducing MMR and IMR through different strategies at community as well as facility level. The major interventions which are implemented currently are as follows:

Village Health and Nutrition Day (VHND)

These days are organized once in a month in every AWC on a fixed day basis (Tuesdays and Fridays) with joint effort of ANM, AWW and ASHA. The VHND provides quality ANC & PNC services for expecting and lactating mothers, counselling on family planning needs, Adolescent Health Day for adolescents, monitoring growth of child development where services like general health checkups (Weight for age, BMI, Anaemia detection etc.), provision of essential drugs and micronutrients like IFA, albendazole, calcium are along with counselling and referral of identified high risk cases to appropriate institutions. Line listing and follow up of anaemia cases is also done in this platform.

Comprehensive Abortion Care (CAC)

To provide safe and accessible abortion care services, doctors and paramedics are trained in different methods of MTP upto CHC DP level.

Review of Maternal Deaths

To reduce the incidence of maternal deaths, each and every cause of maternal death is analysed and corrective action is taken accordingly at appropriate level. These reviews are undertaken at various levels so that steps can be taken for avoiding similar deaths in future.

Screening of Syphilis and HIV in Pregnant Women

For early management of syphilis and HIV among pregnant women, at all pregnant women are mobilized for screening test which is presently available up to delivery points. ANMs and ASHAs are mobilizing pregnant women for screening at the facility level and initiation of treatment, if found positive.

ANM Mentoring

This activity aims at improving knowledge and building defined skill sets of HW(F) for providing quality services in VHNDs and Sub-centre.

MAMATA Yojana

This scheme was launched in the year 2011 and is operational in the state to provide monetary support to the pregnant and lactating women of 19 years of age which enables them to seek improved nutrition and promote health seeking behaviour. The beneficiary will receive a total incentive of Rs. 5000 in four installments, subject to the fulfilment of specific conditions. Payment is made by e-transfer from the CDPO to the beneficiary account.

Janani Suraksha Yojana (JSY)

JSY is a safe motherhood intervention scheme implemented with the objective of reducing maternal and neonatal mortality by promoting institutional delivery among all pregnant women with provision of cash incentive of Rs. 1400 and Rs. 1000 for rural and urban area and Rs. 500 for home delivery cases belonging to BPL category respectively. The payment is made to the beneficiaries through Direct Bank Transfer (DBT) method only.

Janani Sishu Suraksha Karykram (JSSK)

JSSK assures cashless services to pregnant women, post-natal women up to 6 weeks after delivery and sick infants up to one year in government health institutions in both rural and urban areas.

New Born Care Corners (NBCC)

A special corner is established in the labour room of all delivery points with a set of equipment for immediate care of the newborn and Healthcare providers conducting deliveries have been trained in Nabjat Sishu Suraksha Karyakram (NSSK) for essential newborn care and resuscitation.

Kangaroo Mother Care (KMC) Units

KMC units have been established in all health facilities with SNCUs for ensuring warmth and early initiation of breastfeeding in low birth weight, preterm hypothermia and other sick newborns.

Findings

It is estimated that about 15 per cent of all pregnancies can develop complications of which five per cent can be life threatening. These complications cannot be predicted but if detected and timely care is provided then maternal deaths and disability can be averted. Further, there are no evidences that antenatal care alone will have considerable impact on reduction of maternal deaths. However, antenatal care is a crucial aspect of birth preparedness and complication readiness where pregnant women can be screened, danger signs can be detected, treated or referred and to ensure that the pregnant woman and her spouse or family members are educated and counselled. (*Source*: Odisha State Strategy for Accelerated reduction of Maternal and Infant Mortality, 2020).

The Maternal and Infant Mortality rate has been decreased significantly in India due to the innovative schemes adopted by the Government of India through the implementation of family welfare programmes. To improve the accessibility and affordability of quality health care especially for those residing in rural areas particularly the poor and vulnerable women and children, the government has launched National Rural Health Mission in 2005. (*Source*: Maternal Mortality in Orissa: An Epidemiological Study, by MY HEART).

Under the study, attempt was made to collect qualitative information pertaining to maternal mortality, infant mortality and challenges faced by the pregnant women, service providers, ASHAs, ANMs, Anganwadi

Workers and other medical staffs or government staffs etc. Members in the focus group discussions in all the Sub-centre villages were House-wives who actively participated in the process of discussion. In all cases SHGs leaders as well as AWW/ANM moderated the focus group discussion. The findings from each focus group discussion on the present theme have been enumerated below:

Year	*Pregnant*	*Registered*	*Child Birth*	*%*	*Reason*			
					Mis-carriage	*%*	*Child Death*	*%*
2017-18	49	48	46	94	2	4	1	2
2018-19	65	65	62	95	1	2	2	3

Data

In the year 2017-18, 49 women were pregnant, 48 were covered under MAMATA Yojana (Government Policy) but 1 (one) could not come under the policy due to under age (below 18). There were only 46 child births and rest 3 were child death. 2 child deaths were due to miscarriage and 1 child death was due to disease.

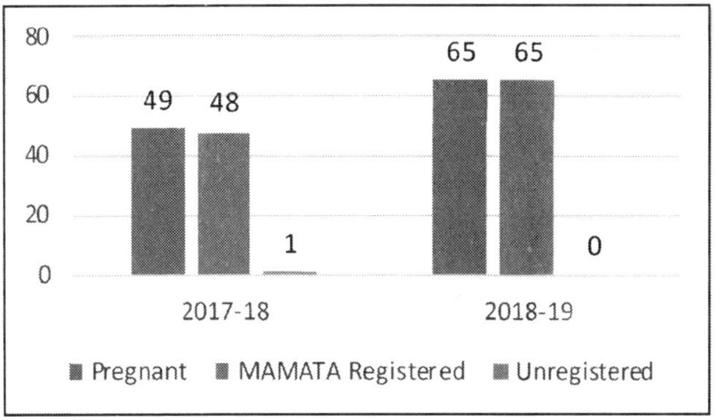

Fig.: Pregnant Beneficiaries Under Govt. Policy

In the year 2018-19, 65 women were pregnant, all were covered under MAMATA Yojana, but there were only 62 child births and rest 3 were child deaths, 1 was miscarriage and 2 were child deaths due to deficiency of vitamins.

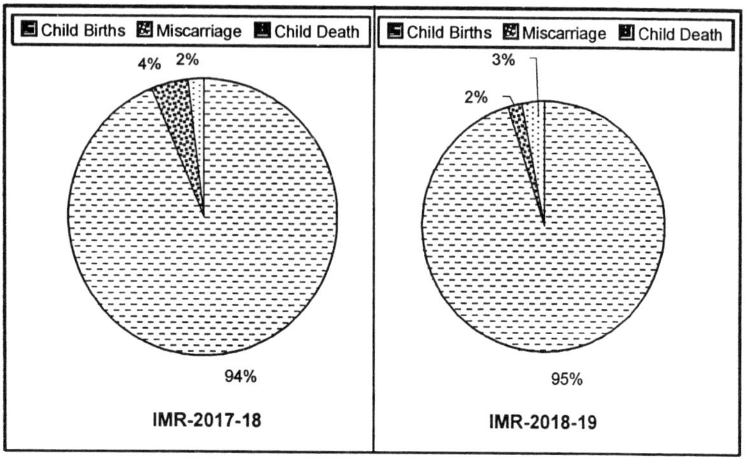

Antenatal Status of Women

Antenatal care generally implies that either a doctor, ANM or any other trained health personnel provides pregnancy related health care so as to avoid complication during pregnancy and child birth. Proper and effective counseling is also an integral part of ANC such as preventive care, diet during pregnancy, delivery and postnatal care. According to guideline envisaged in Reproductive and Child Health Program, ANC should include at least 3 health check-up, measurement of weight, height and blood pressure, administration of 2TT, consumption of IFA tablets and preventive measures for malaria.

Survival Status of Neo-Natal

About 58 per cent of newborn were reported to be alive in the post delivery period whereas only 29 per cent of newborn babies could not survive. It is to mention that in many of the health institutions are not properly equipped to provide neo-natal care. On the other hand, there was lack of health education programme on the aspect of effective neo-natal care and a role of service providers towards community.

Concluding Observations

The present empirical study has reflected the gap between policy formulation and policy implementation. The author concludes the chapter with an optimistic viewpoint suggesting measures to remove the loopholes in Maternal and Child Health Care Policies in Odisha.

Suggestions

- There should be increased awareness programme on maternal health and safe motherhood.
- Treatment at right time during pregnancy and sufficient nutritional food intake by PWs should be major responsibility of elderly members in every family including the husband.
- Services and system in sub-divisional medical centres should be improved and ensure quality maternal healthcare.

REFERENCES

Compendium of Research Projects in RCH (Ministry of Health and Family Welfare, Government of India).

Compendium of Research Projects in RCH (Ministry of Health Family and Welfare, Government of India).

Determinants of Maternal Care in a Region of South India, Jagdish C. Bhatia and John Cleland (Institute of Management, Bangalore, Prof. of Medical Demography, Centre for Population Studies, London School of Hygiene and Tropical Medicine, London, U.K.

Five Year Plans, Three volumes (2002-2007) Vol. I, Vol. II and Vol. III.

International Institute for Population Sciences (IIPS) and Macro International, (2008). *National Family Health Survey (NFHS-3)*, India, 2005-06: Orissa. IIPS, Mumbai.

International Institute for Population Sciences (IIPS), (2010). *District Level Household and Facility Survey (DLHS-3) 2007-08*, Orissa, India. IIPS, Mumbai.

Journal of Women's Health (An analysis of the Determinants of Maternal Mortality in Sub-Saharan Africa), Oct. 2004.

Mapping India's Children-UNICEF in action 2004-2005.

Midterm Appraisal of the Tenth Five Year Plan.

Ministry of Health and Family Welfare, Government of India—*Annual Report 2005-2006.*

Ministry of Health and Family Welfare, Government of India, *Annual Report 2005-2006.*

Mohan, R., Krishna, D.R., Shiva Kumar, A.K., Chatterjee, M., Sundararaman, T., (2011). Human resources for health in India. *Lancet* 377 (9765), 587-598. http://dx.doi.org/10.1016/S0140-6736(10)61888-0.

National Rural Health Mission (2005-2012) *Mission Document.*

National Rural Health Mission, *Mission Document*, Ministry of Health & Family Welfare, Government of India.

Odisha Economic Survey, 2017-18, Planning and Convergence Department, Government of Odisha.

10th Plan strategies for children.

13

An Assessment of Organised *versus* Unorganised Manufacturing Industries in India – State-wise Analysis since 1980

D. Indrakumar

Background

As India was basically agriculture based economy industrial sector was not given its due importance as a result of which virtually there were no major industries in pre-Independence era in the country. However there were many clusters/localities which dominated for artisanal and handicraft work in the country. Mostly all those product-specific clusters adopted the traditional methods to produce their products. Handloom textile products, crafts and artisanal items were the major products which were largely produced in the industrial clusters during the pre-Independence era. However, the modern industrial base which was systematically phased in Europe and America was not developed in the country because of technical issues. Even during British Rule, country has not shown any industrial development. Instead the textile raw materials were taken to United Kingdom from the country and send back as finished textile products. The marginal development in the logistics and infrastructural developments in the country during colonial period was not sufficient to promote industrial base in the country.

Certain industries especially in the field of textile/spinning and weaving were established during the pre-Independence era in the country. They were less in number and spread in few parts of the country. It was not spread over as it was spread in Europe and America after the industrial revolutions. The manufacturing industries in India have been established through huge public sector investments. Especially during the second Five Year Plan period (1956-1961) very large investments were made by the governments to establish industrial base in the country. Heavy industries in the fields like steel, petro-chemicals, electricity, natural gas etc, were established in the country by the huge investment of Government which sowed the seeds of industrial development in the country. Small and ancillary units in and around these big factories emerged from private sector during the 1950s and 1960s which were given protection through strict law and regulations. Even there was quota system to procure the items from these small scale industries in order to safeguard them from heavy industries.

Simultaneously, specialized policy initiatives were also taken up from time to time to attract more private investors in to the field. But the restricted technical base and skilled manpower during early industrial phase in the country affected the growth of the industrial base of the country. Government has taken various steps to address all these issues such as one made in mid-1980s for the easy and abundant availability of foreign technical support. Import of technical knowledge and technical cooperation were simplified in order to make the Indian manufactories more viable which gave a big impetus to the expeditious development of the factories in the country. This in turn attracted some of the multinational companies into India's manufacturing system.

Literature Analysis

In the case of number of enterprises and workers the unorganised manufacturing sectors are much bigger in size the organised segment of manufacturing. Some of the labour intensive industries (Food and Tobacco) the GVA per worker is higher in unorganised than the organized segment. As for as wage rate is concerned organised sectors wage rate is for higher than the unorganised segment of manufacturing (Gupta and Sanjay, 2012). There was a shift in the labour use pattern in the manufacturing industries since 1980s. The rise of unorganised manufacturing and informalisation (Sub-contracting of manufacturing activities, use of temporary and contractual workers in the production process) of organised manufacturing are the two major factors which led to change of labour use pattern in the country (Goldar and Aggarwal, 2010).

Unorganised sector plays a crucial role in provision of employment in labour abundant countries like India. Even after the reforms the unorganised manufacturing sector has shown a sharp rise in creation of employment (Saikia and Das, 2012). The employment in unorganised segment of manufacturing grew much higher than the employment in the organised segment of manufacturing. The employment of unorganised segment was 2.3 time higher than that of organised manufacturing employment in 1978-79 which further raised to 4.54 times higher for the year 1999-2000 (Mathur and Mishra, 2007).

There is fall in the growth of GVA of unorganized manufacturing sector during and after the reform period. From 9.7 per cent during the pre-reform period it fell to 4.4 per cent during the post-reforms period. Similarly the employment also had shown a decline during the post-reform periods. The introduction and implementation of economic policy reforms opened its avenues of stiff competition from the domestic organised sector and the global players as well, led the shrunken sustainability of unorganised manufacturing sector (Raj, 2011). There was a jobless growth in the organised manufacturing sector in 1980s, in contrary there was an increase of 3.5 per cent annual growth rate in per worker wage rate. The capital was substituted labour in this period and which automatically reduced the employment in the sector. During the reform period (1987-1998) there was a steady growth (3.2%) in employment in the organised manufacturing sector. It was argued that the reduction in wage rate may be the reason for the recovery of employment in the sector (Nagaraj, 2000).

Organised manufacturing segment constitute 85 per cent of total capital stock of the manufacturing sector. There was not much difference between pre-recession (2004-05 to 2007-08) and post-recession period (2008-09 to 2012-13) on the capital stock in the manufacturing sector. However, there is divergence among the industries in the stock of capital and growth of capital formation in the sector (Basu, Sengupta, 2016).

Employment in the organised manufacturing sector in India remained virtually stagnant during 1980s. In sharp contrast, there has been a substantial increase in employment in this sector in 1990s. From 1980-81 to 1990-91 employment in the organised manufacturing grew at the rate of only 0.53 per cent per annum which rose to 4.03 per cent per annum during the next five years, 1990-91 to 1995-96. The process of major economic reform initiated in 1991 marked the acceleration in employment growth in organized manufacturing (Goldar, 2000). There was a sharp increase in the employment in the organised manufacturing sectors in recent years. The share of employment size class up to 49 in the total employment size has fallen by 3 per cent and size class of 1000-1999 has increased by 2 per cent during 2002-03 to 2008-09. (Goldar, 2011). In terms of growth of the sector and in employment the economic reforms has achieved very little turn around during the post reform period (Gupta and Kumar, 2010). There is increasing trend of contractualisation of worker in organized manufacturing sector in the country (Panigrahi, 2016). There has been massive concentration of industries in a few large cities of different states (Gadesh, 2012).

There is no significant improvement in employment in the unorganized sector of the country. On the other hand, there is a sharp rise in the informal workforce in the economy (Nayak, 2010). There was huge reduction in total employment in the country from 2004-05 to 2010 which heavily affected the female workforce as found from 4.59 million women out of labour force from manufacturing sector alone (Kannan and Raveendran, 2012). But another views is that there was an absolute increase in employment in the manufacturing sector in the country. In 1999-2000 there were 44 million were employed in the sector which increased to 56 million in 2004-05 (Mehrotra *et al.*, 2012).

The employment in manufacturing has undergone drastic changes during the era of globalisation which forced enactment of flexible labour laws for survival in global market. In India also there is a sharp rise in the use of contractual, casual and temporary labourers (Rajeev, 2009). Indian manufacturing sector is the biggest employment provider in the private sector in the country. During the post-reform period (1991-92 to 2012-13) the manufacturing sector achieved a growth rate of 7.1 per cent (IBEF, 2017). There was no much fluctuation in the employment in the organised manufacturing segment. The increased employment maximum increased in unorganised segment similarly a fall in employment was mostly in unorganised segment of manufacturing (Mehrotra *et.al*, 2014). There was a sharp rise in the total employment in the organised manufacturing sector even though there was a decline in total employment in the country in 2011-12 (GoI, 2014).

An analysis by Mazumdar and Sarkar in 2004 about the employment elasticity in organised manufacturing during three different periods (1974 to 1980, 1980-1986 and 1986-1996) throws light on the trends in the sector. The results show that, the period between 1974 and 1980, the employment elasticity in the organized manufacturing sector was almost unity. It was negative during the second reference period and it was termed as 'jobless growth'. The third period which is also called the reforms period the employment elasticity in the sector has recovered (0.33%) from its negative (-0.16%) during previous period. There was a greater inequality in labour productivity among states in India (Bhalla, 2003).

There was a sharp increase in the productivity of labour in the organised segment of manufacturing industries over a period time. On the other hand, there was a fall in the labour productivity and growth of capital intensity in the unorganised manufacturing during the post-reform period. Growth of total factor productivity of organised manufacturing was better in 2000s than in the 1990s' post-reform periods (Kathuria, Raj, and Kumal Sen 2010).

By and large the study is based on secondary data. Annual Survey of Industries (ASI) and National Account Statistics (NAS) of Central Statistical Organisation (CSO) have been used for the analysis of the paper. ASI data from 1980-81 to 2015-16 (36 years) is considered for the present chapter.

Organised/Registered *versus* Unorganised/Unregistered Manufacturing

In an agrarian economy, the industrial development is mostly related to agriculture and allied industries which are by and large small and family type enterprises. Industries like textile industry which were slightly bigger in size and in volume of investments and employment were considered as factory sector during the early years of industrialisation while other industries were categorically classified into tiny, cottage and small scale industries. As per the industrial classification, all these industries fall fewer than two broad categories organized or registered manufacturing industries and unorganised or unregistered manufacturing industries. Based on the investment, employment and operational nature this classification is made. Since the beginning the unorganised/unregistered industrial sector has an edge over the organised/registered sector in the country. Still the country has around 85 per cent of the industrial units of the manufacturing sector under this unorganised/unregistered segment of manufacturing.

The most recent data (data for the year 2015-16) of the manufacturing shows that there are 19.66 millions of manufacturing enterprises under the unregistered segment of manufacturing whereas it is 0.23 million under the registered manufacturing segment of the manufacturing. Hence in terms of other indicators like the capital invested and productivity the organised manufacturing sector is far ahead compared to unorganised segment of the manufacturing. In terms of the employment, the organised segments provide employment to almost 14.30 million whereas it is 36.04 million in unorganised segment of manufacturing. This is clear from the data that, country has highest share of the manufacturing employment under the informal sector. The growth rate of both the segments of the manufacturing since 1950s is presented in Fig. 13.1. As already mentioned the organized/registered manufacturing sector had registered higher rate of growth during the entire reference period.

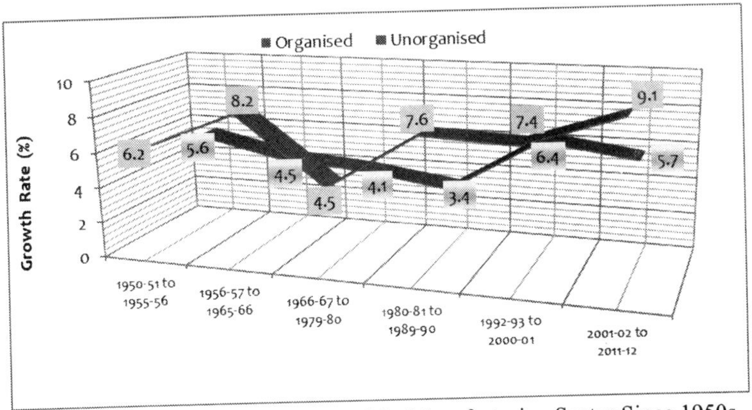

Figure 13.1: Growth Rate (CAGR) of the Manufacturing Sector Since 1950s

Source: Time Series Data of NSSO on Survey of Unorganized Enterprises and ASI Data on Registered Manufacturing.

Gross Domestic Product

Contribution of gross domestic product by the unorganised manufacturing was higher than the organised manufacturing segment of manufacturing up to mid of 1980s starting from 1950-51. After the introduction of various policy initiatives the industrial sector gained popularity in the country. Especially after the adoption of liberalisation process of the manufacturing sector in mid of 1980s, the organised manufacturing industries were started in large numbers and their volume of production has also increased. In the year 1950-51 the unorganised manufacturing contributed Rs. 16403 crore which rose to Rs. 26673 crores and Rs. 38787 crore for 1960-61 and 1970-71 respectively. Even in the year 1980-81 the unorganised manufacturing sector contributed higher than that of organised manufacturing with Rs. 54542 crore. In the year 1990-91 GDP contribution from organised manufacturing was higher than unorganised manufacturing. During the mid of 1980s and early years 1990s, the GDP contribution of the organized manufacturing was around 65 per cent of the total manufacturing. It continuously increased over the years and in 2011-12 the share of GDP reached 85 per cent of the total manufacturing (Table 13.1).

Table 13.1: Gross Domestic Product (GDP) of Organised and Unorganised Manufacturing Sectors since 1950s (2004-05 Constant Price – Values in crores)

Year	*Registered*	*Unregistered*	*Year*	*Registered*	*Unregistered*
1950-51	10317	16403	1983-84	73809	65797
1951-52	10590	16997	1984-85	79444	65617
1952-53	10639	18046	1985-86	81639	68102
1953-54	11107	19952	1986-87	85648	72399
1954-55	12343	20694	1987-88	91372	75371
1955-56	13856	21531	1988-89	102059	78366
1956-57	15400	22427	1989-90	114458	81353
1957-58	16119	23111	1990-91	120905	84090
1958-59	16583	24735	1991-92	119382	80467
1959-60	18256	25630	1992-93	121842	84387
1960-61	20581	26673	1993-94	135536	93877
1961-62	22294	28777	1994-95	153210	107550
1962-63	24466	30081	1995-96	177620	115207
1963-64	27234	32275	1996-97	196693	121373
1964-65	29481	33982	1997-98	191557	124420
1965-66	30447	33298	1998-99	198203	130202
1966-67	30474	33867	1999-2000	208257	139476
1967-68	29481	35600	2000-01	223687	136464
1968-69	31475	37052	2001-02	234943	142687
1969-70	36941	38017	2002-03	254225	149883
1970-71	37821	38787	2003-04	272180	160881
1971-72	38504	40847	2004-05	292344	171281
1972-73	39731	42854	2005-06	327739	191084
1973-74	41690	44488	2006-07	379374	211545
1974-75	42107	46929	2007-08	417528	214247
1975-76	42533	48581	2008-09	422055	223756
1976-77	47845	50572	2009-10	506679	239912
1977-78	51054	53384	2010-11	555240	246509
1978-79	56625	61036	2011-12	607589	249309
1979-80	55434	58158	2012-13	660350	2621449
1980-81	54542	59709	2013-14	717692	275650
1981-82	59245	64299	2014-15	780014	289846
1982-83	64041	63092	2015-16	847747	304774

Source: National Accounts Statistics, 2015-16, Central Statistical Organization, Ministry of Statistics and Programme Implementation, Government of India

The growth of the GDP of the organised and unorganized manufacturing sector is presented in Fig. 13.2. Even though the GDP share of the unorganised manufacturing was higher than the organised manufacturing and the growth was slower than that of the organised manufacturing. For the period 1971-72 to 1980-81, the growth rate was almost equal for both the segments of the manufacturing. There was a continuous rise in the contribution of the GDP of the manufacturing.

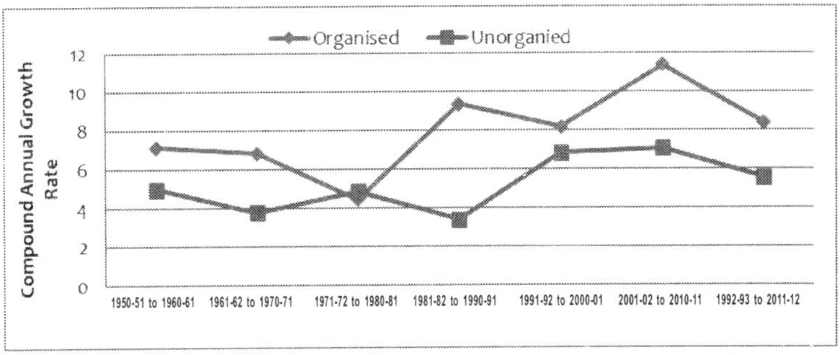

Figure 13.2: Growth Trend of Gross Domestic Product since 1950-51

Source: Time Series Data, National Accounts Statistics, Central Statistical Organisation, Government of India.

Gross Capital Formation

The gross capital formation of the manufacturing sector is presented in the Fig. 13.3. Like the other indicators, the share of organised manufacturing sector has the maximum capital formation of the manufacturing sector. Starting from the 1980s the organised segment of the manufacturing has the three-fourths of the capital formation of the sector. There was fall in the share contribution of the unorganised manufacturing sector and increased in the 2000-01 and again started falling afterwards.

Value of Output and Net Value Added

The value of output produced by the manufacturing sector along with the net value added shows that there was consistent rise in both the indicators for both the segments of manufacturing. The organised segment of manufacturing has achieved a faster and higher growth for both value of output produced as well as net value addition since 1980s. Especially

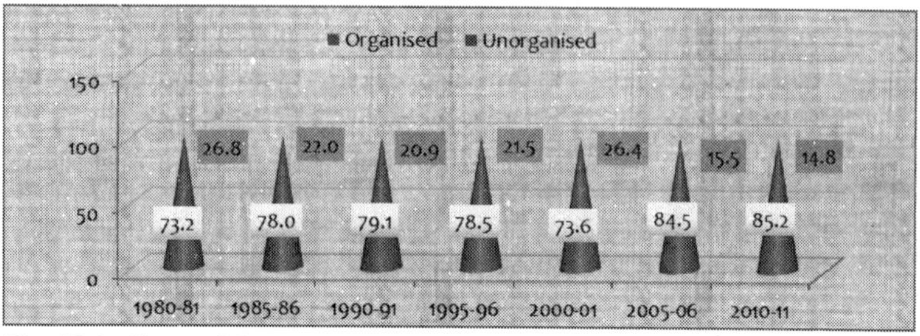

Fig. 13.3: Share of Gross Domestic Product since 1980-81 (%)

Source: Time Series Data, National Accounts Statistics, Central Statistical Organisation, Government of India.

during the post-reform period the organized segment of the manufacturing has registered a very significant growth in terms of output produced whereas the unorganized manufacturing has performed well during the pre-reforms era (Table 13.2).

State-wise Assessment

The state-wise proportion of organized segment of manufacturing industries is shown in Table 13.3. Data analysed for 22 big states shows that Uttarakhand has the maximum share of 40 per cent of their manufacturing industries under the organised/registered category followed by Kerala and Maharashtra with 33 per cent. Similarly, Jammu Kashmir, Himachal Pradesh and Tamil Nadu also have around 30 per cent while Assam, Delhi and Karnataka have more than 20 per cent manufacturing enterprises under the organised/registered segment of the manufacturing in the country.

Jharkhand followed by Odisha has the least proportion of the organised manufacturing sector. Just around one per cent in Jharkhand and 4.3 per cent in Odisha are under the organised segment of manufacturing. Bihar (4.7%), Rajasthan (8%), Andhra Pradesh (10%), and West Bengal (around 10%) also have less proportion of organised manufacturing sector. Surprisingly, Uttar Pradesh which has more industrial units has just 9 per cent of the industrial units under organised segment of manufacturing. It is clear from the data that vast majority of the manufacturing enterprises in almost all states are from the unorganised segments. There is a need of specialized policy framework to address problem of these enormous micro and small manufacturing enterprises in the country. In order to recognise them as an industry for availing

Table 13.2: Value of Output Produced by the Manufacturing since 1980-81.

(2004-05 Constant Price, Value is Rs. crores)

Year	*Value of Output*		*Net Value Added*	
	Registered	*Unregistered*	*Registered*	*Unregistered*
1980-81	61047	11129	8582	10735
1981-82	74255	13072	10106	12525
1982-83	86078	13385	11591	12743
1983-84	94688	15066	14663	14331
1984-85	112470	16274	16855	15366
1985-86	128702	18018	18440	16889
1986-87	141988	20359	19849	18999
1987-88	162065	22812	22635	21278
1988-89	196825	28050	27477	24134
1989-90	244354	30142	34542	27744
1990-91	288989	34278	39469	31483
1991-92	321968	36310	41469	32968
1992-93	363931	43911	46200	40118
1993-94	410021	49506	55548	45297
1994-95	503254	58924	72092	54016
1995-96	628283	73854	91787	67622
1996-97	694579	81800	105145	74696
1997-98	763915	91142	100223	83250
1998-99	816208	100588	105925	91791
1999-2000	925883	112719	106118	102982
2000-01	1050923	122704	124243	111313
2001-02	1118732	120955	133637	108099
2002-03	1246610	129128	151381	115733
2003-04	1425645	142953	174902	127470
2004-05	1657655	160881	205844	140651
2005-06	1885953	618227	246015	153313
2006-07	2360689	672710	311499	181928
2007-08	2726660	791809	357748	212317
2008-09	3195260	975519	407017	225214
2009-10	3644324	1049435	463886	245251
2010-11	4550578	1193596	553152	281378
2011-12	5164863	1332514	612068	312477
2012-13	5934428	1547049	702654	348412
2013-14	6818658	1796124	806647	388479
2014-15	7834638	2085300	926031	433154

Source: National Accounts Statistics—2015-16, Time Series Data, Central Statistical Organisation.

financial and loan support from commercial banks there is a need of the policy supports. It will again sustain and make an impact on the quality of the products and services produced by these enterprises.

Table 13.3: Distribution of Registered Manufacturing Enterprises by States

Sl. No.	*State/UT*	*2015-16 (%)*		
		Rural	*Urban*	*Total*
1.	Andhra Pradesh	7.9	12.7	10.0
2.	Assam	14.7	70.2	25.4
3.	Bihar	4.1	6.3	4.7
4.	Chhattisgarh	11.3	34.1	18.6
5.	Delhi	1.5	23.5	23.4
7.	Gujarat	6.4	20.4	17.1
8.	Haryana	6.3	21.3	14.2
9.	Himachal Pradesh	25.1	64.4	29.5
10.	Jammu & Kashmir	26.8	34.3	29.4
11.	Jharkhand	0.4	5.0	0.9
12.	Karnataka	12.7	34.2	22.0
13.	Kerala	28.3	36.5	32.6
14.	Madhya Pradesh	4.3	29.2	13.8
15.	Maharashtra	19.0	45.1	32.6
16.	Odisha	3.5	8.5	4.3
17.	Punjab	3.1	25.6	15.1
18.	Rajasthan	2.5	12.7	8.0
19.	Tamil Nadu	21.8	33.1	28.9
20.	Uttar Pradesh	3.8	16.1	8.7
21.	Uttarakhand	25.4	65.4	40.3
22.	West Bengal	6.1	19.8	9.6
	Total	**8.3**	**24.6**	**15.1**

Source: NSSO Report No. 581 on Economic Characteristics of Unincorporated Non-Agricultural Enterprises (Excluding Construction) in India.

Type of Industry-wise Distribution

The share of organised manufacturing industries in the total manufacturing by type of industry is presented in Table 13.4. All the manufacturing industries are classified into 25 sub-categories of industries. The highly technical and capital-intensive industries have the maximum share of organised segment of industries at national level. Manufacturing of machinery and equipment industries dominates in the share of organised manufacturing sector. A vast majority of 82 per cent of the total industries in this category are in organised segment. Similarly, manufacturing industry of motor vehicles, trailers and semi-trailers stands at second with 78 percentages of organised manufacturing industries. Capital intensive industries like, manufacturing of coke and refined petroleum products, printing and recorded Media, manufacturing of computer an electronic optical products also have majority of industries in organised segment of manufacturing.

Table 13.4: Share of Manufacturing Industries by its Nature and Type, 2015-16

NIC Activity Category	*Percentage of Enterprises*	
	Registered	*Unregistered*
1. Cotton ginning, cleaning and bailing	38.1	61.9
2. Manufacture of food products	30.2	69.8
3. Manufacture of beverages	14.1	85.9
4. Manufacture of tobacco products	2.7	97.3
5. Manufacture of textiles	14.6	85.4
6. Manufacture of wearing apparel	9.4	90.6
7. Manufacture of leather and related products	13.2	86.8
8. Wood and products of wood, cork	9.2	90.8
9. Manufacture of paper and paper products	14.9	85.1
10. Printing and reproduction of recorded media	64.9	35.1
11. Mfg. coke and refined petroleum products	68.0	32.0
12. Manufacture of chemical and chemical products	11.5	88.5
13. Mfg. Pharmaceuticals, medicinal and botanical products	34.3	65.7
14. Manufacture of Rubber and Plastic Products	36.5	63.5
15. Mfg. other Non-metallic mineral products	14.3	85.7
16. Manufacture of basic metals	40.7	59.3
17. Manufacture of fabricated metal products	38.2	61.8
18. Manufacturing of computer, electronic optical products	58.9	41.1
19. Manufacture of Electrical Equipment	55.8	44.2
20. Manufacture of Machinery and Equipment n.e.c.	82.4	17.6
21. Mfg. of Motor Vehicles trailers and semi-trailers	77.9	22.1
22. Manufacture of other Transport Equipment	25.9	74.1
23. Manufacture of furniture	15.7	84.3
24. Other Manufacturing	23.3	76.7
25. Repairing, Installation of machinery and equipment	19.7	80.3
All Manufacturing	**15.1**	**84.9**

Source: NSSO Report 581 on Economic Characteristics of Unincorporated Non-Agricultural Enterprises (Excluding Construction) in India.

Note : Mfg. is manufacturing.

In the case of labour intensive industries, a vast majority of the industries are in unorganised category. Manufacturing of tobacco products have just only 3 per cent of the total industries (a total of 3.27 million enterprises) in organised manufacturing category. Similarly, manufacturing of wood, products of wood, cork and manufacturing of wearing apparels has just 9 per cent of the industries under organised segment of manufacturing. Surprisingly, manufactusring of chemical and chemical products also have less proportion of organised segment of industries. Manufacturing of leather and leather related products, manufacturing of beverages, manufacturing of paper and paper products and manufacturing of furniture also have less share of organized segment industries.

Unorganized Manufacturing Enterprises by State

A brief description of the unorganized manufacturing industries of the country is given in this part. The data for the post-reforms period are mostly considered for analysis. The state-wise distribution of manufacturing enterprises is presented in Table 13.5. There were 17.07 million unorganised manufacturing enterprises in the country in 2005-06 and it has increased to 17.21 million in 2010-11. In the year 2015-16 country has 19.66 million unregistered manufacturing enterprises. Enterprises had an annual growth rate of just 0.2 per cent between 2005-06 to around 3 per cent between the periods of 2010-1 to 2015-16.

The state-wise data indicates that, West Bengal had maximum of the unorganised manufacturing enterprises amounting to 2.75 million enterprises out of 17 million total enterprises in the year 2005-06 which increased to 2.76 million in 2010-11 and to 4.12 million out of 19.66 million total enterprises in the year 2015-16. Uttar Pradesh stands at second position with the share of 2.36 million in the year 2005-06. However, the Uttar Pradesh has shown a decline in the number of unorganised manufacturing enterprises after 2005-06. It has come down to 2.34 million in the year 2010-11 and to 22 million in 2015-16.

Similarly many more states have shown a decline in the share of the unorganised manufacturing enterprises after 2005-06. Half of the States and Union Territories had reported a decline in the number of unorganised manufacturing enterprises. Entire North Eastern States except Tripura had reported a decline in the number of enterprises. Jharkhand, Bihar and Odisha have also registered a negative growth in the number of the unorganised manufacturing enterprises during the reference period. All the industrially developed states had registered slightly better growth rate in the number of enterprises. Union Territories like Chandigarh, Dadar and Nagar Haveli had registered a higher rate of growth for the number of manufacturing enterprises.

States which have shown a negative growth during 2005-06 to 2010-11 had revived during 2010-11 to 2015-16. An even state from the North Eastern States which has shown negative growth during previous five years has increased number of units of manufacturing enterprises. Many states have registered better growth during the recent years it is the unregistered manufacturing sector. Small States and Union Territories have shown higher growth than the industrially developed States during 2010-11 to 2015-16.

Table 13.5: State-wise Distribution of Unorganized Manufacturing Enterprises

State/UT	*2005-06*	*2010-11*	*2015-16*	*CAGR*	
				2005-06 to 2010-11	2010-11 to 2015-16
A & N Islands	2316	2901	2600	4.6	-2.2
Andhra Pradesh	1533239	1620332	2164142	1.1	6.0
Arunachal Pradesh	859	1419	977	10.6	-7.2
Assam	370781	218559	203187	-10.0	-1.4
Bihar	772397	448080	768427	-10.3	11.4
Chandigarh	1373	5236	6733	30.7	5.2
Chhattisgarh	207481	164678	194792	-4.5	3.4
D. Nagar Haveli	969	1663	4629	11.4	22.7
Daman Diu	2639	2129	1635	-4.2	-5.1
Delhi	97636	204697	181113	16.0	-2.4
Goa	10308	8720	11760	-3.3	6.2
Gujarat	654358	1416655	1240891	16.7	-2.6
Haryana	230110	189662	182923	-3.8	-0.7
Himachal Pradesh	107442	91393	93904	-3.2	0.5
Jammu Kashmir	173412	223103	234393	5.2	1.0
Jharkhand	585948	335233	494131	-10.6	8.1
Karnataka	961761	860837	1248744	-2.2	7.7
Kerala	658692	502080	545820	-5.3	1.7
Lakshadweep	397	470	737	3.4	9.4
Madhya Pradesh	854559	884062	833154	0.7	-1.2
Maharashtra	1126462	1385243	1243261	4.2	-2.1
Manipur	52518	41014	64059	-4.8	9.3
Meghalaya	36987	19456	15836	-12.1	-4.0
Mizoram	5101	4003	8283	-4.7	15.7
Nagaland	9906	7162	16053	-6.3	17.5
Odisha	957229	615179	486352	-8.5	-4.6
Puducherry	13572	15502	24511	2.7	9.6
Punjab	293237	387320	383688	5.7	-0.2
Rajasthan	636470	627358	750970	-0.3	3.7
Sikkim	4103	1190	2413	-21.9	15.2
Tamil Nadu	1481933	1652241	1744620	2.2	1.1
Tripura	45370	69780	50084	9.0	-6.4
Uttar Pradesh	2359375	2341139	2209519	-0.2	-1.2
Uttarakhand	69087	97719	72143	7.2	-5.9
West Bengal	2752793	2764054	4178391	0.1	8.6
All India	17070820	17210269	19664875	0.2	2.7

Source: NSSO Reports No. 541 and 581 on Economic Characteristics of Unincorporated Non-Agricultural Enterprises (Excluding Construction) in India.

There was not much growth in the employment in the unorganised manufacturing enterprises during the post-reforms periods. The number of workers engaged in the sector declined from 36.4 million in 2005-06 to 34.9 million in 2010-11. Similarly enterprises, in West Bengal, Uttar

Pradesh, Tamil Nadu, Andhra Pradesh, Maharashtra and Karnataka have the maximum share of workers in the sector (Table 13.6).

Table 13.6: State-wise Distribution of Workforce in Unorganised Manufacturing Enterprises

State/UT	*2005-06*	*2010-11*	*2015-16*	*CAGR between*	
				2005-06 to 2010-11	2010-11 to 2015-16
1. A N Islands	6037	6431	5979	1.3	-1.4
2. Andhra Pradesh	2938945	3104102	3441171	1.1	2.1
3. Arunachal Pradesh	3301	3994	2108	3.9	-12.0
4. Assam	632481	422025	385949	-7.8	-1.8
5. Bihar	1453073	751265	1217000	-12.4	10.1
6. Chandigarh	2599	8574	22484	27.0	21.3
7. Chhattisgarh	458366	351693	421335	-5.2	3.7
8. D Nagar Haveli	2264	4750	10881	16.0	18.0
9. Daman Diu	8550	3673	2940	-15.5	-4.4
10. Delhi	457208	745141	711586	10.3	-0.9
11. Goa	28487	19062	29170	-7.7	8.9
12. Gujarat	1852132	3214985	2645402	11.7	-3.8
13. Haryana	544024	467773	418405	-3.0	-2.2
14. Himachal Pradesh	165433	154179	140296	-1.4	-1.9
15. Jammu & Kashmir	318869	338342	338338	1.2	0.0
16. Jharkhand	949345	602820	754036	-8.7	4.6
17. Karnataka	1974369	1509006	2176332	-5.2	7.6
18. Kerala	1391006	977902	1011574	-6.8	0.7
19. Lakshadweep	712	1293	1009	12.7	-4.8
20. Madhya Pradesh	1740646	1534863	1453950	-2.5	-1.1
21. Maharashtra	2901417	3218880	2493117	2.1	-5.0
22. Manipur	81370	60895	89832	-5.6	8.1
23. Meghalaya	90437	39103	28634	-15.4	-6.0
24. Mizoram	9447	7275	12392	-5.1	11.2
25. Nagaland	16307	10122	28780	-9.1	23.2
26. Odisha	2023541	1266014	847052	-9.0	-7.7
27. Puducherry	44709	34418	46463	-5.1	6.2
28. Punjab	600810	773754	686875	5.2	-2.4
29. Rajasthan	1295335	1219722	1339887	-1.2	1.9
30. Sikkim	7626	4091	3343	-11.7	-4.0
31. Tamil Nadu	3369519	3513927	3403099	0.8	-0.6
32. Tripura	144860	112937	76080	-4.9	-7.6
33. Uttar Pradesh	5287901	5225929	4708925	-0.2	-2.1
34. Uttarakhand	147838	173233	127351	3.2	-6.0
35. West Bengal	5493833	5006261	6959544	-1.8	6.8
All India Level	36442799	34888434	36041319	-0.9	0.7

Source: NSSO Reports No. 541 and 581 on Economic Characteristics of Unincorporated Non-agricultural Enterprises (Excluding Construction) in India.

Unorganised Manufacturing Enterprises by Type

Number of unorganised manufacturing enterprises and proportion of workers engaged in enterprises is presented in Table 13.7. In 2010-11, labour-intensive industries constituted a large proportion of the unorganised manufacturing enterprises. Manufacturing industries of textile and apparel items represents more than 40 per cent of the enterprises of the unorganized manufacturing enterprises. Manufacturing of wearing apparel industry alone had the share of 25 per cent of total enterprises. Manufacturing of tobacco products is in the third position with the share of 13 per cent closely followed by the manufacturing of food products with 12 per cent. Similarly manufacturing of woods and products of woods, corks is also had around 10 per cent of the total enterprises. It is clear that a vast majority of the enterprises of the unorganised manufacturing segments are from labour intensive industries. Highly technical and capital intensive industries are very limited in number.

There is a sharp increase in the number of unorganized manufacturing enterprises in 2015-16. 2.54 million new enterprises had entered within a span of five years during 2010-11 to 2015-16. Mostly the labour intensive enterprises have shown a better growth during this period. Again the manufacturing enterprise of apparel items dominates with almost 29 per cent of the units. Enterprises which produce the tobacco products also had shown an increase during the period with an increased share of 17 per cent in 2015-16 from 13 per cent in 2010-11. Manufacturing of fabricated metal products and other transport equipment industries also had shown improvement during the period. However, manufacturing enterprises of wood and wood products and manufacturing of textiles had shown a fall in number of enterprises during reference period.

The data on number of workers per enterprise show stagnation during the reference period. On an average only two workers are in each enterprise in the country. However, few industries have engaged with little more workers per factory. Eight out of 25 industrial categories in 2010-11 and seven out of 25 of enterprises groups in 2015-16 engaged 4 or more workers per factory. Capital intensive industries engage more workers per factory than the labour intensive enterprises. Manufacturing of coke and refined petroleum products, manufacturing of pharmaceuticals and medicinal plants and enterprises which engage in production of non-metallic mineral products are having maximum of 5 workers per factory in 2010-11. The manufacturing of machineries and equipment enterprises has 7 workers per factory in 2015-16. Enterprises of cotton ginning, cleaning and bailing have shown a steep increase in the number of workers per factory. Number of workers has increased to 6 workers per factory in 2015-16 from just 2 in 2010-11. Similarly, manufacturers of coke, refined petroleum products, manufacturers of electrical equipment and machineries and equipment also had shown some improvement.

Table 13.7: Distribution of Enterprises and Workers by State

NIC Activity Category	*No. of Enterprises*		*No. of Workers*		*No. of Workers per Enterprise*	
	2010-11	*2015-16*	*2010-11*	*2015-16*	*2010-11*	*2015-16*
M1	5879	1684	13372	9422	2	6
M2	2030286	2274396	4420455	4767455	2	2
M3	210909	185532	372106	343642	2	2
M4	2247706	3275118	3083896	3945784	1	1
M5	2641683	2603535	5862524	4977912	2	2
M6	4320323	5610296	6535563	7864479	2	1
M7	116202	155692	324833	459493	3	3
M8	1586446	1190888	2832487	2178195	2	2
M9	119299	107332	341824	243419	3	2
M10	155756	161187	487544	460043	3	3
M11	1925	2173	10066	11958	5	6
M12	210800	172706	481496	372020	2	2
M13	4633	6345	22265	22146	5	3
M14	178870	124800	558006	419000	3	3
M15	593910	612577	2845864	2806205	5	5
M16	56968	51517	128678	176647	2	3
M17	622432	789407	1824212	2020586	3	3
M18	13447	14238	63985	36119	5	3
M19	35393	37609	130111	179445	4	5
M20	75096	80523	301927	546484	4	7
M21	18393	21611	95645	95689	5	4
M22	9711	6378	40894	22424	4	4
M23	605768	870882	1207197	1652884	2	2
M24	1050002	948893	2330467	1872382	2	2
M25	298432	359556	573017	557486	2	2
Total	**17210269**	**19664875**	**34888434**	**36041319**	**2**	**2**

Source: NSSO Reports No. 541 and 581 on Economic Characteristics of Unincorporated Non-agricultural Enterprises (Excluding Construction) in India.

Organized/Registered Manufacturing

All the major achievements landmarks of the Indian manufacturing happened after the adoption of the new economic reforms. Minor liberalization process initiated in the mid-1980s and New Economic Policy of 1991 had changed the structure and features of the Indian manufacturing. From a controlled and regulated system of functioning it was transformed into a free and exit system of operation by the manufacturing sector in the country. Initially public sector undertakings acted as the agent for the industrial development in the country. Many large and heavy industrial establishments were developed by the government. Inadequate participation of the private sector in the industrial development in the beginning forced the government to initiate appropriate action to strengthen the contribution of the private sector for the industrial development of the country. Government has slowly started withdrawing the control over the industrial sector. Registration formalities and approvals for starting an industry were simplified in order to attract more new players in the field which proved fruitful. The brief profile of the organised manufacturing industries of the country since 1980-81 to 2015-16 is described.

The number of factories registered in the country has shown a sharp increase especially after the adoption of the new economic reforms. There were 6526 registered factories in the country at the time of Independence which had increased to 30 thousand in seventies. Similarly, the total employment (total persons employed) in the sector also increase to 1.64 million in 1949 to 2.18 million in 1980s. In 1974-75 there were 64224 factories in the country with the total employment of 10.82 million. The share of workers was 44 per cent of the total employment. In the year 1992-93 there were 119494 factories and which increased to 127182 in 2001-02 and at present (in 2015-16) country has 233116 registered organised manufacturing industries.

The period of 1980s is called the era of pre-liberalization featured with regulated/controlled and highly protected industrial setups. The industrial growth stagnated during this period. The industrial development has not taken direction towards expected line which forced government to take various measures towards strengthening the manufacturing sector. As already discussed the industrial policies 1980s have introduced some specific policy supports and incentives to the industries in order to attract more players in to the sector. It was the beginning to start a policy framework towards further change in the policy framework related to the industries. The planners and policy makers had adopted strategy to favour the industries in each feature policy frameworks.

During the 1990s, the period of complete liberalization, there was a sharp rise in the number of factories registered in the country. Registration of new factories continuously increased up to 1995-96. The new economic reforms of 1991 might have attracted many new investors in the manufacturing sector. There was a fall in the number of factories in 1996-97 which again recovered in 1997-98. In the last two years there was fall in the number of factories in the organised segment of manufacturing.

Experts opine that the real impact of the economic reforms could be witnessed only after a period of decade. Impact of the economic reforms may be visible in 2000 which is 10th year of implementation. There were many structural changes in the economy during the first ten years of post-reform period. Agriculture has stagnated in all aspects and contribution from the industrial sector also becomes stagnant and the services sector has registered unprecedented growth. In order to enhance the contribution of the industrial sector many policies and measures were also announced as and when required. Huge policy support has been provided to the industrial sector especially the manufacturing sector has given complete autonomy to operate. Many public sector undertakings have been privatised and disinvested. All these steps have really made some changes in the organised manufacturing sector of the country.

The number of registered manufacturing factories has reached a peak in 2000s. In 2000-01 there were 131728 factories in the country which increased to 140160 in 2005-06 an addition of 8432 new factories within a period of five years. In the year 2010-11 the factories have increased to 211660 an addition of 71500 new factories were registered. Almost 14300 new industries were registered per annum during the five years period 2005-06 to 2010-11. Many multinational companies and corporate started their new manufacturing companies in the country. Lifting of cap and barriers in foreign direct investments (FDI) in almost all sectors of the economy was one of the main reasons for the augmentation the registration of new factories. Highly potential market economy, growing young population flexible labour and industrial laws and availability of technical and skilled manpower are some other factors which might have been the reasons for the increase in the number of manufacturing factories in the country. There is a peak in the growth chart (Fig. 13.6) because of the economic growth during 2008-09 which also reached a double digit growth. Entire economy of the country showed upward trend during the period.

The state-wise distribution of industries shows a steady increase in new industrial establishments. Almost all states have registered new industries during the period 2000-01 to 2015-16. At national level more than one lakh new industrial establishments were established during the period (Table 13.8).

Table 13.8: State-wise distribution of Industries during 2000-01 to 2015-16

States	*2000-2001*	*2005-2006*	*2010-2011*	*2015-2016*	*Increase 2000-01 to 2015-16*
I. Big States					
Andhra Pradesh	14029	15790	26286	31214	17185
Bihar	1535	1669	2805	3623	2088
Chhattisgarh	1275	1478	2358	3037	1762
Delhi	3498	3312	3920	3776	278
Goa	524	543	583	654	130
Gujarat	14090	14055	21282	24426	10336
Haryana	4448	4304	5967	7953	3505
Himachal Pradesh	507	808	2210	2767	2260
Jammu & Kashmir	356	519	795	945	589
Jharkhand	1500	1590	2504	2831	1331
Karnataka	7010	7835	10722	12973	5963
Kerala	4853	5643	6917	7580	2727
Madhya Pradesh	3221	2951	4212	4426	1205
Maharashtra	18528	18711	27892	28210	9682
Odisha	1665	1862	2536	2948	1283
Punjab	7137	8332	12770	12521	5384
Rajasthan	5112	6005	8172	9049	3937
Tamil Nadu	20601	21265	36843	37331	16730
Uttar Pradesh	9635	10503	13756	15291	5656
Uttarakhand	744	900	2739	2978	2234
West Bengal	6091	6077	8232	9300	3209
II. North E. States					
Assam	1435	1864	2795	3890	2455
Tripura	239	307	472	558	319
Other NE States	218	234	338	668	450
III. Union Territories					
D N Haveli and Daman Diu	2177	2658	3397	3224	1047
Other UTs	842	945	1157	963	121
All India	**131728**	**140160**	**211660**	**233116**	**101388**

Source: Annual Survey of Industries, Time Series Data, Central Statistical Organisation.

There was drastic growth in the manufacturing industries in the country in recent years. As compared with the unorganised manufacturing the organised manufacturing industries have expanded at large scale. The implementation of new economic reforms in 1991 has helped the manufacturing sector to grow much faster. There is sharp rise in the large scale manufacturing industries in the country after this reform. Country has become one of the most favoured industrial destiny of the world for certain manufacturing items like automobile industries.

NOTES AND COMMENTS

Registered/Organized Manufacturing: The registered or organised manufacturing sector and the unregistered manufacturing sector are complementary to each other. These together constitute manufacturing sector. The manufacturing sector covers all manufacturing, processing and repair and maintenance services units irrespective of their employment size, investment and location.

Unregistered Unorganised Manufacturing – Unregistered or unorganised manufacturing are being complementary to registered manufacturing sector—thus, by implication, covers all those units which are not covered under the registered manufacturing sector. In other words, the unregistered manufacturing sector covers all the manufacturing, processing, repair and maintenance services units employing less than 10 workers and using power or less than 20 workers and not using power. It, by implication, also covers own account enterprises (OAE) engaged in the manufacturing activity. However, conversion of sugarcane into indigenous *gur*, slaughtering of animals and dressing of meat carried out by farmers and individuals are excluded from this sector as they are included under agriculture and allied activities

Gross Capital Formation **(GCF)** refers to the aggregate of gross additions to fixed assets (i.e., fixed capital formation) and change in stocks during the counting period. Fixed assets comprise construction and machinery and equipment including transport equipment.

Value of Output comprises total ex-factory total values of products and by-products manufactured as well as other receipts such as receipts from non-industrial services rendered to others, work done for others on materials supplied by them, value of electricity produced and sold, sale value of goods sold as purchased and the addition in the stock of semi-finished goods.

Net Value Added is arrived by deducting total input and depreciation from total output.

NIC Activity Category : **M1**—Cotton ginning, cleaning and bailing, **M2**—Manufacture of food products, **M3**—Manufacture of Beverages, **M4**—Manufacture of Tobacco Products, **M5**-Manufacture of Textiles, **M6**—Manufacture of Wearing Apparel, **M7**—Manufacture of Leather and related products, **M8**—Manufacturing of Wood and Products of Wood, Cork, **M9**—Manufacture of Paper and paper products, **M10**—Printing and reproduction of recorded media, **M11**—Manufacturing of Coke and refined petroleum products, **M12**—Manufacture of chemical and chemical products, **M13**—Manufacturing of Pharmaceuticals, medicinal and botanical products, **M14**—Manufacture of Rubber and Plastic Products, **M15**—Manufacturing of other Non-metallic mineral products, **M16**—Manufacture of basic Metals, **M17**—Manufacture of fabricated metal products, **M18**—Manufacturing of computer, electronic and optical products, **M19**—Manufacture of Electrical Equipment, **M20**-Manufacture of Machinery and Equipment n.e.c., **M21**—Manufacture of Motor Vehicle trailers and semi-trailers, **M22**—Manufacture of other Transport Equipment, **M23**—Manufacture of furniture, **M24**—Other Manufacturing and **M25**—Repairing, Installation of machinery and equipment.

Classification of NIC 2 Digit as per NIC 1998 and NIC 2004: *15*—Manufacture of Food Products and Beverages, *16*—Manufacture of Tobacco and Tobacco Products, *17*—Manufacturing of Textiles, *18*—Manufacturing of Wearing Apparels; Dressing and Dyeing of Fur, *19*—Dressing of Tanning of Leather manufacture of luggage, handbags, saddlery, harness and footwear, *20*—Manufacturing of Wood and Wood Products and Cork, manufacturing of Articles of Straw and Plaiting Materials, *21*—Manufacturing of Paper and Paper Products, *22*—Publishing, Printing and Reproduction of Recorded Media, *23*—Manufacture of Coke, Refined Petroleum Products and Nuclear Fuel, *24*—Manufacture of Chemicals and Chemical Products, *25*—Manufacture of Rubber and Plastic Products, *26*—Manufacture of Other Non-Metallic Mineral Products, *27*—Manufacture of Basic Metal, *28*—Manufacture of Fabricated Metal Products, except machinery and equipment, *29*—Manufacture of Machinery and Equipment n.e.c, *30*—Manufacture of Office, Accounting and Computing Machinery, *31*—Manufacture of Electrical Machinery and Apparatus n.e.c, *32*—Manufacture of Radio, Television and Communication Equipment and Apparatus, *33*—Manufacture of Medical, Precision and Optical Instruments, Watches and Clocks, *34*—Manufacture of Motor Vehicles, Trailers and Semi-Trailers, *35*—Manufacture of Other Transport equipment, *36*—Manufacturing Furniture and Manufacturing n.e.c and *37*—Recycling.

Classification of NIC 2 digit industries as per NIC 2008 categories: *10*—Manufacture of Food Products, *11*—Manufacture of Beverages, *12*—Manufacture of Tobacco Products, *13*—Manufacturing of Textiles, *14*—Manufacturing of Wearing Apparels, *15*—Dressing of Tanning of Leather and related Products of Leather, *16*—Manufacturing of Wood and Wood Products and Cork, manufacturing of Articles of Straw and Plaiting; Materials Except Furniture, *17*—Manufacturing of Paper and Paper Products, *18*—Printing and Reproduction of Recorded Media, *19*—Manufacture of Coke, Refined Petroleum Products, *20*—Manufacture of Chemicals and Chemical Products, *21*—Manufacture of pharmaceuticals, medicinal chemical and botanical products, *22*—Manufacture of Rubber and Plastic Products, *23*—Manufacture of Other Non-Metallic Mineral Products, *24*—Manufacture of Basic Metal, **25**—Manufacture of Fabricated Metal Products, except machinery and equipment, *26*—Manufacture of computer, electronic and optical products, *27*—Manufacture of Electrical Equipment n.e.c., ***28***—Manufacture of Machinery and Equipment n.e.c, ***29***—Manufacture of Motor Vehicles, Trailers and Semi-Trailers, ***30***—Manufacture of Other Transport equipment, ***31***—Manufacture of Furniture, ***32***—Other manufacturing n.e.c., ***32***—Repair and installation of machinery and equipment.

Jobless Growth: The term 'jobless growth defined as the economy is growing and showing a tangible improvement in the growth of gross domestic product without creating much employment opportunities. It is the level that the unemployment remains at higher level but the economy is showing growth. The term was first coined by Nicolas S. Perna an Economist from United States during early 1990s.

REFERENCES

Bhalla, Sheila (2003) 'The Restructuring of the Unorganized Sector in India', *Report of the Institute for Human Development (IHD)*, New Delhi

CSO (Time Series Data) Annual Survey of India', Central Statistical Organization, Ministry of Statistics and Programme Implementation, Government of India.

Gadesha, Jignesh. H (2012) 'Importance of Large Scale and Small Scale Industries in India', *International Multidisciplinary Research Journal,* Vol. 11, No. 2.

GoI (2014) 'Economic Survey 2012-13' Ministry of Finance, Government of India, New Delhi.

Goldar, Bishwanath and Aggarwal, Suresh Chand (2010) 'Informalisation of Industrial Labour in India: Are Labour Market Rigidities and Growing Import Competition to Blame? The Paper presented in *Annual Conference on 'Growth and Development' at Indian Statistical Institute*, New Delhi between 16-18 December, 2010.

Gupta, Poonam and Kumar, Utsav (2010) 'Performance of Indian Manufacturing in Post Reform Period', MPRA Paper No. 24898, Munich Personal RePEc Archive, Accessed from online at http://mpra.ub.uni-muenchen.de/24898/ on 15th December 2018.

Gupta, Ruchika and Sanjay (2012), 'A Comparative Study Between Organized and Unorganized Manufacturing Sectors in India', *the Journal of Industrial Statistics,* Vol. 1, No. 2, pp. 222-240.

IBEF (2017). 'Manufacturing: Advantage India', India Brand Equity Foundation, New Delhi.

Kannan, K.P and Raveendran, G. (2012) 'Counting and Profiling the Missing Labour Force', *Economic and Political Weekly,* Vol. 42, No. 6, pp. 77-80.

Kathuria, Vinish, Raj, S.N. Rajesh and Kumal Sen (2010) 'Organized versus Unorganized Manufacturing Performance in the Post-Reforms Period', *Economic and Political Weekly,* Vol. 40, No. 24, pp 55-64.

Mathur, Ashok and Mishra, Sunil Kumar (2007), 'Wages and Employment in the Indian Industrial Sector: Theory and Evidence', *Journal of Labour Economics,* Vol. 50, No. 1, pp. 83-110.

Mehrotra, Santosh *et al.* (2012) 'Creating Employment in the 12th Five Year Plan', *IAMR Occasional Paper No. 3/2012*, Institute of Applied Manpower Research, Delhi.

Mehrotra, Santosh *et al.* (2014) 'Explaining Employment Trends in the Indian Economy: 1993-94 to 2011-12', *Economic and Political Weekly,* Vol. 49, No. 32, pp. 49-57.

Nagaraj, R. (2000) 'Organized Manufacturing Employment', *Economic and Political Weekly,* Vol. 35, No. 38, pp. 3445-3448.

Nayak, P.K. *et al.* (2010) 'Inclusive Growth and Its Regional Dimensions', *RBI Occasional Paper Series* Vol. 31 No. 3, Reserve Bank of India, pp. 91-156.

NSSO (2012) *Reports No. 549 on Economic Characteristics of Unincorporated Non-Agricultural Enterprises (Excluding Construction) in India*, National Sample Survey Organization, Ministry of Statistics and Programme Implementation, Government of India.

NSSO (2018) *Reports No. 581 on Economic Characteristics of Unincorporated Non-Agricultural Enterprises (Excluding Construction) in India*, National Sample Survey Organization, Ministry of Statistics and Programme Implementation, Government of India.

Panigrahi, A.K. (2016) 'Contract Workers in India's Organized Manufacturing Sector', *The Journal of Industrial Statistics,* Vol. 5, No. 2, pp. 138-153.

Rajeev, Meenakshi (2009) 'Contractual Labour in India: A Pragmatic view', *Paper Presented at First Annual Meeting of the Asian Law and Economic Association at Seoul,* National University, Korea.

Raj, Rajesh (2011) 'Structure, Employment and Productivity Growth in Indian Unorganized Manufacturing Sector: An Industry Level Analysis', *CMDR Monograph Series No. 50*, Centre for Multi-Disciplinary Development Research, Dharwad (Karnataka).

Saikia, Dilip and Das, Kalyani Kangkana (2012) 'Role of Unorganized Manufacturing in Expanding Employment Opportunities in Assam', *MPRA Paper No. 41861*, Munich Personal RePEc Archive, Munich University Library, Munich (Germany).

14

Legal Interventions and Women Empowerment against Witch Hunting in Rajasthan

Tanvi Yadav and *Nagendra Ambedkar Sole*

Introduction

Witch hunting is a superstitious practice that prompts the abuse and death of more than hundred women in India every year. It is hundred years old practice which includes molesting and killing a woman believed to have evil magic power. "Witch" means a woman, locally known as "*Dayan*", "*Daken*", "*Dakin*" or otherwise, who has been identified by any person or persons believing her to be in possession of or as having any evil power for causing any harm to any person or property as per Section 2(a) of the Rajasthan Prevention of Witch Hunting Act, 2015.

"Witch hunting" means any act or conduct on the part of any person: (i) identifying, accusing or defaming a woman as a witch, (ii) harassing, harming or injuring such woman whether mentally or physically or by damaging her property.[1] The notion of Witch-hunting initiated in Europe and almost ended in the 18th century. The term witch or *dayan* has been referred in the world literature and in cultural practices since the dawn of civilization.[2] In the famous Salem witch trials of the 1692-93 in colonial Massachusetts in America, women were the main victims.[3] In early Europe and Colonial America, women who opposed the church were considered as witches, were regarded as one who brings adversity and thus to protect the society those women were burnt. Later, women were held responsible for all the mishaps, like famine, flood, and epidemic diseases which caused the death of beings. The only solution to these apprehensions was killing women who were blamed to have caused the calamities.

This practice of killing is not new to Indian society rather it has its deep roots in history. Like Europe, the practice of witchcraft has been pervasively customary in India as well.[4] As per K.S. Singh,[5] witchcraft and witch hunting came in India with the British rule during colonial period. During the colonial period, the mass witch hunt has been evidenced in 1857 by some historians in Chotanagpur.[6] At present, witch hunting is more prevalent in following twelve states of India, like Jharkhand, Bihar, Haryana, West Bengal, Madhya Pradesh, Maharashtra, Gujarat, Odisha, Chhattisgarh, Assam, Uttar Pradesh and Rajasthan.[7]

Patriarchal society, illiteracy, superstitions, and property matters has been considered the main causes of such menace, beside the personal reasons such as rivalry, antagonism, enviousness and sexual suppression. The societies where witch hunting is rampant believe in black magic usually blamed on the witches to cause misfortunes, sickness and even death by casting evil eye.[8] 'Witch-hunting' involves the branding of women as witches by 'Ojha' or witch doctor certainly a male and subjecting her to numerous forms of physical and mental torture such as beating, rape, molestation, naked parade and ostracism etc. Witch hunting is a violence which affects the person's reputation, property, family and life. In 21st Century, when in all nook and corners of life, women empowerment has been given the first place; it is unfortunate that the practices based on superstitions as witch hunting still take place.

Witch Hunting as a Superstition

A superstition is an illogical and unreasonable faith or belief in something which cannot be tested by science. Superstition is based upon notions of luck, chance and fate, arising from attempts to explain nature and human existence within the knowledge people possessed in the distant past.[9] Superstition is a well-known term in a normal individual's vocabulary which includes magic, ritual, myth, and occult practices commonly accepted in the society and usually regarded as erroneous beliefs—irrational, primitive, and based on insufficient information.

The evil eye is the superstitious belief that someone can project harm by simply looking at another individual or their property.[10] Whilst the evil eye is often labelled as purely superstitious, as observed by Maloney, 'what is one person's superstition or occult idea is another person's belief or religion.'[11] Superstitions are very much prevalent, especially in India as it is a religious, cultural and traditional country. India is a country where the number of religious places is more than the number of educational institutions and hospitals which shows the inclination of people towards the fantasies and magic.

Even though superstition is not always harmful, but it can become life-threatening at times when it is perpetuated with the personal vengeance on socially disadvantaged peoples. Witch-hunting is such a superstition which is affected on victims from vulnerable sections of society. The vulnerable sections of the society are usually identified as witches with an aim to denounce them from the community and take control over their land, property etc. This is the reason why mostly single women and widows are branded as witches to take their land and property. Witch hunting is also understood as a manifestation of the low social status of women whereby male attitude of dominance and violence against women is legitimised by calling her a witch.[12]

Witch hunting is an organized act of violence against women in which an individual is blamed for witchcraft and the whole community endorses the punishment for that person. This social malevolence is often embedded in the traditional and cultural belief system of the society. In the light of that fact it is, indeed, difficult to handle such cultural violence. With hunting can also take place in form of mob lynching in which one or two people have their vested interests but others participate in this violence due to superstitions.

Incidents in Rajasthan

Many cases of witch hunting in rural area in India go unreported to police. However, National Criminal Record Bureau reports laid down that more than 2000 women were killed in India in witch-hunting cases between 2005 and 2015.There are myriad stories of witch hunting in rural India, where thousands of women have faced violence or been killed after being declared "witches".

> Kesi Chadana, a 40-year old woman was declared witch in 2014 in the State of Rajasthan. Her fellow villagers locked her family in their house and took their phones away, and then they began torturing her. Her neighbours and relatives beat her and stripped her naked, and made her wear a garland of shoes, carry heavy stones on her head, and parade through the neighbouring villages on a donkey. They were planning to burn her at a stake later that evening, but police caught them.

According to reports in the local press and social workers, over 30 people were arrested and later sentenced to jail terms for participating in the attack.[13]

> Noji Regan, a widow in her 60s was also branded a witch by a few men in her village. They dragged her by her hair and beat her with sticks. They accused her of casting an evil eye on the animals because one of the men's buffalos had stopped giving milk.

The men were later arrested for branding her a witch and attacking her, according to local media reports and social workers who followed her case, but the fallout from the accusation remains.[14]

In 2017, two cases of witch hunting took place in Ajmer within a week in which the torture and subsequent death of 40-year old Kanya Devi, and the confinement of an 80-year old woman for 18 days after being branded a witch, was reported.[15]

A 75 year old *dalit* woman, Sunita was locked up in a small room for 10 days without food and facilities by the villagers after branding her witch in Bhoti village of Bhilwara district.[16]

In another instance, Lakshmi Bai (name changed), 65, has been forced to live in Bhilwara for 12 years after being driven out of her native Dariba village on the suspicion of being a witch. Living with her husband as a social outcast, she attended the caste panchayat five times pleading that the odious tag be removed, but to no avail.[17]

Presently a 75-year old woman is living a miserable life in Bhilwara district of Rajasthan. She has been declared a witch by her own relatives and people torture and beat her up whenever she steps out of her house.[18]

There are many other women who become the target of witch hunting by their own people for certain reasons. They are blamed when buffalo or cow stops giving milk, when a child or young is sick, when some loss happens to any villager or community such as loss of crops, stealing at home or any other loss. Many women lost their lives even if some of them survive they live an isolated life in the community for their entire life.

Legal Intervention in Witch-hunting

Some international instruments, such as the Universal Declaration of Human Rights (UDHR) 1948, provide protection against any discrimination and promotes equality before the law. It also confirms the right to life and liberty to every human being. International Covenant on Civil and Political Rights (ICCPR), India associated with it in 1979, promotes equality between men and women by ensuring equal rights to men and women in civil as well as the political sphere and prohibits others from subsuming anyone's basic rights. Article 7 explicitly mentions prohibition of cruelty, inhuman or degrading treatment. In addition to UDHR and ICCPR, India signed Convention on the Elimination of All Forms of Discrimination against Women (CEDAW) in 1993 and agreed to eliminate discrimination and social cruelty against women.

Despite signing these international instruments, there is no specific and national level legislation that penalizes witch hunting except grievance that of the provisions of the Indian Penal Code, 1860 as an alternative for the victim. The different sections invoked in such cases are Section 302 which charge for murder, Section 307 attempt for murder, Section 323 hurt, Section 376 which penalizes for rape and Section 354 which deals with outraging a woman's modesty.

At the national level, due to the pressure from NGOs and other organisations working against witch hunting, the Prevention and Protection of Witch Hunting Bill, 2013 was drafted to providees: more effective measures to prevent and protect women from witch hunt practices, to eliminate their torture, oppression, humiliation and killing by the society by the trial of offences related to witch hunt practices and providing for punishment for the relief and rehabilitation of women victim of such offences and for any other matters connected therewith or incidental thereto by members of Human Rights Defense International[19] which is still pending. It aims at establishing national legislation relating to witch-hunting.

In different states legislation are available to cope with the problems of witch-hunting such as, the Prevention of Witch (Dayan) Practices Act, 1999 in Bihar, the Prevention of Witch-Hunting Practices Act, 2001 in Jharkhand, the Chhattisgarh Tonahi Pratadna Nivaran Act, 2005 in Chhattisgarh, the Odisha Prevention of Witch-Hunting Bill, 2013 in Odisha, the Maharashtra Prevention and Eradication of Human Sacrifice and other Inhuman, Evil and Aghori Practices and Black Magic Act, 2013 in Maharashtra, the Assam Witch-Hunting (Prohibition, Prevention and Protection) Bill, 2015 in Assam. Rajasthan passed Rajasthan Women (Prevention and Protection from Atrocities) Bill, 2006 to prevent atrocities against women. Recently, Rajasthan Prevention of Witch Hunting Act, 2015 was enacted especially to end witch hunting in the State.

As per National Human Rights Committee Report, in last 15 years approximately 2,500 women were killed in name the of witch-hunting. As per reports[20], in the last two years, more than 127 witch hunting incidents occurred in the state of Rajasthan. In rural Rajasthan, the incidence of witch hunting has become an organised crime. Along with recorded cases, there are many instances which are not recorded due to fear. In tribal and rural areas, where literacy rate is low and where people are guided by blind faith and superstition, victims accused of witchcraft are subjected to inhuman atrocities ranging from gang rape, mob lynching, naked parades, blackening of face, shaving of head, beheading and consuming human excreta. It is ironical, on one hand our country is a democratic country and talks about equality, right to life and liberty but on the other hand, it takes away the same rights from others.

Empowerment and Witch Hunting

Women have been considered a critical resource that has imminent potential to contribute constructively in the development process of a country. Empowerment of women and inculcation of scientific temper among the people is the key to root out such practices from the society. Empowering a woman has considered '*sine qua non*' for the development of a country.

Empowerment of women flows from power, it includes—equipping women to be economically independent, self-reliant and to have a positive esteem in the society.[21] Self-esteem is vital for women empowerment in any given society. On the one hand, empowerment of women is the talk of the day; on the other hand, practices like witch hunting is very much prevalent in our society.

The real meaning of empowerment is not only the economic development of women but also include social and cultural development as because of old age traditions and customs still has been used as a tool to suppress women from every aspect.

Witchcraft, thus, emerges as a multifaceted issue which gets linked with both the concerns for superstition and social disempowerment of women. Hence the promotion of scientific temper becomes as important as ensuring the empowerment of fringe communities. The overall institutional approach by the Government places witchcraft within the general category of crime against women. But the emotional stress and social boycott of the victims rarely gets captured in this dehumanizing framework. The stigma and social apathy faced by the victims puts them in a perpetual state of pain, agony and oppression. Empowerment, in this context, can be achieved by a process which enhances the ability of disadvantaged individuals or groups to challenge and change existing power relationships that place them in subordinate economic, social and political positions.[22]

Law and criminal justice system have failed to respond effectively to the menace of witch hunting. The occurring of the cases of witch hunting is a big question mark on our claim of literacy, humanity and gender sensitivity. It shows the failure of the state to spread education and health facilities and to inculcate respect for women and to promote scientific temperament. It is extremely unfortunate that even today there are interior regions where hundreds of women are branded as witches, humiliated, tortured, ostracized and in some cases even killed mercilessly in the name of superstition, to get rid of the evil spell cast by them.

Conclusion

Witch hunting is a test case of the crimes committed against women. In other crimes, women despite being a victim, retain their identity as women, but in Witch hunting a woman loses her very identity of a woman or a human being as she is declared to be a *Dayan* or *Churail* and thus rendered as a non-being or an evil being. The empowerment of women is possible only when such menace against her are curbed out. Witch hunting is an atrocity against women and a gross violation of human rights and against UNDHR, 1948 and India has no national laws to prevent such menace.

Rajasthan High Court laid down that, "the evil practice of declaring the woman a witch and killing her is an offence which cannot be tolerated. If effective progress in these matters is not reported, we may consider declaring the state of Rajasthan not only slow in taking such measures but also backward and ineffective in bringing out appropriate legislation and taking steps on atrocities committed on women."[23]

Rajasthan Prevention of Witch-hunting Act, 2015, Section 4, provides the punishment for witch hunting which is a minimum imprisonment of one year which can be extended up to 5 years and a minimum of Rs. 50,000 fine or both. The success story of the Rajasthan Prevention of Witch Hunting Act, 2015 revolves around the case of *State of Rajasthan* vs. *Shankar*. The observations which were made by the Hon'ble Division Bench in this judgement were that the superstitions and ill-traditions prevail in our society. Illiteracy and backwardness are high in ratio. It is on the part of the governance is to eradicate all these ills.

A strong belief in ghosts, spirits and occult is deeply embedded in the society. Along with criminal legal reforms, there is a need to bring other reforms also such as education and awareness. Sensitizing of police and welfare department and establishment of NGOs for this purpose could prove beneficial. The issue could be brought into the school curriculum to raise awareness to change the perspective of society and the belief over superstition. Protection officers and counsellors must be appointed especially for such crimes which are related to superstition. For the overall development of the country there is a need of quality population and for that country need to make strong their citizens socially, economically and politically.

NOTES

1. Section 2(d) of The Rajasthan Prevention of Witch Hunting Act, 2015.
2. Dr. Sudhansu Ranjan Mohapatra, Witch Hunting: A tool of terrorization across the world and its Legal Ramification, Vol. 1, *IJAR* (2014).
3. Susan Drucker-Brown, Witchcraft, Subversion and Changing Gender Relations, 63 AFRiCA: *J. OF THE INT'L AFR. INST.* 531, 546 (1993).
4. R.N. Saletore, *Indian Witchcraft,* 1-28 (Abhinav Publications, New Delhi, 1981).
5. The author and editor of the project "Peoples of India".
6. S. Sinha, *1857 Witch-Hunts, Adivasis, and the Uprising in Chhotanagpur,* 42 *EPW*, 1672-1676 (May 2007), A. Mallick, *Witch-Hunting in 1857*, 43 *EPW*, 118-119 (Sept., 2008).
7. Parthasarathy, Sindhuja. (2016). Witch hunt Burn in India. *The Week.* Retrieved from https://www.theweek.in/theweek/current/witch-hunting.html.
8. P.C. Joshi, S. Kaushal, S. Katew & O.H. Devi, *Witchcraft Beliefs and Practices among Oraons*, 4(2), *Studies of Tribes and Tribals*, 145-149 (2006).
9. Alexander Lesser, 'Superstition' (1931) 28(3) *The Journal of Philosophy,* 618.
10. Clarence Maloney, *The Evil Eye* (Columbia University Press, 1976).
11. *Ibid.*
12. Chaudhuri, Soma (March 6, 2013). *A curse in the family: Can survivors of witch hunts in India change traditional beliefs to stop the brutal practice*? Accessed from http://www.aljazeera.com/programmes/101east/2013/01/2013121101834161718.htmlon 5.4.13
13. https://broadly.vice.com/en_us/article/zmw4nw/women-in-india-modern-witch-hunts accessed 5th July, 2018.
14. *Ibid.*

15. 50 cases of witch-hunting in Rajasthan in over a year, not one conviction, *The Indian Express*, August 31, 2017
16. Branded Witches and dragged to hell, Mohammed Iqbal, *The Hindu*, 1st October, 2017
17. *Ibid.*
18. Lalima, *rishtedaro ne 75 salkeammako Dayan bola, Ghar se nikalte hi pitne legte hai log*, 16th January, 2019, ODDNAARI, https://www.oddnaari.in/latest/story/rajasthan-old-lady-is-being-called-witch-by-herrelativ-es-128823-2019-01-6?fbclid=IwAR2W_GTEGKXhNMLblcBWOnDqGT0bxP8Wx4_CrsBnb8w4xfjYiLi48MPPYzE. (20.01.2019).
19. Draft of Prevention and Prohibition of Witch Hunting Bill, as drafted by a legal team of HRDI, Human Rights Defense International, http://www.hrdi.in/?p=6449 accessed on 25/03/2018.
20. https://www.hindustantimes.com/jaipur/127-witch-hunting-cases-in-rajasthan-in-last-2-years-activists-slam-police/story-FUW1cXSxIIPC0xdUY7dKGJ.html accessed on 28.06.2018
21. Dhruba Hazarika, Women Empowerment in India: A Brief Discussion, (April. 27, 2018, 3.31 PM) https://www.ripublication.com/ijepa/ijepv1n3_1.pdf
22. Agarwal, Bina (1995). Gender, Property, and Land Rights. Bridging a Critical Gap in Economic Analysis and Policy in *Out of the Margin. Feminist Perspectives on Economics* (eds.) Susan Feiner, Notburga Ott and Zafiris Tzannatos, Routledge.
23. *State of Rajasthan* v. *Shankar* 2010.

REFERENCES

Anand, Ankita & Habib, Narseen. (2017). Witch Hunting: Beyond the Law. *Indian Foundation Journal*, Vol V.

Agarwal, Bina (1995). Gender, Property, and Land Rights. Bridging a Critical Gap in Economic Analysis and Policy in *Out of the Margin. Feminist Perspectives on Economics* (eds.) Susan Feiner, Notburga Ott and Zafiris Tzannatos, Routledge.

Chakraborty, J. & Borah, Anjuman. (2013). Witch Hunting is Assam: Strategising Alternative Media for Women Empowerment and Overcoming Superstition. *Journal of North East India Studies,* Vol. 3(2).

Chaudhuri, Soma (March 6, 2013). A curse in the family: Can survivors of witch hunts in India change traditional beliefs to stop the brutal practice? Accessed from http://www.aljazeera.com/programmes/101east/2013/01/2013121101834161718.htmlon 5.4.13

Gaskill, M. (2010). *Witchcraft: A Very Short Introduction,* New York: Oxford University Press.

Mohapatra, S.R. & Sharma, Jayashree. (2014). Witch Hunting: a tool of terrorization of across the world and its legal ramification. *International Journal of Academic Research*, Vol.1, Issue-3(1).

Nathan, D, Kelkar, G. & Satija, S. (2013). Witches: Through Changing Contexts Women Remain the Target. *IHD Working Paper Series, Working Paper No. WP 004/2013,* Institute for Human Development, New Delhi.

Parthasarathy, Sindhuja. (2016). Witch hunt Burn in India. *The Week.* Retrieved from https://www.theweek.in/theweek/current/witch-hunting.html.

Saikia, Bipasha. (2018). Witch Hunting: The Silent Form of Gender Based Violence and the Need to Bridge the Rural Urban Divide. *Rostrum's Law Review.*

Schnoebelen, Jill. (2009). Witchcraft allegations, refugee protection and human rights: a review of the evidence. *New Issues in Refugee Research, UNHCR, The UN Refugee Agency, Policy Development and Evaluation Service.*

Shrestha, R. (2004). Witch Hunting: A study of cultural violence against women with reference to Nepal and India. *Research Paper, Institute of Social Sciences, Netherlands.*

Singh, Rakesh K. (2011). Witch-Hunting: Alive and Kicking. *Women's Link,* Vol 17.

15

A Critical Appraisal of the Subaltern Resistance in India

A Study of the Identity Movement of the Tea Garden Community of Assam

Phulmoni Das

Theoretical Understanding of Subaltern Resistance in India

Subaltern struggle led by the subaltern groups is not new to Indian history as it has been deeply marked in a long historical time. But in proposition to it, the struggles of these subaltern groups have not been added to the mainstream discourses of history writing for quite some time. It was the Subaltern Studies Group who first tried to make a serious attempt to trace the missing linkages of Subaltern struggle and to bring it to the mainstream discourses. Broadly speaking the approach initiated by the Subaltern historians is referred to as 'subaltern historiography', which seeks to maintain a balance by highlighting the role of the politics of the people as against elite politics played in Indian history. They asserted how the elite politics has failed to acknowledge the contribution made by the people (masses) on their own way which is independent of the elite politics. In parallel to the domain of elite politics in colonial period there always existed another form of politics in which the principal actors were not the dominant groups of the society. These actors are the 'subaltern' classes and groups constituting the masses of the labouring population and the intermediate strata in the town and country—the people'.[1] Subaltern historiography considers subalternity of the masses as an autonomous domain which neither originates from elite politics nor depends on them. According to Ranajit Guha, the mobilization of the domain of elite politics is achieved vertically but the subaltern politics takes place at the horizontal level. Guha also admitted that due to the diversity of the social composition among the subaltern groups and lack of uniformity in ideological element in terms of quality and density in the subaltern groups has sometimes led to the pursuit of their narrow sectional and economic interest as well as sectarian splits which destabilize the horizontal alliances of the subaltern groups.[2] Therefore, Guha also made the observation that the two domains of politics have not been isolated from each other but most often overlapped with each other. It is mainly the elite domain which always had tried to mobilize and integrate the domain of subaltern into the elite domain of politics to accomplish their own interests. However, the subaltern groups managed to come away from the domination of elite control and able to put their characteristic imprints on the campaigns initiated by the elite domain.[3] The peasant and tribal tenant rebelled against elite domination many times, for example, uprisings of Bhumij, the Kol insurrection, the Santal revolt of 1855 and the Indigo disturbances of 1859-62 and the Deccan riots of 1875 etc. can be referred as some of the subaltern struggles which are accomplished by the masses not with the help of the politics of elite. Thus, the main emphasise of subaltern historiography is to reconstruct the history 'from below' or to reformulate the 'history of the people with the politics of the leftout', so it is an attempt to make the history again for those subaltern groups, their politics and movement which has never been given importance and recognized.

People's resistance is a unique phenomenon which takes the form of collective dimensions in complex socio-cultural settings. People's resistance are the collective expressions for survival of their existence which is carried out not on the individual level but as collective venture that takes the shape of a 'movement'. The movement is an expression of either one or many interconnected forms of resistance based on specific ideological expression. Therefore, movement, resistance and ideology are thc three interrelated factors that can determine the dynamics of social change. The functioning of the state cannot be fully understood without the understanding of the politics of the masses. It is sometimes the perception, beliefs, aspirations and the views of the subaltern classes which come into the conflict with the state apparatus. Most of the time, the collective action of people is often regarded as alienated, estranged, excluded and outside the polity. The movement of the masses has been ignored and neglected for not having their own set of voice or politics and it has been misunderstood that the movement of the masses has been manipulated by the ruling classes. But, this is an oversimplification and deviation and stumbling block to the efforts of making a democratic and egalitarian social order. Because masses have their own set of politics and it is independent of elite politics as also referred by Ranajit Guha. Again most of the time social movements are said to be backed by certain objectives, ideology, programmes, leadership and organization which are interdependent influencing each other. But Ranajit Guha has his own observation of looking into the subaltern struggle, although these components are found in all types of movements or insurgencies, including the so called 'spontaneous' rebellions, their forms vary from very unstructured to well organized.[4] Guha looked into the different perspective and the arguments which believes that the peasant insurgencies were spontaneous and lacked political consciousness and organization. Against these contentions, Guha brilliantly offered the study of peasant insurgency in colonial India. The study provides two basic premises:

(a) Subaltern politics was quite different from the elite politics.
(b) Peasant consciousness had an autonomous domain of its own.

The peasant or tribal insurgency not to be treated merely as the 'objects' of history as Guha believes that they should be rather treated as the 'maker' of their own history bestowed with the transformative consciousness of their own. Guha has extensively discussed both these arguments in his classic, 'Elementary Aspect of Peasant Insurgency in Colonial India'. In this study peasant resistance of nineteenth century has been re-appraised and Guha theorized the incidence of peasant revolts in colonial India which became the landmark effort of the Subaltern historiography to reconstruct 'the other history', i.e. history of the subaltern people. Subaltern historiography provides useful framework for studying social movements in general and tribal and peasant insurgencies in particular. It also attributed to the complex phenomenon of peasant or ethnic protest movement or at least significant part of it in contemporary India.[5]

Peasant resistance in colonial period were labelled as 'backward looking and unprogressive' and their consciousness as 'pre-political' and 'superstitious' by the colonial historiographers and colonial authorities.[6] To Guha the term 'pre-political' is misleading. As Eric Hobsbawm in his analysis in the book, '*Primitive Rebels: Studies in Archaic Forms of Social Movement in the 19th and 20th centuries*' noted that, the rebel peasants uprisings in colonial period were 'pre-political' in nature, because their uprisings had no 'elaborate blueprint' to replace the existing superstructure.[7] Contesting that, Guha asserted that the rebel peasant had a clear knowledge of his activity intended principally to destroy the authority of the superordinate elite'.[8] Here the word 'Pre-Political' highlighted the absence of political consciousness or will. 'Pre-political' category according to Hobsbawm included those movements which lacked any organised ideology or consciousness and he even went to observe that social banditry lacked in organization or ideology and he claimed that 'banditry is rather a primitive form of organised social protest'. Though Guha acknowledges that Hobswam's reading may be valid in the historical context he set out to analyse but the expression 'pre-political' is not made any sense in terms of peasant uprisings of colonial India. Because the peasant and tribal revolt against *sarkari*, *sahukari*, and *zamindari* oppression to which they were subjected and exploited can be looked as the rebellion against the exploited power structure of landlord and *zamindars*. Different uprisings of that time such as Bhumij, the Kol insurrection, the Santal, Deccan riots etc. of nineteenth centuries cannot be termed as pre-political rather they were the subaltern struggle which was an attempt to break the power relationship of the existing structure. However, Guha also admits that the tribal and peasantry movements of twentieth centuries have been different from the earlier nineteenth centuries in terms of maturity, consciousness and organization. But those struggles were essentially political in character and they were significant in history and therefore, those struggles cannot be altogether denied as 'pre-political' phenomenon in history. It was a struggle against the triad nexus of the landlord, moneylender and colonial government. Guha in his book '*Elementary Aspect of Peasant Insurgency in Colonial India*' has highlighted six elementary aspects of consciousness of the rebel peasants. These are negation, ambiguity, modality, solidarity, transmission, and territoriality. At the same time, he shows that the peasant consciousness which have been labelled as 'negative consciousness' in the elitist discourses as a hostile power sometimes became manifested at the time of insurrection. Therefore, Guha's framework has the relevance in studying the peasant, tribal or ethnic movement of colonial period. Late colonial India also faced numerous 'transformative' rebellions, particularly in tribal areas. Colonial rule and its commercialization adversely affected the tribal societies and their life which later on became the reason for the various tribal uprisings in colonial period. Because of the oppressive colonial policies, the Adivasis were deprived from their forest rights which led to the rise of fundamental questions of land and forest on which they were traditionally been dependent for their livelihood. The struggles led by the subaltern groups symbolized on how they have been fighting for their existence since historical times. However, the history of the peasant and tribal insurgencies in India were replete with 'myths, rituals, rumours, hopes for a Golden Age and fears of an imminent End of World'.[9] Conventionally, these factors are rendered as meaningless by the historians by declaring them as manipulative actors to rouse the peasantry. But it is the attribution of Subaltern historiography which has considered the importance of these elements which not only potentially unite the rebels but also divide them. Subaltern Studies scholars were among the first to acknowledge the role superstitions and religious beliefs as legitimate causes in understanding rebel consciousness, even when such beliefs defied rational explanations by social scientist.[10] Many of the issues raised by the Subaltern historians such as Shahid Amin's account of rumours and beliefs about colonial India's great personality or symbolic figure, M.K. Gandhi, again Gyanendra Pandey's accounts of sectarian movements related to predominantly agrarian communities in northern India, and in David Hardiman's analysis of tribal uprisings in western India under the apparent command of a local goddess. In Shaid Amin's famous essay, 'Gandhi as Mahatma: Gorakhpur District, Eastern UP, 1921-22', shows how the Mahatma Gandhi's image as great leader, great soul was the factor which empowered the peasant to undertake 'direct action' against the existing order of village society. In fact sometimes it evoked the multiple acts of violence which are carried out in the name of Gandhi. For example, in Gorakhpur a 'criminal tribe' called Badhik looted a market in Gorakhpur and attracted violence to anyone who opposed their immediate goal. Likewise, they attacked the moneylenders, judges, local landlords and Englishmen who are the symbols of authority in rural hinterland. At the same time they justified their acts as that it was the command of the Gandhi in their dreams or in miracles to carry out the act of violence as they were also chanting the slogans in the name of Gandhi or 'Gandhi's Swaraj'.[11] Again David Hardiman has discussed a particular tribal movement of South Gujarat during 1922-23 which is known as Devi movement. Devi according to the Adivasi was a female divinity called Salabai who possessed immense power. It is under 'Devi's' command and inspiration which led the Adivasis to agitate against the local liquor and landlords.[12] But according to Hardiman, unfortunately historians have not written much about such tribal movements. It is not always about the limitation of archival information. More importantly these occurrences are not accepted as the standard 'nationalistic or socialistic' historiographies of colonial India. There is no recognition in nationalist history about the fact that peasant and Adivasis fought against colonial domination on their own. Therefore, the Subaltern historians were interested in developing a rebel historiography because they believe that conventional studies of Indian nationalism have been shaped by the dictates of colonialist and bourgeois-nationalist elitism.

Subaltern social movements and struggles in India continued to proliferate even after post-colonial period. The conflict becomes acute when it came to the edge of the subaltern questions with the post-colonial state apparatus. 'The failings of the modernizing mission of the Nehruvian State' and also the failure of the state to meet the demands and needs of the masses most often led to process of 'struggle and negotiation' between subaltern masses and the state.[13] Again on the other hand the 'elite revolts' of neoliberal restructuring with that of rising trends of Hindu communalism, both of which reflect and are vehicles for the interests and aspirations especially of the middle class and higher caste Indians were noteworthy.[14] Simultaneously, there are other dimensions of multiple forms of 'subaltern politics' which is again representing another long history of struggle of the oppressed against the established existing order. One form of struggle that Corbridge and Harris have mentioned in the book '*Reinventing India*' is what they called as 'empowerment from without'. The contentions are for the *dalits* and *Adivasis* of India who are situated at the bottom of the social pile in India, even after the constitutional provisions for job reservations, reservations of educational places and seats in political assemblies and more generally the extension of the franchise to them, secular education and the laws aimed at the abolition of caste-based discrimination for the advancement of the democratic process in India. Such measures according to Corbridge and Harris have not made any change in the lives of these groups in a significant way. But these measures still had a significant impact on 'the terms of engagement between India's scheduled and non-scheduled communities by allowing an awareness of potential collection strength among the scheduled communities and improving their bargaining position *vis-à-vis* dominant groups.[15] Corbridge and Harris also mentioned another process i.e. 'empowerment from within' which is identified with the electoral success of Bahujan Samaj Party (BSP) which is mainly *dalit* based party of Uttar Pradesh, although electoral success of the BSP cannot be equated with the improvement of living standards of the poor. But it is an electoral upsurge in which backward caste and class groups are participating more actively in electoral politics and they are able to bypasses the politics of local elites which establishes them as a voice to be reckoned with. India with its post-1991 neo-liberalization of economy marked a new shift in the role of state. With the onslaught of globalization, liberalization and privatization the trend is to roll back the state, and it is with that process marginalized sections became more vulnerable and the legitimacy of the state was questioned. The post-1991 neoliberalization of the Indian political economy has accelerated the process of development which is very much for the interest of the capitalist and corporate sector that has led to the large scale development dislocation, displacement, dispossession and it has also resulted into the frequent resistances and struggle from the subaltern groups such as *adivasis* and *dalits* for their rights. A large number of subaltern movements in India such as ethnic/ tribal movements or the recent farmers movement, women movements, that have gathered momentum since Independence provides wide spectrum for the rise of subaltern politics in India. However, most of these contemporary movements come fairly close to what T.D. Tella has referred to as 'the revolutions of rising expectations' which are often unleashed by developmental imbalances resulting from the modernization's process in the third world.[16]

Tea Garden Community as Subaltern and their Quest for Identity

Subaltern Resistance is not a new phenomenon in India. It is since colonial period different subaltern social groups have been fighting for their rights. It is in this context even after Independence subaltern groups have been struggling for achieving their rights. For the welfare state like India, the presence of the Subaltern groups like *Dalits*, *Adivasis*, landless, dispossessed, workers, Scheduled Caste, Scheduled Tribe, rural and urban poor, women and others who are subordinated and excluded from the domain of power have been compelled to accept their inferiority by the dominant social groups and elites of the society. Sumit Sarkar within this standpoint has tried to focus on the tea-garden communities of India as the Subaltern. Reference may be made to the Subaltern Studies project published in Subaltern Studies volume III where Sumit Sarkar says:

> *I am employing the term 'Subaltern' as a convenient short-hand for three social groups: tribal and low-caste agricultural labourers and share-croppers; landholdings peasants, generally of intermediate-caste status in Bengal (together with their*

> *Muslims counterparts) in* ***labour in plantations,*** *mines and industries (along with urban casual labour).*[17]

Tea Plantation in India was the outcome of the Colonialism. The process of tea plantation and the recruitment of workers in the plantation of India demonstrate the ways of colonial government's economy of exploitation and also shows the socio-economic backwardness and underdevelopment of the recruited tea garden working community in India. The Colonial Government had created and sustained the hierarchical plantation structure in the tea plantation of India. They have created this hierarchical structure through the indenture labour mobilisation. This hierarchy had been maintained by the colonial plantation authority under the strict disciplinary rule. Strict control through penal laws was exercised to keep the tea garden workers away from desertion and disobedience. Due to the exploitative regime of the plantation authority made against the tea garden workers of India, they had been suffering from diseases, malnutrition and mortality. Tea plantation had achieved a profitable state by putting the tea garden workers in the state of subalternity and marginality, through the coercive recruitment process, very low labour wages and deplorable living and working conditions.

To understand the status of the tea garden community of Assam, one has to keep in mind that because they have been in Assam for more than a century, their identity remains as fluid as it used to be in the colonial era. They have been struggling for their specific identity since colonial days which have pushed the community to the state of subaltern. The Assam tea plantation brought a conglomeration of different ethnic groups mostly from the densely populated neighbouring provinces. The major chunk of workers brought to Assam was drawn mainly from the Chotanagpur and the Santhal Paraganas of colonial India. The recruits in the tea plantations were mainly tribal peasants who were driven out of land and compelled to migrate in search of livelihood through a complex set of colonial policy.[18] Although the community is generally referred to as a single entity but they are the composition of different ethnic groups. Most of the ethnic groups constituting the composite identity are scheduled either as 'tribe' or as 'caste' in the states where they originally belonged. It is observed that there are around 59 ethnic groups belonging to such tribal category and similarly 40 groups to caste category living in Assam which are denied of such status in this state.[19] In Assam they are officially recognized as Other Backward Community (OBC). Their population in

1971 was found to be around 30 lakh and according to 2011 Census tea garden community constitute about 18 to 20 per cent of the total population.[20] The segregationist attitudes of the wider Assamese society towards the tea garden community persisted till the second half of the 20th century, since when a very gradual process of change in public perception regarding them could be observed. It is with the rise of an educated section amongst the tea garden community, along with the changing democratic process and the social movements and political upheavals in the state since the late 1970s have led to the emergence of an inclusive 'tea tribe' identity. It submerged the tribal or caste categories of tea workers, providing the basis for their political attitudes and actions which moved the community to assert for their identity. It is their longstanding demand of both the tea garden workers and the ex-tea garden workers community to include them in the list of Scheduled Tribes and Scheduled Castes in Assam like their counterparts in the neighbouring tea growing states of West Bengal and Tripura, who enjoy the status of SC or ST depending upon their actual status on this count in their respective places of origin. Deprivation of this identity has led to another phase of movement among the tea garden community of Assam. Ever since India became Independent these people lost their Scheduled Tribe status in Assam and thus they were deprived of their educational, economic and political privileges guaranteed by the Constitution of India, instead they were classified as OBC.[21] This situation has made the tea garden community increasingly restive in recent years.

In the colonial period, it was specially the tea workers and not the ex-tea garden workers in Assam who were given certain constitutional rights. The issue of rescheduling the tea garden tribes was raised in the 1930s when the Schedules were being prepared. The Reform Officer of that time, in-charge of drawing up the list, expressed resentment over the fact that 600,000 ex-tea garden coolies have been excluded though the names of most of our coolie castes appear as scheduled in their home province.[22] It is basically done for the excluding the ex-tea garden castes from political concession and they had no one to represent their cause. Further the European lobby did not see much reason to promote their interest in the government.[23] Hence, the removal of ex-tea garden caste from the lists of Scheduled Castes and Scheduled Tribes remained a constitutional mishap, which is not even rectified in the post-Independence period. On the other hand the reservation of seats for the tea workers' representatives in the provincial legislature was also removed in independent India. It has been observed that many of those claiming to be Scheduled Tribe status in their places of origin say that the ex-tea garden workers are also 'tea tribes'. On the other hand, many who claim to be of non-tribal origin vehemently deny the termed as *Adivasis*. As per an official account around 12 per cent of Indian tribals live in the Northeast, but they do not include the *Adivasis* who are Munda, Oraon, Santhal and other tribals of Jharkhand origin but are not in the schedule in Assam.[24] The *Adivasis* are probably 50 to 60 per cent or 30-40 lakh of the 'tea tribes', i.e. present and past plantation labourers who are estimated to be about 60 lakh in Assam.[25] *Adivasis* can be broadly divided into two communities in Assam, namely, the tea garden workers and the ex-tea garden workers who later on after completing their contract term has settled in and around the plantation area after procuring a little land mostly through government schemes. They are forcefully migrated to Assam as indentured workers and of extremely of harsh kind, during colonial period. Poverty, illiteracy, political disenfranchisement and immense socio-economic political problems characterize the conditions of *Adivasis* in Assam. In the face of misery perpetrated by the colonial state, *Adivasis* started migrating to Assam and began to work as the tea plantation workers. Their socio-economic conditions were unquestionably in a very pitiable state. The *Adivasis*, who are aboriginals of this country, are still struggling for the ST status in the State. The demand for Scheduled Tribe status by the *Adivasis* is not a new phenomenon. The basis of their demand is that, if the communities such as Santhal, Oraon, Munda, Gor, Kol, Bhil, Tanti, Kurmi etc could be included in the ST list in other states like West Bengal, Odisha and Jharkhand, why should they be deprived of this privilege in Assam ? *Adivasis* are the worst sufferer in BTAD area where they have to face the ethnic cleansing which is again an inhuman treatment meted towards them in post-colonial state. The Bodo Militants in BTAD have separately targeted diverse communities at different points of time. From the history of violence of western Assam, it can be distinctly marked that the Bodo militants perpetually picked up soft targets while going in for massacres. Attacks were unleashed on the communities that included Koch-Rajbanshis, *Adivasis*, Muslims, Bengali Hindus, Nepalis etc. The worst sufferers among the communities have been the Muslims and Adivasis. Series of incident which can be termed as ethnic cleansing happened against the *Adivasis* in 1996-98, Beltola incident of 2007 and forced eviction of 2010, clashes between Bodos and Adivasis in 2014 are some examples which grossly violated the human rights of *Adivasis* in Assam. The conflict between the two communities, i.e. Bodos and Adivasis have created a serious havoc in the state which resulted to the large scale of displacement of both the communities. The violence that occurred between the two communities and the consequent displacement brought two pertinent issues to the fore—the non-recognition of Adivasis, including the tea-tribe and ex-tea-tribe communities in Assam as STs and non-granting of land rights under the ST and deprivation of other Traditional Forest Dwellers (Recognition of Forest Rights) Act to Adivasi and Bodo forest dwellers in denuded forest areas. According to Forest Rights Act, 2006, the Adivasis are entitled to claim their rights on the forest land which they possess' before December 13, 2005. However, the Adivasis of Assam are denied their rights under the Forest Rights Act as well. In fact, Adivasis were not given rights and entitlements on the forest lands which they have been cultivating for decades and it is the reason which makes the Adivasis of these region are highly unsecured.[26] The terror attacks and the subsequent violence triggered the displacement of about 8,000 Adivasis from 26 villages and 1,200 Bodos from nine villages, all of them forest-dwellers in the Ultapani reserved forest under the Haltugaon Forest division in Kokrajhar district, within an eight-kilometre radius from Saralpara.[27] The northern bank of Brahmaputra, where Bodos are the majority mostly falls under the tribal belt and block created immediately after independence. This tribal belt and blocks were created to safeguard the tribals from various ways of coercion from other advance communities which is mentioned under the provision of VI Schedule and Article 19(5) of Constitution of India. One of the most important provisions of the VI Schedule is that in that demarcated belts and blocks, non-tribals have occupied a good portion of land and have legal documents of the same for which today tribals are becoming minority in the tribal belts and block itself.[28] But the sad part is that poor implementation of that provision of VI Schedule has further aggravated the violence of the two communities which led to the killing and the loss of innocent lives and property. The ethnic conflict between the two communities left many displaced, homeless and has created a rift between the two communities. These conflicts are seen recurring again in November 24, 2007, when about 5000 Adivasis comprising men, women and children were attacked in Beltola of Guwahati while they were attending a peaceful procession in demand of Scheduled Tribe Status.[29] They were attacked by the local people of Beltola including shopkeepers. Consequently, 300 Adivasis were brutally wounded, hit by bamboos, iron rods and bricks. More than one dead and a teenage Adivasi girl Laxmi Oraon was stripped, chased and kicked.[30] It was a shameful episode which brought a sharp reaction from the civil society condemning the incident and urged for the sake of maintaining communal harmony not to term the incident as an Assamese-Adivasi community clash.[31] The procession was organized by the All Adivasi Students Association of Assam (AASAA) to press for the inclusion of Santhali *Adivasis* and the 'Tea Tribes' in the list of Scheduled Tribes (Plains). Adivasi protesters had bows and arrows, bamboo poles with sharpened ends; the odd axe and machete which are according to the protesters are cultural symbols not for attacking or hurting any individuals. In fact this practice of carrying primitive arms in a political procession has been a recent innovation.[32] The Beltola incident showed the sporadic violent episode which also depicts nature of subaltern movement. The march was a peaceful one for a legitimate cause but it turned violent soon after it started. A section of the protesters resorted to acts of vandalism, and to this invited brutal retaliation from residents of the Beltola locality. The leadership was unable to control the unruly elements and had no influence upon some section of participants in the processions. Procession was infiltrated by some elements which sought trouble and finally, the purpose of the procession was not meted.[33] Because of the failure of the security personnel and police to intervene and control the situation led to the later tragedy. The Adivasis who have been neglected by the state for decades and all this outrage expressed through their movement is the manifestation of their frustration and deprivation. The Post-Independence period and in the era of globalization which has placed the region in a state of transition has opened the ethnic communities such as Adivasis, to break free and to cross the delimit of colonial boundaries. The Beltola incident clearly demonstrates the Adivasis search for an identity through their demand for the ST status and at the same time reflects the failure of the state to grant their demands.

In pursuance of the demand of the Adivasis to secure their identity through granting them as Scheduled Tribe status in Assam has been articulated by the emergence of the leaders of the educated section of the community. The attempt to articulate the socio-political aspirations of the community has started as early as in the decade of 1930s by the leaders such as Chanu Kheria. He was the first matriculate from the community. He submitted a memorandum before Assam Franchise Committee in 1934 to enlist the Tea Garden and Ex-Tea Garden Labourers in the Dalit category.[34] Four years later, another highly educated leader P.M. Sarwan, who was also the first post-graduate from the community launched a new platform Assam Chotnagpuri Sabha in 1938, which can be regarded as the first organization originated from the community.[35] The application of the word 'Chotanagpuri' evidently used to evoke the memory of their place of origin and thereby mobilize the support of the community. The first students organization emerged from the tea garden community were the Assam Chotanagpuri Chatra Sanmilan or Chotnagpuri Students' Association founded in the year of 1947 in Dibrugarh. The main objective of the organization at its initial phase was to bring all the Tea and Ex-Tea Community Students to a common platform and to initiate a socio-political and economic consciousness among them, to drive away the social evils that have deeply entered into their society. The Chotnagpuri Students Association was remained active for a very short period. In 1954 another Students organization was formed under the leadership of Dinanath Choudhury and Chatragopal Karmakar at Golaghat in the name, Assam Chah Bonua Chatra Sanstha and later the name was changed to 'All Assam Tea Garden Community Students Association' by amending the constitution of the organization in 1958. But in 1984, it was again changed into 'Assam Tea Labour Tribes Students Association' and finally, it was converted to 'Assam Tea Tribes Students Association' (ATTSA) and presently it is the largest student organization representing the community. The aim and objectives of the ATTSA is determined to emancipate the tea garden community from exploitation and deprivation. ATTSA has been putting forward number of demands before Central and State Governments from time to time. The most significant demand among them is the demand for Scheduled Tribe (ST) status for the tea and ex-tea garden community of Assam and they have submitted several memorandums to the Government of India and State Government regarding different issues and demands of the community.

Again in Grahampur, near Gossaigaon another organization called 'All Assam Munda, Oraon and Santhal Association' was floated by Mithius Tudu, a prominent leader of Munda community in the year 1957. This organization later named as 'Assam Adivasi Council' in 1959. This organization made a serious effort to expedite the process of enlisting the 'Adivasis' as Scheduled Tribe by submitting memorandum before Central Government.

After the Kokrajhar riot between Bodos and the Adivasis in 1996 another student organization called Adivasi Students Association of Assam (AASAA) emerged around 1997-98 from Gossaigaon. Presently AASAA is widening its support base in various parts of Assam mostly in the ex-tea workers. The main demands of AASAA are recognition of Schedule Tribe status of the Adivasis in Assam and rehabilitation of the victims of Bodo-*Adivasi* riots in Kokrajhar District.

It has been observed by and large that *Adivasis* has become conscious of their separate ethnic identity under a separate banner as a means of accelerating their development. Conduction of different groups and bodies such as Adivasi Mahasabha, Adivasi Mahila Mahasabha, Mundari Sahitya Sabha, Adivasi Sahitya Sabha, All Chautal Students Union etc. are some of the organization where they have been articulating their demand for Scheduled Tribe status as well as different issues of *Adivasis* encompassing their economic, social, cultural and political issues which gives a new dimension to the Identity movements of tea garden community of Assam. Therefore, the demand of the tea garden community for Scheduled Tribe and Scheduled Caste status can be looked into the larger framework within which the debate is being conducted and which drew the attention of continued reliance on a highly questionable stock of colonial knowledge about Indian society and culture. As noted scholar Sanjib Baruah rightly observed that the 'demand of tea garden community of Assam should be a source of embarrassment, as well as cause for serious introspection'.[36] Their movement is the clear manifestation of deprivation and is the movement against the betrayal and deception by the privileged and powerful section of the society.

Identity Movement of the Tea Garden Community and Understanding the Autonomy of the Subaltern Movement

If the identity movement of tea garden community of Assam is analysed from the subaltern studies perspective then the question of subaltern autonomy needs to be interpreted. Viewed from the perspective of the subaltern studies, conduction of different *Adivasi* mahasabhas, different protest march, can be seen as the manifestation of the autonomy of the subaltern agency. Since some of these events happened before the reported fieldwork, and the researcher could not participate in the events, the events are reconstructed through the narratives of the different members of these groups who belonged to the tea garden community. The visual materials such as photographs and pamphlets of those conventions were analysed too. It can be seen that through these movements and celebration of festivals of different ethnic groups of tea garden community, they has tried to reconstruct their identity in cultural and historical terms. By creating an ideological framework for the establishment of an 'alternative counter culture' along with the celebration and adoption of Assamese culture and language a new politics is seen to be developing. So the present study has looked into the question whether the *Adivasis* can be analysed as constituting an alternative independent cultural and political domain as observed by noted Subaltern historian Ranajit Guha and whether the subaltern inevitably is an integral part of the dominant discourse and is unable to speak in his /her own words? as pointed by Spivak.[37] According to Ranajit Guha the colonial Indian State is unable to create an all inclusive universal hegemonic discourse rather political dominance has been exercised and it created conditions for the emergence of an independent autonomous political and cultural subjectivity of the subaltern.[38] But it is after Independence different subaltern groups started to assert their rights and to question the hegemony of the state. Regarding subalterns pertinent discussion on 'autonomy' of the subaltern movement, the arguments put forwarded by Gyan Prakash, a noted historian and Subaltern School proponent aptly describes the changes in the conceptualization of the subaltern:

> *'Subalternist search for a humanist subject-agent frequently ended up with the discovery of the failure of subaltern agency: the moment of rebellion always contained within it the moment of failure. The desire to recover the subaltern's autonomy was repeatedly frustrated because subalternity, by definition, signified the impossibility of autonomy. Subalterns' resistance did not simply oppose power, but was also constituted by it'.*[39]

Therefore, the subaltern autonomy cannot be understood in its own. Understanding of the Subaltern cannot come into being its own. The consensus has been arrived on the dependence of the subaltern on the dominant discourse. Arising of the Subaltern started to be visualized not outside but inside the dominant discourse, 'in its interstice' as Gyan Prakash has mentioned. Although it has been argued that the subaltern has arisen within the dominant discourse, the power of the subaltern clearly reveals their ability to exert pressure on the dominant structures as well. Therefore, the cultural, economic and political assertion of the tea garden community do not happen in vacuum and are not inspired by their own subjectivity. Rather they emerge as a response to the hegemony of the dominant discourse. Noted subaltern scholar Partha Chatterjee expressed his view on the changes in the conceptualization of the subaltern. Presently the political activism of the subaltern is no longer manifested the actual confrontational rebellion, as it was in the case of peasant insurgency discussed by Ranajit Guha. In contemporary time subalterns use bureaucratic and institutional means in fulfilling their objectives. Using of that strategy and tactics resembles the elite politics. As happened with the context of the movement of the tea garden community of Assam where the earlier protest and strike were most often sporadic and although some of the strikes and movement of tea garden community are spontaneous outburst of their anger but most of their movement such as enhancement of wages, demand for bonus, demand for their land rights and forest rights and assertion of Scheduled Tribe status is guided and articulated by different organizations. The leaders of the different organizations such as ACMS, ATTSA, AASAA, Adivasi Mahasabha, Adivasi Sahitya Sabha etc. has mobilized different issues and grievances of the community and presented in front of the government through memorandum, letters and discussion. Thus, the politics of subaltern and elite shows significant inter-connectedness with each other. It is also not true that the political autonomy of the subaltern never existed, rather in post-Independence period it has been affected by many elements. Peasant uprisings of colonial time and present social movements reflected the differences in terms of the conceptualization of subaltern. Guha's view on Subaltern as an autonomous political and cultural agent is deconstructed by the Spivak and O'Hanlon as they focused on recent shifts to the interdependency between the subaltern and the dominant culture.[40]

The prevalent discussion on tea garden community's different movement and the celebration of different community festivals and programmes and the formation of different socio-political organization stressed their cultural practices marks their essential differences from the dominant mainstream Assamese society. These movement showed the attempt of the tea garden community as subaltern to unite among themselves as a community against the powerful structure of the society. The community frequently invokes the motives of the suffering, humiliation and other forms of victimhood which act as the factor to unite the subaltern group which they can relate. On the other hand the identity of the tea garden community as subaltern group is highly fragmented, as the process of acquiring an *Adivasi* identity or tea tribe identity signifies politicization of the subaltern identity of the community. It also depends on the context where it has been used. Because some of the leaders and educated section of the community cannot be termed as subaltern or the subaltern identity can be assumed by non subaltern groups, as they become elite to their community but on the other hand they might be subaltern in terms of the reference to the other dominant section of the society.

Conclusion

Therefore, the important argument for the analysis of subaltern resistance in today's India, points to the fact that power and resistance are practices which takes place within a set of social relationships. It is in that context power and resistance of subaltern can be seen where cultural and political symbols and horizons of understandings violate the boundaries between dominant and subaltern groups, and are continually constructed, deconstructed and reconstructed systematically through the exercise of power and resistance.

NOTES

1. Guha, Ranajit, 'On Some Aspects of the Historiography of Colonial India', in Ranajit Guha (ed.) *Subalten Studies I: Writings on South Asian History and Society*, OUP, Delhi, 1982, p. 5-6.
2. Guha, Ranajit, *Elementary Aspect of Peasant Insurgency in Colonial India*, OUP, New Delhi, 1983, pp. 3-9.
3. *Ibid.*, pp. 5-6.
4. Shah, Ghanshyam, *'Social Movement in India'*, Sage Publications, New Delhi, http://archive.org >stream>movement.
5. Dhangare, D.N, 'Subaltern Consciousness and Populism: Two Approaches in the Study of Social Movements in India', *Social Scientist*, Vol. 16, No. 11 (Nov, 1988), pp. 18-35.
6. *Ibid.*
7. Hobsbawm, Eric, *Primitive Rebels: Studies in Archaic Forms of Social Movement in the 19th and 20th Centuries,* New York: Praeger, 1963.
8. Guha, Ranajit, *Elementary Aspect of Peasant Insurgency in Colonial India*, OUP, New Delhi,1983, pp. 3-9.
9. Guha, Ranajit, 'The Pros of Counter-Insurgency', in Ranajit Guha (ed.), *Subaltern Studies II : Writings on South Asian History and Society*, OUP, Delhi, 1982, p. 39.
10. Majumdar Rochona, 'Subaltern Studies as a History of Social Movements in India', South Asia: *Journal of South Asian Studies'*, Vol. 38, 2015, p. 14.
11. *Ibid.*
12. *Ibid.*
13. Corridge Stuart, and John Harriss, *Reinventing India: Liberalization, Hindu nationalism and Popular democracy,* Cambridge: Polity Press, 2000.
14. Corridge, Stuart, et al. *Seeing the State: Governance and Governability in India*, Cambridge: Cambridge University Press, 2005.
15. *Ibid.*, 210-211.
16. Dhangare, D.N., 'Subaltern Consciousness and Populism: Two Approaches in the Study of Social Movements in India', *Social Scientist*, Vol. 16, No. 11 (Nov, 1988), pp. 18-35.

17. Sarkar, Sumit, 'The Condition and Nature of Subaltern Militancy: Bengal from Swadeshi to Non-Co-operation, c,1905-22', in Guha, Ranajit (ed.) *Subaltern Studies III, Writing on South Asian History and Society*, OUP, New Delhi, 1984, p. 272.
18. Deka, Kangkan, 'Colonialism, Migration and the Problematics of the Making of an Identity: Tea Tribes and 'Adivasis' of Assam', in Srama, Chandan Kumar, (ed.) *Souvenir*, North East History Association 29th Session, 2008, p. 175.
19. Kar, R.K. and Sarma, J.L. in R.K. Bhadra and S.R. Mondol (ed.), *'Stratification, Hierarchy and Ethnicity in North East India'*, pp. 69-84.
20. Goswami T.C. *Chah Janagusthi Jivan Charya*, p. 0.10.
21. Kerketta, Robert, 'The Adivasis in Assam: Their Past, Present and Future' in Thomas Pullopillil (ed.), *Identity of Adivasis in Assam*, New Delhi, Indian Publishers Distributors, pp.10-20.
22. Dev, Bimal and Lahiri, Dilip K., *Cosmogony of Caste and Social Mobility In Assam*, Mittal Publications, Delhi.
23. Sharma, Pratim Dhurba, 'Demand of Tea Tribes for Scheduled Tribe Status in Assam: A Reviews, in Goswami Sandhya (ed.), *'Troubled Diversity'*, OUP, New Delhi, p. 113.
24. Fernandes, Walter, 'Assam Adivasi Identity Issues and Liberation', *Vidyajyoti Journal of Theological Reflection*, February 2003.
25. *Ibid.*
26. Adivasi struggle in Assam, www.indiatogether.org 2008.
27. Talukdar Sushanta, 'Tribal Turmoil', *Frontline*, Vol. 24-Issue 24, December 8, 2007.
28. Assam; *Hand Book of Government Circulation 1981-1990.*
29. Nilsen, Gunvald Alf, *Adivasi in and Against the State,* Critical Asian Studies, 44:2, 251-282, retrieved from Jstore.
30. *Ibid.*
31. Mishra, Udayan, 'The Adivasi struggle', *Economic and Political Weekly,* Vol. XLII, No. 51, 22-8 December, 2007.
32. Gohain, Hiren, 'A Question of Identity: Adivasi Militancy in Assam', *Economic and Political Weekly*, December 8, 2007.
33. Mishra, Udayan, 'The Adivasi struggle', *Economic and Political Weekly,* Vol. XLII, No. 51, 22-8 December, 2007.
34. Sharma, Debabrata, *Asomia Jatigathan Prakria aru Janagosthigata Anusthan Samuh*, Ekloibya Prakashak, Guwahati, p. 367.
35. *Ibid.*
36. Sanjib Baruah, *Adivasi Politics in Assam*, telegraphindia.com, December 10, 2007.
37. Kristina Garalyte, *Subaltern Autonomy: Dalit Students Identity Politics in India* http//ejournals.vdu.it>article.
38. *Ibid.* p. 57.
39. Prakash, G, Subaltern Studies as Postcolonial Criticism. The *American Historical Review*, 99(5), 1475-1490, Retrieved from Jstore database.
40. Kristina Garalyte, '*Subaltern Autonomy: Dalit Students Identity Politics in India*', http//ejournals.vdu.it>article.

16

Interrogating Citizenship: A Glimpse of Vantangia Community

Deepak Kumar Pandey

Since the outset of the societal institutions with power structure, the question of individual status *vis-à-vis* these structures have been enquired into. The quest to find some theorization and to maintain the equilibrium between these two; leads too many theories, some tilted towards one end and some towards another. Some theories make efforts to have a proper balance between these two. From ancient Greek theorists to modern theorists, effort has been made to draw and point the line on which this balance could be made. What is the role of society, state or structures embedded with power? What are its need and limitations? For what purpose these are made? How their legitimacy be claimed? What is the role and status of individual *vis-à-vis* these structures? And if the individuals (on whom these powers have to be used) are the source of legitimacy; can they take their legitimacy out of these structures? What, if these structures will not work according to wish and needs of these individuals? And many more questions arise and have been enquired into deeply. Reciprocal needs, the basic chord of societal structure leads to the Aristotlian conclusion that man is social and political animal. What makes this social 'animal' along with reciprocal needs, which makes it 'political'? How to manage these reciprocal needs? Who will control and coordinate these needs? Need to control and coordinate these needs amongst the social 'animals' lead to power structure. But again, by which mechanism this power structure is to be used? How this mechanism will locate the individual in this power structure? Whether it is a kind of contract or kind of subjection? Again question arises, up to what level these power dynamics can be exercised? What would be the controlling areas and what would be the periphery of individual domain? Should any space be left out for those individual, upon which these controlling power is to be exercised?

The need to control; control with the exercise of power creates the space for power structures like states and the cry for space for individual to define the limits, leads to the notion of liberty, justice and other entitlements, which they may claim from these structures. Claim for entitlements, which necessitate social 'animal' to be 'political'; under the power structure of social life pave the way for the evolution of state and its citizenship in its various forms. The acceptance of the state as both a supreme and an impersonal form of authority brought with it a displacement of the more charismatic elements of political leadership.[1] Milton, Harrington and other defenders of "free states" hardly ever use the term "state" when speaking of the institutions of civil government. Believing as they do that such institutions must remain under the control of the whole community if its members are to preserve their birthright of liberty, they always prefer the term "commonwealth" as a means of referring not merely to bodies of citizens, but also to the forms of political authority by which they must be governed if they are to remain "in a free state".[2] Most of the idealists identified true individuality, citizenship and self development with freedom. Real freedom was not the absence of compulsion but the maximum of power for all members of society to make the best of themselves. Rational activity was determined by choices.[3] Citizenship encompasses the body of rights and political entitlements of claimants under a definite political boundary. Rights, like laws and institution, were bound up with the realization of individuals and their needs. When freedom became universal, citizenship grew from a local into national institution.[4]

Second issue relates to the question that does every claimant individual has a right to claim? Or it is housed to those claimants, who are recognized by these power structures (like state). L.T. Hobhouse wrote in his seminal work, *Liberalism* that liberal doctrine was:

> *a belief that society can be safely founded on this self-directing power of personality, that it is only on this foundation that a true community can be built....it rests not on the claim of A to be let alone by B, but on the duty of B to treat A as a rational being....The rule of liberty is just the application of rational method.*[5]

But as per going through the lines of Hobhouse, can we claim our community to be community in true sense having the right of application of rational method. Though, as in Green's analysis, the capacity for rights in individuals was a social phenomenon; guided and moralized through institutions of society, claims recognized by the power structures become political entitlements in political domain. In fact though having the social relevance of recognition of entitlements, it has a very less or negligible moralizing element in political domain. Even in practice the rationality of the method is even determined by the power structures of the society, having different institutions of their kind to make their own patterns and belief system to maintain hegemony, undermining the rationality and liberty in practice. There is a long confrontation between duties as a subject owed to state or authoritative structures and duties of state towards their subjects (or citizens) as the sole authority in political domain. Here this differentiation leads to concept of citizen and subjects in political structure. Citizenship can be traced back to the political ideas of Ancient Greece (Aristotlian concept of citizenship) which believes that an interest in public affairs is a basic feature of individual existence. Aristotle defined the citizens as those who participate in political affairs of the state, not all the individuals. Citizenship is a relationship between the individual and state, in which two are bound together by reciprocal rights and duties. The legal conception of an individual is one, who owes allegiance to and receives protection from state. Conditions of citizenship are determined for each state in accordance with its own legal provisions. Citizens differ from subjects and aliens in that they are full members of their political community, or state, by virtue of the possession of basic rights. The term 'citizen' over the term 'subject' has been frequent since the American and French Revolutions, being assumed that latter suggests a condition of subservience which the former does not. One can be subject to an unconstituted power, without having any rights, but the citizenship is the idea of mutual responsibility invoked in the legal definition. The differentiation between citizens and subjects (non-claimants and without any entitlements or negligible entitlement) is very much visible from beginning in the discourse of polity. State and power structure demands the duties as subjects and provide the entitlements as rights of citizens. In the proposed work an effort will be made to explore and distinguish the citizenship theory in different structures of Indian society especially relating to the *Vantangia* Community (of east U.P. region). Analyzing Indian scenario from the above perspective, a glimpse of political entitlements of *Vantangia* people have been made in this paper, to analyse that, despite having the provision of differentiated rights for different groups according to their social cultural structures and needs (religion, linguistic, marginalized), how and why some section of people like *Vantangia* and *Mushar* do not have their political entitlements as citizenry of this state. It is true that as Sarah Joseph argues that, Indian society has been undergoing continuous and profound change since independence and this, along with pressures generated by representative democracy, has brought new challenges for the state.[6] The differentiated system of rights was introduced in the Constitution, and the flexibility which the political system has shown, have been applauded by many analysts. There is no question but that the state and political system in India have shown considerable legal and institutional, and political ingenuity in responding to demands for recognition and share of power. But the problem of demand formation is a continuous one and is strengthened by democratic process.[7] While political mobilization and demands may be framed in the language of identities and cultural recognition, the sense of grievance and injustice which they reflect may also stem from more structured social relationships which influence the long term distribution of assets and opportunities in the society.[8] In this chapter attempt will be made to analyse and enquire the citizenship of *Vantangia* people in different contexts having political entitlements they possess. Vantangia community, which has been evolved as community during British period, arises out of the colonial needs as of *Girmitiya* and *Teenkathiya* Community. British people have developed and encouraged three types of bonded labour "*Bandhua majdur*", called: (1) *Girmitia,* (2) *Teenkathia,* and (3) *Vantangia* for their colonial purposes.

- "*Girmitias*" labourer were taken abroad by Britishers and they were used their as tools of British for their benefits. Their condition was not good during colonial period, but became better after independence of colonies.
- "*Teenkathias*" were used for the purpose of indigo plantation in eastern UP and Bihar. But due to efforts of Mahatma Gandhi and his "Champaran Movement", *Teenkathia* system was abandoned.
- "*Vantangias*" were bonded labourers in Terai belt of UP, Bihar and Nepal, for the plantation and look after of "Saal trees" plantation. This act was mainly prevalent in the Terai belt of eastern UP region, due to poverty and dismal human condition. Even after Independence this system prevailed in this area. It continues from 1918 to 1985.

Nowadays this community is mainly confined in some blocks of eastern UP and also in some pockets of Terai region of Uttarakhand.

Though the existence of people living in forest areas has been denied by the state, the fact is this, that after almost six decades of the Independence, thousands of the families living in the forest villages of the state of Uttar Pradesh (Eastern UP) and also in some terai regions of Uttarakhand are struggling to prove their existence in the State. There are about 35 forest villages in 4 districts, namely Behraich, Maharajganj, Gorakhpur and Pilibheet of the UP which in spite of their valuable role in ecological maintenance and their active participation in the freedom struggle of India; are still bereft of their true independence. 6752 families of forest villages are still waiting for their recognition as citizen of the country. They are not being considered as citizen of the village panchayat, hence ration cards are not being provided to them and thus their access to any of the Government welfare schemes are denied. Their names are not included in the Kutumb (Family) Register and therefore, their address and identity could not be certified and without any proof of residence they are not able to apply for any Government or Non-government jobs. Irony is that they can vote and have their voting rights for parliamentary and assembly elections, but do not have the right to vote in local elections, because in legal sense of framework they do not have any village. Perhaps, this group may be only group in India which despite having voting rights for Central and State legislatures, don't have right to constitute their local bodies as per 73rd Amendment to Constitution.

Historical Context of *Vantangia* People: With the inception of *Jamindari* system during colonial period for the sake of revenue, most of the farmers became landless and large number of them converted into agricultural labourer. As per British announcements, large number of the labourers left their native places and they were provided vacant land in the forest areas where they can construct their houses and use the land for the agricultural purposes. In return these people have to perform work like–

- Plantation of Sal, Khair and Teak trees in land allotted to them in Terai Region, but predominantly Sal trees (resolution 03 of proceedings of 1st Taungya Conference),
- Construction and roads and other infrastructures required,
- Maintenance of Forest and preventing the fire in Jungle, and
- Helping British Officials in the hunting.

Taungya (*term for Agriforestation*) is Burmese word, which means development of forest and plants simultaneously with crop production.

Taungya term is now widely used to describe the practice, in many tropical countries, of establishing tree plantations by planting and tending tree seedlings together with food crops. Crop cultivation is limited to few years (maximum upto 5 years, in general it is 1-2 years). It is a kind of shifting cultivation in which labour is allowed for crop cultivation for a definite time period. In India Dr. Brandis has introduced the system of *taungya* in 1890 and raised the first taungya plantation in 1896 in north Bengal. Though it introduced in India earlier, the process of forest development through tangiya process was initiated in 1918 in the Gorakhpur region. There are three types of Taungya.

(a) *Departmental Taungya*: Under this, agricultural crops and plantation are raised by the forest department. Forest department hire the labour on daily wages for the required crop cultivation along with the plantation, it also keeps the land free of unwanted vegetation.
(b) *Leased Taungya*: The forest land is given on lease to the person for raising agricultural crop for number of years and also to ensure care of tree plantation.
(c) *Village Taungya*: This is the most successful of all the three *Taungya* systems. Under this the people who have settled down in a village inside the forest for this purpose raise crops. Usually each family has about 0.8 to1.7 ha of land has raise trees and cultivate crops for 3 to 5 years.

Though the process of forest development through *Taungya* (Tangia) process was started in 1896, it initiated during 1920s in the Gorakhpur region. The process was replication of the experiences of the forest development in the countries like Burma, Uganda, Sri Lanka, Kenya, Thailand etc. Under this process, the department provided half-acre land to every adult labour. He had to develop the land as per the prescribed process in a period of 5 years and after the development of particular forestland they have to shift to the other areas. They were bound to have continuous and periodic displacement and settlement. For their subsistence, they are allowed to grow crops and vegetables, but even the crop selection was done by the British people. Even after the independence there was no change in the position of *Tangia* labour they were continuously displaced after every five-year. They have been forced for migration because of the threat perception felt by forest officials (that they will acquire and take land).

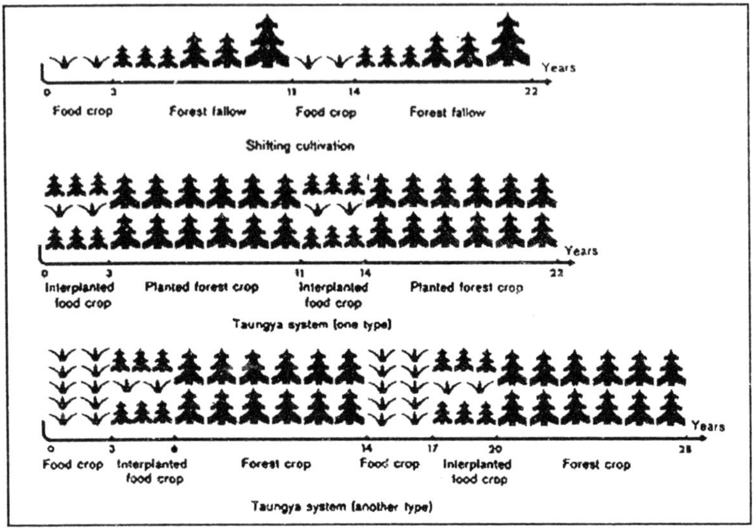

In the proceedings of *Tangia Conference*,[9] held at Nainital in 1933 and 1936, they were considered as cheapest labourer. In the year 1980 the Tangias raised their voice for this exploitation but the forest department declared them encroachers of the forest land. After 1985, these practices were stopped by forest department, but at the same time efforts were made to evacuate forest from these people. And from here the vulnerable *Vantangia* migrant community became perhaps the most insecure community of eastern UP region. In 1980, forest department tried to sign agreement with them, but proved in vain. With that agreement they want to dispose them from their land. On 6 June, 1985 forest department fired on them, burnt their houses, and as per official records 2 *Vantangia* people were died and 24 injured, many of them lost their houses. *Vantangia* is a community which lost much and gained negligible, but paradox is that they have not been even considered tribal. Their societal structure is same as the caste structure of Eastern UP predominantly having OBCs and SCs with some Muslim population also. They bear the same caste structure from where their predecessors came from. There is a continuous demand from this community that they have to be recognized as separate community as tribal status. Normally, there is cordial relation with other societal members. But in social practices and traditions of the same caste community, *Vantangias* are not permitted. Society is in fact closed internally for the *Vantangia* community. There is only superficial integration of society. Main problem for Vantangia community is marriage of their children, because people of the same caste in different societal structure are not willing to make any marital relations. Vantangia are forced to marry only in the Vantangia community, sometimes to different caste person from the Vantangia community only. So they have been internally excluded from other societal structures. Marshall divides the citizenship into three parts–civil, political and social. Civil element is composed of the rights necessary for individual freedom–liberty of the person, freedom of speech, thought and faith, the right to own property and to conclude valid contracts, and the right to justice. Political element means the right to participate in the exercise of political power, as a member of a body invested with political authority or as an elector of the members of such a body. By the social element mean the whole range from the right to a modicum of economic welfare and security to the right to share to the full in the social heritage and to live the life of a civilized being according to the standards prevailing in the society.[10] Analyzing through the Marshallian framework of civil, political and social, it is clearly visible that *Vantangia* community people failed in complying those conditions of citizenship. To have a better in-depth analysis we should go through the data showing their socio-political and economic conditions.

The socio-demographic structure of *Vantangia* people is as below:

Total Families–6752

Hindu Families—87.4% Muslim Families—12.6%

The caste-wise distributions of these families

Scheduled Tribe—3.3% Scheduled Caste—63.8%
Backward Caste—32.6% General—0.3%

Education Level of these Families

Illiterate—55.1%	Primary—28.6%	Jr. High School—9.7%
High School—4.8%	Intermediate—2.4%	Graduate & above—0.4%

Women Education

Illiterate—92.2%	Primary—4.3%	Jr. High School—2.4%
High School—0.8%	Intermediate—0.3%	Graduate & above—0.0%

Their children have not been associated with education system even by the British, because of the fear that they will loose the very cheap labour. Even after Independence, only formality of providing education has been made by forest officials by appointing one teacher to provide them basic education (till 1985). Level of education continues to be low and in dismal condition because of the same kind of psychology of loosing cheap labour. Their children came into ambit of Sarva Shiksha Abhiyan only for a limited period of 2001-2009, through optional system of Vidya Kendra. After 2009 their children are neither getting any proper basic education through Government Schemes and schools nor they are getting benefited by MDM and other schemes.

Government Schemes in Forest Villages

There are no government schemes running in these villages. This is mainly because these forest villages are on the land of forest department. These villages are not under the strict framework of revenue villages. Because of this status, in case of any disaster like fire, which is very usual in summers because of the habitat they have, they are not deemed fit for any type of compensation as per the norms of State Government.

- Ration Card in 2002.
- They do not have access to Domicile certificates, Caste certificates, Income certificates, Indira Awas Yojana etc.
- Ration card is only available to people of 8 villages and 80 family, 550 individual persons under its ambit.
- They have not been considered for BPL survey.
- They are not considered tribal, so they can not take the benefit of reservation policy for different benefits.
- Not a single person from *Vantangia* community is in government job.
- MNREGA, job card has also been made for some villages. But they get their job rights (in limited way) only in 2010-11.
- After 2011 Forest Department did not provide them work under MNREGA, pleading that they have to find work under this scheme at the village level.
- But technically they are not living in any revenue village as per law, so where would they go for their job rights as proclaimed by Government?
- Their children are not benefited either by ICDS (Aanganbadi Karyakram) or Mid Day Meal.
- Enrollment as Voter (for Parliamentary and Assembly elections only) and Voter ID in 2002.

Health Status in the Forest Villages

Health of the people of these forest villages is in the hands of the quacks as government health facilities are not available for them. There is no question of primary health services or vaccination in these villages except the polio vaccination as these villages are covered in the pulse polio campaign. There are no primary health centres or community health centre for them. According to unofficial record (as told by *Vantangia* People), on average 10-20 children become the victim of *Japanese Encephlytis* every year in this region.

Health Status

Complete vaccination (up to Measles)	4.4%
Partial Vaccination (DPT/Polio)	5.3%
Deliveries by ASHA or trained Birth Attendants at hospital	1.3%
Deliveries by ASHA or trained Birth Attendants at Home	Nil
Infant Mortality Rate	166% per 1000 live births
Vaccination of Pregnant Women	1.6%

Political Status of these Villagers

In all the 34 villages, except Hathiyavahva and Baluvahia of Mithor development block of Maharajganj district, eligible people of 32 villages are included in the voter list but they can cast their votes only for Assembly and Parliament elections but not eligible to exercise their voting rights in the election of local bodies. They first voted in 2002 for Assembly elections of UP and in 2004 for the Parliament of the nation.

Livelihood Means

- *Vantangia* used to survive by cultivating cereals and vegetables (suited to interest of forest officials) on the land allotted to them locally called *patta bhumi.*
- They are very good cultivators of vegetables and their expertise in vegetable cultivation produce above average produce of vegetables.

- Due to different forest rules; their produce cannot reach to proper market.
- They can bring their vegetables in market on bicycles only, vehicles are not permitted.
- There is no proper way of marketing.
- Most of the produce go to forest officials or go to the mediators on very low price, resulting in very low income to *Vantangias*.
- Economically insecure, bereft of most of the basic needs.
- They have to pay bribe for so many concessions provided by forest officials.

Forest and Vantangia

Vantangia and forest are inseparable; which is visible in their name, but paradoxically despite their contribution for forest and environment, forest rules have not been always cordial for them, perhaps never. In 1980, forest department tried to sign agreement with them, but not become successful. On the basis of the said agreement they want to dispose them from their land. They get exploited and harassed by forest officials due to their demands. On 6 June, 1985, some forest people opened fire on them, burnt their habitats in Campierganj range, resulting death of 2 *Vantangia* and injuring 24 people. Till today 14 cases of 18 forest villages are pending in court and decision came only in one case almost after six years of the incidence, on 31st December, 1991, when district court sentenced nine involved persons to life imprisonment. They are not in the condition to battle for their concerns legally, owing to their poor and dismal situation. Because of the immense pressure from social activists, media and others, Govt. accepts their habitat in forest under Forest Right Act 1985. After long struggle of these *Vantangia* people, some of the *Vantangia* people got their land rights (*Bhumi-Pradhikar or Patta*) as per Forest Rights Act, 2006, which got Gazette notification on 1st January, 2008. Despite the provision in Gazette notification about their land rights, many of them are still struggling to ensure their name for the land right because of their inability to bribe the *'babus'* of the system. Conflict of Forest with this community is still going on, making their human security at stake always.

The dismal socio-economic scenario and their level of education, where women are almost illiterate exceptionally only few having '*Akshar Gyan*' (basic literacy of letters only) is enough to depict and paint the whole picture of *Vantangia* people. Political exclusion of *Vantangia* people fling them to the periphery of the political power structure. Political theorization in modern contemporary scenario assumed the citizenship as universal, having some sort of entitlements in form of rights, liberty, justice, fairness, food, shelter, employment etc. Citizenship in modern theories is assumed having the notion of equality, having same political entitlements in the same political structure. In theory, ignoring every kind of difference and disparity in any terms, individual possess the same citizenry rights and thus have a right to claim for the political entitlements in political domain. But despite this noble theorization; in practice, in almost every kind of society many layered structures of relationship between power structure and individual is found, terming it to secondary or tertiary kind of citizenship, based on the political entitlements they possess and denied. Many types of groups have formed within a group, itself having found them in disadvantaged position. Vantangia is one such marginalized and disadvantaged group found under the Indian citizenry. Hegel regarded the problem of poverty as one of the most central in society and political theory. Poverty, in his view was a central feature of modern civil society, and the deprivation experienced by the poor was not just to be seen as physical deprivation, however important this may be; rather poverty involves the breaking down of various ties of citizenship—the acquisition of skill, education, access to justice and organized religion—all of which are mediating links which integrate individuals into the state.[11] There are no ties to connect the state and individual in case of *Vantangia*. State, which seems necessary and justified on the grounds of protecting its people, fails in doing so in case of *Vantangia* people, rather different power structures pose threat to the survival and existence of this community. The human security of Vantangia people, in its various dimensions, is at stake. Threat to their existence and dignified survival is found on each and every step.

Despite having same citizenry rights in theory under the same political structure, the policy of 'inclusion' and 'exclusion' for some section leads to some serious questions and even threat to citizenship and its structures. Universal citizenship in view of Iris Marion Young carries at least two meanings in addition to the extension of citizenship to everyone: (a) universality defined as general in opposition to particular; what citizens have in common as opposed to how they differ, and (b) universality in the sense of laws and rules that say the same for all and apply to all in the same way; laws and rules that are blind to individual and group differences.[12] Citizenship locates the status of individual, where it belongs in the socio-political structure. Modern concept of impersonal state, unaffected by any kind of charismatic leadership opens up the new domains of citizenship in which irrespective of the person ruling, citizens (and subjects) have same duties to fulfill and *vice versa* having impersonal quality of state, it provides the same entitlements to all irrespective of the differences found, that is what the basis of equality. But as per the pace of time and milieu around, the notion of citizenship, being basic remains the same has changed a lot. In participatory democratic systems citizens, develop and exercise the capacities of reason and on the basis of this reason and social milieu around, they demand certain claims as entitlements. The ideal of the public realm of citizenship as expressing a general will, a point of view and interest that citizens have in common which transcends their differences, has operated in fact as a demand for homogeneity among citizens.[13] Citizenship is an expression of the universality of human life; it is a realm of rationality and freedom as opposed to the heteronomous realm of particular need, interest and desire.[14] While the virtues of citizenship accepts and express the universal human values, the voices have been raised from different sections and groups in context of their specific physical and social needs for the differential treatment, which lead to differentiated citizenship as demands in feminist or subaltern approach. The differential treatment and differentiated citizenship works in two directions, one from state to individual in which certain groups become deprived with their certain political entitlements, they feel important for their dignified life and in the other way around differentiated citizenship demanded by certain groups (often disadvantaged excluded groups) demands not only equal political entitlements like liberty, shelter, employment, but also demands more preferential treatment than others (case of demand of reservations in India). It is not enough to search for more participatory and deliberative modes of exercising democracy as long as the problems of inclusion and exclusion, of both ensuring access to the material means for a decent living and of broadening the means and forms of democratic expression are not taken up as crucial for the survival and equality of democratic life. Citizens often express their concerns in this respect through repertoires that are not reducible to debate based on rational argument.... How can citizenship and democracy be redefined so as to take into account the emerging versions of a *demos* which is no longer based on clear-cut definitions of national citizenship?[15]

Different social groups have different needs, cultures, histories, experiences and perceptions of the social relations which influence their interpretation of the meaning and consequences of policy proposals and influence the form of their political reasoning.[16] Participatory democracy advocates for inclusion and participation of all citizens in political life for the rational fair decision enhancing their capabilities for the good life. Participatory democracy thrives on the principle of equality, consider generality and commonness of citizens, ignoring and sometimes suppressing the differences among the citizens.

Benjamin Barber makes a clear distinction between the public realm of citizenship and civic activity, on the one hand and a private realm of particular identities, roles, affiliations and interests on the other. Citizenship by no means exhausts people's social identities, but it takes moral priority over all social activities in a strong democracy. The pursuit of particular interests, the pressing of the claims of particular groups, all must take place within a framework of community and common vision established by the public realm.[17] Barber further argues that, a community of citizens owes the character of its existence to what its constituent members have in common.[18]

It is very true that society cannot be formed on the principle of sameness: individual and group differences are bound to be there, but problem arises that how these differences are accommodated within acceptable common framework, in which one group or individual does not feel oppressed or marginalized. Iris M. Young found the traits of oppression to a group when: (1) the benefits of their workforce move to others without reciprocally benefiting them (exploitation). (2) Excluded from participatory in major social activities (marginalization). (3) Live under the authority of others, having little or negligible autonomy (powerlessness). (4) As a group, they are stereotype at the same time that their experience and situation is invisible in the society in general and they have little audience to share their perceptions (cultural imperialism). (5) Group members suffer random violence and harassment motivated by group hatred or fear.[19] Despite differences and diversity cherished within the liberal paradigm, group oppression is also very much visible in these societies. Though liberal societies are claimed to be better than the totalitarian society, many embedded structures (of power domination) prevent not only enjoyment of political entitlements but even from claiming those political entitlements, in the name of rules, laws, law and order, social and community life. Anne Phillips recognizes that in a society marked by vast inequalities the assertion of political equality is necessary but not enough. When group-based exclusions exist, as in the case of women in almost all societies, we need special measures aimed at equalizing, or at least improving, the position of these subordinated groups. It is our concern for equality that warrants and justifies the deviation from the principle of identical treatment.[20]

Controversies about citizenship centre upon the rights it implies and its value as a political principle. Citizenship is both simple as well as complicated in state structure where the level of relationship between Individual and political system determined the citizenry entitlements. The new innovative ideas of providing entitlements through Aadhar or through Population Register with the help of high technologies indeed open up a new debate to think over it, because there is uneven citizenry in India which needs to be rectified first to make the use of these high technologies broad based. Citizenry in India opens up new dimensions of thinking about citizens. There are different citizenship theories, suited to different situations and needs which try to explain Indian citizenry since inception of Indian Citizenship Act, 1955. In the Marshallian framework of *social citizenship*; citizenship is meant as entitlement to equity and sense of belongingness. The idea of social citizenship proclaims that citizens are entitled to a social minimum, expressed in terms of social and welfare rights. Marxists criticize citizenship on the grounds that it masks the reality of unequal class power. Feminist criticizes citizenship on the basis of patriarchal oppression. John Hoffman in his framework considers *citizenship as a moving concept*, with the expansion of equality. We can also find the category of *super citizens, insurgent citizens and subordinate citizens* and relate it to the Indian condition. The grievance and injustices faced by *Vantangia* people is also entangled into the complex social structures in the framework of their cultural recognition and identity. Despite having the same caste structure of the society, they are different in their cultural identity, made because of their status and relationship *vis-à-vis* state power. The denial of opportunities and assets in form of any kind of entitlements including political, make them a special category which despite having the constitutional rights are facing the problem of homelessness (having no space for them either politically or socially), despite having state in political sense are bereft of their basic citizenry rights. They do not even know what the citizenry rights mean to them. Same bureaucratic colonial attitude is faced by them till today in Independent India. Citizenship has itself become, in certain respects the architect of legitimate social inequality.[21] But the social inequality faced by Vantangia people is not legitimate in any case. The basic human equality of membership has been enriched with new substance and invested with a formidable array of rights....It has been clearly identified with the status of citizenship.[22] In the case of *Vantangia* people their membership in society is not founded on the basic human equality having substantial and formidable array of rights. Their quest and struggle for membership based on the human equality and their claim for political entitlements in form of rights and other basic needs, needed for human existence is still going on. Their life is not dignified, as other members of the society under the provision of Article 21 (of Indian Constitution). Their life and dignity are hovering in the judicial courts and bureaucratic files. In fact the miserable condition of their life and their existence compels us to say that they are secondary or tertiary citizens of this country. Citizenship requires a bond of different kind, a direct sense of community membership based on loyalty to a civilization which is a common possession. It is a loyalty of free men endowed with rights and protected by a common law.[23] Citizenship is a status bestowed on those who are full members of a community. All who possess the status are equal with respect to the rights and duties with which the status is endowed. There is no universal principle that determines what those rights and duties shall be, but societies in which citizenship is a developing institution creates an image of an ideal citizenship against which achievement can be measured and towards which aspirations can be directed.[24] This bond of membership between *Vantangia* and rest of the communities is missing, that got reflected in various social activities. Though there is the common law, but *Vantangia* people are not free as the other denizens. They are neither full members of the community as per definition of Marshall. Their achievements are unparallel, but their aspirations are sinking without any direction. Though there may be limitations of data related to political and social entitlements of *Vantangia* community, yet it will open up the understanding of their status in citizenry framework.

Conclusion

Let us draw some conclusions on the basis of evolution of understanding of citizenship theory and the cross examining the status of *Vantangia* people. State and political structures should ever ready and open to accommodate the citizenry in the new developments and needs of the societal structure. State and its legal citizenship should not work as barrier for accommodating diversities and new developments, rather political and social structures should move and evolve in tandem to have better citizenry rights and political entitlements. Conceptualization of *'Public Sphere'* by Habermas as a space for deliberation and democratic citizenship masks many of the inequalities and hierarchies. Citizenship should be viewed and should come out of its legal trap to accommodate its 'own' people, for their better life and subsistence. Coming out of legal trap does not mean that being illegal; rather it means that, legal structures should not be in the confines and their own shackles. There should be enough elasticity to cover the emerging and ongoing socio-political needs, moves and developments. We have to perceive the polity and its structures 'out of the box' of procedures and lock of the authority (or political power). Because of *Vantangia*, thousands of acre of land between Dehradun to Gorakhpur gets blessed with vast area of natural forest. But despite all their contributions to society and nation, they are still struggling for their citizenry rights and entitlements. Even after 66 years of Independence they are forced to be second rate citizens. They are still waiting for their new dawn, in which they are seen and considered as equals to citizens. There is a need to break this 'disconnect', which is prevailing between the 'demos' and the polity. There is a need to adopt the sustainable local development approach, in which the 'people' at the periphery get the entitlements and opportunities in decision-making and a chance to have dignified life as a human being enriching citizenship in ever evolving mode, with new array of rights in their socio-political domain. "Democracy, in the modern sense, is going to be the institution of a space whose social function has had to emancipate itself from any concrete content....What is at stake is more than procedures; it is the institution of signifiers of a social lack resulting from the absence of God as fullness of Being."[25]

From the human security perspective, they need urgent attention of Government, society and other institutions. Bringing governance out of the shackles of legality and turning it into humane governance can only bring their citizenry entitlements. They should have been given the land rights and the duty to protect the forests to which they are emotionally and almost culturally associated, then only dawn of true independence will reach to these 'wretched of the earth' and then only being citizen become meaningful term for them.

NOTES

1. Skinner, Quentin, 'The State', In Goodin, E. Robert and Pettit Phillip (eds.), *Contemporary Political Philosophy: An Anthology*, Oxford: Blackwell Publishers, 1997, p. 19.

2. c.f. Skinner, Quentin, 'The State', in *Contemporary Political Philosophy: An Anthology*, Goodin, E. Robert and Pettit Phillip (eds.), Oxford: Blackwell Publishers, 1997, pp. 13-14.
3. Vincent, Andrew and Plant Raymond, 'A Metaphysical Theory of Politics' (ch.), in *Philosophy, Politics and Citizenship: The Life and Thought of the British Idealists*, Oxford: Basil Blackwell Publishers, 1984, p. 27.
4. Marshall, T.H., 'Citizenship and Social Class', In Goodin E. Robert and Pettit Phillip (eds.), *Contemporary Political Philosophy: An Anthology*, Oxford: Blackwell Publishers, 1997, p. 296.
5. Hobhouse, L.T., *Liberalism*, London: Thornton Butterworth, 1911, p. 123.
6. Joseph, Sarah, 'Multiculturalism and Diversity', in *Accommodating Diversity*, Mahajan, Gurpreet (ed.), New Delhi: Oxford University Press, p. 114.
7. *Ibid.*, pp. 114-115.
8. Bebbington, Anthony, "Social Movements and Politicization of Chronic Poverty", *Development and Change*, vol. 38, No. 5, 2007, pp. 791-818, c.f. Joseph, Sarah, 'Multiculturalism and Diversity', In Mahajan, Gurpreet (ed.), *Accommodating Diversity*, New Delhi: Oxford University Press, p. 115.
9. See Proceedings of *First Taungya Conference* (31st August to 2nd September 1933) and *Second Taungya Conference* (12th to 14th August 1936), held at Nainital, Chaired by Mr. Smythies, Source: Archives of Forest Research Institute (FRI), Dehradun.
10. Marshall, T.H., 'Citizenship and Social Class', In Goodin, E. Robert and Pettit Phillip (eds.), *Contemporary Political Philosophy: An Anthology*, Oxford: Blackwell Publishers, 1997, p. 294.
11. c.f. Vincent, Andrew and Plant Raymond, 'The Charity Organization Society: Poverty and Citizenship' (ch.), in *Philosophy, Politics and Citizenship: The Life and Thought of the British Idealists*, Oxford: Basil Blackwell Publishers, 1984, p. 94.
12. Young, Iris Marian, 'Polity and Group Difference: A Critique of the Ideal of Universal Citizenship', In Goodin, E. Robert and Pettit Phillip (eds.), *Contemporary Political Philosophy: An Anthology*, Oxford: Blackwell Publishers, 1997, p. 256.
13. *Ibid.*, p. 257.
14. *Ibid.*, p. 258.
15. Santos, Boaventura De Sousa and Nunes, Joao Arriscado, 'Introduction: Democracy, Participation and Grass Roots Movements in Contemporary Portugal', In Santos, Boaventura De Sousa and Nunes, Joao Arriscado (eds.), *Reinventing Democracy: Grassroots Movements in Portugal*, Oxon: Routledge, 2006, p. 6.
16. Young, Iris Marian, 'Polity and Group Difference: A Critique of the Ideal of Universal Citizenship', In Goodin, E. Robert and Pettit Phillip (eds.), *Contemporary Political Philosophy: An Anthology*, Oxford: Blackwell Publishers, 1997, p. 260.
17. Barber, Benjamin, *Strong Democracy* (Chs. 8 and 9), Berkely: University of California Press, 1984.

18. *Ibid.*, p. 232.
19. Young, Iris Marian, 'Polity and Group Difference: A Critique of the Ideal of Universal Citizenship', In Goodin E. Robert and Pettit Phillip (eds.), *Contemporary Political Philosophy: An Anthology*, Oxford: Blackwell Publishers, 1997, p. 262.
20. Phillips, Anne, *Multiculturalism without Culture*, Princeton: Princeton University Press, 2007.
21. Marshall, T.H., 'Citizenship and Social Class', In Goodin, E. Robert and Pettit Phillip (eds.), *Contemporary Political Philosophy: An Anthology*, Oxford: Blackwell Publishers, 1997, p. 293.
22. *Ibid.*
23. *Ibid.*, p. 304.
24. *Ibid.*, p. 300.
25. Laclau, Ernesto and Zac, Lilian, 'Minding the Gap: The Subject of Politics', In Laclau, Ernesto (ed.), *The Making of Political Identities*, London: Verso, 1994, p. 36.

17

Democracy, Secularism and Religio-Political Corruption in India

A Critique of the Narendra Modi Regime

Sujit Lahiry

Introduction

Discourses and debates on democracy and secularism have proliferated in the post-independent India, even though they were a primary concern of the colonial India too. The colonial power, i.e. the Britishers came to India in the guise of doing business through its flagship company, the East India Company. But, very soon, they established their colonial rule over the nascent Indian state. They instilled the poisonous venom of Hindu-Muslim communal polarization and riots across every nook and corner of India. This policy of 'Divide and Rule' became the basis of the Britishers to establish their colonial empire in India. The entire anti-colonial struggle waged by the Congress and the Left is full of struggles against such anti-society and anti-religious policies of the Britishers. Another pertinent point which we need to ponder is that religion was and still is a very important aspect of an individual's life in both pre-independent as well as in post-independent India. The reason behind it is that India was a semi-feudal society during the British rule over India.

This chapter treats the mixing of religion and politics, i.e. religious politics as a manifestation of political corruption, especially as illustrated in contemporary India. It critically analyses the endemic communal and divisive politics of the Sangh Parivaar, ever since 2014, when the Narendra Modi government came to power. The Modi-Amit Shah duo had unleashed a reign of terror, which can be referred to as 'Hindu Terrorism'. This chapter accordingly has been divided into three sections. The first section deals with the philosophical debates on secularism to the contemporary discourses on secularism and democracy in India. It seeks to tease out the notions of secularism as it had evolved in contemporary India. The second sections provide a detailed analysis of the notions of democracy and secularism under the present regime of Narendra Modi at the Centre. How religio-political corruption has been unveiled in the present Central Government of Modi is the subject matter of discussion here. It especially critiques the notion of secularism as it has been championed by the fascist government of Modi. The concluding remarks have been put forward in the third and last section.

I

What constitutes secularism? What is meant by communalism? How they are intrinsically related? How secularism has been interpreted philosophically ever since the medieval political theory, Renaissance and modern political theory? What are the various provisions provided by our founding fathers of the Constitution to preserve a secular polity? How they have been threatened by the Hindu fanatics and fundamentalists? How the notions of secularism have affected democracy in India? These are some of the questions which have been addressed in this section.

Let me begin with some fundamental presumptions. The first argument is that communalism and secularism are both thesis and anti-thesis of each other. Both cannot exist in conjunction with each other. A secular polity will thereby mean that the state will be a neutral arbitrer in religious matters of the individual. Religion is the personal domain of every individual and the state has no role to play in matters of promoting and practicing anyone religion. However, the state can interfere only when anyone religion tries to make a super-imposition over other religions. In other words, the dominant majority religion should not thrust aside the fragmented and minority religion. Minority rights need to be respected and protected at all costs and with utmost sincerity in all states. And, this becomes the responsibility of the state, that every individual is free to practice and propagate their own religion. If the state fails in its duty then it becomes ominous on the part of the individual to resist such hegemonic assertions of anyone religion.

The debate on religion and politics has been the concern of many Western political thinkers. St. Thomas Aquinas, St. Augustine and Machiavelli are some of the earliest thinkers who have debated extensively on the role of state *vis-à-vis* the church (Christian religion). As St. Thomas Aquinas has elucidated that the church is superior and the state is subordinate. However, this view is contested by Machiavelli, who was a product of Renaissance. This convinced him to the idea that politics and religion are two distinct entities, and, he debunked Christianity. His theory of religion supports his theory of a strong state. However, Marx, a modern political thinker has opined that religion is the opium of the masses. And, religion is the resort of the weak individuals.

Karl Marx, a renowned political economist, had argued that, religion is the very basis of feudal and semi-feudal society. In such a society, the mode of production is large-scale agriculture-based economy. These contradictions in society can be removed only when there is a mechanized system of production, as it prevails in a capitalist society. Here, the mode of production is large-scale industrialized system of economy. And, only capitalism will lead to the eventual emergence of a socialist society, wherein the notion of religion will be relegated to the background. The socialist society will eventually usher in communism, i.e. the formation of a classless and state-less society, in which the individuals would no longer fight with each other on the basis of religion. That will lay down the basis of a truly humane and egalitarian society. This author feels very strongly that mixing of religion and politics will give rise to religious fundamentalism, as is depicted by the rise of Hindu fundamentalism in India. The rise of Hindutva signals the beginning of a fascist and narcissist government, as it is depicted by the contemporary BJP-led government at the Centre in India.

Secularism in the West is at a better position as compared to India, since most of the states in the West and the North are industrialized and developed countries. And, in industrialized states, religion is gradually pushed to the periphery. Religion, though it exists in the developed countries, is essentially a matter of private sphere and not a matter in the realm of public domain. In other words, secularism in the West is a means of securing multiculturalism, which means celebrating religious diversity. However, the rise of Far Right under Donald Trump in the US, and, Trump's open advocacy of an anti-Muslim stance and his support for the Hindu Right in India, has led to racist violence in America. Trump's support for white supremacists and his contempt for Muslims, Jews, or minorities, has led to an unprecedented and widespread condemnation from the world community. It has led to a dominant majoritarian democracy, which has only endangered the religious minorities. It is no secret that that Trump has received support from the Republican Hindu

Foundation, an Indian Hindu diaspora organization that has extended unequivocal support to Trump, both before and after the US Presidential elections were held on November 8, 2016.

Let me now move on to a different terrain of secularism and ask us the question what does a secular state entails? This question has been beautifully summarized by Marc Galanter through a review of Donald Eugene Smith's work, which is being reproduced below:

> Professor Smith discusses Indian aspirations and practices in terms of their conformity to the 'secular state'. His 'working definition' of the secular state involves 'three distinct but inter-related, sets of relationships concerning the state, religion and the individual'. First, as regards the relation between *religion and the individual*, '[t]he secular state....guarantees individual and corporate freedom of religion'. Second, as regards the relation between *the state and the individual*, the secular state 'dealt with the individual as a citizen irrespective of his religion'. Finally, as regards the relation between the *state and religions*, the secular state 'is not constitutionally connected to a particular religion, nor does it seek either to promote or interfere with religion'. It is these three—religious freedom, state indifference to religious affiliation, and separation (that is, neither interference, nor promotion)—that constitute the 'doctrine', 'theory', 'principles', and 'conception' of *the* secular state to which he repeatedly refers and against which he measures Indian practices. This conception is derived from the 'liberal democratic tradition of the West' and it is also said to be 'essentially that which can be derived from the Indian Constitution itself' (Galanter, 1999: 234-235).

In other words, secularism means that the state will ensure religious freedom and, the individual will be completely free to practice and propagate any religion. According to Rajeev Bhargava, secularism 'means principled distance, a flexible but value-based relation that accommodates intervention as well as abstention' (Bhargava, 1999: 7). On the other hand, secularism, according to Donald Eugene Smith has three connotations—'religious freedom, state indifference to religious affiliation, and separation (that is, neither interference, nor promotion)'. Ashis Nandy makes a distinction between two forms of religion—i.e., 'religion as a faith' and 'religion as an ideology' (Nandy, 1999: 321-

344). So long religion is a faith, it is a personal domain and choice of the individual. But, the moment religion becomes an ideology to usurp political power, it becomes violent and fascist, as is exhibited by the upsurge of the Hindu Right (Sarkar, 1993: 1768-77). This is also exhibited by the Akali Dal's policy of religious mobilization of the Sikhs through SGPC, right since its inception in Punjab (Chatterjee, 1999: 378). Partha Chatterjee has argued that 'the Hindu Right cannot only deflect accusations of being anti-secular, but can even use the arguments for interventionist secularization to promote intolerance and violence against minorities' (Chatterjee, 1999: 347). This chapter treats the mixing of religion and politics, i.e. religious politics as a manifestation of political corruption, especially as illustrated in contemporary India. It critically analyzes the endemic communal and divisive politics of the Sangh Parivaar, ever since 2014, when the Narendra Modi government came to power. The Modi-Amit Shah duo had unleashed a reign of terror, which had led to the rise of 'Hindu Terrorism'.

The partition of the Indian subcontinent in 1947 led to the emergence of two sovereign states—India and Pakistan. The horrors of partition are being felt even after 70 years of Independence. It led to communal rights between the Hindus and Muslims, which was essentially a legacy of the colonial rule era. As Steven I. Wilkinson (2013: 268) has pointed out, 'Under the British, India had a system of communal reservations in politics and administration, and a system of "class recruitment" in the army whose effect (and its intention) was to accentuate communal divides and preserve their own rule. The partition itself led to the killing of perhaps 200,000 people and the mass migration of 13 million more, in a process that was to continue well into the 1950s. The killing of Mahatma Gandhi by a Hindu fanatic, Nathuram Godse, associated with the RSS, in 1948, discredited the Hindu Right.

The framers of the Constitution of India had completely vowed to create India as a 'socialist' and 'secular' state, as defined in our Preamble. Further, the Indian state had provided 'Right to Freedom of Religion' under Articles 25 to 28 as a Fundamental Right, which cannot be negated and infringed at any cost. It essentially gave the citizens of India the freedom to practice and propagate any religion without any hindrance from the state. And, the state was supposed not to enforce the religion of the dominant majority, meaning thereby that the ideals of Hindu nationalism will not be forced upon the religious minorities, especially the Muslims. Minority rights and the secular ethos ought to be maintained at all costs, so that individuals are able to preserve their religious identity.

It is India's misfortune that the present NDA government at the Centre has obliquely tried to remove the word 'Secular' from the Constitution of India. Prakash Singh Badal, the former Chief Minister of Punjab, often resorts to his phrase, '*Raj Nahi, seva*' (not rule, but service). This is an attempt to legitimize his rule over the people of Punjab. It can be expressed by using Italian Marxist thinker, Antonio Gramsci's subtle way of legitimizing his rule and establishing his 'hegemony'. The dominant ruling elite often tries to so disperse their moral, political and social values throughout society in such a way that subordinate groups (i.e. the minorities) and classes would never question their authority, and would also accept the voices of the ruling elite as their own. The ruling elite dominates through a clever interplay of rule through coercion (i.e. political society) and rule through consent (i.e. civil society). There is a similarity in the manner by which the Indian Prime Minister, Narendra Modi and Parkash Singh Badal tries to legitimize their rule by using religion as a metaphor. While, Badal's phrase has been discussed above, Narendra Modi often says during election campaigns that 'give me a chance, I will be your chowkidar'. These assertions are essentially to hegemonize their rule over the vast mass of Indian citizens. In other words, Hindu terrorism and the concomitant religious intolerance constitute the two very serious challenges for our society and polity. They can be countered only by a counter-hegemonic struggle by a United Opposition, including the Congress and the Left, to re-establish the secular credentials of the Indian state.

What is meant by Hindu nationalism—this question has been beautifully summarized by Paul R. Brass. To quote him:

> Hindu nationalism has offered the prospect of uniting the country around the idea that all those who consider themselves "Hindus", whatever their sect, language, or caste are joined in fact by systems of beliefs, philosophical principles, and rituals going back to the Vedas, that they share a common history preceding both the British and the Muslim invasions, and that, as the "majority" population of the country, their beliefs and history ought to provide the ideological basis for an Indian state properly conceived as a Hindu state (Brass, 1990: 228).

The Indian state under its first Prime Minister, Jawaharlal Nehru, followed this principle, both in letter and spirit. Nehru was successful in reducing communal conflicts and riots, essentially because of his strong belief and commitment to secularism and socialistic policies. Mrs. Indira Gandhi, Nehru's successor, was also able to maintain this tradition with utmost sincerity. However, the rise of Jan Sangh and BJP in the subsequent years led to communal polarization between the Hindus and Muslims. 'Communal politics', as Andre Beteille, has pointed out, 'seemed to take a Hindu-Muslim pattern in the north but have a caste pattern in the south, and he noted that even within the south there was substantial regional variation, with Muslim political mobilization strongest in those areas such as Kerala and parts of Andhra, where the non-Brahmin movement had been weakest' (Beteille cited in Wilkinson, 2013: 262).

The demolition of Babri Masjid in Ayodhya on 6th December, 1992, by the Hindu *karsevaks*, with the tacit support of the BJP-led Kalyan Singh government was one of the most black spots in the history of Indian democracy and secularism. The Hindu fanatics vowed to create a Ram temple at the disputed site in Ayodhya and committed one of the worst Hindu-Muslim communal riot and aggravated the communal polarization between these two religious communities. The Sangh Parivaar turned to a policy of aggressive Hindutva to gain electoral dividends, and appease the hardline Hindu community, its traditional support base. The 1990s also saw an unprecedented wave of caste reservation in the form of Mandal Commission, brought in by the V.P. Singh government. There is no denying the fact that reservations based on caste criteria need to be continued for the Dalit community, as these are essentially part of an affirmative action to bring them at par with other caste communities. Quite naturally, the debate in Indian democracy turned to Mandir *versus* Mandal mobilization—i.e., religion *versus* caste configuration. The 1990s thus witnessed the rise of BJP and militant Hindu nationalism. As Paul R. Brass has argued,

> The various forms of religious and political mobilization that were developed in these earlier waves of violence have persisted into the present, but they have been subordinated to more direct appeals to Hindu religious sentiment and solidarity that confront and directly offend Muslim religious sentiments. These have included *yatras* (journeys) from one Hindu religious site to another or from one emotionally charged national site to another, of which the most famous was the *rathyatra* of the BJP leader L.K. Advani in 1990 from the Hindu temple of Somnath in the western state of Gujarat to the Babri mosque at Ayodhya. Although this *yatra* was aborted before it reached UP, it gathered

> a massive following of Hindus and was accompanied by rioting in its wake at numerous sites through which it passed (Brass, 2003: 13).

Christophe Jaffrelot has argued "that embracing Hindutva and the organizational energies of militant organizations such as the RSS, VHP, and Bajrang Dal seems to be especially attractive to BJP leaders when the party has suffered reverses, and therefore looks unlikely to win on other issues" (Jaffrelot cited in Wilkinson, 2013: 263). If we look at Gujarat, the BJP came to power on the basis of a militant Hindutva and one of its hardline leader, Narendra Modi committed one of its worst communal riots in the state in 2002 in the form of Godhra carnage, which will be remembered as the second most black spot in the chequered history of Indian democracy. The Godhra carnage threw all the narrative of secularism and democracy into dustbin and resulted in a massive massacre of the Muslims in Gujarat. The experience was so horrific, that all secular, democratic and radical intelligentsia were critical of that large-scale genocide. As Partha Chatterjee elucidates, "the current campaign of the Hindu Right is directed not against the principle of the secular state, but rather towards mobilizing the legal powers of that state in order to systematically persecute and terrorize a specific religious minority within its population" (Chatterjee, 1999: 348). What Chatterjee specifically implies is that the Hindu majoritarian democracy is terrorizing the minority religious community, by implicating the Islamic religion.

II

It is a mockery of Indian democracy that the perpetrator of Godhra carnage, Chief Minister Narendra Modi is now the Indian Prime Minister. Modi-Amit Shah duo carried out very brutally the murder of Indian democracy by killing innocent Muslims, through the Godhra massacre. However, Modi's posture of aggressive and militant Hindutva has paid off, as he was projected as the BJP's Prime Ministerial candidate in the 2014 Lok Sabha elections. Immediately after the Lok Sabha elections, the Sangh Parivaar's pseudo-academic Dinanath Batra started the policy of projecting an aggressive Hindutva in the educational curriculum. Not only this, Wendy Donigger's book was banned, essentially because it provided a thorough and comprehensive critic of the rising tide of Hindu nationalism and Hindutva. It was followed by many renowned academicians returning their awards and felicitations, because of their antipathy to growing Hindu terrorism.

Moreover, the BJP government and the entire Sangh Parivar has been involved in communalization and saffronization of our society, polity and education. The issue of saffronization of the education system first was pronounced in the NDA government led by former Prime Minister, Atal Bihari Vajpayee, during the five year period spanning from 1999 to 2004. Murli Manohar Joshi, the Human Resource Development (HRD) minister, during the Vajpayee era, was marked by a massive wave of saffronization. The NCERT text-books were rewritten and there was a very hardened wave of Hindutva, which could be reflected in the NDA government's move to rewrite history by glorifying the contribution of RSS's ideologues, such as M.S. Gowalkar, Deen Dayal Upadhyaya, Shyama Prasad Mukherjee etc.

The same move of saffronization has been initiated with a much more renewed vigour, ever since the Narendra Modi government came to power in 2014. The imposition of teaching Sanskrit in schools and the *Gita* should be declared as a national scripture are indications of saffronization of our education system. The RSS-affiliated academics now head majority of the educational institutions and research institutes. Further, the suicide of a *Dalit* research scholar, Rohith Vemula, in the University of Hyderabad reflects that notes of dissent and independent view point, most notably the Leftist view point, have now become a subdued phenomenon. The *Dalits* and minorities, especially the Muslims, are living in a state of horrified fear. This is further substantiated by the fact many Left rationalists, like Narendra Dabholkar, Govind Pansare and M.M. Kalburgi, have been openly murdered.

The entire politics of religious conversion through '*Ghar Vapsi*' and '*Love Jihad*' by the Sangh Parivar testify to our observation. The repeated remark by RSS Chief Mohan Bhagwat, and, VHP chief Praveen Togadia; as well as senior BJP leaders to construct a 'Hindu Rashtra' has given rise to Right-Wing Hindu terrorism and fundamentalism. In the recent past, senior BJP leaders have obliquely tried to delete the words 'Secular' and 'Socialist' from the Preamble of our Constitution. All these are leading to fascist tendencies all over the country (Lahiry, 2015: 82).The Planning Commission was disbanded and replaced by a new institution, the National Institution for Transforming India (NITI Aayog). This essentially reflects that most of the institutions established during the Nehruvian era will now become a thing of the past.

Moreover, the issue of mob-lynching has become a regular phenomenon in most of the states. The brutal murder of Mohammad Ikhlaq in Dadri and many other people by the so-called '*Gau-Rakshaks*' have now become a regular phenomenon. They are openly targeting the Muslim minorities on the assumption that they are consuming beef. One pertinent question which arises here is that how can the state decide what an individual should consume or not? Is not it an intrusion into individual's private sphere? The 'Gau-Rakshaks', who primarily belong to the Sangh Parivaar's outfits, like, RSS, VHP, Bajrang Dal, Hindu Yuva Vahini, are openly roaming scot-free and have unleashed a reign of terror in majority of the states in India. Most of the BJP-ruled states have banned the consumption of beef and made it a punishable offence. Kerala is one state where beef consumption is allowed. Suhas Palshikar makes a very pertinent point. He argues that,

> The creative deployment of the arsenal of culture and tradition can call the BJP's bluff about Hindutva (as a religio-cultural prerequisite of our collective being). It can also contest the exclusionary nationalism that the BJP seeks to construct and spread. The nationalism of Gandhi and Nehru is distinct because it does not prescribe preconditions of religion, language or sect as necessary ingredients to being a nationalist (Palshikar, 2017).

However, a ray of hope can now be seen in the fact that in the recently conducted students union elections in Panjab University, Chandigarh in 2018, the BJP-backed ABVP (Akhil Bhartiya Vidyarthi Parishad) have been defeated and the Left candidate has won. This essentially reflects the revival of socialist politics over the rising tide of Hindutva. And, a ray of hope is being reflected by the fact that the Congress-Samajwadi Party-Bahujan Samaj Party-Rashtriya Lok Dal candidate has won the Kairana bye-election in Uttar Pradesh. This reflects the victory of Opposition unity, as it had led to consolidation of secular votes.

In the recently concluded Assembly elections in five states in November-December 2018, the Congress party won in the three largest Hindi heartland states of Rajasthan, Madhya Pradesh and Chhattisgarh, while losing in Telangana and Mizoram. The BJP made a complete rout and lost in all the five states. Reading these Assembly election results, we can certainly argue that the voters of all the five states have rejected the aggressive Hindutva of the Sangh Parivaar and the divisive politics of Modi government. Just before the elections, the BJP made a big push for building up the Ram Temple at Ayodhya in Uttar Pradesh, even though the matter is sub-judicial. Narendra Modi and Amit Shah addressed many rallies in all these states. However, the BJP's loss meant that the Modi-

Amit Shah magic had failed to reap any electoral dividends. The verdict certainly has revived the prospects of Congress party. Certainly, the credit goes to Rahul Gandhi, the president of Congress party. Rahul Gandhi made a distinct combination of old and young guards to steer the Congress party to an emphatic and resounding victory. There was a strong wave of anti-incumbency blowing in the three Hindi heartland states of Madhya Pradesh, Chhattisgarh and Rajasthan over the failure of these three BJP governments on the issue of rural distress, farmer's suicides and agrarian crises, unemployment, demonetization and GST (Goods and Services Tax), corruption at both the national level (Rafale deal as well as those who have duped the people of India by siphoning off crores of rupees, like Nirav Modi, Mehul Choksi etc) as well as corruption at the regional and state level (like Vyapam scam in Madhya Pradesh). Coupled with all these, there has grown the rising tide of Hindutva wave and brutal crackdown on Muslims, minorities and *Dalits* over issues of cow and beef politics. These developments in Indian politics have not only revived the fortunes of the grand old Congress party, but have also enabled the Congress party to bargain from a position of strength over issues of seat sharing with its allied partners. Having won the semi-final election in winter 2018, the chances of UPA-III have only brightened with Rahul Gandhi to be elevated as a consensual candidate for the position of Prime Minister in the 2019 Lok Sabha election.

III

What then is the way ahead? The arguments in the preceding pages of this paper clearly convey the point that there is a rising level of religious intolerance prevailing in contemporary India, under Narendra Modi's leadership. And so powerful is this discourse of Hindu terrorism, that alternative narratives of secularism and socialism are crushed with an iron hand. What we need to do is to promote and embrace multiculturalism in all forms and at all levels. Religious diversity and religious pluralism needs to be promoted in right earnest, so as to tide over the notions of communalism and build a new democratic India on the basis of secularism and socialism. We earnestly hope that 2019 will lay the foundations of a secular India and defeat of the fascist BJP-led coalition.

REFERENCES

1. Bhargava, Rajeev (1999). 'Introduction', in Rajeev Bhargava (ed.), *Secularism and Its Critics*. New Delhi: Oxford University Press, pp. 1-28.

2. Brass, Paul R. (1990).*The Politics of India since Independence*. New Delhi: Cambridge University Press.
3. ——(2003). *The Production of Hindu-Muslim Violence in Contemporary India*. New Delhi: Oxford University Press.
4. Chatterjee, Partha (1999). 'Secularism and Tolerance', in Rajeev Bhargava (ed.), *Secularism and Its Critics*. New Delhi: Oxford University Press, pp. 345-379.
5. Galanter, Marc (1999). 'Secularism East and West', in Rajeev Bhargava (ed.), *Secularism and Its Critics*. New Delhi: Oxford University Press, pp. 234-267.
6. Lahiry, Sujit (2015). 'Perspectives of Globalisation and Governance in India', *Man & Development* 37(2): 77-86.
7. Nandy, Ashis (1999).'The Politics of Secularism and the Recovery of Religious Toleration', in Rajeev Bhargava (ed.), *Secularism and Its Critics*, New Delhi: Oxford University Press, pp. 321-344.
8. Palshikar, Suhas (2017). 'BJP Bhagao: How and Why?', *Economic and Political Weekly*, 52 (37), September 16.
9. Sarkar, Sumit (1993). 'The Fascism of the Sangh Parivar', *Economic and Political Weekly*, January 30: 163-167.
10. Smith, Donald Eugene (1963). *India as a Secular State*, Princeton: Princeton University Press.
11. Wilkinson, Steven I (2013). 'Communal and Caste Politics and Conflicts in India', in Paul R. Brass (ed.) *Routledge Handbook of South Asian Politics: India, Pakistan, Bangladesh, Sri Lanka, and Nepal*. New York: Routledge, pp. 262-273.

18

Gender and Political Economy

Dimensions of Exploitation

Venkatanarayanan, S. and *Valentina Fusari*

Introduction

Gender-based distinction and its resultant inequity have been prevalent in social and economic history until this date visibly. It is reflected in every sphere of our day-to-day life, reinforcing the patriarchal traits of our society. The present capitalist (Neoliberal Phase) political economy, which has inequality as its functional component, makes use of this social cleavage of gender to create more burden, adding to the existing gender based woes, for women. Gender-based divisions constantly are produced and reproduced in every sphere through cultural practices and economic activities. It occurs at all levels of the social structure as a "system" of practices that are far-reaching, interlocked, and that exist independently of individuals. Creation and sustenance of inequality between genders maintaining the dominance of one gender has been an important trait of patriarchy (Walby, 2002, Warton, 2005, Rawat, 2014, Semali & Shakespeare, 2014). The resource allocation reeks of gender biasness at household level, within local and national budgets (Cagatay, 2000). The market-based neoliberalism perpetuates gender bias through economic policies, labour market, and employment choices for men and women. Thus, the gender relations pervade all aspects of economic life, making economies gendered structures. Understanding gender and its operational aspects will clearly reveal the gender based inequality and its discriminatory aspects in our society. The aim of this chapter is to promote a theoretical reflection, accompanied by brief examples related to Global

North and Global South, to understand how neoliberalism and patriarchy reinforce marginalization of women even in those contexts where this mechanism of reproduction may appear mitigated. Thus, the convergence between neoliberalism and patriarchy is itself a lens through which to investigate specific aspects of women's socio-economic and cultural life.

Comprehending Gender and its Functioning

Gender as a system of social practices creates and sustains gender dissimilarities, on the basis of which, the relations of inequalities are organized (Ridgeway & Smith-Lovin, 1999). In this view, gender involves the creation of both difference and inequalities. Historically, such gendered thinking was based on three beliefs regarding women and men, which dominated the cultural sphere of influence, and they are men and women have different psychological and sexual natures; men are inherently dominant or superior sex; and male-female difference and male dominance are natural (Bem, 1993).

Every society and its cultural practices embrace certain veiled conjectures with regard to sex and gender, which are embedded in cultural discourses, social institutions, and individual psyches that indiscernibly reproduce the dominance of male supremacy, to continue for next generation. According to Bem (1993), these conjectures could be classified as androcentrism, gender polarization and biological essentialism. Androcentrism or male-centred perception considered male experience as neutral or standard, and perceives female experience as deviation from male standard. Gender polarization considers the male-female difference as organizing principle for social life of culture. It is reflected in the mode of dress, social roles, expressing emotions and experiencing sexual desires in every society. Biological essentialism rationalizes and legitimizes androcentrism and gender polarization by demonstrating them as natural due to biological differences between male and female. These conjectures reproduce themselves in any society to sustain the male-female differences creating different life situations for them. The enculturation[1] process sustains and transmits these notions to next generation.

Historically, women suffered exclusion and discrimination due to above notions. Traditionalist views maintained that male domination is universal and natural as it was created by god. They glorified women's reproductive capacity and considered motherhood as women's chief goal in life. The sexual division of labour based on biological difference was believed to be functional and just (Lee & De Vore, 1968). Men's greater physical strength made them hunters, warriors and protectors of 'vulnerable' female. Nevertheless, the dubious claims of male superiority were disproved by feminist anthropologists, as food-gathering and small hunting by women and children formed the main food supply, and hunting by male was only auxiliary (Rosaldo, 1980). Both sexes contributed equally and women's position in society was respected during ancient hunting gathering period.

During the 19th century, after the development of science and technology, based on rationality, the religious arguments were weakened and 'scientific' arguments were developed to prove women's inferiority and male supremacy. Darwinian theories strengthened the belief system that species survival was more central than the individual self-fulfilment. Scientific defence of patriarchy was propagated, assigning women maternal role and excluding them from economic and educational opportunities that best suited for species survival. Menstruation, menopause and pregnancy were considered as diseases or abnormality, which made women inferior (Lerner, 1986). But the modern technology and its implements have transformed the functional significance of biological difference between male and female in bringing about equality among them in day-to-day activities. Mother milk substitute, fertility control techniques, change in the division of labour due to modern science and technology are some of the instances, which have challenged the gender-based sexual division of labour.

Marxists have identified the origin of private property, as the beginning of women's subordination, resulting in the gender-based sexual division of labour. Engels's *Origin of the Family, Private Property and the State* has been the important theoretical source in understanding the subordination of women for Marxists. The classless communist societies before the origin of private property as explained by the ethnographic study of Bachofen and Morgan formed the basis for Engels's generalization regarding the historic subordination of female sex. The development of animal husbandry led to development of commerce and private property ownership, which made men to institutionalize monogamous family for controlling women's sexuality to secure private property for himself and his heirs (Engels, 1972). Further, prostitution was institutionalized as an opposite to family, to create a 'pure' and 'respectable' image only for family women, also controlling her sexuality within the patriarchal monogamous family. Unfortunately, these developments were not explained and proved in detail by Engels and the ethnographic basis of these ideas has been disproved as sexual division of labour varied enormously in different cultures depending on their ecological environment (Lerner, 1986: 22). But still Engels made a significant contribution in comprehending the position of women in our society historically.

Structural anthropologist Lévi-Strauss' work on kinship structures, *The Elementary Structures of Kinship*, envisages kinship system as one based on the exchange of women between men, thus producing a theory of sex oppression. He regards the two relevant elements: the "gift" and the "incest taboo" as defining features of the concept of the exchange of women. According to him, the incest taboo, which is the root of all social organizations and formation of culture, is a way to ensure the exchange of women between groups, rather than within families. Prohibition of incest was the beginning of women's subordination, where they were exchanged for marriage like commodity trade. Lévi-Strauss identified incest as positive movement towards the creation of human culture. Furthermore, he considered that the sexual division of labour creates gender by dividing sexes into two mutually exclusive binary categories towards the system of marriage, thus making heterosexuality a norm (Levi-Strauss, 1969). Nevertheless, exchange of women is more of traffic in women for the benefit of men, which is considered as origin of human culture by Lévi-Strauss. Rubin (1975) contradicts this position and argues that exchange of women cannot be the basis for a definition of culture or system. It could be a part of the social relations of sex/gender system[2] (Rubin, 1975: 159). The kinship systems cannot be narrowed down to the exchange of women, as they are a complex system of relationships. Lévi-Strauss' work has given direction to understand the separation of sex and gender, which formed the basis for the passivity of women, historically.

The psychoanalysis theories help in understanding how the kinship structures are reproduced and transmitted to next generation. The feminine development, according to Freud, is not a biological reflex, as boys and girls are bisexual during pre-oedipal phase.[3] Lacan explains that the transformation of biological sexuality, towards a gender-based psyche, happens through the enculturation process within every kinship system. The Oedipus complex develops during the child's confrontation with the sexual rules of his/her kinship system. Women's psychological structure was constructed from phallocentric point of view as deviant, always struggling to compensate for the penis deficiency, making them inferior and male with penis as superior (Miller, 1973). The psychological structure of hierarchy is being created by the social relationships within the kinship system, rather than biological differentiation.

Thus, gender-based women's subordination is considered as one of the most important axis of power relations in social life. In all societies, gender relations play a role in the division of labour, distribution of work, income, wealth, education, public goods and services, and so on. In most societies, women are likely to work longer hours than men, have lower earnings, education, wealth and less access to credit, information and knowledge (Cagatay, 2000). Gender biases in social life are transmitted through a variety of institutions, other than family, like markets, state etc.

The type of gender inequality may differ across diverse strata within the society, but they are always more severe among the poor compared to rich. As a result, gender inequality overlaps with economic deprivation in producing worse forms of poverty for women. Gender inequality is part of the processes, which causes and deepens poverty in a society and must, therefore, be part of measures to eradicate poverty (Kabeer, 2003, Puri, 2017). Therefore, gender is not only used in the study of individuals' attributes, but also to understand the institutions' attitudes as they are also gendered. This inequality is reflected in many aspects of our social life like family, employment, education, and health where women are deprived, excluded and forced to be inferior to men. These aspects of social life, which reflect the gender-based subordination, can be witnessed in all hitherto existing social formations, including the contemporary capitalist political economy (neoliberalism), for their benefit and development.

Capitalism and Women's Subordination

The contemporary capitalist system and its functioning have been critically looked by Western socialist feminist theorists to understand women's survival experience and the significance of patriarchal subordination of women within it to sustain and expand the capitalist system. The material base for men's control over women is exhibited through two-fold restrictions over women's access to labour market and women's sexuality. In capitalist societies, the institutions of family and monogamous marriage act as an efficient control mechanism over women's labour and sexuality (Tusscher, 1986). The male domination is perpetuated by monogamous family by controlling women's access to resources and establishing women's sexuality as reproducers and men's pleasure satisfying object, further hampering access to paid labour. Sexual harassment at workplace, rape, and lack of provision for childcare, are some of the exclusionary patriarchal practices that exclude and marginalize women from labour force outside family. Such social relations are further strengthened through the patriarchal values of institutions such as religious system, education system, health system, state, and so on (Barrett, 1980).

The Marxist theory of value, which revealed the exploitative structures of capitalist mode of production, was critically viewed by the feminists as incomplete and gender biased theory. It consists of extended reproduction or accumulation and subsistence reproduction, where the valorisation process happens in extended reproduction as analyzed by Marx. But the reproduction of life and working capacity of workers happen in subsistence reproduction, which is the basic necessity for the value creation in extended reproduction. The subsistence reproduction, which includes biological reproduction and social reproduction of the family, is largely associated with women's work and includes pregnancy, childbirth, nursing and education of children, production and transformation of food for the household, clothing, housing, physical and psychological demands associated with sexuality (Werlhof, 1980). A more extended definition of social reproduction includes the social management that is maintaining kinship linkages, developing neighbourhood network and carrying out religious and social obligations in the community (Momsen, 1991). The subsistence reproduction process lays the foundation for the valorisation process to happen in extended reproduction (Bennholdt-Thomsen 1981). The Marxist theory of value has failed to emphasize the importance of subsistence reproduction, which makes it gender biased in its analysis of capitalist mode of production.

Women and Wage Employment

For women, even when they have full-time jobs, the main responsibilities in the household remain on their shoulders, so women's participation in the productive workforce is affected by their reproductive tasks[4]. For instance, at the end of the 20th century in Gambia, the average woman had 10 to 14 complete pregnancies, and as a consequence spent the most of her (re)productive years carrying a child in her womb or breastfeeding a baby (Momsen, 1991: 30). Similarly, in Zambia, the burden of both productive and reproductive task determined the high incidence of ill-health among rural women and the poor family nutrition (Africa Progress Report, 2012). The domestic division of labour can reduce women's occupational activities: as they are burdened with domestic duties, they have less time and forces to think about their own careers. However, this is not a prerogative of the Global South countries or of the historical populations, but the emergence of role incompatibility is also found in the contexts such as Italy, France, and Turkey.

In fact, the neoliberal withdrawal of state has made the life of women in Italy difficult forcing many to involve in involuntary part-time employment to manage family-care work. In 2010, Italian women accounted for 78.1 per cent of all part-timers and 80.5 per cent in service sector. The Italian women aged 20-74 do around 5 hours and 20 minutes of family work on average each day compared to 1 hour and 35 minutes for men. With such deep rooted patriarchal structures, the withdrawal of neoliberal state is going to have negative impact on women (Tania, 2011).

In France, statistics show the difficulty of changing gender roles. While there is a growing involvement of women in the labour market, the terms of this commitment differ from those of men (part-time work, more frequent withdrawals etc.). The degree and the different ways in which men and women participate in the labour market result in a lower income for women, who are more dependent than men on their spouses' incomes, and have a negative impact also on their respective social benefits. At the same time, the involvement of men in the family sphere is evolving very slowly, although this factor is decisive for promoting women's participation in the labour market. Thus, it is in this dynamic that gender inequalities are anchored (Vieille, 2018).

In Turkey, there have been considerable structural changes since 1960s, related to the incompatibility between women's roles as mother and worker. The available evidence on the relationship between fertility and employment among Turkish women suggest a two-way negative association: The characteristics of jobs that favour compatibility between worker and mother roles increase the risk of conception. Existing employment is temporarily increased by fertility, due either to pregnancy or having an infant. Fertility in all its dimensions decreases the risk of entry into employment. Therefore, contextual changes related to the incompatibility of the roles of mother and worker has transformed the fertility-employment relationship in Turkey from being insignificant to being strongly negative (Ozgoren, Ergocmen & Tansel, 2018). Therefore, the interrelated systems of patriarchy and capitalism create a cycle of subordination, as the gendered division of labour; the productive and reproductive labour emphasizes the division of labour among workers granting men occupational superiority.

Women are more likely to find themselves in vulnerable employment (including unpaid family work) and poorly paid positions compared to men. As a result, female workers lack enough social protection and suffer from low pay compared to men, and from difficult working conditions violating their fundamental rights (UN, 2012). Data show that the gap between women's and men's vulnerable employment is widest in North Africa (in 2011, 44% of women were in vulnerable jobs as compared to 26% of men) and in Western Asia, where the rates were respectively 41 per cent and 22 per cent. However, the highest share of vulnerable employment for women is in Sub-Saharan Africa, where it reached 85 per cent (UN, 2012: 12). Looking through the Millennium Development Goals Report (2012), it is possible to assert that women's share in paid jobs outside of the agricultural sector increased slowly on a global basis, from 35 per cent in 1990 to 40 per cent in 2010, but there are differences among regions. Women and men are approaching parity in the developed regions and in the Caucasus and Central Asia. On the contrary, in Western Asia, Northern Africa and Southern Asia, only 20 per cent or less of non-agricultural manpower is female in 2010. The quality work should provide decent pay and offer development and progression according to International Labour Organisation (ILO). However, most of the times the nature of women's work does not satisfy the criteria for quality work and involves low paid "pink-collar" jobs. The austerity measures of neoliberalism had a drastic impact on childcare provisions in Britain. The House of Commons library and UK Women's Budget Group estimated that 78.5 per cent cuts in welfare disproportionately affected women in Britain. When state withdraws from childcare responsibility, the women end up in part-time irregular works to manage family and earn (Louise, 2018).

The problem is that even where women represent a large share of wage workers they are discriminated as compared with men. Although they may enter the labour market with the same educational and skill levels as men, they used to face more barriers in reaching top-level positions. As a result, women occupy only 25 per cent of senior management position, while women's jobs tend to be at the lower end of the labour market (i.e. less remunerative, poor working conditions), and in a narrower range of occupations and activities (the so called "women's employment ghettos", i.e., services, garment making, food processing) (Kramer, 2011). In fact, the rise of factory-based production for worldwide market has allocated sex-stereotyped work for women reinforcing the gender based sexual division of labour (Frobel, Heinrichs & Kreye, 1980). Women were also preferred in many types of works in factory system due to their nimble fingers, which are suited for a particular type of work, their docile nature willing to accept tough work disciplines, which is more suited for tedious, repetitious, and monotonous work (Elson & Pearson, 1981). The dialectical relation between factory work and women's subordination produces three different tendencies. The tendency to intensify, decompose and recompose the existing forms of gender subordination. They intensify by utilizing and encouraging the exisitng patriarchal values, so the family motivate the daughters or wives to participate in the factory-based production process (Lim, 1978). They decompose by expanding the choice of women in choosing their marital partner and also avoiding early marriage (Blake, 1979). It will not completely undermine the patriarchal institution of arranged marriages in the Global South, as it only makes women more competitive in the marriage market, commodifying them. They recompose the gender subordination by using the interaction of women employees with men at work place, to put more restrictions over them and their sexuality. The factory girls are considered to violate the norms of gendered female and as less respectable within the patriarchal societal setup (Lim, 1978). In traditional societies, a girl that decides to accept a job, considered not coherent with her family role, risks to be seen as a "loose woman". Moreover, once men meet women in their workplace, they may fall back on gender-based social expectations, and think that their female colleagues are sexually available. Otherwise, men in higher positions may insist to have sexual favours in return for job security, contributing in this way to generate turnover among the women workers. As a result, families that need the female members' salary but at the same time want to protect their reputation can encourage women to find an employment in certain sectors, facilitating the "ghettoization of women" (Kramer, 2011).

Furthermore, the assumption that breadwinners are male, that women are homemaker and dependent on men, even if it is more theoretical than practical, creates problems associated with using occupation to classify women. For instance, in Kamwokya (Uganda), women have become "occupation pluralists" as they have to participate in different smaller business or changing from one activity to another depending on demand in order to contribute to household expenditures (food and basic necessities, school fees for their children). Nevertheless, men still wield power, so women do not feel that their contribution makes them more powerful in their households (Kyomuhendo, 1999).

Although urbanization can ease women entering the formal labour market, it is also true that for poor, uneducated female migrants to the cities, prostitution probably offers one of the best-paid employments, and often it is the only job available to send money to the families in the rural areas (Buccianti & Fusari, 2008). Thus, the gender based discrimination and exclusion of women result in further sexual exploitation of women.

In developing countries, the capitalist production reduces and decentralizes the women's role in production, leading to marginalization. According to Momsen (1991), this marginalization can cover four dimensions in urban female employment: firstly, because of physical weakness, moral danger, or lack of facilities, women are barred from entering certain types of employment; secondly, as women are mostly employed in the "periphery of the labour market", the informal sector, the lowest-paid and most insecure jobs become their reign. Thirdly, if an employment becomes feminized because of the high concentration of female manpower, it will be soon considered of low status. Finally, there is a marginalization due to economic inequality accompanying occupational differentiation in terms of wages, working conditions, benefits and job security, between men and women. According to Thistle (2006), even when women become chief economic agent of family and work longer and harder, female labour in the public sphere is equated with the informal unwaged work she performs in the private sphere. The National Association of Schoolmasters Union of Women Teachers (NASUWT) report (2008) "Women Teachers' Careers" showed that, in Britain, only 8.5 per cent of female teachers attain leadership scale compared to 20 per cent of male teachers after five to nine years of working in primary education. It is 70 per cent of men and 40 per cent of women after 20 years. This pattern is replicated in secondary sector also. As a result, women are under-represented in senior and headship roles. There are 75 per cent of female head teachers in primary and only 40 per cent in the secondary sector. A study by Ortiz & Cummins (2013) examined 128 developing countries based on International Monetary Fund fiscal projections and country reports to understand the public spending decisions of governments. The study revealed that after the financial crisis in 2008, the majority of the countries started reducing their expenditures through wage bill cuts or caps, reducing subsidies, cutting down social safety nets and reforming old-age pensions. Wage bill cuts can affect health, nutrition, educational, other needed services, subsidy cuts will make many essential goods unaffordable, and pension cuts will make the old age people more vulnerable. Most of them will have adverse impact on children and women.

Women and Export Processing Zones (EPZ)

The rise of special "economic zones" called Export Processing Zones (EPZ) has given more scope for use of cheap female labour within it, as they are free from the labour laws of the country in which they are based. Verbal abuse, unpaid overtime, sexual harassment, forced sex, and physical violence are common phenomenon in EPZs. In Kenya, which employs more than 40,000 workers in EPZs, 95 per cent of women are facing workplace harassment and in Lesotho, EPZ women are normally subjected to complete strip searches in the name of security. 70 per cent of men consider sexual harassment of women workers in EPZs as "normal and natural" (Karega, 2002). The Maquiladora factories in EPZ, established through the North American Free Trade Agreement (NAFTA) in 1992, which is on the US-Mexico border has been in news for violence against women. More than 400 female workers have "disappeared" from its inception (True, 2012). In spite of some financial independence gained by women due to wage labour, these are considered challenging the "traditional" male authority. Salzinger's work on Maquiladora labour shows that feminization is one of the best strategies of neoliberal capital as "the trope of productive femininity"—that is, the "icon of the 'docile and dexterous' woman worker" as both preferred and expected embodiment of export-processing labour" (Bhattacharya, 2013).

The capitalist phase of neoliberal political economy tries to create a protected domain of law, liberty and private property rights for individuals. It is against the concept of social justice under the welfare state model, as it is against the smooth working of spontaneous order in liberal society (Davidson, 2013). Lack of positive discrimination under the social justice has created three important hurdles for women to achieve liberty under neoliberal structures. The first is to create governmental discrimination in evolving protective laws for protecting women against any form of discrimination. The second is to protect them from institutional discrimination by employers, and the third one is interpersonal discriminatory behaviour, which involves the socialization of women in workplace and discrimination at personal level (Waylen, 1986).

The neoliberal insistence on the supremacy of markets has weakened the subsistence economy in Global South, which resulted in more gender based discriminatory practices in everyday life situations. According to the conditionalities of Structural Adjustment Programmes (SAPs), many governments in the Global South have privatized water, which is the essential ingredient to cooking, cleaning and care work. The state's withdrawal imposes more pressure on women to get these resources for the family's sustenance. For example, in rural Senegal, women walk up and down 10 kilometres (6.2 miles) to fetch water for the family. Moreover, many developing and under-developed countries have devalued their currencies according to fulfil the conditionalities for the loan from IMF. This has resulted in high prices for the imported goods, and reduced the consumption, as food, fuel, and medicines form the bulk of imported goods for Global South (Bhattacharya, 2013).

According to ILO, the gender pay gap is prevalent globally and in most regions and many occupations, women are paid between 70 and 90 per cent of men's wages, with many Asian and Latin American countries falling below this range. Women represent 40.4 per cent of the worldwide workforce in which 46.3 per cent are in the services sector, 35.4 per cent are in the agricultural sector and only 18.3 per cent in the industrial sector (ILO, 2009). Women are found to work in majority in the sectors, reflecting the gender based traits such as secretaries, teachers and nurses. Moreover, even within these sectors, they are paid less as compared to their male colleagues (IWPR, 2009). This gender-based discrimination depends on the notion of associating women's nature of work to unpaid care based work in family and community (UNIFEM, 2005). The United Nations Development Programme (2006) has identified *direct gender discrimination* in labour markets and *occupational segregation* as important reasons for gender pay gap. Direct discrimination takes place when people with same level of educational attainment and work experience are treated differently due to their gender. The occupational segregation, rather prevalent in all fields, is more subtle and complex to address with specific actions.

The neoclassical economic theory assumes that in competitive conditions, workers are paid according to their productivity, so as in general women have lower education levels, training and on-the-job experience, which justifies their inferior position. Therefore, the neoliberal approach uses the idea of differences in human capital to explain gender differences in employment: as women are underprivileged because of their reproduction responsibilities, physical strength, education, turnover, and so on, they can be subordinated in the labour market (Kramer, 2011). This approach has been criticized, because it ignores the socio-cultural aspects that can affect the socio-economic position of women before entering the labour market (Whitehead, 1979). According to a study by Costa & Silva (2008), using a simulated model to understand the benefits of an increase in gender equality in the workforce, in five Latin American countries, they reached the conclusion that "reducing gender inequalities implies benefits not only for women but also for men, children and the elderly, and for the poor as well as the rich."

Conclusion

The neoliberal political economy not only sustains the already existing patriarchal divisions within different societies, but also aggravates the gender division to make the conditions worse for women. The implementation of SAPs in Africa and Asia has deprived/reduced the state funded benefits to a larger extent. This in result has affected the women to a larger extent, strengthening the case for arguments for feminization of poverty in neoliberal times. The arguments and evidences have pointed out how the socio-cultural structure, which discriminates women, is intensified under capitalism and specifically during neoliberal phase. In order to eliminate the gender biasness within the society and to create equality, we need a concrete effort to restructure our political economy accordingly, along with the fight against patriarchy. By this approach, decent work, that is a key element to achieving a fair globalization and poverty reduction, can be put in place for both men and women as it requires job creation, rights at work, social protection and social dialogue, with gender equality as a crosscutting objective.

NOTES

1. Anthropologically, it is the process by which people learn and acquire values and behaviours appropriate to live in their culture. Enculturation is related to socialization that needs different formal and informal institutions such as parents, peers, school, and so on.
2. A system which consists of a set of arrangements by which a society transforms biological sexuality into products of human activity, to satisfy the transformed sexual needs.
3. According to Freudian theory, the Oedipus complex is a complex of emotions aroused in a young child by an unconscious sexual desire for the parent of the opposite sex.
4. Only Cuba on ideological basis stated in its Family Code that husbands should undertake a fair share of household chores in order to reduce women's double burden of productive and reproductive work, but the legislation cannot be enough to remove traditional gender role division.

REFERENCES

Africa Progress Panel (2012). *Jobs, Justice, and Equality. Seizing Opportunities in Times of Global Change.* Geneva: Africa Progress Panel.

Barrett, M. (1980). *Women's Oppression Today: Problems in Marxist Feminist Analysis.* London: Verso.

Bem, S.L. (1993). *The Lenses of Gender: Transforming the Debate on Sexual Inequality.* London: Yale University Press.

Bennholdt-Thomsen, V. (1981). Subsistence Production and Extended Reproduction. In K. Young, C. Wolkowitz, & R. McCullagh, *Of Marriage and the Market: Women's subordination internationally and its lessons* (pp. 41-54). London: Routledge & Kegan Paul.

Bhattacharya, T. (2013, December 28th). *Explaining Gender Violence in the Neoliberal Era.* Retrieved January 5th, 2014, from International Viewpoint: http://www.internationalviewpoint.org

Blake, M. (1979). *Asian Women in Formal and Non-Formal Sectors—Review and Proposals for Research-Education-Mobilisation.* United Nations Asian and Pacific Centre for Women and Development.

Buccianti, C., & Fusari, V. (2008). *Lineamenti di Etnodemografia.* Padova: Cedam.

Cagatay, N. (2000). *Budgets as if people mattered: Democratizing Macroeconomic Policies.* New York: UNDP.

Costa, J., & Silva, E. (2008). *The Burden of Inequality for Society.* Retrieved December 18th, 2013, from United Nations Development Programme: www.ipc-undp.org/pub/IPCPovertyInFocus13.pdf.

Davidson, N. (2013). The Neoliberal Era in Britain: Historical Developments and Current Perspectives. *International Socialism*, 139.

Elson, D., & Pearson, R. (1981). The Subordination of Women and the Internationalisation of Factory Production. In K. Young, C. Wolkowitz, & R. McCullagh, *Of Marriage and the Market: Women's subordination internationally and its lessons* (pp. 18-40). London: Routledge & Kegan Paul.

Engels, F. (1972). *The Origin of the Family, Private Property and the State.* New York: E. Leacock, Ed..

Frobel, F., Heinrichs, J., & Kreye, O. (1980). *The New International Division of Labour.* Cambridge: Cambridge University Press.

ILO. (2009). *Global Employment Trends for Women.* Retrieved December 25th, 2013, from International Labour Organisation: http://www.ilo.org/wcmsp5/groups/public/—dgreports/—dcomm/documents/publication/wcms_103456.pdf

Isabel Ortiz & Matthew Cummins (2013). Austerity Measures in Developing Countries: Public Expenditure Trends and the Risks to Children and Women, *Feminist Economics*, 19:3, 55-81, DOI: 10.1080/13545701.2013.791027

IWPR. (2009). *The Gender Wage Gap by Occupation.* Retrieved December 26th,

2013, from Institute for Women's Policy Research: http://www.iwpr.org/pdf/c350a.pdf

Kabeer, N. (2003). Gender Equality, Poverty Eradication and the Millennium Development Goals: Promoting Women's Capabilities and Participation. *Gender & Development*, Discussion Paper Series 13, Economic and Social Commission for Asia and Africa.

Karega, G.R. (2002). *Violence Against Women in the Workplace in Kenya: Assessment of Workplace Sexual Harassment in the Commercial, Agriculture and Textile Manufacturing Sectors in Kenya.* International Labour Rights Fund.

Kramer, L. (2011). *The Sociology of Gender.* Oxford: Oxford University Press.

Kyomuhendo, G. (1999). Decision-Making in Poor Households: The Case of Kampala, Uganda. In S. Jones, & N. Nelson, *Urban Poverty in Africa. From Understanding to Alleviation* (pp. 113-125). London: Intermediate Technology Publications.

Lee, R., & De Vore, I. (1968). *Man, The Hunter.* Pocatello: Idaho State University Press.

Lerner, G. (1986). *The Creation of Patriarchy.* New York: OUP.

Levi-Strauss, C. (1969). *The Elementary Structures of Kinship.* Boston: Beacon Press.

Lim, L. (1978). *Women Workers in Multinational Corporations in Developing Countries—The Case of the Electronics Industry in Malaysia and Singapore.* Michigan: University of Michigan.

Louise Dalingwater, "*Neo-liberalism and Gender Inequality in the Workplace in Britain*", *Revue Française de Civilisation Britannique* [Online], XXIII-1 | 2018, Online since 20 March 2018, connection on 04 December, 2018. URL : http://journals.openedition.org/rfcb/1802 ; DOI : 10.4000/rfcb.1802

Miller, J.B. (1973). *Psychoanalysis and Women.* Harmondsworth: Penguin.

Momsen, J. (1991). *Women and Development in the Third World.* New York: Routledge.

NASUWT. (2008). *Women Teachers' Careers.* Retrieved December 15th, 2013, from National Association of Schoolmasters Union of Women Teachers: http://www.nasuwt.org.uk

Özgören, A.A., Ergöçmen, B., Tansel, A. (2018), Birth and Employment Transitions of Women inTurkey: The Emergence of Role Incompatibility. *Demographic Research*, 39(46): 1241-1290.

Puri, L. (2017). Women: Major Drivers and Beneficiaries of Poverty Eradication, Reliefweb, http://www.ipsnews.net/2017/10/women-major-drivers-beneficiaries-poverty-eradication/ (last accessed on 20 December, 2018)

Rawat, P.S. (2014). Patriarchal Beliefs, Women's Empowerment, and General Well-Being. *Vikalpa*, 39(2): 43-55.

Ridgeway, C., & Smith-Lovin, L. (1999). The Gender System and Interaction. *Annual Review of Sociology*, 25: 191-216.

Rosaldo, M.Z. (1980). The Use and Abuse of Anthropology: Reflections on Feminism and Cross-Cultural Understanding. *SIGNS*, 5(3): 412-13.

Rubin, G. (1975). The Traffic in Women: Notes on the Political Economy of Sex. In R. Reiter, *Towards an Anthropology of Women* (pp. 157-209). New York: Monthly Review Press.

Semali, L.M., Shakespeare, E.S. (2014). Rethinking Mindscapes and Symbols of Patriarchy in the Workforce to Explain Gendered Privileges and Rewards. *International Education Studies*, 7(2): 37-53.

Tania Toffanin (2011) The Role of Neoliberal Capitalism in Reproducing Gender Inequality in Italy, *Journal of Contemporary European Studies*, 19:3, 379-392, DOI:10.1080/14782804.2011.610607

Thistle, S. (2006). *From Marriage to the Market. The Transformation of Women's Live and Work.* Berkeley: University of California Press.

True, J. (2012). *The Political Economy of Violence Against Women.* New York: Oxford University Press.

Tusscher, T.T. (1986). Patriarchy, Capitalism and the New Right. In J. Evans, J. Hills, K. Hunt, E. Meehan, T.T. Tusscher, U. Vogel, *et al.*, *Feminism and Political Theory* (pp. 66-84). London: Sage Publications.

UNDP (2006). *The Gender Pay Gap over Women's Working Lifetime*. Retrieved December 20th, 2013, from United Nations Development Programme: http://www.ipc-undp.org/pub/IPCOnePager20.pdf

UNIFEM (2005). *Women, Work & Poverty*. Retrieved December 20th, 2013, from United Nations Development Fund for Women: http://www.un-ngls.org/orf/women-2005.pdf

United Nations (2012). *The Millennium Development Goals.* New York: United Nations.

Vieille, P. (2018), La Protection Sociale comme «Régime de Genre», Fellows le regard de chercheursinternationaux sur l'actualité. http://fellows.rfiea.fr/dossier/devenir-parents-rester-inegaux/article/la-protection-sociale-comme-regime-de-genre (last accessed on 20 December, 2018).

Walby, S. (2002). *Towards a Theory of Patriarchy*. London: Blackwell Publishers.

Waylen, G. (1986). Women and Neo-Liberalism. In J. Evans, J. Hills, K. Hunt, E. Meehan, T.T. Tusscher, U. Vogel, *et al.*, *Feminism and Political Theory* (pp. 85-102). London: Sage Publications.

Werlhof, V.C. (1980). Notes on the Relation between Sexuality and Economy. *FBC Review* IV(1): 32-42.

Wharton, A. (2005). *The Sociology of Gender: An Introduction to Theory and Research.* USA: Blackwell.

Whitehead, A. (1979). Some Preliminary Notes on the Subordination of Women. *IDS Bulletin*, 10(3): 10-13. and Phillips, A., & Taylor, B. (1980). Sex and Skill. Notes Towards a Feminist Economics. *Feminist Review*, 6: 79-88.

19

Decentralisation and Democracy

The Gandhian Way

M.R. Biju and *M.R.B. Anantha Padmanabha*

A democratic polity involves decentralisation or de-concentration of power in a way that the affairs of the local people are managed by means of their positive participation. It implies the extension of democracy at the grassroots level in view of the fact that the people's participation signifies the constitution of a democratic government not merely at the top but at the foundation level of the political system.

Gandhiji firmly believed that the present state was unwanted because it was a highly centralised one in its organisation and structure. He condemned the state because it was based on force and as such believed that everything could be achieved only by forceful methods. Gandhiji felt that in the present set-up state authority had been centralised and the power passed on to a few individuals and there was every danger that such power might be misused. Mahatma made first reference to Democratic Decentralisation in February 1916, while appreciating the working of the ancient Panchayat System existed in India. He was of the opinion that, "India, basically a republican country as it is because it has sure that the problem of village sanitation would have been solved long ago and India would have been enjoying self-government suited to its requirements, had village panchayats been acting as a living force."

In his presidential address at Belgium Congress, Gandhi referred to the panchayat system as the right medium for securing speedy and cheap justice as well as for avoiding reliance on government for the settlement of mutual dispute. During his term of office, as the President of the Indian National Congress, he extensively toured the whole country. That reinforced his conviction that India would be benefited, a great deal if the villages were governed by the Village panchayats. However he felt that, the reorganisation of the village administration could not be taken in isolation. He was sure that Indian village life had great vitality and character. It was because of this that it has persisted all these long ears and had weathered many a storm. Gandhi's view of democratic decentralization developed over the years. He laid emphasis on Panchayati Raj till the last movement of his life. Simple living and high thinking was the ideal the very foundation and essential of Gandhian approach to decentralisation.

Concept of Ideal Society

Gandhi condemned the present state being based on violence and wanted to have an ideal society in which state will be based on non-violence in which there will be maximum independence for the individuals. To him, it will be a state based on village autonomy and each village enjoying maximum possible autonomy. The villages will be combined together to form a sort of loose federation based on moral strength. There will be no need and necessity for the police or military forces. Instead or centralisation there wili be decentralization and the way of living will be very simple. The people shall practise self-discipline and control and everybody will be most willing to perform his duties by persuasion. The police men and all executive officers will act as the servants of the people, and national arms will rarely be used. According to him it will be an ideal society or *Ram Rajya* in which he says: "Justice is prompt, perfect, cheap, there is freedom of worship and speech and of the Press, all this is because of the reign of self-imposed law of moral restraint such a state must be based on truth and non-violence and must consist of prosperous, lofty and self contained and village communities."

Democratic System

Gandhiji favoured democratic system in his ideal society. He believed that it was the only compromise formula in which individual freedom was attained and at the same time the authority of the state was not altogether dispensed with. For him in a democracy if properly followed, there can be no difficulty in adjusting individual freedom with state authority. He, however, had a different opinion about democracy. To him:

> "The nearest approach to the purest anarchy would be democracy based on non-violence in such a state everyone is his own ruler. He rules himself in such a manner that he is never a hindrance to his neighbour. In the ideal state, therefore there is no political power because there is no state. He wanted to have a stateless society where the individual will be an end and his self-realisation is the sole object. He believed that in a stateless society there will be proper adjustment between law, freedom and social restraint on the basis of *dharma*."

Gandhi opposed all types of concentration of power, since to him, centralisation is a menace and danger to democracy. Concentration of power, in his view distorts all democratic values. So he argues, possession of power makes men blind and deaf, they cannot see things which are under their very nose, and cannot hear things which invade their ears. In other words centralization as a system consistent with non-violent structure of society.

Moreover he was convinced that moral progress was possible only in a decentralised setup. In a nutshell, the affairs that without decentralisation it is impossible to ensure individual liberty and mental and moral growth of man. Similarly, it is equally essential for the realisation of the ideal democracy, for the rule of the people, which it stands for, is not possible without adequate opportunities to individuals to participate in the management of their own affairs.

Gandhi rather pleads for decentralisation of both economic and political power. For the success of political decentralisation, in his view, depends upon economic decentralisation. This follows from his conviction that a highly centralised political setup is likely to bring dictatorship of one kind or another by self-interested and power-hungry minority imposing itself on deluded and subservient majority.

While elaborating his ideas on decentralisation, Gandhi keeps in mind two different structures—First, the power state structure of the West. Basically he rejects it on the ground that it leads to centralisation of power, exploitation of the weak, denial of individual freedom and moral degradation. It is democratic in its external framework but dictatorial in actual practice. Second is the panchayati raj model—building up from below. In other words, it can be called democratic decentralisation. Basically, Gandhi is drawn towards this model. One important feature of this model is the economic self-sufficiency at the grassroot level. To him this is the only way to eliminate exploitation of the weaker sections in society and to bring happiness to their millions.

Further his de-centralisation implies the fundamental principle of self-sufficiency. But, it is not absolute sufficiency. It is mostly confined to the basic needs such as food, clothing and shelter. He reiterated that if a new democratic equalitarian social, political order free from exploitation, had to be established on firm foundations de-centralisation in economics must go side by side with de-centralisation in politics. Even success of political de-centralisation depends upon economic de-centralisation In other words without economic de-centralisation, political de-centralisation would be meaningless. The manifesto of the Congress Parliamentary Board, 29 July, 1934 which was drafted by Gandhi declared: In order to end the exploitation of the masses political freedom must include real freedom of the starving millions. Similarly his advocacy of *charka* and village industries only demonstrate his living faith in decentralisation of economic power.

Gandhi is not against modern science and technology. His attitude is entirely rational and scientific. His main thrust is that science and technology, instead of becoming masters should function as the servants of the people. Basically he has no objection to machines as such. But he argues that, it is wrong to carry the process of mechanisation of industry so far as to kill the cottage industries and concentrate them within a narrow field. Accordingly, he wants villages to be production centres and towns to be clearing houses for such products instead of being the reverse as today.

Therefore, Gandhi's concept of democratic decentralisation bears the stamp of his passionate belief in non-violence, truth and individual freedom. He calls it PR village Swaraj. He wants to see each village a little republic self-sufficient in it vital wants organically linked with the higher bodies and enjoying the maximum freedom of deciding the affairs of the locality. According to Gandhi, real India lives in its villages. So villages held an important place in Gandhi's scheme of life and social organisation. He was a strong and ardent supporter of rural atmosphere, rural. We and rural development for him Indian villages were the backbone of India or real India. He believed if the villages perished India will perish too. It will be no more India. Her own mission in the world will get lost.

Till 1936, Gandhi had not made up his mind or he was not clear about the character of the structure of Indian polity. At the Faizpur Congress Session in 1936, he expressed that India must have a polity suited to her genius. But he could not give its blueprint. This shows that he was clear about the spirit but not of the form of Indian polity. He only indicated that the Western mechanism of democracy was not suitable for

India. This meant that India must seek its own institutional framework to realize the values of democracy. He made some loud thinking in this connection. The institution of the village panchayat which had provided a democratic structure at the grassroot level for centuries in India, showed him direction. The institution of panchayat, for him, was the fundamental unit of democratic decentralisation.

Further in 1942, during the course of an interview with Louis Fisher he remarked that voluntary co-operation and co-operation induced by Nazi methods was the essence of the panchayat system. Here again he pleaded for the distribution of power among the villagers. He said, you see, the centre of power now is in New Delhi, or in Calcutta and Bombay, in the big cities. I would have it distributed among the seven hundred thousand villages of India. That will mean that there is not power. In other words, I want the seven hundred thousand dollars now invested in the Imperial Bank of England, withdrawn and distributed among the seven hundred thousand villages. Then each village will have its dollar which cannot be lost. Emphasizing this point, he said, the seven hundred thousand dollars invested in the Imperial Bank of India, could be swept away by a bomb from a Japanese plane. Whereas if they were distributed among the seven hundred thousand shareholders, nobody could deprive them of their assets. This will then be voluntary co-operation between these seven hundred thousand units, voluntary co-operation will produce real freedom and a new order vastly superior to the new order in Soviet Russia.

The above mentioned interview, reveals Gandhi's deep faith in decentralised democracy based on village panchayats drawing their power from the initiative and willing co-operation of the people. He fully subscribed to the principle that power resides in the people and it must belong to the people. It seeks expression through democratic decentralisation or panchayati raj. Again in 1946, Gandhi while rejecting Western political institutions of parliamentary democracy, laid stress on the concept of decentralised democracy consisting of concentric village republics. He elaborated his plan for independent India at the time of transfer of power. He asserted that independence must begin at the bottom. Thus every village would be a republic or panchayat having full powers. It follows, that every village had to be self-sustained and capable of managing its affairs even to the extent of defending itself against the whole world. Thus ultimately, it is the individual who is the unit. But, Gandhi,s points out that this does not exclude dependence on and willing help from neighbours or from the world. Under the Gandhian constitution, the scheme of government was briefly as follows:

1. First the primary political unit was to be the village panchayat whose members would be elected by the adults of the village. The panchayat would control chowkidars, patwans, police and schools. It would also assess and collect land revenue, supervise co-operative farming, irrigation and interest rates as well as *Khadi* and other village industries.
2. Secondly, above the village panchayat came a hierarchy of indirectly elected bodies. First came taluks and district panchayats, each comprised sarpanchs of the next lower panchayats and having only advisory powers over them. Members from the district and municipal panchayats would make up the provincial panchayats, which would elect President to serve as head of the provincial government. Presidents of a provincial panchayat would comprise the all India Panchayat whose President would be the head of state and of the government, which would be ministerial in character. Among the responsibilities of provincial panchayats would be transport, irrigation, natural resources and co-operative bank.

The national panchayat would be responsible for such things as defence, currency, customs, the running of key industries of national importance and the co-ordination of provincial economic development plans. For Gandhiji centralisation as a system is inconsistent with non-violent structure of society. Centralisation of power, political or economic is the source of all kinds of exploitation resulting in curtailment of individual liberty, unemployment and poverty. Decentralisation counters all kinds of exploitation, restores human freedom and dignity and promotes human values like fellow feeling and co-operation. Thus the essence of non-violence is decentralisation. To quote Gandhiji, The end to be sought is human happiness combined with full mental and moral growth. I use the adjective moral as anonymous with spiritual. The end can be achieved under decentralisation. Centralisation as a system is inconsistent with non-violent structure of society" (*Harijan*, 18 January, 1942).

Gandhiji gave importance to regeneration of village which is possible only with the help of a decentralised economic and political setup. Rural India can prosper only through the revival of gram panchayats and creation of self-sufficient and self-governing village republics. In the West villages were exploited to serve the interest of the urban communities. Gandhiji did not want the same experiment to perpetuate in India. In the case of India the twin objectives of growth with social justice have to be achieved simultaneously. It has been said that the strategy of development has to be both mobilisational in the sense of reaching out to choose regions or sections of her people who have been bypassed in the process of development and has also to aim at efficiency of resource use in areas and sectors which have developed (Y.K. Alagh, 1993).

When Gandhiji talked of self-sufficient village units, what he had in mind was that a village community should not depend on the higher government for those needs which it could satisfy with local resources and local efforts. He visualised decentralised planning with local participation. This would put pressure on local representatives to respond to local needs. For him, the word *swaraj* implied self-rule and self-restraint and not freedom from all restraints. Gandhian view of decentralisation implies "Voluntarily giving responsibility to the people to make decisions of their own affairs, subject to certain broad guidelines, which would not conflict with the overall framework of the society" (C. Thimmaiah, 1979).

To Gandhiji the economy should have base at the village level. Gandhiji envisaged a self-sufficient village which is very strong. Economic and political power in such a village is shared equally. The basic principles of village *swaraj* are supremacy of man, physical labour, equality, trusteeship, decentralisation, *swadeshi*, self-sufficiency, co-operation, *satyagraha* and equality of religions. Gandhiji chose the village to be the basic operational unit in India to be developed along the lines of decentralisation and self-sufficiency. Gandhiji wrote in *Harijan* on 28 July, 1946 as, "Independence must begin at the bottom, thus every village will be a republic or panchayat having full powers." "Every village of India will almost be a self-supporting and self-contained unit exchanging only such necessary commodities with other villages where they are not locally producible."

The village system should also provide sufficient leisure to the villagers so that they can take up creative work. He was painfully hurt by the criminal neglect of the peasant and artisans of rural India. A policy of decentralisation and modernisation of rural industries would provide immediate solution to the grave problems of unemployment, under-employment, poverty, inequalities, and exploitation, revival and encouragement of village industries would create opportunities for self-employment. This would make man independent and free so that his creativity and expression are stimulated.

Gandhian economic philosophy has nationalistic dimensions. He was in favour of promoting the spirit of *Swadeshi*. Each village is capable to produce all the essential commodities it requires. People should try to substitute village products for those produced in the city. Gandhiji aptly observed in *Harijan* on 30 November, 1934 as: "We begin with ourselves and thus use say handmade paper instead of mill made use village reed, where possible instead of the fountain pen or the pen holders, ink made in the village instead of the big factories and so on...."

Thus, Gandhian Economics was need-oriented and not want-oriented. According to him, distribution can be equalised only when production is localised. As pointed out by him in *Harijan* on 2 November, 1934: "When production and consumption both become localised the the temptation to speed up production, indefinitely and at any price, disappears". All the endless difficulties and problems that our present day economic system presents, too would then comes to an end... there would be no unnatural accumulation or hoards in the pockets of the few, and want in the midst of plenty in regard to the rest, as is happening today."

In his ideal society Gandhiji said everyone will keep only what was required by him for his day-to-day life. No one will keep unnecessarily accumulated wealth or surplus goods. He felt that the rich should have only what was their minimum basic necessity and the rest of the wealth they should distribute among the poor and deserving. He, however, pleaded that it was not at all justified 10 use force for getting surplus wealthy from the rich but the effective method was that of persuasion. The consciousness and sense of justice of the right should be arrested and they should themselves feel that they had no justification in keeping surplus wealth with them. In other words, the rich should act as trustees of the surplus wealth which they had with them.

As far as his ideas about Trusteeship was concerned, Gandhiji believed that everyone who owns a capital should feel that he is, I trustee of the capital, which belongs to the society as a whole the people should realise that they should possess only that much of capital and property which is needed by them. No one should use capital disregard of collective social interests. For him difference between the minimum and maximum wages should be reasonable. Gandhi, therefore, said that the character of production will be determined by the social necessity. He said that everyone should have balanced. diet, a good house to live, facility for education and inadequate medical relief. Everyone should believe that everything belonged to God. There was no idea in appropriating money from capitalists to the workers, if the former behaved properly and in the collective social interest. He was opposed to class antagonism but instead promoted class collaboration and co-ordination.

Two-fold Idea of Gandhiji

Gandhiji was the most vocal votary of making the village panchayats the basic unit self-government and social organisation. His idea behind making the village panchayat the kingpin of administration was two-fold. One was to convert the Congress, after independence into a social service organisation which would primarily work towards strengthening the panchayats at the village level and thus usher in the progress. The other was to generate acceptance for his idea that any organised government which would emerge to rule India after independence should have the panchayats as its basic unit of government.

Gandhi submitted two plans, one in January 1946 and the other in 1948 to the committee trusted with revising the constitution of the Congress. The second plan presented on the day of his assassination, is now called his testament. This plan called for disbanding the Congress and making it as a social service organisation with a nationwide network of the panchayats. Gandhi's idea was so simple and uncomplicated. To him, each village panchayat would form a unit: two such panchayats would constitute a working party with and elected leader who would co-ordinate their efforts and who would also be available for national service such second grade leaders could affect a chief to regulate and command all the groups.

The Congress Constitution Committee which at that point of time was constituted with Sitaramayya, Tandon, Narendra Dev, Diwakar, S.K. Patil, S.H. Ghose and Jugal Kishore as members did not accept Gandhiji's suggestion and found no reason for the Congress to give up its political identity and become social service organisation. The Committee come to a however, compromise by establishing "Primary Congress panchayats in a village or a group of villages as the basic organisational unit of the party." Later the AICC comeout with a Bulletin No. 5 of November, 1947 which states that:

> "If India's destiny is to be fulfilled and it is to take its proper place in the comity of nations, then its unity is essential and there is no other organisation more fit for this difficult task than the Congress. India requires, for its gradual and orderly political, social and economic all-round progress, one big political party large enough to guarantee a stable government and strong enough organisationally to maintain its hold and influence over the people. Such a party, of course, must have a programme of radical

change aiming at social justice and eradication of exploitation in all its forms."

Thus, Gandhiji's idea of converting the Congress into a social service organisation having its moorings in the panchayats died in its infancy.

Gandhian Constitution for Free India

As regards his second idea, one of his followers, Narayan Agarwal drafted a "Gandhian Constitution for Free India." As observed by eminent jurist Granville Austin, Gandhiji found in it nothing that jarred him or was inconsistent with what he would like to stand for. It can, therefore, be safely assumed that this constitution truly reflected Gandhiji's views on the form of government he wanted India to adopt after independence.

Agarwal espoused Gandhiji's cause by making the village panchayat the primary political unit, whose members would be elected by the adults of the village. Above the village panchayat came a hierarchy of indirectly elected bodies. First the taluk, municipal and district panchayats each comprising the sarpanchs, of the next lower panchayats and having only advisory powers over them. Members from district and municipal panchayats would make up the provincial panchayat which would elect a President to serve as the head of the provincial government. The Presidents of the provincial panchayats would comprise the All India panchayat whose President would be the head of the state and of the government which would be ministerial in character. Among the responsibilities of the provincial Panchayats would be transport, irrigation, natural resources and a co-operative bank. The National Panchayat would be responsible for such things as defence, currency, customs, the running of key industries of national importance and the co-ordination of provincial economic development plans.

The advantage of this system, according to N.L. Rajah, would have been manifold. A few of them are:

1. It would have kept the evil party politics at bay;
2. Even if parties achieved prominence within the system it would not have jeopardised the interests of the party or those of the public;
3. It would have established self-government;
4. It would have made adult suffrage more meaningful;
5. It would have given the people a sense of participation in government and made them socially and politically responsible;

6. It would have ensured a decentralised government;
7. It would have created ideal bureaucratic structure of a perfect pyramid with more powers of governance vested in the lower layers as against the present inverted pyramid structure we have adopted which leaves us with thousands of civil servants in Delhi and the state capitals against a handful in the districts.

But these are only few advantages which the country would have joined with the adoption of Gandhiji's model for governance. The Constituent Assembly's alternative was in the European and American tradition, with the principles different from those envisioned by the Mahatma. The basic features of all these constitutions in their accent on centralisation.

The debate on the form of government lent within the Constituent Assembly regard full 30 months (from July 1946 to November 1948), before the draft Constitution came into being. In the draft Constitution prepared by the Experts Committee, no serious consideration was bestowed on Gandhiji's model for decentralised governance and the majority were overwhelmingly in favour of a centralised government, which the Constituent Assembly strongly felt most suited to guaranteed unity, stability, social progress and economic gains and being about a social revolution.

Thus, Gandhiji's idea of decentralised government with the village panchayat as primary political unit. It also did not take off. The paradox is that in the early Constituent Assembly debates, everyone spoke in favour of panchayats and recognized its worth as an ancient Indian institution. But beyond that the speakers refused to give any great political power to this institution. Their speeches in favour of the panchayat did not amount to rejection of the Parliamentary government. The critics also supported other aspects of the draft Constitution that were negotiations of a Gandhian government system, centralised planning, great power status for India, expropriation of property, the development of heavy industry etc. (N.L. Rajah, 1977).

But the framers of Indian Constitution had incorporated an Article in the Constitution to pacify the Gandhian followers. It was Article 40, which states that lithe state shall take steps to organise village panchayats and endow them with such powers and authority as may be necessary to enable them to function as "units of self-government". But this goal remained as one of the innumerable mandates of the Constitution to which the state has been consistently indifferent. The makers of government, administrators and even statesmen have indifference and apathy towards this noble Gandhian dream, up to the presentation of the controversial 64 Constitution (Amendment) Bill, 1989 during the Prime Minister of Rajiv

Gandhi. It provides a constitutional status to the Panchayati Raj Institutions. The draft Bill makes the establishment of PRIs mandatory. Membership is to be by elections with the Chief Election Commissioner is to be in-charge. The CAG is to audit the accounts and submit his report to the Governor, who in turn would have it laid before the State Legislature. It provides for a three-tier structure of PRIs—village, intermediate and district levels. The term of the panchayat is to be five years. Reservation of seats (30%) have been made for members of the SC and ST as well as women. The panchayats will be having functions, powers, and authority to enable them to function as institutions of self-government. But when the bill was presented before the Parliament for its approval it got support of the Lok Sabha but fell in the Rajya Sabha (in which the Congress did not command majority). Soon the Congress found itself out of power. But the idea of giving constitutional status to the PRIs was not forgotten. The new government headed by V.P. Singh introduced yet another Bill—the Seventy-fourth Amendment in September 1990. But the Bill could not be passed due to the untimely collapse of the Ministry. In the general elections in 1991, the Congress Party assumed office once again. The government was headed by P.V. Narasimha Rao, introdroduced yet another Bill Constitution (Seventy-third Amendment) in 1991. With the support of all major parties the Bill was passed by Parliament in December 1992 and became operative in 1991, on its ratification by fifty per cent of the states.

Important features of the 73rd Constitution Amendment Act can be summed up as follows:

Structure

(a) Firstly, there will be a Gram Sabha in each village. It will be a body consisting of all persons registered as voters in the panchayat area at the village level.

(b) There shall be a three-tier, system of Panchayati Raj Village, intermediate and district levels—in all states except states having population of 20 lakh, which shall have the option not to have intermediate level bodies.

(c) There shall be direct election to fill all the seats in all three tiers and state have been empowered to have option for *ex-officio* person like Chairperson of the panchayat body, MLA's, MP's and MLCs as *ex-officio* members.

(d) Panchayats have been given option to have *sarpanch* of the village panchayats to be elected either directly or from amongst the elected members.

Reservation for SC/ST

The Constitutional amendment clearly provides for reservation of seats for SC/ST in panchayats on the population basis. Further, one-third of the total seats reserved for SC/ST shall be reserved for women belonging to corresponding reserved seats of SC/ST. Thus, women from SC/ST shall have reservation from their reserved seats. This is a unique provision that it would have been more happy position if the Constitution amendment makers should have thought fit to extend this provision to the election to Assemblies and Parliament.

Reservation for Women

Thirdly, as per the New Act one-third of the seats are to be reserved for women. Reservation should be on the rotation basis. Similarly not less than one-third of the offices of Chairman are to be reserved for women. These too are to be on rotation basis. But later reservation for women was extended to 50 per cent.

Duration of Panchayats

Fourthly, the Act provides for a uniform five-year term for PRIs. Thus, there is no provision of any extension of period of five years and elections shall have to be made before the expiry of period. Elections should be conducted under the supervision of the State Election Commission appointed by the State Governor.

Appointment of Finance Commission

According to Article 343-1 a Finance Commission has to be constituted to review the financial position of the panchayats and to make recommendations to the government. The recommendations should be submitted to the Governor who shall place it before the State Legislature.

State Election Commission

As cited earlier, according to the Act, there shall be a separate election commission to conduct elections to the PRIs. The Commission will work without any fear or favour for preparation of electoral rolls and the conduct of elections.

Thus, the Panchayati Raj, 1992 constitute a major milestone in the history of rural local government of the country. Because it makes elections to the PRIs mandatory every five years. This guarantees the right of local self-government institutions to exist Independent of the whims and political colour of the state government. Further the Amendment has made the PRIs financially solvent. Moreover the statutory compulsory representation of the weaker sections are assured in the PRIs. Lastly yet another warning nature is that PRIs have been made more broad based which will rescue them from possible domination by socially and economically well-off sections. Consequent upon the passing of the new Act, almost all state governments have enacted their Panchayati Raj legislations, to fulfil the dreams of Mahatmaji.

Constitutionalisation of Panchayats: A Review from 1992-2020

The working of panchayats in India in the last few decades more specifically from its constitutionalisation in 1992 to the present (2020) shows that the PRIs had undergone several agonies and sorrows. There were a number of disturbing factors contributed to it. Most important among them include:

1. Postponing panchayat elections in an irregular manner by several states of India.
2. Introduction of several parallel structures by Government of India, Ministries at the National Level and the development departments at the state level connected with a series of developmental schemes and programmes. It resulted in the emergence of parallel structures of governance which has by-passed the very purpose of decentralisation and democracy. Some of the major programmes which came under the parallel structures include:
   (a) creation of district level developmental agencies,
   (b) creation of watershed development agencies and programmes,
   (c) formation of joint forest management committees,
   (d) launching of new initiatives in the educational sector, and
   (e) launching of local area development schemes of MP's and MLA's.

In the light of experiences from 1992 to 2020 there is a general feeling that the 73rd and 74th Amendment Acts incorporated in Part IX of the Constitution need a fresh look to strengthen the provisions as well as to achieve the objectives set out in Article 243. The problem areas are:

1. The gram sabha and its jurisdiction enhancing its utility and effectiveness,
2. The desirability of uniform 3 tiers and integration between different levels of panchayati raj system,
3. Presence of MP's and MLA's on the panchayats
4. Reservation for OBCs,
5. Which way should Article 243G and the XI Schedule be modified to enable panchayats to become institutions of self-governance, and
6. Nyaya Panchayats should have a specific provision in the constitutional mechanism.

Despite of these troubles and limitations of the old order to yield to the new, several development points to a situation of poise and optimism. New programmes with the participation of people are being taken up in several states in a meaningful way after the new panchayats came into being. Participatory and sustainable local level development planning with the slogan "planning by the people and for the people is a noticeable achievement. The attempt to empower the local bodies by ensuring that they prepare and prioritise a shelf of integrated schemes in a scientific manner has assumed the dimensions of a movement and attracted nationwide attention. The 73rd and 74th Constitution Amendment Acts are only a necessary condition to bring into existence vibrant local governments. The political will is an equally important factor for the local bodies to take roots. But even where the political will is totally absent hitherto imposing developments to strengthen panchayats have taken place. It entered in a phase of negation after 2014. The NDA government has not paid any serious attention to strengthen both urban and rural local bodies due to reasons unknown. It has to be taken seriously by the political leadership both at the national and state level.

Conclusion

We have seen in the Seventy four years after Independence that Gandhiji's isolated foresight, courage, determination and wisdom were the motivating and guiding spirit behind the Indian leaders, which compelled them to do justice to accomplish the uncherished dreams of Gandhiji. Certainly it is a step in the right direction. Gandhiji was neither mumpsimus nor stoic. His approach to life was fully humanistic and holistic. The economic principles underlying Gandhian holistic economics are decentralisation, self-sufficiency co-operation, equality, *swadeshi* and trusteeship. His tress on utilisation of resources prudently, primacy of human resources. a decentralised development process and the need for hinging about an egalitarian society would be relevant to the conditions prevailing in most developing countries including India Any approach, other than a holistic to development does not cut muchice.

REFERENCES

Barnabas, A.P., *Social Change in a North Indian Village*, IIPA, New Delhi, 1969.

Biju, M.R., *Dynamics of New Panchayati Raj System: Reflections and Retrospections*, Kanishka Publishers, Distributors, New Delhi, 1998.

Biju, M.R., *Parliamentary Democracy and Political Change in India*, Kanishka Publishers, Distributors, New Delhi, 1999.

Dey, S.K., *Community Development*, Kitab Mahal, Allahabad, 1960, *Power to the People*, Orient Longmans, New Delhi, 1969.

Dube, S.C., *India's Changing Village*, Allied Publishers, Bombay, 1967.

Gandhi M.K., *Panchayati Raj*, (Compiled by R.K. Prabhu) Navjeevan, Ahmedabad, 1959.

Gandhi M.K., *Rebuilding Our Villages*, Navjeevan, Ahmedabad, 1952.

Inamdar, N.R., *Functioning of Village Panchayats*, Popular Prakashan, Bombay, 1970.

Institute of Social Sciences, *Status of Panchayati Raj in the States and Union Territories of India*, 2013, Concept, New Delhi, 2013.

Maddick Henry, *Panchayati Raj*, Longman Group Ltd., London, 1970.

Rajah, N.T., Gandhiji's Concept of Governance Remains a Dream, *Southern Economist*, 15 August, 1997.

Sharma, M.L., *Gandhi and Democratic Decentralisation in India*, Deep & Deep Publications, New Delhi, 1987.

Sinha, Durganand, *Indian Villages in Transition*, Associated House, New Delhi, 1969.

The Hindu, 21 January, 1997.

Index